W9-AGF-612

Mathematics
UNLIMITED

HOLT, RINEHART and WINSTON, Publishers
New York • Toronto • Mexico City • London • Sydney • Tokyo

AUTHORS

Francis "Skip" Fennell
Chairman, Education Department
Associate Professor of Education
Western Maryland College
Westminster, Maryland

Barbara J. Reys
Assistant Professor of Curriculum
and Instruction
University of Missouri, Columbia, Missouri
Formerly Junior High Mathematics Teacher
Oakland Junior High, Columbia, Missouri

Robert E. Reys
Professor of Mathematics Education
University of Missouri
Columbia, Missouri

Arnold W. Webb
Senior Research Associate
Research for Better Schools
Philadelphia, Pennsylvania
Formerly Asst. Commissioner of Education
New Jersey State Education Department

ILLUSTRATION

Bob Aiese: pp. 96, 97, 101, 112, 113, 162, 163, 190, 191, 210, 211, 223, 230, 231, 394, 395, 406, 407, 417 ● Donald Crews: pp. 44, 45, 308, 314, 431, 433, 434, 436 ● Jack Davis: p. 92 ● Jim Deigan: pp. 378, 379 ● Nancy Didion: pp. 22, 74, 75, 150, 208, 209, 240, 241, 242, 300, 301 ● Hovik Dilakian: pp. 130, 142, 143 ● Mark Giglio: pp. 78, 118, 119, 192, 193, 232, 233, 322, 324, 332, 348, 424 ● Deirdre Newman Griffin: pp. 31, 194, 216, 217, 250, 296, 358, 359, 367 ● Hal Just: pp. 4, 46, 160, 161, 172, 173, 248, 272, 273, 354, 355 ● Jim Ludtke: pp. 61, 94, 116, 134, 135, 147, 176, 177, 204, 326, 342, 343 ● Linda Miyamoto: pp. 60, 154, 155 ● Michele Noiset: pp. 392, 393 ● Michael O'Reilly: pp. 2, 3, 20, 72, 156, 157, 202, 238, 239, 290 ● Rosanne Percivalle: pp. 14, 82, 83, 386, 387 ● Dixon Scott: pp. 140, 141, 181, 218, 246, 247, 252, 259, 268, 288, 306, 307, 320, 321, 352, 377, 404 ● Marti Shohet: pp. 200, 201 ● Joe Snyder: p. 117 ● Arthur Thompson: pp. 34, 52, 53, 65, 114, 115, 234, 235, 333, 397 ● James Torok: p. 435 ● Paul Vaccarello: pp. 12, 381 ● Vantage Art Inc.: pp. 66, 151, 269, 302, 313, 329, 335, 362, 364, 396, 417, 420 ● Fred Winkowski: pp. 266, 267, 410, 411 ● Nina Winters: pp. 124, 125, 214, 215, 254, 255, 297, 425 ● Lane Yerkes: pp. 88, 89, 180, 279, 284, 365, 412. **Chapter Opener Illustrations:** Michael Haynes: 1, 37, 69, 109, 153, 189, 229, 265, 305, 341, 375, 403. **Cover Illustration:** Jeanette Adams.

PHOTOGRAPHY

AP/Wide World Photos: p. 136 top ● Bettman Archives: p. 390 ● Lee Boltin: p. 362 ● Carousel/Irmgard Groth: p. 346 ● Bruce Coleman, Inc./Joseph Tomala Jr.: p. 415 ● Duomo/David Madison: p. 42; Steven E. Sutton: p. 58 ● Walter Frerck: pp. 98-99 ● Focus on Sports: pp. 41, 48, 50, 51 ● Granger Collection: p. 318 ● Michal Heron: pp. 9, 128, 274-275, 292, 350-351, 384-385 ● HRW Photo/Russell Dian: p. 169 ● Don Kincaid: p. 356 ● Lucas Film Ltd.: pp. 279, 280 left ● Image Bank/Bupitis: p. 16; Alan Choisnet: p. 179; Brett Frooner: p. 139; Don King: p. 138 bottom; Colin Moyneux: p. 168; Art Wolfe: p. 138 top ● Image Works/Alan Carey: p. 136 bottom ● Metropolitan Museum of Art/Rogers Fund (1914): p. 328 ● Lawrence Migdale: pp. 294 ● Museo National De Antropologia/Carousel: p. 346 ● New York Color Works/L. Druskis: p. 8 ● Marvin E. Newman: p. 212 ● Odyssey Productions/Robert Frerck: pp. 220-221, 330, 331, 414 ● Omni-Photo Communications, Inc./Ken Karp: pp. 10-11, 24-25, 54, 80-81, 84, 132-133, 170-171, 286, 408-9; John Lei: pp. 18-19, 26, 28, 29, 38-39, 70-71, 126, 158-9, 166-167, 198-199, 242-243, 244-245, 270, 282-283, 376-377, 383 ● Photo Researchers, Inc./Michael Austin: p. 144; Gerry Cranham: p. 40; Wm. J. Jahoda: p. 120 bottom; Edward Lettau: p. 6 ● Phototeque: p. 280 right ● Scala/Art Source: p. 345 ● Stock Market/Roy Morsch: p. 236; Randy O'Rourke: p. 16; Gabe Palmer: p. 196; Christopher Springmann: p. 278; Alexas Urba: p. 278; Luie Villota: p. 276 ● Stock Shop/Tom Tracy: p. 339 ● Wheeler Pictures/Paul Solomon: p. 418 ● Woodfin Camp & Associates/Nathan Benn: p. 236; Mark & Evelyn Bernheim: p. 120 top; Jonathan Blair: p. 356; Ira Block: p. 87; John Ficara: pp. 76-77; Michal Heron: p. 66, 106, 110; John Marmaras: p. 213; Wally McNamee: pp. 7, 86; Mi Setitelman: p. 90; Mike Yamashita: p. 312 ● Leo de Wys/Nicholas de Gregory: p. 302.

Copyright © 1987 by Holt, Rinehart and Winston, Publishers
All rights reserved
Printed in the United States of America

ISBN 0-03-006442-2

6 7 8 9 0 032 9 8 7 6 5 4 3 2

CONTENTS

4 DIVIDING WHOLE NUMBERS

5 DIVIDING WITH DECIMALS
Metric Measurement

6 NUMBER THEORY, FRACTIONS

Good health requires a combination of exercise and nutrition. Analyze your current diet and the quality and quantity of the exercise you do regularly. Then make a plan for improving both your diet and your exercise program.

1 PLACE VALUE, ADDITION AND SUBTRACTION
Whole Numbers

Numbers to Hundred Thousands

The human respiratory system works day and night without a thought from us. In one month, the lungs take in oxygen at least six hundred forty-seven thousand, eight hundred fifty times.

Write the numeral for this number.

Hundred thousands	Ten thousands	Thousands	Hundreds	Tens	Ones
6	4	7,	8	5	0

Commas separate large numbers into groups of three digits.

In 647,850:

the value of the digit 6 in the hundred thousands place is 600,000.
the value of the digit 4 in the ten thousands place is 40,000.
the value of the digit 7 in the thousands place is 7,000.
the value of the digit 8 in the hundreds place is 800.
the value of the digit 5 in the tens place is 50.
the value of the digit 0 in the ones place is 0.

Standard form: 647,850
Expanded form: 600,000 + 40,000 + 7,000 + 800 + 50

Checkpoint Write the letter of the correct answer.

Identify the expanded form.

1. 630,891

a. 600,000 + 30,000 + 800 + 90 + 1
b. 600,000 + 3,000 + 800 + 90 + 1
c. 60,000 + 30,000 + 800 + 90 + 1
d. 60,000 + 3,000 + 800 + 90 + 1

Identify the standard form.

2. 800,000 + 300 + 60 + 8

a. 83,680
b. 800,368
c. 803,068
d. 800,000,368

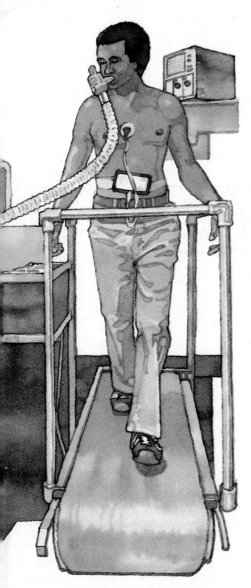

Write the value of the blue digit.

1. 369,418   **2.** 725,001   **3.** 803,060   **4.** 914,735

5. 862,741   **6.** 305,000   **7.** 486,321   **8.** 224,683

Write the number in standard form.

9. six hundred fifty-eight thousand, three hundred

10. seventy-nine thousand, forty-four

11. two hundred twelve thousand, six hundred nine

12. nine hundred thousand, sixty

13. 600,000 + 40,000 + 3,000 + 800 + 5

14. 900,000 + 9,000 + 900 + 60 + 2

15. 30,000 + 7,000 + 80 + 7

Write the word name for the number.

16. 263,410   **17.** 980,063   **18.** 435,000

19. 306,809   **20.** 512,422   **21.** 776,009

Write the number in expanded form.

22. 386,047   **23.** 299,810   **24.** 506,304

25. 816,124   **26.** 108,622   **27.** 741,616

Combine the digits in each to write the greatest possible number.

★28. 6,8,9, and 3   **★29.** 6,7,9,4, and 2   **★30.** 3,5,8,6,2, and 9

CHALLENGE

Ancient Greeks represented their numbers with these symbols.

1 = α   2 = β   3 = γ   4 = δ   5 = ε

6 = ζ   7 = η   8 = θ   9 = ι   10 = κ

What number does each Greek symbol represent?

1. κθ   **2.** κγ   **3.** κα   **4.** κι   **5.** κβ

Numbers to Hundred Billions

A. Red blood cells are constantly dying and being replaced by your body. Every day, about 172,800,000,000 new red blood cells are produced.

The place-value chart below can help you to understand the meaning of each digit in this number.

Period	Billions			Millions			Thousands			Ones		
Place value	hundred billions	ten billions	billions	hundred millions	ten millions	millions	hundred thousands	ten thousands	thousands	hundreds	tens	ones
	1	7	2,	8	0	0,	0	0	0,	0	0	0

Write: 172,800,000,000.

B. Each group of 3 digits is called a **period.** Period names help you to read large numbers.

You can write 172,800,000,000 with this short word name: 172 billion, 800 million.

Another example:

Write the short word name for 46,308,715,940.
46 billion, 308 million, 715 thousand, 940

4

Write the value of the blue digit.

1. 163,745,268,061
2. 391,465,000
3. 435,628,100,350

4. 927,431,539,877
5. 543,268,304,100
6. 119,368,541,111

7. 648,639,047,715
8. 836,103
9. 256,055,296,173

For 694,358,723,688, write the digits in the

10. millions period.
11. thousands period.
12. billions period.

Write the short word name for the number.

13. 528,632,981,620
14. 763,245,861,116
15. 986,411,629

16. 943,785,126,987
17. 543,269,446,038
18. 271,364,062,525

Read the data. Write the number in standard form.

19. One drop of blood contains about five million red blood cells.

20. The average adult sleeps for about thirteen thousand, three hundred eighty-three hours every five years.

21. The human eye can see more than seven million, five hundred thousand color differences.

22. During an average lifetime, the human heart beats about two billion, five hundred million times.

CHALLENGE

To write 1 billion, write 1 followed by nine zeros: 1,000,000,000.

The table below shows the number of zeros in the periods beyond billions.

Period	Quintillions	Quadrillions	Trillions	Billions
Number of zeros	18	15	12	9

Use the information in the table to help you write the number.

1. 3 quintillion, 645 quadrillion, 109 trillion

2. 46 quadrillion, 763 trillion, 436 billion

Comparing and Ordering Numbers

A. The table shows the approximate number of births in some states in 1981. Which state had a greater number of births, Arkansas or Connecticut?

Compare 35,386 and 37,604.

State	Births
Arkansas	35,386
California	422,066
Connecticut	37,604
Kentucky	58,047

Symbols for Comparing	
>	greater than
<	less than
=	equal to
≠	not equal to

Line up the digits.	Compare the digits from left to right. Find the first place where they differ.	Compare the digits.
35,386	35,386	5 < 7
37,604	37,604	

The numbers compare in the same way.

35,386 < 37,604   or   37,604 > 35,386

Connecticut had a greater number of births.

B. You can compare two numbers at a time to order a series of numbers. Write 50,107; 8,714; 51,911; and 48,729 in order from the least to the greatest.

Line up the digits. Compare to find the least.

50,107
 8,714
51,911
48,729

> 8,714 has no ten thousands. It is the least number.

Continue to compare to order the remaining numbers.

48,729 < 50,107
48,729 < 51,911
50,107 < 51,911

From the least to the greatest:

8,714 < 48,729 < 50,107 < 51,911.

The steps are the same to order numbers from the greatest to the least.

51,911 > 50,107 > 48,729 > 8,714

Compare. Write >, <, or = for ●.

1. 1,400 ● 998
2. 135,098 ● 53,876
3. 3,901,823 ● 6,857,243
4. 10,001 ● 10,100
5. 6,354 ● 6,354
6. 7,819 ● 62,478
7. 546,831 ● 545,831
8. 624,738 ● 62,478
9. 734,826 ● 734,926
10. 26,015 ● 26,115

Compare. Write >, <, or = for ●.

11. 278 million, 799 thousand ● 278 million, 875 thousand
12. 120 billion, 30 thousand ● 99 million, 80 thousand
13. 15 billion, 64 thousand ● 15 billion, 11 million

Write in order from the least to the greatest.

14. 58,906; 101,001; 60,732
15. 789,213; 798,321; 799,831; 789,312
16. 64,358; 64,538; 64,483; 63,584

Write in order from the greatest to the least.

17. 234,321; 189,000; 234,543; 99,789
18. 910,235; 911,325; 901,532; 911,523
19. 51,781; 51,871; 51,187; 51,817

CHALLENGE

Due to improvements in health care, world population has increased rapidly in the past 180 years. Use the chart to answer the questions.

1. In which of these years was world population less than 1 billion?

2. During which years was it between 1 billion and 2 billion?

Year	World Population
1800	910,000,000
1850	1,130,000,000
1900	1,600,000,000
1950	2,510,000,000
1982	4,600,000,000

★3. Between which years did the population increase by more than 1 billion?

PROBLEM SOLVING
Using the Help File

If you have trouble solving a problem in this book, try using the Help File at the back of this book. It will give you hints that will help you find an answer.

Read the problem. Then see how these students used each section of the Help File.

Sarita is deciding what to have for a snack. She wants to have fewer than 200 calories. Can she have an apple and an orange?

Calories	
Apple	115
Banana	176
Orange	70

Megan did not understand what the question was asking. Using an idea in the **Questions** section of the Help File, she decided to write down what she needed to know.

I need to know if an apple and an orange together have fewer than 200 calories.

Cy did not know what math to use to find an answer. An idea in the **Tools** section told him to add the calories of an apple and of an orange together.

$$115 + 70 = 185$$

Connie did not know what to do after adding the calories of an apple and an orange. The **Solutions** section told her to compare the number to 200.

$$185 < 200$$

Len wanted to check to be sure that he computed correctly. The **Checks** section showed him how to check his computation.

$$185 - 115 = 70$$

The total minus one of the addends produced the other addend. The computation was correct. All the students agreed that Sarita can have an apple and an orange.

Write the letter of the section of the Help File that would best help each student.

1. Tina wants to make sure that an answer she has found is correct. Which section of the Help File should she use?

   a. Tools
   b. Questions
   c. Checks

2. Randy doesn't understand the fifth problem in his homework at all. Which section of the Help File should he use first?

   a. Checks
   b. Solutions
   c. Questions

Solve. Use the Help File if you need assistance.

3. A woman's heart has a mass of about 260 grams. A man's heart has a mass that is about 52 grams more than that. What, approximately, is the mass of a man's heart?

4. If you consume 3,500 more calories than you use, you will gain 1 pound. Jim gains 2 pounds in a month. How many more calories did he consume than he used?

5. It takes a 150-lb person 66 minutes of bike riding to burn 542 calories. A 75-lb person takes twice as long to burn the same number of calories. For how many minutes would a 75-lb person have to ride a bike to burn 542 calories?

6. Sally weighs 95 lb. She recently lost 5 lb. How much did she weigh before she lost the weight?

7. The human body has more than 600 muscles. Helena's muscles weigh 38 lb. The rest of her body weighs 57 lb. How much does Helena weigh altogether?

8. The Red Cross found that in Hinton, 97 blood donors had type AB blood and 84 donors had type O blood. Of the donors in Milltown, 88 had type O blood and 79 had type AB blood. How many donors in all had type AB blood?

Addition and Subtraction

A. Michael jogged 2 miles on Monday and 4 miles on Wednesday. How many miles did he jog?

You add to find the total amount. Add 2 + 4.

$$2 + 4 = 6$$

↑ addend   ↑ addend   ↑ sum

$$\begin{array}{r} 2 \leftarrow \text{addend} \\ +4 \leftarrow \text{addend} \\ \hline 6 \leftarrow \text{sum} \end{array}$$

Michael jogged 6 miles.

B. Addition has these properties:

Commutative Property If the order of the addends is changed, the sum remains the same.	$5 + 4 = 4 + 5$ $9 = 9$
Identity Property If one of the addends is zero, the sum is equal to the other addend.	$7 + 0 = 7$ $0 + 9 = 9$
Associative Property If the grouping of the addends is changed, the sum remains the same.	$(2 + 3) + 6 = 2 + (3 + 6)$ $5 + 6 = 2 + 9$ $11 = 11$

C. You subtract to compare amounts, to find how many are left, or to find how many more are needed.

Addition can help you with subtraction.

$14 - 8 = $ ■ Think: $8 + $ ■ $ = 14$.
Since $8 + 6 = 14$, then $14 - 8 = 6$. ← **difference**

D. When you subtract, remember:

If zero is subtracted from a number, the difference is that number.	$5 - 0 = 5$
If a number is subtracted from itself, the difference is zero.	$6 - 6 = 0$
Subtraction is not commutative. $7 - 3 = 4$ $3 - 7 \neq 4$	$\neq$ means not equal to

Add or subtract.

1. 4 $+1$	**2.** 7 $+2$	**3.** 8 $+8$	**4.** 6 $+7$	**5.** 2 $+4$	**6.** 1 $+3$	**7.** 5 $+4$
8. 14 -9	**9.** 7 -6	**10.** 4 -2	**11.** 17 -9	**12.** 11 -7	**13.** 8 -3	**14.** 7 -1

15. $5 + 0$ **16.** $9 - 6$ **17.** $9 + 7$ **18.** $9 - 1$ **19.** $9 + 3$

20. $8 + 8$ **21.** $6 - 4$ **22.** $1 + 0$ **23.** $10 - 3$ **24.** $3 + 8$

Identify the property used. Find the missing number.

25. $6 + \blacksquare = 6$ **26.** $5 + 8 = 8 + \blacksquare$ **27.** $(4 + 7) + \blacksquare = 4 + (7 + 5)$

28. $5 + \blacksquare = 5$ **29.** $4 + 3 = 3 + \blacksquare$ **30.** $(8 + 2) + \blacksquare = 8 + (2 + 9)$

Find the missing number.

31. $8 - 0 = \blacksquare$ **32.** $3 - \blacksquare = 0$ ★**33.** $7 - 6 = 6 - \blacksquare$

Solve.

34. Sue and Lars rode their bicycles the same number of miles. Sue rode 8 miles on Saturday and 9 miles on Sunday. If Lars rode 9 miles on Saturday, how many miles did he ride on Sunday?

35. If a team of two students can do 15 chin-ups, they earn a fitness medal. Al did 7 chin-ups. Shelly did 9. Did Al and Shelly earn a fitness medal?

CHALLENGE

You can use letters to show how the Commutative Property works.

$$3 + 2 = 2 + 3$$
$$\downarrow \quad \downarrow \quad \downarrow \quad \downarrow$$
$$a + b = b + a$$

Use letters to show how the property works.

1. Associative Property

2. Zero Property

More Practice, page 437

Front-End Estimation

A. You have $10 to buy soaps and shampoo from the drugstore. Will that be enough to pay this bill?

You can estimate using the front-end method to find out.

Add the front digits (dollar amounts).

$$
\begin{array}{r}
\$\,3.45 \\
4.63 \\
+\ 2.88 \\
\hline
\$\,9.
\end{array}
$$

Adjust by grouping the cents amount to dollars.

$$
\begin{array}{r}
\$\,3.45 \\
4.63 \\
+\ 2.88 \\
\end{array}
$$

$\left.\begin{array}{r}\$\,3.45 \\ 4.63\end{array}\right\} \rightarrow$ about \$1

$+\ 2.88 \rightarrow$ about \$1

Adjustment: about \$2.

Estimate: \$9 + \$2 = \$11.

$10 is not enough money to pay this bill.

B. You can estimate the sums of whole numbers in the same way.

$$
\begin{array}{r}
8,182 \\
1,426 \\
+\ 7,319 \\
\hline
16
\end{array}
\qquad
\left.\begin{array}{r}
8,182 \\
1,426 \\
+\ 7,319
\end{array}\right\}\text{about 1,000}
$$

Adjustment: about 1,000.

Estimate: 16,000 + 1,000 = 17,000.

C. You can also estimate differences using the front-end method.

Subtract the front digits.

$$
\begin{array}{r}
8,366 \\
-\ 2,876 \\
\hline
6
\end{array}
$$

Adjust by looking at the hundreds.

$$
\begin{array}{r}
8,366 \\
-\ 2,876 \\
\end{array}
$$

366 < 876

So, adjust downward.

Estimate: less than 6,000.

Another example:

$$
\begin{array}{r}
5,789 \\
-\ 2,567 \\
\hline
3
\end{array}
\qquad
\begin{array}{r}
5,789 \\
-\ 2,567 \\
\end{array}
$$

789 > 567

So, adjust upward.

Estimate: more than 3,000.

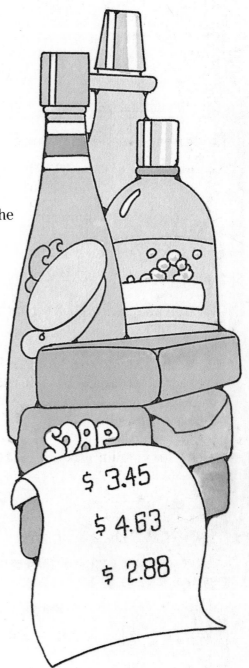

$ 3.45

$ 4.63

$ 2.88

Estimate the sum or difference. Write the letter of the best estimate.

1. 6,275 + 4,187 + 8,540   **a.** less than 20,000   **b.** more than 20,000

2. 18,547 + 2,795   **a.** less than 20,000   **b.** more than 20,000

3. 950 + 4,758 + 2,597   **a.** less than 10,000   **b.** more than 10,000

4. $22.75 + $7.67 + $4.89   **a.** less than $30.00   **b.** more than $30.00

5. 6,534 − 2,185   **a.** less than 4,000   **b.** more than 4,000

6. 842 − 367   **a.** less than 500   **b.** more than 500

7. 4,327 − 1,427   **a.** less than 3,000   **b.** more than 3,000

Estimate the sum or difference.

8.
```
    895
    927
+ 2,750
```

9.
```
  45,276
   5,895
+ 47,879
```

10.
```
  75,295
  10,458
+ 12,075
```

11.
```
  $9.78
   4.37
+  4.29
```

12.
```
  $890.54
    98.50
+  101.39
```

13.
```
  9,625
− 4,187
```

14.
```
  45,265
− 26,185
```

15.
```
  87,534
− 25,895
```

16.
```
  $457.98
−  228.74
```

17.
```
  $3,560.92
−    876.95
```

Solve.

18. Miranda went to the Health-Plus vitamin sale and bought all the B-complex vitamins that she had seen in an advertisement. Was $12 enough to pay for her purchase?

★19. Which vitamin was discounted the most?

HEALTH-PLUS VITAMIN SALE

Vitamin	Reg.	Sale
A	$6.29	$4.89
B$_1$	5.35	4.59
B$_6$	5.35	4.59
B$_{12}$	5.35	4.29
C	3.39	2.50
E	6.39	4.89

CALCULATOR

Find a number that will give you an answer within the range.

              Range

1. 478 + ☐   900 − 950

3. 1,387 − ☐   750 − 800

              Range

2. 605 − ☐   100 − 150

4. 2,791 + ☐   7,000 − 8,000

Rounding and Estimating

A. On the average, a person in the United States lives a total of 74 years, or 27,028 days. To the nearest thousand, for how many days does a person live?

Round 27,028 to the nearest thousand.

Find the thousands place.	Look at the digit in the hundreds place.	If the hundreds digit is • 5 or greater, round up; • less than 5, round down.
27,028	**27,028**	**0 < 5** Round down.

A person in the United States lives for an average of 27,000 days.

Another example:

Round 56,784,355 to the nearest million.

Find the millions place.	Look at the digit in the hundred thousands place.	
56,784,355	**56,784,355**	**7 > 5** Round up.

56,784,355 to the nearest million is 57,000,000.

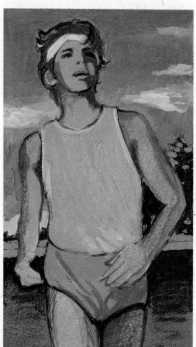

B. You can use rounding to help you estimate sums. Always round to numbers that make sense and are easy to compute. Be flexible as you round. Here are three ways to estimate the same problem.

$$\begin{array}{r} \$84.95 \\ +\ 52.78 \end{array}$$

$80	$85	$85
+ 50 or	+ 55 or	+ 53
$130	$140	$138

The estimate $130 would not be enough money to buy the items at these prices. Both $138 and $140 are reasonable estimates.

C. You can also use rounding to estimate differences.

Here are two ways to estimate the same problem.

$$\begin{array}{r} 8,257 \\ -\ 3,195 \end{array}$$

8,000	8,300
− 3,000 or	− 3,200
5,000	5,100

Both 5,000 and 5,100 are reasonable estimates.

Round to the nearest thousand.

1. 5,649   **2.** 31,506   **3.** 34,407   **4.** 791,239

Round to the nearest hundred thousand.

5. 5,326,498   **6.** 8,269,308   **7.** 3,742,896   **8.** 15,463,203

Round to the nearest million.

9. 72,896,420   **10.** 301,940,055   **11.** 824,196,538   **12.** 256,682,439

Round to the nearest ten dollars.

13. $18.59   **14.** $346.00   **15.** $76.77   **16.** $508.29

Estimate. Write the letter of the best answer.

17. 345 + 589   **a.** less than 1,000   **b.** more than 1,000

18. 6,685 + 4,389   **a.** less than 10,000   **b.** more than 10,000

19. $9.76 + $8.88   **a.** less than $20   **b.** more than $20

20. 875 − 295   **a.** less than 500   **b.** more than 500

21. 82,956 − 21,658   **a.** less than 60,000   **b.** more than 60,000

22. 81,214 − 32,587   **a.** less than 50,000   **b.** more than 50,000

Estimate.

23.   74,075
    + 26,953

24. $63.80
    +   7.45

25.   41,278
    −   9,847

26. $774.33
    −   98.67

Solve.

27. A hospital ship sailed 28,490 miles in one year and 17,385 miles the next year. About how far did the ship travel in these two years?

28. Last month, Dr. Hanson spent $919.04 on medical supplies. If his total supply budget is $1,500.00, about how much money is left?

CALCULATOR

I rounded five of the numbers in the box to the nearest thousand. The sum was 44,000 when I added the rounded numbers. Which number was not included?

2,614	7,143
3,891	9,814
4,584	19,614

PROBLEM SOLVING
Using Outside Sources Including the Infobank

Sometimes you have to obtain information from outside sources to be able to solve a problem. Written sources include books, magazines, catalogs, and newspapers. Often, you can find information by contacting government agencies, museums, or other organizations.

> In 1984, Americans spent $124 billion to eat in restaurants. Did people in New England spend more per person than people in the South?

To answer this question, you need to know how much money people in those regions spent to eat in restaurants.

You might be able to find this information in an almanac or a recent magazine on the subject.

Data from several outside sources have been gathered together to form an Infobank on pages 431–436. You can use this information to solve many problems in this book.

Once you have found the information you need, you can solve the problem.

$659 = money spent per person in New England
$498 = money spent per person in the South
$659 > $498

New Englanders spent more per person than Southerners spent to eat in restaurants in 1984.

Would you need a reference source to answer each question? Write *yes* or *no*.

1. Edward Brooke served for 12 years in the United States Senate. For how much longer did Edmund Muskie serve as a senator?

2. Frank Church served in the United States Senate from 1958 to 1981. Robert Taft and Howard Baker served for a combined total of 19 years. For how much longer did Church serve than Taft and Baker?

3. Christopher Columbus discovered the New World in 1492. How many years elapsed between Columbus's first voyage and his second voyage?

4. Sir Roger Bannister was the first person to run a mile in less than 4 minutes. In 1954, he ran a mile in 3 minutes 59.4 seconds. How much faster can a person run the mile today?

Solve each problem. Use the Infobank if you need additional facts.

5. The peak of the highest mountain that Sam ever climbed was 7,265 feet above sea level. His brother, Mike, climbed a peak that was 8,530 feet above sea level. Who climbed higher, Mike or Sam?

6. Water use is monitored in the East and in the West of the United States during a comparable 20-hour period. Which activity uses the most water in the eastern United States?

7. Over a typical 20-hour period, which activity in the United States uses the most water?

8. Which part of the United States uses less water for energy in a typical 20-hour period?

9. New Englanders spent $659 per person to eat in restaurants in 1984. In which region of the United States did people spend more to eat in restaurants during that time?

10. In which region of the United States did people spend the smallest amount of money to eat in restaurants in 1984?

11. Linda wants to buy a notebook for $3.45 and a pen for $1.19. Is $5 enough to pay for her purchase?

12. About how much was spent per person to dine out in the Central region of the United States during 1984?

Adding Whole Numbers

A. Julie keeps track of the calories in her diet. Her breakfast, of oatmeal and milk, contained 272 calories. At lunch, she ate a cheese sandwich and an apple. Lunch contained 469 calories. What was the total number of calories in Julie's breakfast and lunch?

Add 272 + 469.
First, estimate the sum: 300 + 500 = 800.

Add the ones. Regroup, if necessary.	Add the tens. Regroup, if necessary.	Add the hundreds. Regroup, if necessary.
$\begin{array}{r} 1 \\ 2\,7\,2 \\ +\,4\,6\,9 \\ \hline 1 \end{array}$	$\begin{array}{r} 1\ 1 \\ 2\,7\,2 \\ +\,4\,6\,9 \\ \hline 4\,1 \end{array}$	$\begin{array}{r} 1\ 1 \\ 2\,7\,2 \\ +\,4\,6\,9 \\ \hline 7\,4\,1 \end{array}$

The total number of calories was 741.
The answer is reasonably close to the estimate.

Other examples:

$$\begin{array}{r} 1 \\ 2\,7 \\ +\,5\,8 \\ \hline 8\,5 \end{array} \qquad \begin{array}{r} 1 \\ 3\,0\,5 \\ +\ \ 2\,6 \\ \hline 3\,3\,1 \end{array} \qquad \begin{array}{r} 1 \\ 7\,5 \\ +\,6\,7 \\ \hline 1\,4\,2 \end{array}$$

B. You add money the same way you add whole numbers. Remember to write the dollar sign and the cents point.

$$\begin{array}{r} 1 \\ \$54.36 \\ +\ \ 21.57 \\ \hline \$75.93 \end{array} \qquad \begin{array}{r} 1\ 1 \\ \$657.51 \\ +\ \ 128.94 \\ \hline \$786.45 \end{array}$$

Checkpoint   Write the letter of the correct answer.

Add.

1. $\begin{array}{r} 337 \\ +\ 249 \end{array}$

2. $\begin{array}{r} \$47.28 \\ +\ \ \ 2.35 \end{array}$

3. $\begin{array}{r} 52{,}029 \\ +\ 34{,}365 \end{array}$

4. 616,255 + 153,479

1.	2.	3.	4.
a. 576	**a.** $49.53	**a.** 86,094	**a.** 769,624
b. 586	**b.** $49.63	**b.** 86,384	**b.** 769,634
c. 686	**c.** $50.63	**c.** 86,394	**c.** 769,734
d. 5,716	**d.** $4,963	**d.** 86,494	**d.** 770,734

Add.

1. 22
+ 17

2. 61
+ 27

3. 735
+ 51

4. 866
+ 42

5. 132
+ 61

6. 649
+ 217

7. 208
+ 716

8. 709
+ 621

9. 637
+ 15

10. 432
+ 249

11. 1,333
+ 2,493

12. 6,344
+ 261

13. 2,150
+ 4,470

14. 7,445
+ 3,381

15. 3,491
+ 1,121

16. 1,764 + 2,463

17. $66.41 + $14.95

18. 1,422 + 594

19. 12,547 + 25,843

20. 42,625 + 35,665

21. $478.63 + $212.27

22. 356,081 + 7,974

23. 918,597 + 24,987

24. $13,184 + $994

25. 5,508 + 98,801

26. 40,852 + 4,194

27. 2,781 + 31,152

★**28.** 37 thousand + 4 thousand, 543   ★**29.** 5 million, 3 thousand + 427 thousand

Solve.

30. Jan interviews students in her school. Of those interviewed, 355 say they exercise regularly and 287 say they do not. How many students are interviewed?

31. David is watching his weight. For lunch, he has a 209-calorie cheeseburger and a 155-calorie salad. How many calories does David's lunch contain?

FOCUS: MENTAL MATH

To add numbers that end in 8 or 9, you can use a technique called **compensating.**

78
+ 64

Think: 80 is easier to add than 78.

80
+ 64
144

Add 2 to 78 to make it 80.

144
− 2
142

Then subtract 2 from the sum to compensate.

Remember: If you add a number to an addend, subtract it from the sum.

Compute mentally.

1. 207 + 109

2. 118 + 63

3. 49 + 315

4. 822 + 179

Column Addition

Conklin Hospital runs a nursing school. One year, the hospital trained 127 nurses. The next year, 130 nurses were trained. During the third year, the hospital trained 84 nurses. How many nurses were trained at Conklin Hospital during the three years?

Add 127 + 130 + 84.

Add the ones. Regroup, if necessary.	Add the tens. Regroup, if necessary.	Add the hundreds. Regroup, if necessary.	Check by adding up.
1	1 1	1 1	1 1
127	127	127	127
130	130	130	130
+ 84	+ 84	+ 84	+ 84
1	41	341	341

During the three years, 341 nurses were trained at the hospital.

Other examples:

$$
\begin{array}{r}
\text{\tiny 2 1 2 1} \\
\$192.95 \\
251.90 \\
+\ \ 457.39 \\
\hline
\$902.24
\end{array}
\qquad
\begin{array}{r}
\text{\tiny 1 2 1} \\
14{,}535 \\
107 \\
2{,}694 \\
+\qquad 82 \\
\hline
17{,}418
\end{array}
\qquad
\begin{array}{r}
\text{\tiny 2 2} \\
459 \\
328 \\
142 \\
+\ \ 98 \\
\hline
1{,}027
\end{array}
$$

Checkpoint Write the letter of the correct answer.

Find the sum.

1.	2.	3.	4.
315	$420.39	212,861	212,861
207	207.25	430,315	30,455
+ 469	+ 30.50	+ 505,642	+ 793

1.	2.	3.	4.
a. 901	a. $657.04	a. 1,147,718	a. 243,009
b. 971	b. $657.14	b. 1,147,828	b. 244,109
c. 981	c. $658.14	c. 1,148,818	c. 343,019
d. 991	d. $932.54	d. 11,248,818	d. 1,310,411

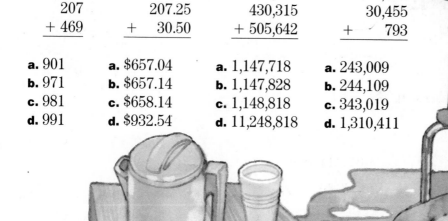

Add. Check your answer by adding up.

1.	49 77 + 47	2.	369 698 + 875	3.	140 402 + 864	4.	916 535 + 319	5.	$3.18 2.02 + 5.94

1. 49 · 77 · + 47

2. 369 · 698 · + 875

3. 140 · 402 · + 864

4. 916 · 535 · + 319

5. $3.18 · 2.02 · + 5.94

6. 12,180 · 41,192 · + 8,740

7. 25,672 · 63,823 · + 15,620

8. 417,827 · 9,571 · + 71,163

9. 64,336 · 2,571 · + 56,924

10. $844.81 · 375.88 · + 74.82

11. 621 · 83 · 743 · + 37

12. 93 · 1,291 · 4,468 · + 276

13. 2,067 · 43,957 · 66 · + 4,999

14. 5,851 · 783 · 12 · + 8,962

15. $833.97 · 921.68 · 9.90 · + 0.75

16. 54,897 + 32 + 4,908

17. 90,220 + 308 + 51,245

18. 16 + 43 + 2,913 + 5

19. 80 + 463 + 8,097

20. 16 + 404 + 590

21. $109.05 + $0.89 + $56.30

22. 678 + 89 + 2,447

23. 67,909 + 74 + 331

24. $86.45 + $567.90 + $0.74

Solve.

25. Dr. Smith begins a three-week jogging program. She jogs 17 miles the first week, 15 miles the second week, and 20 miles the third. How many miles does Dr. Smith jog in the three weeks?

26. Hospital workers are running a four-week drive to raise funds for a health center. They raise $490.50 the first week, $675.89 the second, $1,055.35 the third, and $729.75 the fourth. How much do they raise?

MIDCHAPTER REVIEW

Write > or < for each ●.

1. 370,643 ● 369,999

2. 613,090 ● 613,019

Write in order from the least to the greatest.

3. 1,010; 2,000; 999

4. 63,971; 63,791; 63,197; 63,917

Estimate the sum.

5. 36,985 · + 53,947

Find the sum.

6. 103 · + 18

7. 47,452 · + 3,449

8. $5,206.48 · + 884.52

Subtracting Whole Numbers

A. The average 11-year-old American is 142 centimeters tall. Ben is 161 centimeters tall. How much taller is Ben than the average 11-year-old American?

Subtract 161 − 142.
First, estimate the difference: 160 − 140 = 20.

Regroup. Subtract the ones.	Subtract the tens.	Subtract the hundreds.	Check by adding.
5 11 **1 6 1̸** **− 1 4 2** **9**	5 11 **1 6̸ 1̸** **− 1 4 2** **1 9**	5 11 **1 6̸ 1̸** **− 1 4 2** **1 9**	1 **1 4 2** **+ 1 9** **1 6 1**

Ben is 19 centimeters taller than the average 11-year-old American.

The answer is reasonably close to the estimate.

HEIGHTS OF 11-YEAR-OLDS

— 161 cm

— 142 cm average

— 123 cm

Other examples:

3 15 5 13 **4̸,5̸ 6̸ 3̸** **− 1,7 0 9** **2,8 5 4**	8 10 **6 7,9̸ 0̸ 5** **− 1 3,1 2 4** **5 4,7 8 1**	5 12 **9 8,6̸ 2̸ 7** **− 3 9 6** **9 8,2 3 1**

B. You subtract money the same way you subtract whole numbers. Remember to write the dollar sign and the cents point.

6 15 **$8.7 5̸** **− 5.4 9** **$3. 2 6**	12 8 2̸ 15 **$2 9̸.3̸ 5̸** **− 2 8.3 9** **$ 0.9 6**	11 8 1̸ 15 **$6 7 9̸.2̸ 5̸** **− 3 2 5.4 9** **$3 5 3. 7 6**

Checkpoint Write the letter of the correct answer.

Subtract.

1.   365
     − 148

2. $95.23
     − 32.05

3.   48,924
     − 31,537

4. 586,342 − 245,259

1.	**2.**	**3.**	**4.**
a. 217	**a.** $63.18	**a.** 17,387	**a.** 141,193
b. 223	**b.** $63.22	**b.** 17,413	**b.** 341,083
c. 227	**c.** $127.28	**c.** 17,497	**c.** 341,117
d. 513	**d.** $6,318	**d.** 80,461	**d.** 341,197

Subtract.

1.	499 − 274	2.	681 − 146	3.	624 − 319	4.	999 − 102	5.	$6.78 − 3.31

6.	7,856 − 2,327	7.	8,844 − 3,612	8.	5,551 − 3,408	9.	6,447 − 2,339	10.	$86.77 − 14.61

11.	75,682 − 24,543	12.	95,649 − 24,432	13.	78,884 − 56,107	14.	48,891 − 14,219	15.	$584.78 − 461.46

16.	366,721 − 143,547	17.	576,434 − 313,185	18.	689,277 − 516,144	19.	754,869 − 432,246	20.	$7,876.17 − 3,034.57

21. 997,364 − 33,228   **22.** 56,981 − 345   **23.** 168,752 − 2,314

24. 868,844 − 2,618   **25.** 985,983 − 814   **26.** $648.74 − $2.30

27. 98,621 − 724   **28.** 8,778 − 3,145   **29.** $1,488.91 − $142.19

Solve.

30. Robert's rate of breathing at rest is 45 breaths per minute. After 20 minutes of exercise, his rate is 72 breaths per minute. What is the difference between Robert's rate of breathing at rest and after exercise?

31. As part of a science project, Linda keeps track of the number of calories in her diet. On Monday, her diet contained 1,350 calories. On Tuesday, her diet had 1,245 calories. How many more calories did Monday's diet have than Tuesday's?

FOCUS: MENTAL MATH

You can subtract numbers that end in 8 or 9 by compensating.

73 − 49	Think: 50 is easier to subtract than 49.	73 − 50 23	Add 1 to 49 to make it 50.	23 + 1 24	Then add 1 to the difference to compensate.

REMEMBER: If you add to a number before you subtract it, you must add the same number to the difference to compensate.

Compute mentally.

1. 56 − 29   **2.** 85 − 38   **3.** 92 − 49   **4.** 236 − 98

Subtracting with Zeros

Cassandra is keeping track of her diet. The recommended daily allowance of calcium for her age group is 1,200 milligrams. Cassandra discovered that her daily diet usually contains only 1,125 milligrams of calcium. How many more milligrams of calcium does she need to meet the recommended daily allowance?

Subtract 1,200 − 1,125.

Regroup the hundreds.	Regroup the tens.	Subtract.	Check by adding.
$\begin{array}{r} \overset{1\ 10}{1,2\cancel{0}0} \\ -1,125 \\ \hline \end{array}$	$\begin{array}{r} \overset{1\ \overset{9}{10}\ 10}{1,\cancel{2}\cancel{0}\cancel{0}} \\ -1,125 \\ \hline \end{array}$	$\begin{array}{r} \overset{1\ \overset{9}{10}\ 10}{1,\cancel{2}\cancel{0}\cancel{0}} \\ -1,125 \\ \hline 75 \end{array}$	$\begin{array}{r} 1,125 \\ +\quad 75 \\ \hline 1,200 \end{array}$

Cassandra needs 75 more milligrams of calcium.

Other examples:

$$\begin{array}{r} \overset{6\ \overset{9}{\cancel{10}}\ \overset{9}{\cancel{10}}15}{7,0\cancel{0}5} \\ -6,128 \\ \hline 877 \end{array} \qquad \begin{array}{r} \overset{4\ \overset{9}{\cancel{10}}\cancel{10}\cancel{10}}{\$9\cancel{5}.\cancel{0}\cancel{0}} \\ -50.75 \\ \hline \$44.25 \end{array} \qquad \begin{array}{r} \overset{6\ \overset{9}{\cancel{10}}\ \overset{9}{\cancel{10}}\ \overset{9}{\cancel{10}}10}{77\cancel{0},\cancel{0}\cancel{0}\cancel{0}} \\ -31,349 \\ \hline 738,651 \end{array}$$

Checkpoint Write the letter of the correct answer.

Subtract.

1. $\begin{array}{r} 700 \\ -412 \\ \hline \end{array}$	2. $\begin{array}{r} \$80.08 \\ -55.29 \\ \hline \end{array}$	3. $\begin{array}{r} 6,800 \\ -4,236 \\ \hline \end{array}$	4. $950,000 - 14,629$
a. 188	a. $24.70	a. 2,474	a. 803,710
b. 288	b. $24.71	b. 2,564	b. 906,481
c. 300	c. $24.79	c. 2,574	c. 935,371
d. 398	d. $25.89	d. 2,654	d. 936,481

Subtract. Check your answers by adding.

1. 630
    − 233

2. 800
    − 697

3. 690
    − 591

4. 800
    − 391

5. 650
    − 571

6. 201
    − 163

7. 4,000
    − 1,653

8. 3,408
    − 1,113

9. 8,057
    − 7,211

10. 7,590
    − 1,346

11. 2,067
    − 1,622

12. 7,990
    − 3,161

13. 56,090
    − 22,652

14. 60,799
    − 22,372

15. 90,000
    − 54,872

16. 79,000
    − 17,278

17. 67,709
    − 13,345

18. 840,500
    − 731,234

19. 757,504
    − 346,272

20. 600,000
    − 382,851

21. 806,090
    − 725,321

22. 490,065
    − 113,242

23. 460,040 − 47,397

24. 11,002 − 9,993

25. 303,280 − 11,990

26. 700,000 − 5,816

27. 999,040 − 233

28. 720,004 − 61,243

To make each statement true,
write >, <, or = for each ●.

29. 983 − 428 ● 653 + 129

30. 306 + 631 ● 939 − 17

31. 356 + 356 ● 1,006 − 227

32. 760,021 − 999 ● 436,308 + 290,715

★33. (1,317 + 9,703) − 901 ● (1,493 + 513) − 807

Solve.

34. A doctor surveyed 1,000 people. The major health concern of 814 of them was keeping the correct weight. How many people did not list keeping the correct weight as their major health concern?

★35. In the same survey, 189 people reported their age as 65 years or older, and 374 people reported their age as 25 years or younger. How many of those surveyed were between 25 and 65?

CHALLENGE

John visits a refreshment stand. According to the problem below, what might John be doing there? Solve the problem. What does the answer represent?

$5.00 − ($1.60 + $1.45) = ▨

PROBLEM SOLVING
Estimation

Sometimes you can estimate to solve a problem. At other times, you need to find the exact answer.

> Think about this problem.
>
> Karen eats lunch at a health-food restaurant. She has $6.85 to spend. She wants to buy a cup of gazpacho soup for $1.35, a chicken salad sandwich for $3.45, and apple juice for $0.75. Does she have enough money?

Estimate by rounding to the nearest dollar. A cup of gazpacho soup costs about $1.00, a chicken salad sandwich costs about $3.00, and apple juice costs about $1.00. The three items cost about $5.00.

Since $5.00 is less than $6.85, Karen will have enough money.

If she wanted to buy a lunch of shrimp and avocado for $5.95 and apple juice for $0.75, would she have enough money?

Estimate. $5.95 ⟶ $6.00
              $0.75 ⟶ $1.00
                      $7.00   estimated sum

$7.00 is very close to $6.85. To find whether Karen would have enough money, you will have to find the exact sum.

         $5.95
      + $0.75
         $6.70

Since $6.70 is less than $6.85, Karen would have enough money.

Read each problem. Use the menu on the right to decide whether you can estimate the answer or whether you need to find the exact answer. Write *estimate* or *exact answer*.

1. Gail wants to order a cup of tomato dill soup and a yogurt-and-fruit platter. She has $6.50. Does she have enough money?

2. Janice ordered a bowl of gazpacho and a tuna melt. She paid for her lunch with a $5 bill and received $2.10 in change. Was that the right amount of change?

3. Sally ordered a shrimp-and-avocado platter and a glass of apple juice. Mark ordered a chicken salad sandwich and spring water. Whose lunch cost more?

	NELL'S	
Soup		
Gazpacho	$1.35 cup	
	$1.65 bowl	
Tomato Dill	$1.45 cup	
	$1.75 bowl	
Sandwiches		
Tuna Melt	$2.25	
Chicken Salad	$3.45	
Cold Platters		
Yogurt and Fresh Fruit Platter	$4.95	
Shrimp and Avocado Platter	$5.95	
Beverages		
Apple Juice	$0.75	
Spring Water	$1.25	

Solve. Estimate if possible.

	Suppose You Had	Could You Buy
4.	$3.57	a cup of gazpacho and apple juice?
5.	$5.22	a bowl of tomato dill and chicken salad?
6.	$5.75	a bowl of gazpacho and a yogurt-and-fruit platter?
7.	$5.82	a cup of tomato dill, a chicken salad sandwich, and apple juice?
8.	$9.10	a bowl of tomato dill, a shrimp-and-avocado platter, and spring water?
9.	$7.25	a bowl of gazpacho, a yogurt-and-fruit platter, and apple juice?
10.	$8.50	a yogurt-and-fruit platter, a tuna melt, and spring water?

Equations

A. The sixth-grade class at Hoover Elementary School took a physical-fitness test. Together, Marcie and Ed did as many chin-ups as Leah. Marcie did 6 chin-ups. Leah did 9 chin-ups. How many chin-ups did Ed do?

You can write an equation to solve this problem.

Marcie's chin-ups	plus	Ed's chin-ups	equals	Leah's chin-ups
6	plus	what number	equals	9
6	+	n	=	9

Think of a related subtraction fact.
$6 + 3 = 9$ So, $n = 3$.
Ed did 3 chin-ups.

$$9 - 6 = 3$$

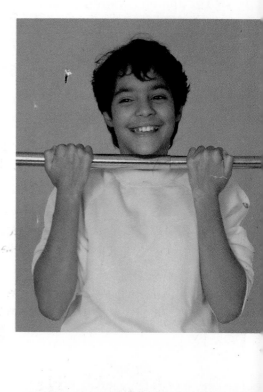

B. You can solve subtraction equations in a similar way. What number minus 4 equals 11?

$$n - 4 = 11$$

Think of a related addition fact.
$15 - 4 = 11$ So, $n = 15$.

$$11 + 4 = 15$$

Another example:

$16 - n = 7$
$16 - 7 = 9$ related subtraction fact
$16 - 9 = 7$
$\quad\quad n = 9$

Checkpoint   Write the letter of the correct answer.

Find the missing number.

1. $n + 5 = 11$ **a.** 3   **b.** 6   **c.** 7   **d.** 16

2. $n - 7 = 2$ **a.** 9   **b.** 10   **c.** 11   **d.** 16

3. $13 - n = 5$ **a.** 8   **b.** 9   **c.** 18   **d.** 135

Find the missing number.

1. $5 + n = 6$ **2.** $n + 6 = 10$ **3.** $8 + n = 15$ **4.** $7 + 8 = n$

5. $n + 6 = 13$ **6.** $4 + n = 11$ **7.** $n + 2 = 6$ **8.** $13 + n = 14$

9. $n + 2 = 12$ **10.** $18 + n = 18$ **11.** $n - 8 = 10$ **12.** $18 - n = 9$

13. $13 - n = 9$ **14.** $15 - 3 = n$ **15.** $n - 6 = 10$ **16.** $n - 4 = 6$

17. $17 - n = 9$ **18.** $17 - n = 8$ **19.** $n - 1 = 10$ **20.** $13 - 5 = n$

21. $11 - 6 = n$ **22.** $n - 8 = 7$ **23.** $5 - 1 = n$ **24.** $16 - n = 14$

25. $13 - 9 = n$ **26.** $10 - n = 6$ **27.** $2 + n = 5$ **28.** $n + 2 = 8$

29. $11 - n = 9$ **30.** $n - 2 = 12$ **31.** $7 + n = 10$ **32.** $16 - 8 = n$

33. $n + 4 = 9$ **34.** $7 - n = 4$ **35.** $20 + n = 25$ ★**36.** $n + 69 = 71$

★**37.** $n - 21 = 29$ ★**38.** $52 + n = 87$ ★**39.** $n + 33 = 69$ ★**40.** $72 - 69 = n$

Write an equation. Solve.

41. When a certain number is subtracted from 17, the difference is 5. What is the number?

42. When 8 is subtracted from a certain number, the difference is 3. What is the number?

43. The sum of a certain number and 9 is 16. What is the number?

44. The sum of a number and 7 is 15. What is the number?

★**45.** In 4 years, Clara will be 17 years old. How old is she now?

★**46.** Larry was 5 years old 12 years ago. How old is Larry now?

CHALLENGE

Make each statement true. Write + or − for ●.

1. $3 \bullet 5 \bullet 2 \bullet 4 = 10$

2. $32 \bullet 12 \bullet 15 \bullet 15 = 50$

3. $90 \bullet 45 \bullet 20 \bullet 50 = 75$

4. $64 \bullet 25 \bullet 50 \bullet 61 = 100$

5. $148 \bullet 67 \bullet 10 \bullet 5 = 200$

CALCULATOR

Estimate the sum or difference to find which result is incorrect. Then use your calculator to find the correct answer.

Example: **a.** 365 **b.** 721
  27   129
+ 145 + 91
537   2,041

Estimates: 400 − 600   800 − 1,100   So, b is incorrect.

Example: **a.** 392 **b.** 465
  − 128   − 203
264   369

Estimates: less than 300   less than 300   So, b is incorrect.

1. a. 415 **b.** 723   **2. a.** 621 **b.** 164   **3. a.** 241 **b.** 624
    612   821   123   897   389   819
  + 425   + 104   587   140   465   912
  1,152   1,648   + 621   + 503   + 193   + 408
                    1,952   1,804   1,288   3,069

4. a. 513 **b.** 248   **5. a.** 691 **b.** 654   **6. a.** 912 **b.** 906
    519   612   245   382   129   413
    513   846   834   455   843   825
  + 419   + 765   + 491   + 778   + 804   + 176
  1,964   2,749   2,503   2,269   2,688   2,404

7. a. 5,138 **b.** 6,045   **8. a.** 25,138 **b.** 37,129   **9. a.** 36,045 **b.** 67,184
  − 1,292   − 2,709   −   465   − 4,423   − 1,293   − 2,651
  6,056   3,336   28,203   32,706   34,752   65,533

10. a. 12,798 **b.** 72,138   **11. a.** 37,041 **b.** 96,405   **12. a.** 69,124 **b.** 56,142
  − 10,469   − 45,169   − 19,820   − 27,371   − 28,071   − 22,041
  3,011   26,969   17,221   79,604   41,053   21,001

GROUP PROJECT

Hiking to a Rescue

The problem: You and 3 friends are hiking in the Grand Canyon. You have been hiking for 2 days, when one of your friends twists an ankle and is unable to walk farther. You estimate that you are 20 miles from the nearest ranger station. You need to plan how to move everyone out of the canyon safely. You must find help. Look at the key facts. Look at the list to decide which items you need to take with you when you go for help.

Key Facts

- If you carry 10 pounds in your backpack, you can walk 3 miles per hour.
- If you carry 20 pounds, you can walk 2 miles per hour.
- If you carry 30 pounds, you can walk only 1 mile per hour.
- It becomes cold in the canyon by nightfall.

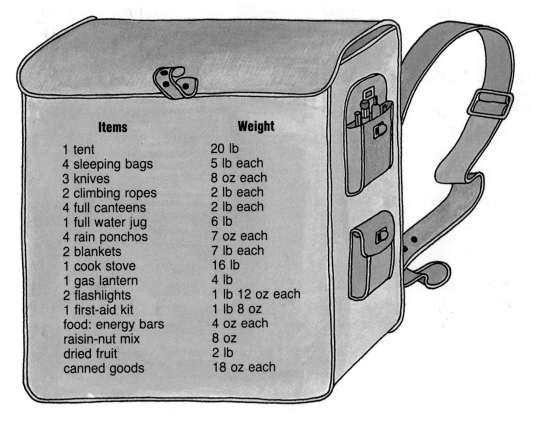

Items	Weight
1 tent	20 lb
4 sleeping bags	5 lb each
3 knives	8 oz each
2 climbing ropes	2 lb each
4 full canteens	2 lb each
1 full water jug	6 lb
4 rain ponchos	7 oz each
2 blankets	7 lb each
1 cook stove	16 lb
1 gas lantern	4 lb
2 flashlights	1 lb 12 oz each
1 first-aid kit	1 lb 8 oz
food: energy bars	4 oz each
raisin-nut mix	8 oz
dried fruit	2 lb
canned goods	18 oz each

CHAPTER TEST

Write the number in standard form. (pages 2 and 4)

1. four hundred twelve million

2. nine thousand, six hundred five

3. $400,000 + 3,000 + 900 + 30 + 6$

4. $200,000 + 60,000 + 800 + 4$

Write the value of the blue digit. (pages 2 and 4)

5. 735,211,332,810

6. 2,111,202

7. 900,000,020,000

Compare. Write $>$, $<$, or $=$ for each ●. (page 6)

8. 780,413 ● 780,341

9. 1,523,654 ● 1,600,423

Write in order from the least to the greatest. (page 6)

10. 312; 299; 906; 1,153; 563

Write in order from the greatest to the least. (page 6)

11. 423,912; 523,912; 423,921

Find the missing number. Identify the property used. (page 10)

12. $451 + 507 = 507 +$ ▨

13. $65 + (101 + 12) = (65 +$ ▨$) + 12$

Write the letter of the best estimate. (page 12)

14. $928 + 428$ **a.** less than 1,400   **b.** more than 1,400

15. $\$85.78 + \$6.79$ **a.** less than $91.00   **b.** more than $91.00

16. $\$71.38 - \$33.69$ **a.** less than $40.00   **b.** more than $40.00

17. $9,752 - 4,681$ **a.** less than 5,000   **b.** more than 5,000

Round to the nearest thousand. (page 14)

18. 5,472

19. 592,094

20. $963,923

Round to the nearest hundred thousand. (page 14)

21. 76,903

22. 2,341,879

23. 8,504,287

Add or subtract. (pages 18 and 22)

24. $\begin{array}{r} 98 \\ + 38 \\ \hline \end{array}$

25. $\begin{array}{r} 827 \\ + 195 \\ \hline \end{array}$

26. $\begin{array}{r} 4,378 \\ + 5,902 \\ \hline \end{array}$

27. $6,341 - 5,087$

28. $59,983 - 29,992$

29. $823,959 - 367,185$

Add or subtract. (pages 20 and 24)

30.   3,002
    − 2,418

31.   705,001
    − 630,204

32.   903
    66
    793
    + 121

33.   6,450
    1,450
    29
    +   83

Find the missing number. (page 28)

34. $n + 8 = 17$

35. $15 - n = 7$

36. $n - 9 = 4$

37. $9 + 10 = n$

Solve. Use the Help File if you need assistance. (page 8)

38. Brian finds out that his heart usually beats 75 times per minute. After he exercises for 20 minutes, his heart beats 130 times per minute. How much faster does his heart beat after exercise?

Estimate. (page 26)

39. Althea wants to buy a carton of orange juice for $1.59, a loaf of bread for $0.99, and a package of cheese for $2.29. Can she pay for all three items with a $5 bill?

Use the Infobank on page 431 to solve. (page 16)

40. In 1984, people from the West-North-Central region of the United States spent $441 dollars per person to eat in restaurants. What was the amount spent per person in the West-North-Central region and the East-North-Central region combined?

BONUS

Add or subtract.

1.   2,803,004
    − 1,917,385

2.   13,609,864
    + 9,795,738

3.   10,000,000,000
    − 2,601,726,168

4.   12,123,876
    + 87,698,669

5. 34,986 + 66,932 + 1,345,638

6. 909,040,101 − 23,856,437

RETEACHING

A. You can write an equation to solve an addition problem.

7 plus what number equals 15?
$$7 + \quad n \quad = \quad 15$$

Think of a related subtraction fact. $\boxed{15 - 7 = 8}$
$7 + 8 = 15$ So, $n = 8$.

B. You can solve subtraction problems in a similar way.

What number minus 9 equals 5?
$$n - 9 = 5$$

Think of a related addition fact. $\boxed{5 + 9 = 14}$
$14 - 9 = 5$ So, $n = 14$.

Find the missing number.

1. $4 + n = 9$	**2.** $n + 3 = 10$	**3.** $6 + n = 14$	**4.** $8 + n = 12$
5. $n + 2 = 11$	**6.** $7 + n = 15$	**7.** $9 + n = 13$	**8.** $2 + n = 9$
9. $8 - n = 3$	**10.** $10 - n = 4$	**11.** $n - 8 = 6$	**12.** $15 - n = 5$
13. $16 - n = 2$	**14.** $n - 4 = 11$	**15.** $19 - n = 18$	**16.** $n - 3 = 13$
17. $10 + n = 16$	**18.** $12 - n = 8$	**19.** $n + 9 = 17$	**20.** $n - 7 = 1$
21. $5 + n = 14$	**22.** $13 - n = 7$	**23.** $11 + n = 15$	**24.** $12 - 3 = n$
25. $n + 12 = 13$	**26.** $18 - n = 9$	**27.** $4 + n = 14$	**28.** $17 - n = 17$

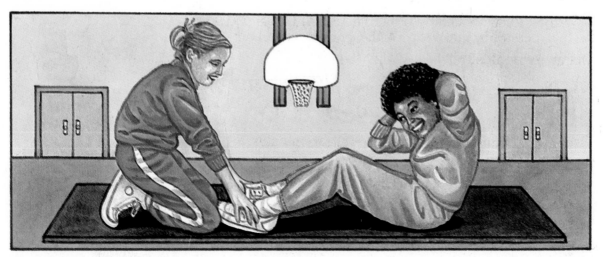

ENRICHMENT

Roman Numerals

The digits 0, 1, 2, 3, 4, 5, 6, 7, 8, and 9 are the basic symbols of the Arabic number system. The Romans developed their own number system in about 500 B.C.

The Roman number system uses seven basic symbols.

Roman Numeral	I	V	X	L	C	D	M
Arabic Numeral	1	5	10	50	100	500	1,000

The Roman number system is not based on place value. You can use the following rules to determine the value of Roman numerals.

If a larger number appears to the *left* of a smaller number, *add* the values of the numbers.

VI	**XXXV**	**DCX**
6	35	610
(5 + 1)	(10 + 10 + 10 + 5)	(500 + 100 + 10)

If a larger number appears to the *right* of a smaller number, *subtract* the smaller number from the larger number.

IV	**XL**	**XC**	**CD**
4	40	90	400
(5 − 1)	(50 − 10)	(100 − 10)	(500 − 100)

A bar over a symbol multiplies its value by 1,000.

$\overline{V} = 5 \times 1,000 = 5,000$ $\overline{X} = 10 \times 1,000 = 10,000$

Other examples:

XXXIV = 34   **CLVI** = 156 $\overline{XV}$**CCXVIII** = 15,218

Use Roman numerals to write the following dates.

1. the year you were born
2. the year men first landed on the moon
3. the year your school was built
4. the year your town was founded
5. the year that the Declaration of Independence was signed
6. the year Columbus first traveled to the new world

CUMULATIVE REVIEW

Write the letter of the correct answer.

1. Write in standard form:
   six hundred forty-three thousand.

   a. 643
   c. 643,000
   b. 64,300
   d. not given

2. Write the value of the blue digit:
   758,492,063.

   a. 90
   c. 900,000
   b. 90,000
   d. not given

3. Write in standard form:
   $50,000 + 900 + 20 + 7$.

   a. 5,927
   c. 50,927
   b. 500,927
   d. not given

4. Order from the least to the greatest:
   40,908; 49,008; 40,098.

   a. 49,008; 40,908; 40,098
   b. 40,098; 40,908; 49,008
   c. 40,908; 40,098; 49,008
   d. not given

5. $6.47
    + 9.54

   a. $15.01
   c. $16.01
   b. $15.91
   d. not given

6. Round 8,948,529 to the nearest
   hundred thousand.

   a. 8,900,000
   c. 9,000,000
   b. 8,950,000
   d. not given

7.   59,467
    − 49,478

   a. 9,989
   c. 10,989
   b. 9,999
   d. not given

8. Round $59.58 to the nearest dollar.

   a. $58.00
   c. $60.00
   b. $59.00
   d. not given

9. Choose the best estimate:
   $6.49 + $42.57 + $37.98.

   a. less than $80
   c. more than
       $100
   b. more than $80
   d. more than
       $800

10. $8 + n = 8$; solve for n.

    a. 1
    c. 8
    b. 4
    d. not given

11. Identify the property shown.
    $(4 + 2) + 5 = 4 + (2 + 5)$

    a. Identity
    c. Commutative
    b. Associative
    d. not given

12. **SIT-UPS**

Pat	Richard	Paul
97	52	100

    Estimate the total number of
    sit-ups.

    a. 150
    c. 250
    b. 200
    d. not given

13. Look at the Infobank on page 431.
    Estimate how much more money
    people from the Pacific region spent
    eating in restaurants than did
    southerners in 1984.

    a. $100
    c. $250
    b. $200
    d. $500

Plan a mini-Olympics. Consider including at least three events. Here are some ideas.

- Walk 0.5 mile.
- Do a standing long jump.
- Throw a softball.
- Do sit-ups for 2 minutes.

The top score is 1 point per event. Decide what contestants must do to earn 0.25 point, 0.50 point, 0.75 point, or 1.00 point.

2 PLACE VALUE, ADDITION AND SUBTRACTION
Decimals

Tenths and Hundredths

Every four years, athletes from around the world participate in the Olympics. In many events, each competitor's time is shown as a decimal.

A. You can write a decimal to represent part of a whole.

The square below is divided into ten equal parts. Each part is one tenth. Six tenths are colored.

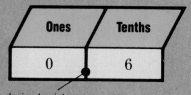

Ones	Tenths
0	6

decimal point

Read: six tenths.
Write: fraction $\frac{6}{10}$; decimal 0.6.

B. You can divide each tenth into ten equal parts. Each part is one hundredth of the whole.

Ones	Tenths	Hundredths
0	6	3

Read: sixty three hundredths.
Write: fraction $\frac{63}{100}$; decimal 0.63.

C. You can write a decimal for a number greater than 1.

Read: one and three tenths.
Write: mixed number $1\frac{3}{10}$; decimal 1.3.

Another example:

Hundreds	Tens	Ones	Tenths	Hundredths
1	4	2	0	7

Read: one hundred forty-two and seven hundredths.
Write: mixed number $142\frac{7}{100}$; decimal 142.07.

38

Write as a decimal.

1.

2.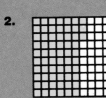

3.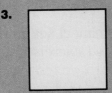

4. $2\frac{3}{10}$

5. $\frac{61}{100}$

6. $9\frac{6}{100}$

7. $10\frac{57}{100}$

Copy and complete this place-value chart. Write each number as a decimal.

Hundreds	Tens	Ones	Tenths	Hundredths

8. $5\frac{3}{10}$ **9.** $243\frac{27}{100}$ **10.** $28\frac{7}{10}$ **11.** $156\frac{5}{100}$

12. $4\frac{79}{100}$ **13.** $\frac{75}{100}$ **14.** $96\frac{3}{100}$ **15.** $1\frac{2}{100}$

16. seven and eight tenths

17. fifty-three and thirty-five hundredths

Write the word name.

18. 0.5   **19.** 1.3   **20.** 78.9   **21.** 0.9

22. 34.06   **23.** 71.11   **24.** 0.87   **25.** 16.08

Solve.

26. In the 1984 Olympic Games, Evelyn Ashford of the United States set the record for the women's 100-meter dash. Her time was ten and ninety-seven hundredths seconds. Write her time as a decimal.

27. United States Olympic star Carl Lewis ran the men's 200-meter dash. His record time was 19.8 seconds. Suppose that he had been 0.1 second faster. What would his time have been?

CHALLENGE

Use these clues to write the "mystery number."

The number has four digits.
The number is greater than 24 but less than 25.
The sum of the four digits is 13.
A 6 is in the hundredths place.

Hundred-Thousandths

A. In 1976, gymnast Nadia Comaneci set an Olympic record for her score in combined exercises. She earned 79.275 points.

The place-value chart can help you understand the meaning of each digit in Nadia Comaneci's winning score.

Tens	Ones	Tenths	Hundredths	Thousandths
7	9	2	7	5

Read: seventy-nine and two hundred seventy-five thousandths.
Short word name: 79 and 275 thousandths.
Write: 79.275.

Other examples:

sixteen and four thousandths
16 and 4 thousandths
16.004

twelve thousandths
12 thousandths
0.012

B. Decimals can be written for ten-thousandths and for hundred-thousandths.

Ones	Tenths	Hundredths	Thousandths	Ten-thousandths	Hundred-thousandths
9	1	0	8	6	3

Read: nine and ten thousand eight hundred sixty-three hundred-thousandths, or 9 and 10,863 hundred-thousandths.
Write: 9.10863.

In 9.10863:

The value of the digit 9 in the ones place is 9.
The value of the digit 1 in the tenths place is 0.1.
The value of the digit 0 in the hundredths place is 0.00.
The value of the digit 8 in the thousandths place is 0.008.
The value of the digit 6 in the ten-thousandths place is 0.0006.
The value of the digit 3 in the hundred-thousandths place is 0.00003.

Read each decimal. Write the value of the blue digit.

1. 5.734 **2.** 7.087 **3.** 0.561 **4.** 21.063

5. 23.907 **6.** 0.001 **7.** 211.703 **8.** 8.749

9. 0.20982 **10.** 231.2312 **11.** 0.0241 **12.** 90.2718

13. 1,985.984 **14.** 0.30078 **15.** 2.38017 **16.** 8.47913

Write each as a decimal.

17. 236 thousandths

18. 352 thousandths

19. 1 and 42 hundredths

20. 2 and 13,948 hundred-thousandths

Write the short word name for each decimal.

21. 9.89 **22.** 0.731 **23.** 8.034 **24.** 6.756

25. 0.4107 **26.** 0.06312 **27.** 2.00408 **28.** 16.934

Solve.

29. Mary Lou Retton of the United States won the gold medal for combined exercises in 1984. Her score was 79.175. What is the value of the digit 5 in her score?

30. Larissa Latynina of the Soviet Union won two gold medals and one silver medal for combined exercises in three Olympiads. Write her best score of 77.031 points as a short word name.

FOCUS: REASONING

There are 25 people in a travel club. The list below shows how many people went to the 1976, 1980, and 1984 Olympics.

1976 only—1   1976 and 1980 only—3
1980 only—1   1980 and 1984 only—3
1984 only—4   All three—2
          None—5

How many people from the club visited the 1976 Olympics?
(HINT: You first need to fill in the missing number in the list—the number of people who went to the Olympics in 1976 and 1984, but not in 1980. Remember that there is a total of 25 people in the club.)

More Practice, page 439

PROBLEM SOLVING
Checking for a Reasonable Answer

When you solve a problem, think about the value of your answer. Is it much too great? Is it much too small? You can often spot a wrong answer just by thinking about the value of it.

Yachtsman William E. Buchan, age 49, was the oldest United States citizen to win a medal at the 1984 Summer Olympic Games. The youngest United States citizen to win a medal there was swimmer Michele Richardson, age 15. How much older was Buchan than Richardson?

a. 14 years   **b.** 34 years   **c.** 64 years

Without finding the exact answer, you can see that choice *a* is too small a number and choice *c* is too large. Choice *b*, 34 years, is the best choice. Always check the value of your answer choices. You will catch many errors.

Read each problem. Without finding the exact answer, write the letter of the reasonable answer.

1. A total of 140 countries competed in the 1984 Summer Olympics. Only 47 countries won medals. How many countries did not win medals?

   a. 47
   b. 93
   c. 187

2. At the 1984 Summer Olympics, the United States won 83 gold, 61 silver, and 30 bronze medals. How many medals did the United States win?

   a. 91
   b. 144
   c. 174

3. The first Olympic Games of the modern era were held in Greece in 1896. How many years before the 1984 Olympics were the 1896 Olympics held?

   a. 12   **b.** 88   **c.** 3,890

4. Since the 1896 Olympics, the United States has won a total of 1,716 medals. The Soviet Union is second, having won 848 fewer medals than the United States. How many medals has the Soviet Union won?

   a. 800   **b.** 868   **c.** 2,524

5. A total of 7,200 athletes competed in the 1984 Summer Olympics. There were 54 athletes with the family name *Kim* and 34 named *Smith*. How many athletes at the games were not named *Kim* or *Smith?*

   a. 88
   b. 7,112
   c. 7,288

6. A total of 20 Olympic records were set at the 1984 Summer Games. That total was 18 less than the number of Olympic records set at the 1972 Summer Games. How many Olympic records were set at the 1972 Summer Games?

   a. 2
   b. 12
   c. 38

7. The United States won the women's basketball gold medal by achieving an 85–55 victory over South Korea. By how many points did the United States win the game?

   a. 10
   b. 30
   c. 140

8. A total of 101,799 fans watched the championship soccer game at the 1984 Olympics. 100,374 fans watched the third-place game. How many fans watched the two games?

   a. 1,425
   b. 202,173
   c. 302,173

9. The Weiss family spent all but 3 days at the 1984 Summer Olympics. The games lasted 16 days. How many days did the Weiss family spend at the games?

   a. 13
   b. 16
   c. 19

10. Mr. Weiss gave the parking attendant at Olympic Stadium a $20 bill. Parking costs $7.50. How much change should Mr. Weiss have received?

   a. $7.50
   b. $12.50
   c. $17.50

11. On the day the Weiss family arrived at the Olympic Games, there was a total of 426,000 visitors. The day before, there were 414,500 visitors. How many visitors were there at the Olympic Games on those two days?

   a. 11,500
   b. 740,500
   c. 840,500

12. Don Weiss bought an official Olympic souvenir program for $6.00, a cap for $8.50, and a pennant for his sister for $3.75. How much in all did he spend?

   a. $14.50
   b. $18.25
   c. $22.25

Comparing and Ordering Decimals

A. In 1984, the Olympic record for the women's 100-meter freestyle swim was 55.92 seconds. In 1976, the Olympic record for the same event was 55.65 seconds. Which is the faster time?

To find the faster time, you must compare decimals. You can use a number line.

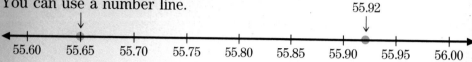

On the number line, 55.65 is to the left of 55.92. So, 55.65 < 55.92. 55.65 is the faster time.

B. Compare 4.735 and 4.784 without a number line.

Line up the decimal points.	Begin to compare at the left.	Continue to compare until you find the first place where the digits differ.
4.735 4.784	4.735 4.784 4 = 4	4.735 4.735 4.784 4.784 7 = 7 3 < 8

So, 4.735 < 4.784.

C. You can write equivalent decimals by writing zeros to the right of the number.

Write three equivalent decimals for 0.4.
0.4 = 0.40 = 0.400 = 0.4000

D. You can order 0.469, 0.4694, 0.46, and 0.4692 by comparing them.

Line up the decimal points. Write equivalent decimals.	Begin to compare at the left. Find the first place the numbers differ.	Continue to compare.
0.4690 0.4694 0.4600 0.4692	0.4690 0.4694 0.4600 — the smallest number 0.4692	0 < 2 0.4690 < 0.4692 2 < 4 0.4692 < 0.4694

From the least to the greatest: 0.46 < 0.469 < 0.4692 < 0.4694
From the greatest to the least: 0.4694 > 0.4692 > 0.469 > 0.46

Write each as an equivalent decimal that has hundredths.

1. 0.9   **2.** 2.6   **3.** 4.8   **4.** 21.6   **5.** 9   **6.** 10.2

Write >, <, or = for each ●.

7. 0.9723 ● 0.9273   **8.** 5.6 ● 5.30151   **9.** 4.1 ● 4.09

10. 88.19 ● 88.190   **11.** 0.10098 ● 0.1098   **12.** 11.011 ● 11.0101

13. 100.001 ● 101.100   **14.** 0.033 ● 0.03312   **15.** 52.8 ● 52.799

Write in order from the least to the greatest.

16. 31.148, 31.15, 32.1, 31.1481, 31.14799   **17.** 7.019, 7.017, 7.190, 7.17

18. 0.5, 0.5505, 0.555, 0.50505, 0.05   **19.** 6.302, 6.032, 6.32, 6.203

Write in order from the greatest to the least.

20. 10.1, 10.1001, 10.01, 10.101, 10.11011   **21.** 0.047, 0.407, 0.47, 0.447

22. 2.99, 2.998, 2.98988, 3.0, 2.9889   **23.** 3.8, 3.023, 3.328, 3.028

Solve.

24. At the 1984 Summer Olympics, Rowdy Gaines won the men's 100-meter freestyle with a time of 49.80 seconds. Did this break the old record of 49.99 seconds?

25. Carl Lewis won the 100-meter run in the 1984 Olympics with a time of 9.99 seconds. Did this break Jim Hines's record of 9.9 seconds, set in 1968?

26. The table to the right gives the winning times for the women's 100-meter run in four Olympics. Use the data in the table to write and solve your own word problem.

WOMEN'S 100–METER RUN

1972	11.07 seconds
1976	11.08 seconds
1980	11.6 seconds
1984	10.97 seconds

CHALLENGE

Use the digits 1, 2, 3, and 4 to make each inequality true.

1. 2.431 > ■ > 2.314   **2.** 3.142 < ■ < 3.412

3. 0.3421 > ■ > 0.3214   **4.** 4.123 < ■ < 4.231

Rounding Decimals

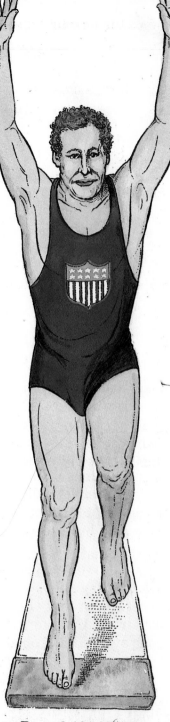

A. In the 1924 Olympic Games, a United States diver, Albert White, won a gold medal in the springboard diving competition with a score of 696.4 points. Rounded to the nearest whole number, what was his score?

Round 696.4 to the nearest whole number.

Look at the digit to the right of the ones place.
If the digit is 5 or greater, round up.
If the digit is less than 5, round down.

696.4

| 4 < 5 |
| **Round down.** |

Albert White scored 696 points to the nearest whole number.

Other examples:

| 56.779 | Think: 56.779; 7 > 5. | Round up to 57. |
| 43.5183 | Think: 43.5183; 5 = 5. | Round up to 44. |

B. To round to the nearest tenth, hundredth, thousandth, or ten-thousandth, find the digit to the right of that place, and compare it to 5.

Round 2.731 to the nearest tenth.
Think: 2.731; 3 < 5.   Round down to 2.7.

Round 1.827 to the nearest hundredth.
Think: 1.827; 7 > 5.   Round up to 1.83.

Round 0.47549 to the nearest thousandth.
Think: 0.47549; 4 < 5.   Round down to 0.475.

Round 3.57185 to the nearest ten-thousandth.
Think: 3.57185; 5 = 5.   Round up to 3.5719.

Checkpoint   Write the letter of the correct answer.

1. Round 525.071 to the nearest whole number.

a. 500
b. 525
c. 525.1
d. 526

2. Round 4.8156 to the nearest tenth.

a. 4.8
b. 4.82
c. 4.9
d. 5

3. Round 101.25687 to the nearest thousandth.

a. 101.256
b. 101.2569
c. 101.257
d. 101.260

Round to the nearest whole number.

1. 0.401   **2.** 4.95   **3.** 0.011   **4.** 10.65   **5.** 9.009

Round to the nearest tenth.

6. 0.69   **7.** 1.0089   **8.** 7.454   **9.** 98.701   **10.** 17.05

Round to the nearest hundredth.

11. 0.394   **12.** 45.90801   **13.** 2.6045   **14.** 78.502   **15.** 29.351

Round to the nearest thousandth.

16. 0.89795   **17.** 51.1472   **18.** 43.0098   **19.** 5.9595   **20.** 1.5745

Round to the nearest ten-thousandth.

21. 0.82095   **22.** 9.89678   **23.** 40.61474   **24.** 10.00089   **25.** 4.10273

Solve. For Problem 29, use the Infobank.

26. John Naber of the United States set an Olympic record in the 1976 games. He swam the 100-meter backstroke in 55.49 seconds. Round this number to the nearest tenth of a second.

27. In 1928, Johnny Weissmuller, who later became famous as an actor who played Tarzan, won the 100-meter freestyle in 58.6 seconds. Round this to the nearest whole number.

28. In the 1936 Olympics, Tetsuo Hamuro of Japan won the 200-meter breaststroke in 2 minutes 42.5 seconds. What was his time, to the nearest second?

★29. Use the information on page 431 to solve. If the scores for these 100-meter butterfly races were rounded to tenths, in which year would the swimmers' rankings change? What would the change be?

ANOTHER LOOK

Write > or < to make each inequality true.

1. 451 ● 449   **2.** 1,596 ● 1,569   **3.** 65,009 ● 65,090

4. 1,317,800 ● 1,370,080   **5.** 3,971,462 ● 3,959,947   **6.** 13,909 ● 13,898

7. 999,999 ● 100,000   **8.** 4,361,461 ● 4,361,641   **9.** 1,122 ● 1,212

PROBLEM SOLVING
Making an Organized List

Sometimes you can use an organized list to solve a problem.

> Six Olympic swimmers raced in the 200-meter freestyle. When the race was over, each swimmer shook hands with all the other swimmers. How many handshakes did they exchange?

Make a list to show all the combinations of handshakes. List the first letter of the name of each swimmer. The 6 swimmers are Gloria, Helga, Isabel, Jackie, Kathy, and Lynn.

Gloria shook hands with each of the 5 other swimmers.

G and H
G and I
G and J
G and K
G and L

Helga shook hands with 4 other swimmers. You don't need to include H(elga) and G(loria) because that is the same as G and H.

H and I
H and J
H and K
H and L

Isabel shook hands with 3 other swimmers.

I and J
I and K
I and L

Jackie shook hands with 2 other swimmers.

J and K
J and L

Finally, Kathy shook hands with Lynn.

K and L

Add to find the total number of combinations.

$5 + 4 + 3 + 2 + 1 = 15$

They exchanged 15 handshakes.

Solve. Use a list if needed.

1. The Olympic volleyball team is receiving their numbers. Debbie is able to pick her own number, but she must choose from the digits 1, 2, and 4. What are the possible 2-digit combinations?

2. The Olympic archery team has 6 members. 3 of them will be able to compete at the games. The other 3 members will serve as alternates. How many possible sets of 3 archers could be named to the first-string team?

3. The Olympic basketball team is practicing passing. Each of the 5 players passes the ball once to everyone else. How many passes are made?

4. Don found 4 coins in the Olympic Stadium stands. The coins were dimes and quarters. What are the possible combinations of coins that Don could have found?

5. There are 4 fencers left in the Olympic fencing tournament. If each fencer faces every other fencer once, how many matches would there be?

6. There are 7 teams left in the Olympic hockey competition. If each team plays every other team once, how many games will be played?

7. At breakfast in the Olympic Village dining hall, athletes are given a choice of orange or tomato juice, toast or a bran muffin, and hot or cold cereal. How many possible breakfast combinations are there?

8. At lunch, the athletes can make a sandwich with rye or wheat bread. They can also choose 2 of 3 fillings: roast beef, turkey, cheese. How many possible combinations of sandwiches could each athlete make?

9. Bruce, John, and Alberto had a practice race before their Olympic event. In how many different orders could they have finished the race?

10. Carla has 1 blue shirt and 1 red shirt. She wears them with either her white or tan pants. How many different outfits can she make from these shirts and pants?

11. Bob won 3 medals at the Olympic Games. What are the possible combinations of gold, silver, and bronze medals that he could have won?

★12. Alice won 4 medals at the Olympic Games. At least 2 of her medals were silver. What are the possible combinations of gold, silver, and bronze medals she could have won?

Estimating Decimal Sums and Differences

A. At the 1964 Olympics in Tokyo, Japanese gymnasts won the gold and the silver medals in the parallel bars. Yukio Endo won the gold medal with a score of 19.675. Shuji Tsurumi won the silver medal with a score of 19.45. Estimate the total number of points scored by the two Japanese gymnasts in this event.

Estimate 19.675 + 19.45.

You can estimate with decimals the same way you estimate with whole numbers.

Use front-end estimation.

Add the whole numbers.

$$19 + 19 = 38$$

Adjust by examining the decimal parts.

0.675 ⟍₁ 0.45

$$38 + 1 = 39$$

Use rounding.

Round each number to the nearest whole number. Then add.

$$19.675 \longrightarrow 20$$
$$19.45 \longrightarrow \underline{+19}$$
$$39$$

The Japanese gymnasts scored about 39 points.

B. You can also estimate to find differences. Estimate the difference: 41.560 − 38.391.

Use front-end estimation.

Subtract the whole numbers.

$$41 - 38 = 3$$

Adjust by examining the decimal part.

$$\begin{array}{r} 41.560 \\ -38.391 \\ \hline .2 \end{array}$$

The difference is a little more than 3.

Use rounding.

Round each number to the nearest whole number.

$$41.560 \to 42$$
$$38.391 \to 38$$

Subtract.

$$42 - 38 = 4$$

About 4.

Both these estimates are reasonable.

Estimate. Write > or < for ●.

1. $4.26 + 5.47$ ● 10
2. $8.87 + 3.75$ ● 15
3. $2.17 + 1.98$ ● 5
4. $4.87 + 5.93$ ● 10
5. $13.65 + 4.89$ ● 20
6. $9.76 + 8.63$ ● 20
7. $2.753 + 2.896$ ● 6
8. $4.473 + 3.477$ ● 9
9. $15.937 + 4.865$ ● 20
10. $24.573 + 4.965$ ● 30
11. $27.953 + 1.276$ ● 30
12. $19.875 + 19.639$ ● 40
13. $5.36 - 2.19$ ● 2
14. $15.76 - 9.89$ ● 5
15. $21.87 - 9.98$ ● 10
16. $3.365 - 0.984$ ● 3
17. $5.297 - 4.538$ ● 1
18. $16.951 - 7.087$ ● 10
19. $38.765 - 17.985$ ● 20
20. $7 - 3.765$ ● 3
21. $82.507 - 50.968$ ● 30
22. $40 - 19.867$ ● 20
23. $12.347 - 1.987$ ● 10
24. $100.275 - 95.69$ ● 5
25. $15.195 - 4.372$ ● 10
26. $14.75 - 1.99$ ● 12
27. $18.67 - 9.12$ ● 11

Solve.

28. Japan won a gold medal for men's team gymnastics in the 1972 Olympic Games, scoring 571.25 points. The Japanese team won again in 1976 with a score of 576.85 points. Estimate, to the nearest whole number, the difference between these two scores.

29. Men's gymnastics is divided into compulsory events and optional events. In 1984, the United States team members won the gold medal. Their score in optional events was 296.1. In compulsory events, they scored 259.3 points. Was their total score more than 550 points?

MIDCHAPTER REVIEW

Write > or < for each ●.

1. 0.6029 ● 0.6031
2. 1.0467 ● 1.0466
3. 420.977 ● 420.982

Round each number to the nearest tenth.

4. 0.361
5. 0.8436
6. 1.34456
7. 12.19
8. 0.956

More Practice, page 440

Adding with Decimals

A. On the first day of the 1984 Olympic luge races, Italian Paul Hildgartner completed the course in 92.453 seconds. On the second day, he finished in 91.805 seconds. What was his total time?

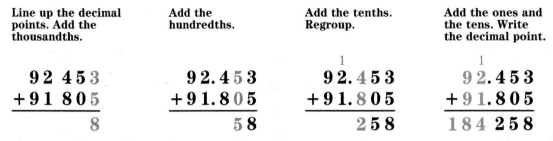

Find 92.453 + 91.805.
First estimate the sum: 92 + 92 = 184.
Then compute the answer.

Line up the decimal points. Add the thousandths.	Add the hundredths.	Add the tenths. Regroup.	Add the ones and the tens. Write the decimal point.
9 2 4 5 3 + 9 1 8 0 5 8	9 2.4 5 3 + 9 1.8 0 5 5 8	¹ 9 2.4 5 3 + 9 1.8 0 5 2 5 8	¹ 9 2.4 5 3 + 9 1.8 0 5 1 8 4 2 5 8

Hildgartner's total time was 184.258 seconds.
This answer is close to the estimate of 184.

B. You may need to write equivalent decimals before adding.

Find 4.56 + 13.6708 + 23.03.

Line up the decimal points. Write equivalent decimals.	Add the decimals.	Add the whole numbers. Write the decimal point.
4.5 6 0 0 13.6 7 0 8 + 23.0 3 0 0	1 1 4.5 6 0 0 13.6 7 0 8 + 23.0 3 0 0 2 6 0 8	1 1 1 4.5 6 0 0 13.6 7 0 8 + 23.0 3 0 0 4 1.2 6 0 8

Checkpoint Write the letter of the correct answer.

Add.

1. 4.25 + 56.7

  a. 9.92
  b. 50.95
  c. 60.95
  d. 99.2

2. 1.0567 + 2.145 + 2.0023

  a. 0.204
  b. 3.2725
  c. 5.193
  d. 5.204

3. $13.25 + $9.07

  a. $21.32
  b. $22.22
  c. $22.32
  d. $2,323

Find the sum.

1. 15.53
  + 61.06

2. 2.62
  + 2.06

3. 80.25
  + 19.81

4. $36.75
  + 32.12

5. $51.34
  + 12.66

6. 60.033
  + 27.82

7. 69.609
  + 3.51

8. 86.1
  + 6.98

9. 62.603
  + 3.7

10. 6
  + 1.15

11. 7.59
  19.49
  + 24.846

12. 0.8
  26.04
  + 93.33

13. 0.0008
  1.5003
  + 3.8299

14. 0.287
  0.1902
  + 0.3939

15. 4.009
  3.9101
  + 1.2019

16. $17.15 + 7.01$

17. $2.691 + 6.99$

18. $2.54 + $6.47

19. $13.01 + $73.71

20. $13.76 + 3.9$

21. $0.97 + 1.91$

22. $68.074 + 5 + 3.008$

23. $71.244 + 6.149$

24. $1.3 + 39 + 33.385$

25. $6.01 + 3.5 = n$

26. $0.08 + 0.92 = n$

★27. $10.56 + n = 11.78$

Solve.

28. The West Germans won the men's double-luge event in the 1984 Olympics. Their times were 41.753 seconds and 41.867 seconds. What is the total of their two times?

29. After three runs, American luger Frank Masley's total time was 140.760 seconds. He made his final run in 46.990 seconds. What was his new total time?

30. The table at the right shows the top three women luge-racers at the 1984 Olympics. Rank them in order from the fastest to the slowest.

1984 WOMEN'S LUGE RACERS

Racer	Country	Time (seconds)
S. Martin	E. Germany	166.57
U. Weiss	E. Germany	167.248
B. Schmidt	E. Germany	166.873

CHALLENGE

Discover the pattern. Then copy each sequence and write the missing numbers in the pattern.

1. 0.2, 0.5, 0.8, ▒, 1.4, 1.7, ▒

2. 0.4, 0.9, 1.4, ▒, 2.4, ▒, ▒

3. 0.17, 0.25, 0.33, ▒, ▒, ▒

More Practice, page 440

Subtracting with Decimals

A. In the 1984 Olympics, Edwin Moses of the United States won the men's 400-meter hurdles with a time of 47.75 seconds. Henry Amike of Nigeria came in eighth with a time of 53.78 seconds. How many seconds faster was Moses?

Subtract 53.78 − 47.75.
First estimate your answer: 53 − 47 = 6.
Compute the answer.

Line up the decimal points. Subtract the hundredths.	Subtract the tenths.	Regroup. Subtract the ones and the tens. Write the decimal point.
$$\begin{array}{r} 53.78 \\ -47.75 \\ \hline 3 \end{array}$$	$$\begin{array}{r} 53.78 \\ -47.75 \\ \hline 03 \end{array}$$	$$\begin{array}{r} {}^{4\;13} \\ 5\cancel{3}.78 \\ -47.75 \\ \hline 6.03 \end{array}$$

Moses was 6.03 seconds faster.
The answer is reasonably close to the estimate.

B. You may need to write equivalent decimals before subtracting.

Find 6 − 1.974.

Line up the decimal points. Write equivalent decimals.	Subtract the decimals.	Subtract the ones. Write the decimal point.
$$\begin{array}{r} 6.000 \\ -1.974 \\ \hline \end{array}$$	$$\begin{array}{r} {}^{9\;9} \\ {}^{5\;\cancel{10}\cancel{10}10} \\ \cancel{6}.\cancel{0}\cancel{0}\cancel{0} \\ -1.974 \\ \hline 026 \end{array}$$ This 0 must be written.	$$\begin{array}{r} {}^{9\;9} \\ {}^{5\;\cancel{10}\cancel{10}10} \\ \cancel{6}.\cancel{0}\cancel{0}\cancel{0} \\ -1.974 \\ \hline 4.026 \end{array}$$

Checkpoint Write the letter of the correct answer.

Subtract.

1. 0.88 − 0.624
   a. 0.264   **b.** 0.256   **c.** 0.266   **d.** 0.536

2. 4.66 − 1.783
   a. 3.123   **b.** 2.883   **c.** 2.877   **d.** 3.987

Subtract.

| **1.** | 8.64
 − 5.12 | **2.** | 11.030
 − 4.256 | **3.** | 0.4821
 − 0.3835 | **4.** | $9.13
 − 5.73 | **5.** | 7
 − 3.1 | **6.** | 15
 − 2.16 |

| **7.** | 10.4
 − 8.561 | **8.** | 9.1
 − 5.7395 | **9.** | $10.00
 − 8.29 | **10.** | $20.00
 − 13.47 | **11.** | 6.0005
 − 4.037 | **12.** | 13.0045
 − 6.056 |

13. $3.51 - 2.62$ **14.** $0.985 - 0.72$ **15.** $12.001 - 8.36$

16. $8.001 - 7.9$ **17.** $8.68 - 7.89 **18.** $9.27 - 7.38

19. $9.01 - 5.1 = n$ **20.** $8.327 - 4.809 = n$ ★**21.** $8.009 - n = 1.767$

Solve.

22. American Valerie Briscoe-Hooks won the women's 200-meter run at the 1984 Olympics in a record time of 21.81 seconds. By how many seconds did she break the 1980 record of 22.03 seconds?

23. In 1976, Mac Wilkins of the United States won the discus throw with a distance of 67.5 meters. He beat silver medalist John Powell by 1.8 meters. How far did Powell throw the discus?

24. At the 1984 Olympics, Doina Melinte of Rumania ran the women's 800-meter run in 1 minute 57.60 seconds. Kim Gallagher of the United States ran that distance in 1 minute 58.63 seconds. What is the difference between their times?

★**25.** In 1984, the United States team set a record of 37.83 seconds in the men's 400-meter relay. Three racers, in turn, ran 100 meters in 10.29, 9.19, and 9.41 seconds. What was the running time of the fourth racer?

FOCUS: MENTAL MATH

When adding decimals that end in 8 or 9, it is sometimes easier to use several operations.

Add $3.4 + 1.9$. Think: $1.9 + 0.1 = 2.0$
      $3.4 + 2.0 = 5.4$.
Now subtract the 0.1 that you added.
$5.4 - 0.1 = 5.3$; so, $3.4 + 1.9 = 5.3$.

Compute mentally.

1. $6.4 + 1.9$ **2.** $7.5 + 1.9$ **3.** $2.6 + 1.9$

4. $4.9 + 1.9$ **5.** $9.3 + 1.8$ **6.** $9.5 + 1.8$

More Practice, page 440

PROBLEM SOLVING
Choosing the Operation

When you are trying to solve a problem, read it carefully. Its wording and the question it asks can give you hints about whether to add or subtract.

> In the 1980 Winter Olympics, Eric Heiden won the 500-meter speed-skating race. His time was 38.03 seconds. Sergei Fokichev won in 1984. He took 0.16 seconds longer than Heiden did to finish the race. What was Fokichev's time?

Hints:

If you know	and you want to find	you can
• how many are in two or more sets	how many in all	add.
• how many are in one set • how many join it	the total number	add.
• how many are in one set • the number taken away	how many are left	subtract.
• how many are in two sets	how much greater one set is than another	subtract to compare.
• how many are in one set • how many are in part of the set	how many are in the remaining part of the set	subtract.

Once you have decided which operation to use, you can solve the problem.

how many are in one set   how many join it   the total number
$$38.03 \quad + \quad 0.16 \quad = \quad 38.19$$

Sergei Fokichev's time was 38.19 seconds.

Decide whether you would add or subtract to solve each problem. Write the letter of the correct answer.

1. Mr. Dithers, a souvenir vendor at the Olympics, earned $167.75 in sales in the morning and $345.85 in the afternoon. How much money in all did he earn?

   a. add   **b.** subtract

2. Herbie bought an official Olympics souvenir program from Mr. Dithers for $4.50. Herbie gave Mr. Dithers a $20 bill. How much change should he receive?

   a. add   **b.** subtract

Solve.

3. Mr. Dithers sold 23 official Olympics caps on Tuesday. Two other vendors, Kate and Arnold, sold 16 caps each. How many caps did the three vendors sell?

4. Kate sold a total of 437 official Olympics souvenir buttons. Arnold sold a total of 389 buttons. How many more buttons did Kate sell than Arnold sold?

5. Total attendance at Tuesday's events was 150,846. Wednesday's attendance was larger than Tuesday's by 12,395 people. What was Wednesday's attendance?

6. At 5:00 P.M. on Friday, the attendance in Olympic Stadium was 105,327. By 8:00 P.M., 9,849 people had gone home. How many people were there in the stadium at 8:00 P.M.?

7. In the 1960 Olympics, Wilma Rudolph won the 200-meter race in 24 seconds. In 1984, Valerie Brisco-Hooks won the 200-meter race in 21.81 seconds. How much faster was Brisco-Hooks's time?

8. The United States won the men's 400-meter relay race in 1984 in a record 37.83 seconds. The last three runners took 27.43 seconds to run their laps. What was the first runner's time?

9. In the 1984 Olympics, Carl Lewis won the long jump with a jump of 8.54 meters. This was 0.36 meters short of Bob Beamon's record jump in 1968. How far did Beamon jump?

10. Evelyn Ashford won the 1984 women's 100-meter race in 10.97 seconds, breaking the old record by 0.03 seconds. What was the old record for the event?

11. In 1900, Walter Tewksbury won the first 200-meter Olympic race. His time was 22.2 seconds. In 1984, Carl Lewis won the 200-meter race with a time that was 2.4 seconds faster than Tewksbury's. What was Lewis's time for the 200-meter event?

12. Carl Lewis also won the 100-meter race in 1984. His time for that event was 9.99 seconds. Thomas Burke won the first 100-meter Olympic race in 1896 with a time of 12 seconds. How much faster was Lewis's time for the 100-meter race?

13. At the right are the top three scorers from the 1984 parallel-bars competition. Which gymnast won the gold medal?
Who won the silver medal?

Gymnast (country)	Points
Mitch Gaylord (U.S.)	19.85
Bart Connor (U.S.)	19.95
Nobuyuki Kajitani (JAPAN)	19.925

PROBLEM SOLVING
Identifying Extra/Needed Information

Eric Heiden won 5 gold medals in the 1980 Winter Olympics. He won the 500-meter speed-skating event in 38.03 seconds. In 1928, Clas Thunberg won the 500-meter race. Thunberg won a total of 7 medals. How much faster was Heiden's time than Thunberg's?

A problem may not contain all the information you need to solve it. Sometimes you can find the information. Other problems may contain more information than you need. It is important to determine what information is needed to solve a problem and what information is given. Follow these steps.

1. Study the question.
How much faster was Heiden than Thunberg?

2. List the facts. Cross out the facts that will not help you.
   a. Heiden won 5 medals.
   b. Heiden's time was 38.03.
   c. Thunberg won 7 medals.
   d. Thunberg won the 500-meter race. (Cross out *a*, *c*, and *d*.)

3. List the facts you need that were not stated in the problem.
Thunberg's time for the 500-meter race

4. Study the facts you have. If you have all the information you need, or if you know where to find it, solve the problem. If not, write *There is not enough information.*

Write the letter of the sentence that describes the problem.

1. In the 1960 Olympics, Wilma Rudolph ran 100 meters in 11.0 seconds. In the 1964 Olympics, Wyomia Tyus won the 100-meter run. Who ran faster?

   a. Not enough information is given to solve the problem.
   b. More information than you need to solve the problem is given.

2. In 1972, Renate Stecher won the 200-meter run in 22.40 seconds. In 1976, she finished third with 22.47 seconds. The winning time that year was 22.37 seconds. Was Renate faster in 1972 or in 1976?

   a. Not enough information is given to solve the problem.
   b. More information than you need to solve the problem is given.

Solve if possible. Identify the needed information.

3. In the 1900 Olympics, Walter Tewksbury ran 200 meters in 22.2 seconds. In 1904, Archie Hahn's speed was 0.6 seconds faster. What was Archie Hahn's speed?

4. In the 1964 Olympics, Wyomia Tyus won a gold medal for the 100-meter run. In 1968, she won it again. How much faster did she run in 1968?

5. In the 1960 Olympics, Abebe Bikila ran the marathon in 2 hours 15 minutes 16.2 seconds. In the next Olympics, his time was 2 hours 12 minutes 11.2 seconds. Frank Shorter's time was 2 hours 12 minutes 19.8 seconds in the 1972 Olympic marathon. How much slower was Bikila's first run than his second?

6. In the 1976 Olympics, Brian Goodell won the 400-meter freestyle swim in 3 minutes 51.93 seconds. The second-fastest time in that event that year was 3 minutes 52.54 seconds. In 1984, George DiCarlo swam 400 meters in 3 minutes 51.23 seconds. How much faster was DiCarlo's time than Goodell's?

7. Al Oerter won a gold medal for the discus throw in four Olympics in a row starting in 1956. What was the last year in which he won a gold medal?

8. Alonzo Babers won the gold medal in 1984 for the 400-meter run. His time was 0.33 seconds faster than Viktor Markin's time four years earlier. What was Alonzo Babers's time?

LOGICAL REASONING

A. Statements are **equivalent** if each is true when the other is true. Statements p and q are equivalent.

STATEMENT p: Today is Thursday.
STATEMENT q: Tomorrow is Friday.

B. The statement "Today is *not* Thursday" is called the **negation** of the statement "Today is Thursday."

If a statement is true, its negation is false.
If a statement is false, its negation is true.

For each statement, write a statement that is equivalent.

1. Yesterday was Monday.

2. 5 is greater than 2.

3. Three months from now will be July.

4. My sister is shorter than I am.

Write the negation of each statement.

5. Tomorrow is not Tuesday.

6. Today is Thursday.

7. Yesterday was Sunday.

If next month is September, write which of the following is *true* and which is *false*.

8. Last month was November.

9. This month is August.

10. Next month is not February.

GROUP PROJECT

An Olympian Task

The problem: You have been hired as a chef for the Olympics. Your first task is to decide on a breakfast menu for the Olympic athletes. Make out a complete plan for the breakfast. Include all aspects of the job: ordering food; hiring cooks, servers, dishwashers, and maintenance people; making out work schedules; and keeping a budget.

Key Facts

- There will be approximately 500 athletes eating breakfast.
- Breakfast will be served from 6:00 A.M. to 9:00 A.M.
- The athletes come from many nations; some of them are on special diets.
- Not all the athletes eat meat, and so, you will have to prepare some vegetarian dishes.

Key Questions

- How many eggs will you need to order each day? loaves of bread?
- What other foods should you order?
- What beverages will you serve?
- Approximately how much extra food should be ordered for those athletes who have Olympian appetites?
- How many cooks will you need to hire? servers? dishwashers?
- How much time do the cooks need to prepare the breakfast?

CHAPTER TEST

Write as a decimal. (pages 38 and 40)

1.

2.

3. $\frac{9}{10}$ **4.** $2\frac{31}{100}$ **5.** $\frac{7}{1,000}$ **6.** 543 ten-thousandths

7. nine and two tenths   **8.** seventy and twelve ten-thousandths

Compare. Write >, <, or = for each ●. (page 44)

9. 2.49 ● 2.5   **10.** 52.9 ● 52.90

11. 7.196 ● 7.1963   **12.** 201.2 ● 200.3

Write in order from the least to the greatest. (page 44)

13. 5.01, 5.1, 5.011, 5.001

Write in order from the greatest to the least. (page 44)

14. 2.498, 2.5, 2.499, 2.4988

Round to the nearest tenth. (page 46)

15. 5.42   **16.** 0.674   **17.** 0.007

Round to the nearest thousandth. (page 46)

18. 5.4321   **19.** 8.0597   **20.** 0.40006

Estimate. Write > or < for each ●. (page 50)

21. 6.52 + 3.67 ● 10   **22.** 9.38 + 12.51 ● 22

23. 4.42 − 0.89 ● 4   **24.** 8 − 6.739 ● 1

Find the sum. (page 52)

25.   4.51
       + 3.29

26.   18.24
       + 31.95

27.   60.4
       + 28.658

28. $89.26
       +   7.74

29. 18.004 + 31.997 + 0.09   **30.** $19.95 + $26.48

Find the difference. (page 54)

31.
$$0.5932$$
$$- 0.4846$$

32.
$$9$$
$$- 7.008$$

33.
$$5.236$$
$$- 4.609$$

34.
$$\$79.95$$
$$- 59.98$$

35. 24.703 − 20.75

36. $134.18 − $34.29

37. Read the problem. Without finding the exact answer, write the letter of the reasonable answer. (page 42)

The Weiss family took two trips to the beach during the 1984 Olympics. They drove 145 miles on the first trip and 117 miles on the second trip. How many more miles did they drive on the first trip?

a. 8 miles   **b.** 28 miles   **c.** 128 miles

38. Solve. If there is not enough information, identify the information you would need. (page 58)

Paul, Jeb, Marge, and Beth formed a relay-race team. They ran the 400-meter relay in 62.35 seconds. Jeb ran his leg of the race in 16.9 seconds. Marge ran her leg of the race in 15.8 seconds. How fast did Paul and Beth run each of their legs of the race?

39. Write whether you would add or subtract to solve. (page 56)

During a day at the Olympic stadium, Katie spent $4.50 for a souvenir program and $12.50 for lunch and refreshments. How much money in all did she spend?

40. Solve. Use a list if needed. (page 48)

The Olympic relay team has 6 runners who can run in the relay race. Each race requires 4 runners. How many combinations of runners can be formed with the 6 members of the team?

BONUS

Add or subtract.

1.
$$5.367948$$
$$+ 4.852397$$

2.
$$15.999999$$
$$+ 79.807965$$

3.
$$8.040506$$
$$- 7.050607$$

4.
$$20.7$$
$$- 6.888888$$

5. 101.010101 + 4.312987

6. 1 − 0.743957

7. $435.79 + $298.54 + $320.60

8. $54,279.98 − $46,399.99

RETEACHING

A. You can estimate decimal sums the same way you estimate whole number sums.
Estimate 17.54 + 25.492.

Using front-end
Add the whole numbers.
17 + 25 = 42
Adjust by examining the decimal parts.
  0.54   0.492
        \ /
         1
42 + 1 = 43

Using rounding
Round each number to the nearest whole number. Then add.
17.54 → 18
25.492 → + 25
         43

| Look at the digit in the tenths place. If it is: 5 or greater, round up, less than 5, round down. |

B. You can also estimate differences.
Estimate 58.984 − 49.295.

Using front-end
Subtract the whole numbers.
    58 − 49 = 9
Adjust by examining the decimal parts.
    58.984
  − 49.295
       .7
More than 9.

Using rounding
Round each number to the nearest whole number.
    58.984 → 59
    49.295 → 49
Subtract 59 − 49 = 10.
About 10.

Estimate. Write > or < for each ●.

1. 8.17 + 1.05 ● 9
2. 4.9 + 2.8 ● 9
3. 18.46 + 20.6 ● 39
4. 1.54 + 0.389 ● 2
5. 75.563 + 24.009 ● 100
6. 4.89 + 3.2 ● 8
7. 7.08 − 6.88 ● 0
8. 18.49 − 12.105 ● 6
9. 30.004 − 0.904 ● 29
10. 79.98 − 9.09 ● 71
11. 12.405 − 9.8 ● 3
12. 16.01 − 7.89 ● 8
13. 0.475 + 8.56 ● 10
14. 18.8 + 38.5 ● 57
15. 7.9 + 82.78 ● 91
16. 99.5 + 27.36 ● 127
17. 46.495 − 3.419 ● 43
18. 89.394 − 88.9 ● 0
19. 39.904 − 29.666 ● 10
20. 85.38 + 29.56 ● 115

ENRICHMENT

Solving Inequalities

An inequality is a number sentence that contains $>$, $<$, or $\neq$. To solve an inequality, use a related equation.

Example:

$4 + n > 9$	
$4 + n = 9$	Write a related equation.
$9 - 4 = 5$	Think of a related subtraction fact.
$n = 5$	
$n > 5$	Rewrite as an inequality.

Any number greater than 5 will make the inequality true. Check: $4 + 6 = 10$, $4 + 7 = 11$. . . .

Another example:

$n - 7 < 6$	
$n - 7 = 6$	Write a related equation.
$7 + 6 = 13$	Think of a related addition fact.
$n = 13$	
$n < 13$	Rewrite as an inequality.

Any number less than 13 will make the inequality true. Check: $12 - 7 = 5$, $11 - 7 = 4$. . . .

Find the value for n.
Check by using three different values for n.

1. $3 + n > 7$
2. $4 + n < 21$
3. $n - 12 > 5$
4. $n + 8 > 31$
5. $n - 35 > 6$
6. $6 + n < 60$
7. $12 + 13 > n$
8. $54 - 13 < n$
9. $n + 2 > 3$
10. $4 \times n > 16$
11. $n \times 6 > 54$
12. $n \div 5 > 5$

Solve.

13. Any number less than this number added to 43 will give a sum less than 87.

14. Any number greater than this number subtracted from 92 will give a difference less than 80.

TECHNOLOGY

Here are some LOGO commands.

FD   This moves the turtle forward the number of steps shown.

BK   This moves the turtle backward.

RT   This makes the turtle turn to the right the number of degrees shown.

LT   This makes the turtle turn to the left.

PU   This moves the turtle without drawing a line.

PD   This tells the turtle to begin drawing lines again.

PE   This tells the turtle to begin erasing.

HOME   This takes the turtle to the center of the screen.

A LOGO program is called a **procedure.** In order for the turtle to draw correctly the picture you want, each command in the procedure must be in the proper order. Two or more commands can be on a line. The last command in a procedure must be END.

Here is one way to tell the turtle to draw a square.

```
TO SQUARE
FD 40   RT 90   FD 40   RT 90   FD 40   RT 90   FD 40   RT 90
END
```

Here is another way to draw a square.

```
TO SQUARE
REPEAT 4 [FD 40   RT 90]
END
```

The REPEAT 4 commands tells the turtle to repeat the commands shown in the brackets 4 times. You can use the REPEAT command with any number you want.

You can write a procedure that allows you to change the lengths of the sides of the squares, too. Use a variable for the lengths of the sides.

```
TO SQUARE :SIDE
REPEAT 4   [FD :SIDE RT 90]
END
```

In this procedure, :SIDE is the variable. When you type the name of the procedure that will command the turtle to draw the square, also type the length of a side.

```
SQUARE 80
```

This will command the turtle to draw a square that has sides that are 80 steps long.

1. Write a procedure that tells the turtle to draw three parallel lines, each 75 steps long, that are 10 steps apart.

2. Write a procedure that tells the turtle to draw a triangle that has angles of 60° and sides of any length. (The turtle should turn 120°.)

3. This octagon was drawn by the following procedure. There are five mistakes in the procedure. Find and correct them. Then use the REPEAT and variable commands to rewrite the procedure.

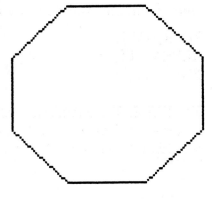

```
TO OCTAGON
RT 40      RT 45      FD 40      RT 45      BK 40
LT 45      FD 45      RT 45      FD 40      RT 45
FD 40      RT 45      FD 40      FD 45      FD 40
END
```

CUMULATIVE REVIEW

Write the letter of the correct answer.

1. Write in standard form: eight million, two thousand, thirty-one.

   a. 8,231
   b. 8,002,031
   c. 80,002,031
   d. not given

2. Write the value of the blue digit: 26,504,738.

   a. 500
   b. 5,000
   c. 50,000
   d. not given

3. Write in standard form: $400,000 + 7,000 + 500 + 8$.

   a. 407,508
   b. 407,580
   c. 470,508
   d. not given

4. Compare: 6,074 ● 6,704.

   a. $6,074 > 6,704$
   b. $6,074 < 6,704$
   c. $6,074 = 6,704$
   d. not given

5. Order from the greatest to the least: 785,813; 795,803; 795,308.

   a. 795,308; 785,813; 795,803
   b. 785,813; 795,803; 795,308
   c. 795,803; 795,308; 785,813
   d. not given

6. $9 + 0 = \blacksquare$

   a. 0
   b. 9
   c. 10
   d. not given

7. Round 589,512 to the nearest thousand.

   a. 589,000
   b. 589,600
   c. 590,000
   d. not given

8.
   $$\begin{array}{r} 26,754 \\ 9,208 \\ + 57,439 \\ \hline \end{array}$$

   a. 92,401
   b. 93,381
   c. 93,401
   d. not given

9. Choose the best estimate: $42,835 - 33,906$.

   a. less than 8,000
   b. less than 10,000
   c. more than 10,000
   d. more than 80,000

10. $n - 3 = 6$; find the missing number.

    a. 3
    b. 6
    c. 9
    d. not given

11. Tim has $29.03. He buys a present for his father that costs $12.98. Estimate how much money Tim has left.

    a. less than $14
    b. more than $15
    c. more than $20
    d. not given

12. In 1975, the population of Centerville was 43,296. In 1980, the population was 41,052. In 1985, it was up to 46,184. How much larger was the population in 1985 than in 1975? Which phrase best describes this problem?

    a. not enough information
    b. enough information
    c. too much information

You are on the committee that arranges class trips for your school. The committee is investigating local places of interest to see such as aquariums, museums, historic sites, and factories. Plan routes for possible trips, and estimate the cost of the trip per person and the cost for the whole class.

3 MULTIPLYING WHOLE NUMBERS AND DECIMALS

Multiplication Facts and Properties

A. A sixth-grade class learns about the different places to visit in Washington, D.C. There are 3 groups that do reports. Each group reports on 5 places to visit. How many places do the groups report on?

You can add: $5 + 5 + 5 = 15$.

You can multiply:

$$3 \times 5 = 15$$

factor   factor   product

$$
\begin{array}{r}
5 \;\longleftarrow \text{factor} \\
\times 3 \;\longleftarrow \text{factor} \\
\hline
15 \;\longleftarrow \text{product}
\end{array}
$$

They report on 15 places.

B. These properties can make multiplication easier.

Commutative Property Factors can be multiplied in any order, and the product is always the same.	$6 \times 5 = 30$ $5 \times 6 = 30$
Identity Property If one factor is 1, the product is always the other factor.	$7 \times 1 = 7$ $1 \times 9 = 9$
Property of Zero If one factor is 0, the product is always 0.	$9 \times 0 = 0$ $0 \times 5 = 0$
Associative Property If the grouping of the factors is changed, the product is still the same.	$(2 \times 2) \times 4 = 2 \times (2 \times 4)$ $\qquad 4 \quad \times 4 = 2 \times \quad 8$ $\qquad\qquad 16 = 16$
Distributive Property To multiply a number by the sum of two addends, multiply each addend by the number and then add the products.	$3 \times (8 + 5) = (3 \times 8) + (3 \times 5)$ $3 \times \quad 13 \quad = \quad 24 \quad + \quad 15$ $\qquad\quad 39 \quad = \quad 39$

Multiply.

1. $\begin{array}{r} 3 \\ \times 2 \end{array}$ **2.** $\begin{array}{r} 8 \\ \times 7 \end{array}$ **3.** $\begin{array}{r} 4 \\ \times 6 \end{array}$ **4.** $\begin{array}{r} 5 \\ \times 8 \end{array}$ **5.** $\begin{array}{r} 4 \\ \times 5 \end{array}$ **6.** $\begin{array}{r} 6 \\ \times 6 \end{array}$ **7.** $\begin{array}{r} 7 \\ \times 5 \end{array}$

8. 9×9 **9.** 4×4 **10.** 3×5 **11.** 4×3

12. 6×9 **13.** $(2 \times 3) \times 8$ **14.** $7 \times (3 \times 3)$ **15.** $2 \times (2 \times 2) \times 8$

Identify the property used. Find the missing number.

16. $9 \times 0 = \blacksquare$ **17.** $8 \times 2 = 2 \times \blacksquare$ **18.** $8 \times \blacksquare = 8$ **19.** $\blacksquare \times 5 = 0$

20. $6 \times (4 + 3) = (\blacksquare \times 4) + (\blacksquare \times 3)$ **21.** $2 \times (4 \times 3) = (\blacksquare \times 4) \times 3$

22. $38 \times \blacksquare = 0$ **23.** $6 \times \blacksquare = 78 \times 6$ **24.** $\blacksquare \times 1 = 123$

★25. $\blacksquare \times (6 + 7) = (5 \times \blacksquare) + (5 \times \blacksquare)$ **★26.** $5 \times (\blacksquare \times 9) = (\blacksquare \times 6) \times \blacksquare$

★27. $34 \times (45 \times \blacksquare) = (\blacksquare \times 45) \times 27$ **★28.** $\blacksquare \times (9 + \blacksquare) = (5 \times 9) + (\blacksquare \times 63)$

Solve. For Problem 30, use the Infobank.

29. One group read about the 3 monuments for Presidents Washington, Jefferson, and Lincoln. They found 9 interesting facts about each. How many facts did they find?

30. Use the information on page 432 to solve. Find the total number of years served by the senators listed.

31. Sally and Raul discovered that they had both seen the same monuments in Washington. Sally visited 3 monuments during each of her 2 days there. If Raul visited only 2 monuments a day, for how many days was his trip?

★32. For a project, 7 students gave oral reports on the National Archives. Of these reports, 3 were 5 minutes long and the rest were 9 minutes long. How long did it take for all the reports to be given?

CHALLENGE

Find the missing number.

1. $6 \times 8 = (6 \times \blacksquare) - (6 \times 1)$ **2.** $6 \times 0 = (6 \times 8) - (6 \times \blacksquare)$

3. $(6 \times 3) - (6 \times 2) = (6 \times \blacksquare)$ **4.** $(7 \times 4) = (7 \times 2) + (7 \times \blacksquare)$

Multiplying with Multiples of 10

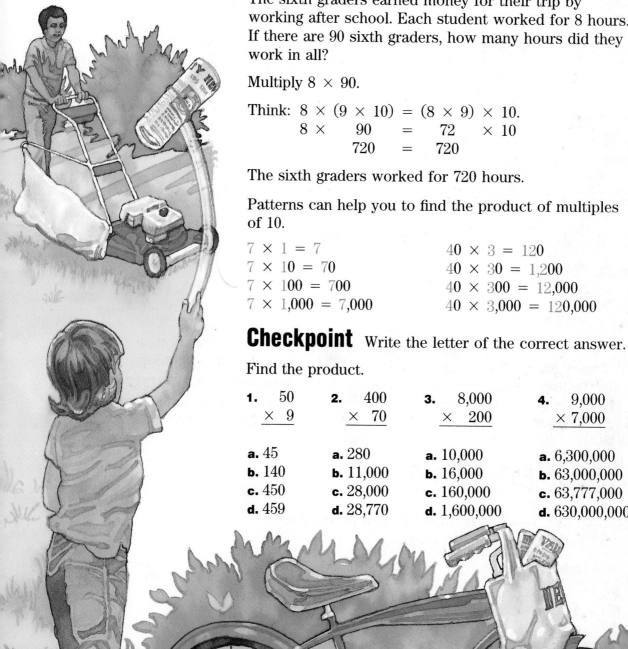

The sixth graders earned money for their trip by working after school. Each student worked for 8 hours. If there are 90 sixth graders, how many hours did they work in all?

Multiply 8 × 90.

Think: 8 × (9 × 10) = (8 × 9) × 10.
      8 ×   90   =   72 × 10
          720   =   720

The sixth graders worked for 720 hours.

Patterns can help you to find the product of multiples of 10.

7 × 1 = 7
7 × 10 = 70
7 × 100 = 700
7 × 1,000 = 7,000

40 × 3 = 120
40 × 30 = 1,200
40 × 300 = 12,000
40 × 3,000 = 120,000

Checkpoint Write the letter of the correct answer.

Find the product.

1.	2.	3.	4.
50 × 9	400 × 70	8,000 × 200	9,000 × 7,000

a. 45	a. 280	a. 10,000	a. 6,300,000
b. 140	b. 11,000	b. 16,000	b. 63,000,000
c. 450	c. 28,000	c. 160,000	c. 63,777,000
d. 459	d. 28,770	d. 1,600,000	d. 630,000,000

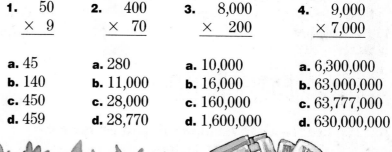

Find the product.

1. 20
   × 6
   (handwritten: 120)

2. 50
   × 7
   (handwritten: 350)

3. 90
   × 4
   (handwritten: 360)

4. 30
   × 5
   (handwritten: 150)

5. 40
   × 6
   (handwritten: 240)

6. 300
   × 60
   (handwritten: 18000)

7. 500
   × 40
   (handwritten: 20000)

8. 800
   × 30
   (handwritten: 24000)

9. 200
   × 90
   (handwritten: 18000)

10. 800
    × 80
    (handwritten: 64000)

11. 5,000
    × 400
    (handwritten: 2000000)

12. 2,000
    × 600
    (handwritten: 1200000)

13. 9,000
    × 30
    (handwritten: 270000)

14. 7,000
    × 300
    (handwritten: 2100000)

15. 2,000
    × 800
    (handwritten: 1800000)

16. 80
    × 9
    (handwritten: 720)

17. 400
    × 70
    (handwritten: 28000)

18. 6,000
    × 800
    (handwritten: 4800000)

19. 4,000
    × 500
    (handwritten: 2000000)

20. 300
    × 30
    (handwritten: 9000)

21. 500 × 5,000 *(handwritten: 2500000)*

22. 60 × 700 *(handwritten: 42000)*

23. 9 × 80 = *(handwritten: 720)*

24. 40 × 7 = *(handwritten: 280)*

25. 10 × 9,000 *(handwritten: 90000)*

★26. 40 × 2 × 800 *(handwritten: 64000)*

Solve.

27. The cafeteria staff prepares 3 kinds of sandwiches for the bus trip. They make 100 of each kind. How many sandwiches do they make altogether?

★28. The students visit the Government Printing Office. They see 9,000 copies of a 900-page report being printed. If only 3,600,000 pages are bound, how many are unbound?

FOCUS: ESTIMATION

You can use front-end multiplication to estimate the product of greatly different factors.

Find the greatest place of each number.

97,426
× 32
(handwritten: 9485?)

90,000
× 30

Multiply.

90,000
× 30
27

Count the zeros. Then write them in.

90,000
× 30
2,700,000

Use front-end multiplication to estimate the product.

1. 3,197
   × 7

2. 9,461
   × 8

3. 62,970
   × 72

4. 48,198
   × 52

★5. 491,821
    × 742

Estimating Products by Rounding

The class visited one of Washington's many art museums. The museum consisted of 19 galleries. There were about 28 works of art in each gallery. About how many works of art did the museum contain?

Because you do not know the exact number of artworks in each gallery, estimate to find the product.

Estimate 19 × 28.

Round each factor to the largest place.	Multiply to get a rough estimate.
$28 \rightarrow 30$ $\times 19 \rightarrow \times 20$	30 $\times 20$ ———— 600

Adjust the estimate.

Because both factors were rounded up, 600 is an overestimate. The answer is less than 600.

The museum contained a little less than 600 works of art.

Other examples:

	Rough estimate	Adjusted estimate
237 × 41	200 × 40 = 8,000	Because both factors were rounded down, 8,000 is an underestimate. The product is more than 8,000, or > 8,000.
37 × $823	40 × $800 = $32,000	One factor was rounded up. One factor was rounded down. No adjustment is needed.

Estimate. Then if needed, write > or < to show how
you would adjust the estimate.

1. 439×610
2. 175×203
3. 476×389
4. 879×212
5. 539×309

6. 98×876
7. 412×398
8. 55×32
9. 78×588
10. 87×18

11. 982×48
12. 96×387
13. 108×634
14. 712×54
15. 997×113

16. 49×37
17. 471×59
18. 147×219
19. 151×269
20. 374×81

21. 527×719
22. 487×779
23. 427×525
24. 487×295
25. 619×717

26. 874×464
27. 214×731
28. 77×38
29. 275×47
30. 531×644

Solve.

31. An Oriental pot in one gallery was
decorated with 9 rows of dragons.
Each row contained about 27
dragons. About how many dragons
was the pot decorated with?

★32. The museum displayed slides of its
exhibits on 6-sided racks. Each
side had 12 rows of slides. Each
row held about 18 slides. About
how many slides were there on
each rack?

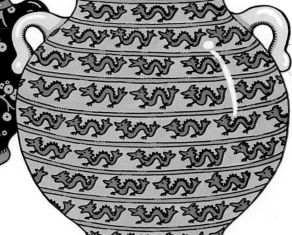

FOCUS: ESTIMATION

Numbers can be rounded in different ways.
Here are four different ways to estimate 26×12.
Each estimate is reasonable.

$30 \times 10 = 300$—about 300
$30 \times 12 = 360$—a little less than 360

$25 \times 12 = 300$—a little more than 300
$26 \times 10 = 260$—a little more than 260

Estimate in two different ways.

1. 31×23
2. 35×45
3. 48×26
4. 77×11

More Practice, page 441

PROBLEM SOLVING
Writing an Equation

Writing an equation can help you solve a word problem. An equation can show how to use the numbers you know to find the number you need.

> Mr. Cohen's sixth-grade class went to the Capitol to hear a senator speak about United States history. There were 32 students in the class. They were joined by another sixth-grade class of 27 students. How many students listened to the senator's speech?

1. List what you know and what you want to find.

There were 32 students in the class. They were joined by 27 more students. How many students were there in all?

2. Think about how to use this information to solve the problem.

You know how many there are in one set and how many join it. You want to find the total number. You can add.

3. Write an equation. Use n to stand for the number you want to find.

number of students in first class		number of students in second class		total number
32	+	27	=	n

4. Solve. Write the answer.

$32 + 27 = 59$
$59 = n$
There were 59 students who listened to the senator's speech.

Write the letter of the correct equation.

1. Josephine and Mike spent $1.25 to ride the subway to the National Gallery. They rode a shorter route back to their hotel and paid $1.05 for the subway. How much did they spend in all?

   a. $1.25 - $1.05 = n
   b. $1.25 + $1.05 = n
   c. $1.05 + n = $1.25

2. On Monday, Harold spent $9.50 for entrance fees to visit some private museums and exhibitions in Washington. On Tuesday, he spent $6.75 for similar fees. How much more money did Harold spend on Monday?

   a. $9.50 - $6.75 = n
   b. $9.50 + n = $6.75
   c. $9.50 + $6.75 = n

Write an equation. Solve.

3. Mr. Cohen's class went to visit the Library of Congress. The students learned that this library was established in the Capitol Building in 1800. By 1897, the library had grown so large that it had to be moved from the Capitol Building to a new building. How long had the library existed in the Capitol Building?

4. Joseph learns that the Library of Congress has about 5,600 books that were printed before the 1500s. The library near his home has only about 150 of these antique books. How many more antique books does the Library of Congress have?

5. Jan and Sue spent 15 minutes riding the subway to the Capitol. On the return trip, they spent 35 minutes on the bus. How much time did they spend on the bus and the subway?

Multiplying by 1-Digit Factors

A. The students observed 2 sessions of the House of Representatives. Present at each meeting were 319 representatives. How many representatives were present at both sessions?

Find the product of 2 × 319.

First, estimate the product.
2 × 300 = 600

Multiply the ones. Regroup the 1 ten.	Multiply the tens. Then add the 1 ten.	Multiply the hundreds.
$\begin{array}{r} 1 \\ 3\,1\,9 \\ \times\quad 2 \\ \hline 8 \end{array}$	$\begin{array}{r} 1 \\ 3\,1\,9 \\ \times\quad 2 \\ \hline 3\,8 \end{array}$	$\begin{array}{r} 1 \\ 3\,1\,9 \\ \times\quad 2 \\ \hline 6\,3\,8 \end{array}$

A total of 638 representatives were present. This answer is reasonably close to the estimate of 600.

B. Multiply money the same way you multiply whole numbers. Then place the dollar sign and the cents point.

$\begin{array}{r} 1 \\ \$1.2\,6 \\ \times\quad 3 \\ \hline \$3.7\,8 \end{array}$
$\qquad$
$\begin{array}{r} 1 \\ \$4\,2.5\,1 \\ \times\quad 2 \\ \hline \$8\,5.0\,2 \end{array}$
$\qquad$
$\begin{array}{r} 1\quad 2 \\ \$3\,1\,4.1\,6 \\ \times\quad 4 \\ \hline \$1,2\,5\,6.6\,4 \end{array}$

Checkpoint Write the letter of the correct answer.

Find the product.

1. $\begin{array}{r}459\\ \times\ 2\end{array}$	2. $\begin{array}{r}\$28.68\\ \times\quad 7\end{array}$	3. $\begin{array}{r}710{,}586\\ \times\qquad 4\end{array}$	4. 6 × \$0.82
a. 808	**a.** \$146.26	**a.** 2,840,024	**a.** \$4.82
b. 918	**b.** \$152.76	**b.** 2,840,344	**b.** \$4.92
c. 981	**c.** \$196.76	**c.** 2,842,344	**c.** \$5.42
d. 81,018	**d.** \$200.76	**d.** 2,882,604	**d.** \$49.20

Find the product.

1. 61
   × 4

2. 31
   × 3

3. 91
   × 8

4. $0.74
   × 2

5. $0.41
   × 4

6. 68
   × 5

7. 26
   × 6

8. 46
   × 5

9. $0.16
   × 5

10. $0.25
    × 4

11. 753
    × 9

12. 918
    × 3

13. 462
    × 3

14. $6.39
    × 8

15. $8.76
    × 7

16. 8,299
    × 2

17. 7,476
    × 8

18. 8,103
    × 1

19. $49.13
    × 8

20. $11.11
    × 8

21. $52,864 \times 3$

22. $37,591 \times 5$

23. $769,322 \times 6$

24. $891,543 \times 4$

25. $4 \times 2 \times 3,584$

26. 189×2

27. $2 \times \$3.84$

28. 25×4

29. $4 \times \$0.74$

★30. $(3 \times 2) \times 8,984$

Solve.

31. A group of students visits 5 rooms in the United States Capitol. Hanging in each room are 12 paintings that depict important events in United States history. How many paintings does the group see?

★32. A senator spoke with 3 groups of 36 students each on Monday. On Tuesday, the senator spoke with 4 groups of 27 students each. On Friday, the senator spoke with 3 groups of 112 students each. How many students in all did the senator speak with?

FOCUS: MENTAL MATH

You can use doubling to multiply a number by 8.

Multiply 8×31. $8 \times 31 = 2 \times 2 \times 2 \times 31$
So, double 31 three times.
$2 \times 31 = 62$ $2 \times 62 = 124$ $2 \times 124 = 248$

Find the product. Try to do the multiplication mentally.

1. 8×21

2. 8×211

3. 8×52

4. 8×104

Multiplying by 2-Digit Factors

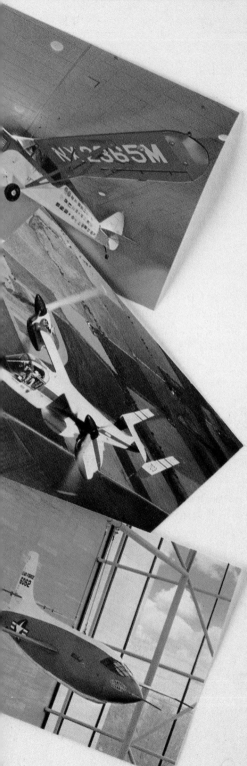

A. At the National Air and Space Museum, students viewed famous airplanes and spaceships. Later, 16 students bought sets of pictures that showed the history of flight. If there are 34 pictures in each set, how many pictures did the students buy?

Multiply 16 × 34.

Multiply by ones.	Multiply by tens.	Add.
34 ×16 ――― 204	34 ×16 ――― 204 340	34 ×16 ――― 204 340 ――― 544

The students bought a total of 544 pictures.

B. You can multiply with money the same way you multiply whole numbers. Remember to place the dollar sign and the cents point.

$2.18
×   71
―――
218
15260
―――
$154.78

You can leave out the zeros as place holders.

$0.95
×   16
―――
570
950
―――
$15.20

$3.89
×   52
―――
778
19450
―――
$202.28

Checkpoint Write the letter of the correct answer.

Multiply.

1.   28
   × 43
	2. $0.89
	  × 36
		3. 456 × 23	**4.** $7.25 × 98

a. 71	**a.** $1.25	**a.** 9,278	**a.** $6.27
b. 104	**b.** $29.54	**b.** 10,488	**b.** $8.23
c. 894	**c.** $32.04	**c.** 11,808	**c.** $695.10
d. 1,204	**d.** $3,204	**d.** 81,368	**d.** $710.50

Multiply.

| 1. | 24 $\times$ 12 | 2. | 12 $\times$ 13 | 3. | 51 $\times$ 16 | 4. | $0.21 $\times$ 14 | 5. | $0.22 $\times$ 14 |

| 6. | 52 $\times$ 28 | 7. | 75 $\times$ 18 | 8. | 48 $\times$ 45 | 9. | $0.60 $\times$ 16 | 10. | $0.29 $\times$ 28 |

| 11. | 799 $\times$ 72 | 12. | 317 $\times$ 31 | 13. | 873 $\times$ 24 | 14. | $1.02 $\times$ 37 | 15. | $3.08 $\times$ 25 |

16. $5{,}384 \times 17$

17. $1{,}545 \times 95$

18. $\$8{,}175 \times 52$

19. $5{,}290 \times 61$

20. $14 \times \$0.91$

★21. $9 \times 20 \times 79$

Solve.

22. One exhibit shows Lindbergh's famous first flight across the Atlantic. Lindbergh flew for 34 hours, at an average speed of 106 miles per hour. How far did he travel?

23. In his first airplane flight, Orville Wright flew for 12 seconds, at a speed of 88 feet per second. Use this information to write your own word problem.

24. In the museum gift shop, jacket patches cost $4.95 each. If 58 students bought patches, how much did they spend in all?

★25. The students saw 15 exhibits and a 20-minute movie *The History of the United States Space Program.* They spent an average of 12 minutes at each exhibit. How much time did they spend in the museum?

FOCUS: MENTAL MATH

You can use the Distributive Property to help you multiply a number by 11.

Multiply 11×25.
Since $11 \times 25 = (10 + 1) \times 25$
  Think: $= (10 \times 25) + (1 \times 25)$
      $= \quad 250 \quad + \quad 25 \quad = 275$

Multiply. Use the Distributive Property.

1. 17×11 2. 11×42 3. 36×11 4. 11×59

Multiplying by 3-Digit Factors

The class visits the Washington Monument. An average of 3,707 people visit the monument each day. How many people visit it in a year?

You can multiply as if the same number of people visit the monument each day.

Multiply 365 × 3,707.

Multiply by ones.	Multiply by tens.	Multiply by hundreds.	Add.
$\begin{array}{r} 3{,}7\,0\,7 \\ \times\ \ \ 3\,6\,5 \\ \hline 1\,8\,5\,3\,5 \end{array}$	$\begin{array}{r} 3{,}7\,0\,7 \\ \times\ \ \ 3\,6\,5 \\ \hline 1\,8\,5\,3\,5 \\ 2\,2\,2\,4\,2 \end{array}$	$\begin{array}{r} 3{,}7\,0\,7 \\ \times\ \ \ 3\,6\,5 \\ \hline 1\,8\,5\,3\,5 \\ 2\,2\,2\,4\,2 \\ 1\,1\,1\,2\,1 \end{array}$	$\begin{array}{r} 3{,}7\,0\,7 \\ \times\ \ \ 3\,6\,5 \\ \hline 1\,8\,5\,3\,5 \\ 2\,2\,2\,4\,2 \\ 1\,1\,1\,2\,1 \\ \hline 1{,}3\,5\,3{,}0\,5\,5 \end{array}$

About 1,353,055 people per year visit the Washington Monument.

Another example:

$$\begin{array}{r} 646 \\ \times\ 403 \\ \hline 1938 \\ 25840\ \ \ \ \\ \hline 260{,}338 \end{array}$$

A shortcut: Since 0 × 646 = 0, you can write a 0 in the tens place. Then multiply by the hundreds.

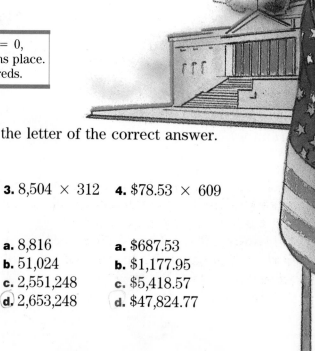

Checkpoint Write the letter of the correct answer.

Multiply.

1. $\begin{array}{r} 534 \\ \times\ 751 \end{array}$ **2.** $\begin{array}{r} \$6.27 \\ \times\ \ 139 \end{array}$ **3.** 8,504 × 312   **4.** $78.53 × 609

1.	2.	3.	4.
a. 1,285	**a.** $81.51	**a.** 8,816	**a.** $687.53
b. 4,272	**b.** $867.93	**b.** 51,024	**b.** $1,177.95
c. 377,834	**c.** $871.53	**c.** 2,551,248	**c.** $5,418.57
d. 401,034	**d.** $87,153	**d.** 2,653,248	**d.** $47,824.77

Multiply.

1. 238 × 645	**2.** 184 × 426	**3.** 179 × 550	**4.** $6.02 × 775	**5.** $1.18 × 302
6. 5,116 × 477	**7.** 7,239 × 416	**8.** 1,517 × 526	**9.** $83.85 × 346	**10.** $39.30 × 765
11. 7,069 × 142	**12.** 206 × 921	**13.** 366 × 102	**14.** $13.97 × 723	**15.** $36.82 × 496
16. 408 × 639	**17.** 2,623 × 346	**18.** 320 × 792	**19.** $86.00 × 447	**20.** $5.33 × 425

21. 283 × 993 **22.** 4,268 × 789 **23.** 239 × $4.08

24. 7,155 × 976 **25.** 6,846 × 812 **26.** 142 × $41.63

Solve.

27. An average of 13,122 people per day visit the Capitol building. How many people visit it during a two-week period?

28. On the average, 10,859 people per day visit the Lincoln Memorial. How many more people visit the Capitol building than the Lincoln Memorial each day?

29. The Jefferson Memorial has on the average 5,571 visitors per day. How many people visit it each year?

CHALLENGE

To raise money for their field trip, Dale, Rosa, and Tim worked together to rake Mr. Bradley's yards. They each charged Mr. Bradley in a different way: Dale charged $3.65 for each hour he worked. Rosa charged $5.50 for each yard she helped rake. Tim charged a flat rate of $15.00. There are 3 yards around Mr. Bradley's house. Each student worked 5 hours. Who earned the most money?

More Practice, page 441

Exponents and Squares

A. The State Dining Room at the White House is set for lunch. There are 10 tables, and 10 places are set at each table. How many people are expected for lunch?

Multiply 10×10.

When a number is being multiplied by itself, you can write it this way:

base $\longrightarrow 10^2 \longleftarrow$ exponent

The **base** is the number being multiplied by itself. The **exponent** tells how many times the base is used as a factor.

Read 10^2 as "ten to the second power," or "ten squared."
$10^2 = 10 \times 10 = 100$

There are 100 people expected for lunch.

B. Write $7 \times 7 \times 7 \times 7$ in exponent form.

Identify and write the base number: 7.
Count how many times the base is used as a factor.
Write the exponent: 7^4.

Read 7^4 as "seven to the fourth power."

C. Multiply to find the number.
$2^5 = 2 \times 2 \times 2 \times 2 \times 2 = 32$

Checkpoint

Write the letter of the exponent form.

1. 5×5

a. 25
b. 5^2
c. 55
d. 5^5

2. $3 \times 3 \times 3 \times 3$

a. 3^3
b. 4^3
c. 81
d. 3^4

Write the letter of the product.

3. 2^4

a. 6
b. 8
c. 16
d. 24

4. 4^3

a. 7
b. 12
c. 16
d. 64

Write in exponent form.

1. two to the third power

2. four to the second power

3. three to the fifth power

4. five to the fourth power

5. eight squared

6. two to the sixth power

Write in exponent form.

7. $5 \times 5 \times 5$

8. $4 \times 4 \times 4 \times 4$

9. $2 \times 2 \times 2 \times 2 \times 2$

10. 6×6

11. $7 \times 7 \times 7$

12. $3 \times 3 \times 3 \times 3 \times 3$

13. 18×18

14. $10 \times 10 \times 10$

15. $9 \times 9 \times 9 \times 9$

Write the product.

16. 3^4
17. 5^2
18. 4^3
19. 2^7
20. 7^2
21. 1^5

22. 9^2
23. 2^8
24. 6^3
25. 1^{12}
26. 4^4
27. 10^3

Solve.

28. Students tour the Bureau of Engraving and Printing. They are shown 8 large sheets of new dollar bills. Each sheet has 8 rows, with 8 bills in each row. How many bills do they see?

29. There are 10 tables at the White House lunch. Each table has 10 settings. Each setting has 5 pieces of silverware. How many pieces of silverware are there in all?

30. The State Dining Room is decorated for lunch. Vases of flowers line the 4 sides of the room, with 8 vases on each side. How many vases are there?

★31. The Bureau of Engraving can print 10^3 stamps each second. How many stamps can the bureau print in 10 seconds?

CALCULATOR

Copy and complete the sales slip for June's postcards. Use a calculator and the price list.

June bought 5 postcards. Of these, 3 sold for one price, and 2 sold for another. June spent $2.65 on the postcards. What was the price and subtotal of each type of postcard?

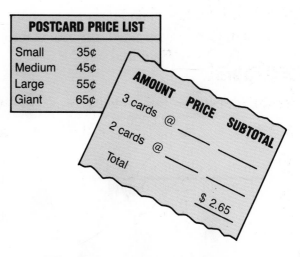

POSTCARD PRICE LIST	
Small	35¢
Medium	45¢
Large	55¢
Giant	65¢

AMOUNT PRICE SUBTOTAL

3 cards @ _____

2 cards @ _____

Total _____

$ 2.65

PROBLEM SOLVING
Estimation

Sometimes you can estimate to solve a problem. When you do, you will have to decide how close to the actual value your estimate needs to be.

> Vicki's class visits the National Zoological Park in Washington. They see two giant pandas named Hsing-Hsing and Ling-Ling. They learn that Ling-Ling eats 46,020 pounds of bamboo per year. Hsing-Hsing eats 4,390 pounds of bamboo per month. Which of them eats more?

You do not need to know exactly how much Hsing-Hsing eats. You can estimate. Round the number of pounds eaten each month to the nearest thousand, and multiply to find the yearly total.

$$4,390 \longrightarrow 4,000 \qquad 12 \times 4,000 = 48,000$$

> Hsing-Hsing eats about 48,000 pounds of bamboo per year. Since you rounded down to estimate, you know that the actual amount is larger. Since 48,000 > 46,020, you can be sure that Hsing-Hsing eats more. Another panda in China eats 49,149 pounds of bamboo per year. Does the panda eat more than Hsing-Hsing?

The first estimate of 48,000 is too close to 49,149. To answer the question, you need a more exact estimate. Round to the nearest hundred.

$$4,390 \rightarrow 4,400$$
$$12 \times 4,400 = (10 \times 4,400) + (2 \times 4,400)$$
$$= 44,000 + 8,800$$
$$= 52,800$$

This estimate is closer to the actual amount. Hsing-Hsing eats about 52,800 pounds of bamboo per year. That is more than the panda in China eats.

Write the letter of the answer to each question.

1. A Siberian tiger eats about 890 lb of meat per month. The zoo has 4 tigers. Which is the best estimate of how much meat the zookeepers should order for the tigers in May?

   a. 3,200 lb
   b. 3,600 lb
   c. 3,800 lb

2. There are 11 different areas on Monkey Island. Brenda notices that each area has about the same number of monkeys. She counts 19 monkeys in the first area. About how many monkeys are there on Monkey Island?

   a. 200
   b. 400
   c. 2,000

Estimate to solve. Explain your answer.

3. The zoo has 6 elephants. Each elephant eats 1,285 lb of hay per week. Will 8,000 lb of hay be enough for the elephants for one week?

4. Brad and Brenda stop for lunch at the zoo cafeteria. They have $12.46. Brenda wants stew for $3.95 and a salad for $1.77. Brad wants soup for $2.30 and an omelet for $3.15. Do they have enough money?

5. In the souvenir shop, Torrie buys a panda T-shirt for $6.95 and a stuffed panda for $8.45. She had $16.20. Does she have enough money left to buy three 45¢ postcards?

6. The zoo needs to move 4 hippos. Each hippo weighs about 4,900 pounds. The zoo truck can carry 18,000 pounds per trip. Can all the hippos be moved in one trip?

7. A turtle needs a tank that is 5 times as long as the turtle. Vicki buys a pet turtle 5.5 in. long. Is a tank 21 in. long big enough for the turtle?

8. An ostrich grows to a height of 9 feet 9 inches. About how many feet taller is this than a 6-foot-tall man?

Multiplying Decimals by 10; 100; and 1,000

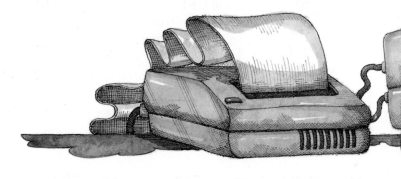

In their senator's office, the class watched a computer help answer the mail. The computer can write 2.5 letters per minute. How many letters can it write in 10 minutes? in 100 minutes? in 1,000 minutes?

$1 \times 2.5 = 2.5$ To multiply:
$10 \times 2.5 = 25$ by 10, move the decimal point one place to the right. 2.5

$100 \times 2.5 = 250$ by 100, move the decimal point two places to the right. 2.50

$1,000 \times 2.5 = 2,500$ by 1,000, move the decimal point three places to the right. 2.500

Write zeros in the product as needed.

You can multiply money in the same way.

$10 \times \$8.75 = \$87.50$
$100 \times \$8.75 = \$875$
$1,000 \times \$8.75 = \$8,750$

Checkpoint Write the letter of the correct answer.

Multiply.

1. $\$4.99$
     $\times \quad 100$

a. $\$0.049$
b. $\$0.49$
c. $\$499.00$
d. $\$4,990.00$

2. 0.075×10

a. 0.0075
b. 0.075
c. 0.75
d. 7,510

3. $6.736 \times 1,000$

a. 0.006736
b. 6.736000
c. 67.36
d. 6,736

Multiply.

1. $\begin{array}{r} 0.75 \\ \times\ 10 \\ \hline \end{array}$
2. $\begin{array}{r} 49.8 \\ \times\ 10 \\ \hline \end{array}$
3. $\begin{array}{r} 0.07 \\ \times\ 10 \\ \hline \end{array}$
4. $\begin{array}{r} 3.68 \\ \times\ 10 \\ \hline \end{array}$
5. $\begin{array}{r} 3.0573 \\ \times\ 10 \\ \hline \end{array}$

6. $\begin{array}{r} 6.63332 \\ \times\ 100 \\ \hline \end{array}$
7. $\begin{array}{r} 40.2 \\ \times\ 100 \\ \hline \end{array}$
8. $\begin{array}{r} 0.0097 \\ \times\ 100 \\ \hline \end{array}$
9. $\begin{array}{r} 38.33333 \\ \times\ 100 \\ \hline \end{array}$
10. $\begin{array}{r} 0.01067 \\ \times\ 100 \\ \hline \end{array}$

11. $\begin{array}{r} 0.0005 \\ \times\ 1,000 \\ \hline \end{array}$
12. $\begin{array}{r} 15.7748 \\ \times\ 1,000 \\ \hline \end{array}$
13. $\begin{array}{r} 8.5 \\ \times\ 1,000 \\ \hline \end{array}$
14. $\begin{array}{r} 12.1 \\ \times\ 1,000 \\ \hline \end{array}$
15. $\begin{array}{r} 0.6 \\ \times\ 1,000 \\ \hline \end{array}$

16. $\begin{array}{r} 0.0045 \\ \times\ 1,000 \\ \hline \end{array}$
17. $\begin{array}{r} 0.9464 \\ \times\ 100 \\ \hline \end{array}$
18. $\begin{array}{r} 11.601 \\ \times\ 10 \\ \hline \end{array}$
19. $\begin{array}{r} 7.08 \\ \times\ 1,000 \\ \hline \end{array}$
20. $\begin{array}{r} 29.9 \\ \times\ 100 \\ \hline \end{array}$

21. 10×0.4
22. $1,000 \times 6.9478$
23. 100×0.628
24. 100×0.0193
25. $1,000 \times 0.0702$
26. 10×6.2031

Solve.

27. Fran picked up a bag full of mail. It contained letters from students concerned about pollution. The bag had 1,000 letters in it, and each letter weighed 0.064 pound. How much did the contents of the full bag weigh?

28. The senator asked the class what they would do to fight pollution. A group of students organized a letter writing campaign. They sent 14 letters to the President, 26 to their senator, and 19 to their governor. Another 28 said they would help pick up litter. How many letters did the students send?

MIDCHAPTER REVIEW

Compute.

1. $\begin{array}{r} 800 \\ \times\ 40 \\ \hline \end{array}$
2. $\begin{array}{r} 9,000 \\ \times\ 700 \\ \hline \end{array}$
3. $\begin{array}{r} 376 \\ \times\ 7 \\ \hline \end{array}$
4. $\begin{array}{r} 6,119 \\ \times\ 6 \\ \hline \end{array}$

5. 17×951 6. 408×395 7. $916 \times 6,591$ 8. $\$39.95 \times 95$

PROBLEM SOLVING
Solving Two-Step Problems/Making a Plan

Many problems cannot be solved in one step.

Before you can answer the question asked, you may have to find needed data. This data can then be used to solve the problem. Making a plan can help you solve this kind of problem.

A group of 36 students and 5 adults go on a trip to the Air and Space Museum. Admission is $2.95 each. What is the cost of admission for the group?

Needed data: the total number of people on the trip

Plan
Step 1: Find the number of people on the trip.
Step 2: Find the total cost of admission for the group.

Step 1: Add to find the total number of people.

$$\begin{array}{r} 36 \\ +\ 5 \\ \hline 41 \end{array} \quad \begin{array}{l} \text{students} \\ \text{adults} \\ \text{total number of people} \end{array}$$

Step 2: Multiply to find the total cost.

$$\begin{array}{r} \$2.95 \\ \times\ 41 \\ \hline \$120.95 \end{array} \quad \begin{array}{l} \text{admission cost for each} \\ \text{total number of people} \\ \text{admission cost for the group} \end{array}$$

The cost of admission for the group is $120.95.

Complete the plan by writing the missing step or steps.

1. On the way to the museum, the group stops for lunch. At lunch, all 41 people order the Combo Deluxe for $2.10 each. Will $90 be enough to pay for everyone's lunch?

   Step 1: Find the total amount spent.
   Step 2: Compare the total amount spent to $90.

2. Mrs. Lopez, the sixth-grade teacher, bought 6 models and 8 posters in the museum gift shop. Each item cost $4.65. How much did she spend?

   Step 1: Find the total number of items bought.
   Step 2: Find the total cost.

Make a plan for each problem. Solve.

3. Jonathan wants to buy a poster of the space shuttle *Columbia* for $3.25 and 5 NASA patches for $0.75 each. How much will they cost?

4. A round trip to the museum costs either $1.50 on the bus or $1.75 on the subway. What is the total cost of travel if a student took 1 trip by bus and 3 trips by subway?

5. Tina wants to buy postcards of antique aircraft. The postcards cost $0.79 each, but a pack of 6 postcards costs $3.99. How much more does it cost to buy the 6 postcards individually?

6. Mr. Garton bought 6 rolls of film in the museum gift shop. Each roll cost $3.29. He paid with a $20 bill. How much change did he receive?

7. Mr. Lima works at the Air and Space Museum. He drives 18.5 kilometers to work each day. How many kilometers does he drive to and from work in 5 days?

8. Rose works in the museum gift shop. She buys 18 boxes of rocket models for $269.10. The models sell for $23.95 each. How much profit does she make for the gift shop on the 18 boxes?

★9. For $4.50, Stephanie had her picture taken in an astronaut's suit. Then, she spent $3.14 for lunch and $6.95 on a T-shirt featuring the museum's logo. She had $20 when she went to the museum. She has $4 left. Did she spend money on anything else?

★10. At the movies, 12 students will see *Hail Columbia*, and 24 students will see *To Fly*. Admission to *Hail Columbia* costs $1.35, and admission to *To Fly* costs $1.75. What is the total cost of admission to both movies?

Multiplying Decimals by Whole Numbers

A. The class pays a visit to the National Zoo. The zoo's 9 elephants are a favorite attraction. The elephant keeper explains that, on the average, each elephant eats 67.75 kilograms of food daily. How many kilograms of food do the elephants eat each day?

Multiply 9×67.75.

First, estimate the product.
$9 \times 70 = 630$

Multiply.

$$
\begin{array}{r}
6\,7.7\,5 \\
\times9 \\
\hline
6\,0\,9\,7\,5
\end{array}
$$

The product has the same number of decimal places as the decimal factor. Place the decimal point.

$$
\begin{array}{r}
6\,7.7\,5 \longleftarrow \text{two places}\\
\times9 \\
\hline
6\,0\,9.7\,5 \longleftarrow \text{two places}
\end{array}
$$

The elephants eat 609.75 kilograms of food daily. This answer is reasonably close to the estimate of 630.

B. Sometimes you must write zeros in the product to place the decimal point correctly.

$$
\begin{array}{r}
0.0\,0\,2\,9 \longleftarrow \text{four places}\\
\times2\,4 \\
\hline
1\,1\,6 \\
5\,8 \\
\hline
0.0\,6\,9\,6 \longleftarrow \text{four places}
\end{array}
$$

Checkpoint Write the letter of the correct answer.

Multiply.

1.
$$
\begin{array}{r}
4.36 \\
\times5 \\
\hline
\end{array}
$$

a. 2.18
b. 20.50
c. 21.80
d. 35.00

2.
$$
\begin{array}{r}
0.569 \\
\times21 \\
\hline
\end{array}
$$

a. 1.707
b. 10.749
c. 11.949
d. 13.049

3. 0.00416×13

a. 0.005408
b. 0.05398
c. 0.05408
d. 0.5408

Multiply.

1. 8.04 × 9	**2.** 6.24 × 4	**3.** 0.8 × 7	**4.** 1.04 × 17	**5.** 0.28 × 28
6. 0.0015 × 7	**7.** 0.0103 × 9	**8.** 0.0012 × 47	**9.** 0.03 × 3	**10.** 0.0051 × 19
11. 8.9731 × 25	**12.** 8.268 × 32	**13.** 0.0099 × 18	**14.** 0.0957 × 36	**15.** 0.035 × 6
16. 0.00703 × 11	**17.** 4.628 × 5	**18.** 0.1222 × 13	**19.** 8.631 × 9	**20.** 0.807 × 4

21. 21×3.23 **22.** 0.004×16 **23.** 4.4×56

24. 11×0.0088 **25.** 8.49×38 **26.** 44×2.569

Solve.

27. The students look at the zoo's famous pandas. Their newborn cub has a mass of only 1.39 kilograms. The mass of the cub's mother is 97 times as great. What is the mass of the mother panda?

28. While in Washington, some of the teachers picked up a mail-order slide catalog. They later decided to order 5 sets of the "Presidential Monuments" and 3 sets of the "Smithsonian Institution" for the school district. What was the total amount they spent?

Capital Slides Catalog		
"Presidential Monuments" (8 slides)	$3.15	two sets for $6
"The White House: Through History" (20 slides)	$6.95	two sets for $13
"Smithsonian Institute" (32 slides)	$10.65	

ANOTHER LOOK

Compare. Write >, <, or = for ●.

1. 28.4 ● 2.84   **2.** 10.01 ● 11.01   **3.** 2.02 ● 2.202

4. 100.01 ● 100.1   **5.** 0.006 ● 0.056   **6.** 0.345 ● 0.0345

7. 419.19 ● 409.19   **8.** 0.079 ● 0.79   **9.** 361.2 ● 361.20

More Practice, page 442

Estimating Decimal Products by Rounding

The cost of chartering a tour bus in Washington is
$38.50 per hour. The class budgeted $300 for bus rental.
Do they have enough money for a tour that might last
5.5 hours?

Because the exact cost of the tour will not be known
until it is completed, you should estimate the final cost.

Estimate 5.5 × $38.50.

Round each factor to the largest place.	Multiply to get a rough estimate.	Adjust the estimate.
$38.50 → $40 × 5.5 → × 6	$40 × 6 $240	Because both factors were rounded up, $240 is an overestimate. The answer is less than $240.

The class has enough money for a bus tour that might
last 5.5 hours.

Other examples:

	Rough estimate	Adjusted estimate
4.2 × 31.064	4 × 30 = 120	Because both factors were rounded down, 120 is an underestimate. The product is more than 120, or > 120.
1.86 × 0.41	2 × 0.4 = 0.8	One factor was rounded up. One factor was rounded down. No adjustment is needed.

Estimate. Then if needed, write > or < to show how you would adjust the estimate.

1. 0.57×29.7
2. 14.9×4.3
3. 0.48×15.7
4. 6.56×2.2

5. 4.7×1.69
6. 0.21×1.48
7. 4.3×1.62
8. 9.3×0.09

9. 8.8×0.184
10. 6.9×3.21
11. 3.01×1.99
12. 0.53×6.2

13. 7.88×5.08
14. 8.1×8.9
15. 2.56×1.215
16. 3.61×0.59

Estimate. Write > or < for each ●.

17. 6×4.27 ● 24
18. 8×3.87 ● 32
19. 6×2.19 ● 12

20. 9×3.216 ● 27
21. 7×8.762 ● 56
22. 9×1.763 ● 18

23. 19×3.818 ● 80
24. 12×2.169 ● 24
25. 29×4.897 ● 150

26. 2.83×4.67 ● 15
27. 4.17×1.027 ● 4
28. 7.83×8.799 ● 72

29. 2.17×6.039 ● 12
30. 7.4×8.23 ● 56
31. 2.195×6.047 ● 12

Solve.

32. The tour bus travels 8.7 miles per gallon of gasoline. The bus used about 1.5 gallons during the class's tour. Was the class's bus tour longer or shorter than 18 miles?

★33. The tour bus takes two routes. One is 13.05 miles long. It travels that route 10 times per month. The other route is 9.75 miles long. It travels that route 19 times per month. About how far does the bus travel in one month?

FOCUS: ESTIMATION

Estimating can help you place the decimal point correctly when multiplying decimals.

Estimate:
4×0.883

Round to:
$4 \times 0.9 =$
36, or 3.6, or 0.36?

Think:
You're multiplying 4 by a number less than 1. So, the product must be less than 4.

Estimate.
3.6

Place the decimal point.

1. $27.6 \times 0.89 = 24564$
2. $3.04 \times 1.2 = 3648$
3. $0.73 \times 0.8 = 584$

Multiplying by a Decimal

The last place the class visited was the Air and Space Museum. There, they saw the Wright brothers' first airplane. They also saw the space capsule in which Col. John Glenn orbited Earth. The capsule is 2.1 meters long. The Wright brothers' plane is 5.8 times as long. How long is the airplane?

Multiply 5.8 × 2.1.

Multiply as you would with whole numbers.

$$\begin{array}{r} 2.1 \\ \times\,5.8 \\ \hline 168 \\ 105 \\ \hline 1218 \end{array}$$

Write the decimal point so that the product has as many places as the sum of the decimal places in the factors.

$$\begin{array}{r} 2.1 \longleftarrow \text{1 place} \\ \times\,5.8 \longleftarrow +\text{1 place} \\ \hline 168 \\ 105 \\ \hline 12.18 \longleftarrow \text{2 places} \end{array}$$

The airplane is 12.18 meters long.

Other examples:

$$\begin{array}{r} 0.045 \longleftarrow \text{3 places} \\ \times\;\;0.23 \longleftarrow +\text{2 places} \\ \hline 135 \\ 90 \\ \hline 0.01035 \longleftarrow \text{5 places} \end{array}$$

> Write zeros in the product if needed.

$$\begin{array}{r} \$4.15 \\ \times\;\;1.15 \\ \hline 2075 \\ 415 \\ 415 \\ \hline \$4.7725 \end{array} \text{ Rounds to } \$4.77.$$

> When multiplying money, round the product to the nearest cent.

Checkpoint   Write the letter of the correct answer.

Multiply. Round to the nearest cent if necessary.

1. 4.81 × 0.7   **a.** 2.867   **b.** 3.367   **c.** 33.67

2. $1.79 × 6.34   **a.** $11.33   **b.** $11.3486   **c.** $11.35

Multiply. Round to the nearest cent if necessary.

1. 34.1 × 0.1	**2.** 3.69 × 7.27	**3.** 9.49 × 5.9	**4.** 6.99 × 1.6	**5.** 0.448 × 14.4
6. 0.089 × 2.2	**7.** 0.069 × 0.4	**8.** 0.03 × 0.9	**9.** 0.008 × 0.07	**10.** 0.131 × 0.7
11. 0.097 × 0.05	**12.** 33.798 × 0.7	**13.** 0.64 × 9	**14.** 0.7 × 0.3	**15.** 1.012 × 8.84
16. 0.353 × 0.06	**17.** 7.516 × 0.002	**18.** 2.705 × 3.78	**19.** $43.74 × 5	**20.** 0.001 × 16

21. 0.025 × 0.2

22. 5.997 × 0.956

23. 12.67 × 0.29

24. $5.15 × 0.15

25. $8.49 × 2.5

26. $391.42 × 0.05

Solve.

27. The museum has an Apollo lunar module that is 7.1 meters tall. Next to it is a Gemini space capsule that is 5.8 meters tall. How much taller is the lunar module than the Gemini capsule?

28. Jenny phones her dad from the museum to say that she will be home the next day. The phone company charges $0.36 per minute for the call. Their call lasts 1.4 minutes. How much does the call cost to the nearest cent?

★29. On the way home, the buses stop for gas. Gas costs $1.27 per gallon. One bus takes 25.4 gallons, another 29.2 gallons, and the third 22.7 gallons. How much does all of the gas cost?

ANOTHER LOOK

Add or subtract.

1. 2.34 + 5.67

2. 7.07 + 0.41

3. 0.98 − 0.45

4. 23.294 − 19.003

5. 0.653 + 2.96

6. 0.675 − 0.0826

PROBLEM SOLVING
Guessing and Checking

Sometimes, making a guess and checking it is a good way to solve a problem. Read the problem to find hints, and make a guess. Then check it. If it does not answer the question, try again.

> A high school club is planning a trip. The club will need 25 hotel rooms. The planning committee assigns members to three inns. They do not reserve the same number of rooms in the three inns. They reserve an odd number of rooms in each inn. They reserve fewer than 12 rooms in each inn. How many rooms do they reserve in each inn?

Think about the hints.
- There are three numbers whose sum is 25.
- No number is the same as any other number.
- Each number is an odd number.
- Each number is less than 12.

Use 11 as your first guess. It is the first odd number that is less than 12. When you subtract 11 from 25, you have 14 left. Think about pairs of odd numbers that add up to 14.

The numbers can't be 7 and 7, because no number is the same as any other number. They can't be 8 and 6, 10 and 4, or 12 and 2, because those numbers are even numbers. They can't be 13 and 1 because no number is more than 12. They can't be 11 and 3 because you already have an 11. That leaves 9 and 5.

Check your answer.
- 11, 9, and 5 add up to 25.
- All the numbers are different.
- They are all odd numbers.
- They are all less than 12.

Solve. If you use the guess-and-check method, show your guesses and checks.

1. Four boxes of supplies have been loaded onto the bus for the trip. The combined weight of the 4 boxes is 45 pounds. Each of the last 3 boxes loaded weighs 2 times more than the box loaded just before it. The last box weighs 8 times more than the first box. How many pounds does each box weigh?

2. The travelers go boating. Some of the boats can carry 3 people each, and the rest can hold 4 people each. If there are 14 boats carrying a total of 50 people, how many boats carrying 4 people are there?

3. Several of the travelers play a trivia game. Everyone has to answer 15 questions. The game leader adds 10 points for each correct answer and deducts 3 points for each incorrect answer. Henry's score is 72 points. How many correct answers and incorrect answers did he give?

4. Some of the travelers went to an outdoor concert. They spent a total of $48 on tickets. For this concert, center-section tickets sold for $12 each. Side-section tickets sold for $8 each. How many of each kind of ticket did the group buy?

5. One morning, it rains and the group must stay indoors. Alicia makes up a number code for her friends to crack. Each letter in the code stands for a different number. Alicia writes this problem in her code: WH + H + H = WW. She thought this code represented only one combination of numbers. Marge found two other combinations. What are the three sets of numbers Marge found?

6. Mittens sell for $4 per pair, and scarves sell for $9 each. Group members paid $78 in all for scarves and mittens. They bought the same number of scarves as pairs of mittens. How many of each item did they buy?

CALCULATOR

You can use the calculator to find a number whose square is equal to 144. First take a guess at what the number might be. Try squaring 10.

Press    The answer is 100.

That's too small. Try a bigger number.

Press

The answer is 225. 15 is too large a number.

Try numbers between 10 and 15 on your calculator. Which number multiplied by itself equals 144? That number is called the **square root** of 144.

Copy and complete the table.

Number	Low Guess	Square	High Guess	Square	Square Root
1. 289	15	■	20	■	■
2. 196	■	■	■	■	■
3. 361	■	■	■	■	■
4. 529	■	■	■	■	■

Try to find the square root of 6. Without the calculator, you know that $2 \times 2 = 4$ and $3 \times 3 = 9$. So the square root of 6 must be a number between 2 and 3. Try decimals between 2 and 3. You will not find an exact square root, but you can get a good approximation.

Number	Low Guess	Square	High Guess	Square	Square Root
5. 8	■	■	■	■	■
6. 5	■	■	■	■	■
7. 11	■	■	■	■	■
8. 10	■	■	■	■	■

GROUP PROJECT

Planning Can Be a Picnic

The problem: Your class is planning an outing to a local park. The class must decide the best way to organize the trip. Will you put one person in charge of planning? Will you form committees? Will the entire class make the arrangements? How will you decide who will perform the five tasks listed below?

Making miscellaneous arrangements

- You need to reserve space in the park.
- You have to ask teachers and parents to chaperone the outing.

Arranging transportation

- There are 40 students going to the park.
- School buses might be available at no charge.

Calculating finances

- The class treasury has $200.
- The park fee is $25.
- The fees for tennis courts and ball fields aren't included in the park fee.
- Buses from a private company rent for $85 per day and seat 30 people.

Planning and preparing food

- Each student could bring his or her own food, or the picnic could be a cooperative effort.
- There are barbecue grills in the park.

Scheduling activities

- The school will provide equipment for tennis or softball.
- A variety of activities should be planned so that individual preferences will be satisfied.

What will you do if it rains on the day of the outing?

CHAPTER TEST

Identify the property. Find the missing number. (page 70)

1. $3 \times 6 = \blacksquare \times 3$ **2.** $5 \times 1 = \blacksquare$ **3.** $0 \times 8 = \blacksquare$

4. $(2 \times 3) \times 4 = 2 \times (\blacksquare \times 4)$ **5.** $4 \times (2 + 5) = (\blacksquare \times 2) + (\blacksquare \times 5)$

Find the product. (page 72)

6.   600
       $\times \ \ 50$

7.   7,000
       $\times \ \ \ 300$

8.   800
       $\times \ \ 70$

Estimate. Then if needed, write > or < to adjust the estimate. (page 74)

9. 229×510 **10.** 481×58 **11.** 382×765

Find the product. (pages 78, 80, and 82)

12.   67
        $\times \ 5$

13. $8.26
        $\times \ \ \ \ 4$

14.   74
        $\times \ 56$

15. $4,192
        $\times \ \ \ \ \ 38$

16.   698
        $\times \ 109$

17. 198×9 **18.** $183 \times \$51.97$

Find the product. (page 84)

19. 5^2 **20.** 4^3 **21.** 3^4 **22.** 10^5

Find the product. (page 88)

23.   5.0698
        $\times \ \ \ \ \ 10$

24.   7.92346
        $\times \ \ \ \ \ 100$

25.   26.8549
        $\times \ \ \ 1,000$

Find the product. (page 92)

26.   9.03
        $\times \ \ \ 6$

27. $0.57
        $\times \ \ \ 48$

28.   0.025
        $\times \ \ \ 8$

29.   9.561
        $\times \ \ \ 89$

Estimate. Then if needed, write > or < to adjust the estimate. (page 94)

30. 5.7×3.89 **31.** 7.7×0.294 **32.** 3.02×3.09

Find the product. (page 96)

33.   65.7
        $\times \ 0.9$

34.   0.824
        $\times \ \ 1.6$

35.   11.689
        $\times \ \ 2.87$

36. $845.50
        $\times \ \ \ \ 0.16$

Make a plan for each problem. Solve. (page 90)

37. The bicycle ride from Steve's house to the shopping mall is 2.3 miles. Last month, Steve made 7 round-trips from his home to the mall and back. How many total miles did he ride?

Write an equation. Solve. (page 76)

38. Steve's class went on a trip to the zoo. They spent 25 minutes in the monkey house and 18 minutes in the reptile house. How much more time did they spend in the monkey house?

Estimate to solve. (page 86)

39. Steve wants to buy 6 postcards at the zoo's gift shop. Each card costs $0.35, including tax. Is $2.00 enough to buy all 6 cards?

Solve. If you use the guess-and-check method, show each guess and check. (page 98)

40. The students learn that the zoo's three Alaskan brown bears have a combined weight of 3,000 pounds. The "papa" bear weighs 300 pounds more than the "mama" bear. The "mama" bear weighs 4 times as much as the "baby" bear. How much does each bear weigh?

BONUS

Multiply.

1. 6,325
×2,079

2. 80,000
× 3,000

3. $29.95
× 1,710

4. 90 × 70 × 60

5. 5,398 × 100,000

6. 0.00955 × 8,423

7. 1.00538 × 2.659

RETEACHING

When you multiply a number by a 3-digit factor, you can drop the placeholder zeros.

Multiply 287 × 5,203.

Multiply by the ones.	**Multiply by the tens.**	**Multiply by the hundreds.**	**Add.**
5,203	5,203	5,203	5,203
× 287	× 287	× 287	× 287
36,421	36,421	36,421	36,421
	416,240	416,240	416,240
		1,040,600	1,040,600
			1,493,261

Multiply.

1. 357
   × 296

2. 738
   × 959

3. 605
   × 812

4. $4.99
   × 320

5. $7.47
   × 125

6. 8,495
   × 567

7. 5,596
   × 101

8. 6,060
   × 888

9. $29.95
   × 632

10. $50.45
   × 931

11. 238
   × 472

12. 723
   × 167

13. 530
   × 859

14. $2.91
   × 705

15. $8.47
   × 686

16. 5,154
   × 383

17. 2,503
   × 927

18. 6,767
   × 816

19. $35.41
   × 748

20. $86.15
   × 969

21. 876 × 579

22. 2,390 × 489

23. $83.26 × 395

24. 772 × 638

25. 9,955 × 911

26. $58.73 × 352

ENRICHMENT

Lattice Multiplication

Lattice multiplication is a quick and different
way to multiply two numbers.

Multiply 387×94.

First, make a grid. Write the digits of
one factor along the top. Write the
digits of the second factor along the right.
Divide each box diagonally.

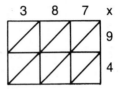

Next, multiply each digit along the top
by the digit in the ones place along the
side. Place the answers in the boxes.

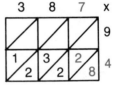

Think:
$4 \times 7 = 28.$

Multiply the rest of the digits in the
same way.

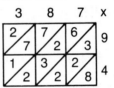

Add along the diagonals.
Regroup if necessary.

Write the digits in order from left to
right. You've found the product: 36,378.

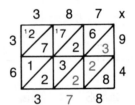

Think:
$3 + 2 + 2 = 7.$

Copy and complete each lattice. Check your product
with a calculator.

1.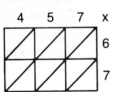

2.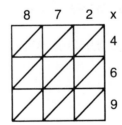

3.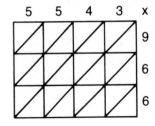

Use lattice multiplication to find the product.

4. $6,975 \times 784$

5. $8,787 \times 5,973$

6. $34,978 \times 952$

105

TECHNOLOGY

In BASIC, the computer uses a set of rules to simplify expressions. First, all operations within parentheses are done. Then, multiplication and division are done, from left to right. Addition and subtraction are done last, from left to right.

Write what the computer will print.

1. PRINT 9 * (9 − 2)

2. PRINT 9 * 9 − 2

3. PRINT 7 / 1 + 10 − 3

4. PRINT (6 − (8 − 4)) + 7

5. PRINT 16 + 8 / 2

6. Write what this program will print when you RUN it.

```
10   LET N = 180
20   LET P = .15
30   LET A = N * P
40   PRINT "15% OF" N "IS" A
```

7. Write a program to solve this problem.

There are 260 lockers in the locker room. Of them, 10% are not being used. How many lockers are unused?

Here is a short program that stores 13 in a variable for age. Then it prints out a message about how old you are.

```
10   LET AG = 13
20   PRINT "YOU ARE" AG "YEARS OLD"
```

If you have several different friends who are different ages, you would need to rewrite the LET statement in line 10 for each of them. For instance, you could rewrite line 10 this way.

```
10   LET AG = 16
```

You could then RUN this for your friend who is 16 years old. It will print this.

YOU ARE 16 YEARS OLD

Here's another way to do the same thing. Instead of rewriting the program each time, you can use a statement that will let you type in a new number each time the program is RUN.

```
10   INPUT AG
20   PRINT "YOU ARE" AG "YEARS OLD"
```

When you RUN this program, a question mark will appear on the screen. The computer is waiting for you to type a number. You can type in any number, and the computer will tell you how old you are. Your screen might look like this.

```
RUN
?   7 ←—— Type, and press RETURN.
YOU ARE 7 YEARS OLD
```

You can RUN the program again.
```
RUN
?   17 ←—— Type, and press RETURN.
YOU ARE 17 YEARS OLD
```

The number you typed was stored in the variable AG.

The INPUT statement prints a question mark and waits for you to type something in. As soon as you press RETURN or ENTER, the computer stores your number in a variable and goes on to the next statement.

8. Write another line in the program so that when the program is RUN, your screen might look like this.

```
RUN
WHAT IS YOUR AGE
?   75
YOU ARE 75 YEARS OLD
```

CUMULATIVE REVIEW

Write the letter of the correct answer.

1. Write as a decimal: four hundred twenty-seven thousandths.

   a. 0.0427   **b.** 0.427
   c. 400.027   **d.** not given

2. 5.24 + 6.1689

   a. 11.1713   **b.** 11.4089
   c. 11.489   **d.** not given

3. Compare: 9.4074 ● 9.4047.

   a. 9.4074 > 9.4047
   b. 9.4074 < 9.4047
   c. 9.4074 = 9.4047
   d. not given

4. Write as a decimal: three and five hundredths.

   a. 0.35   **b.** 3.05
   c. 3.5   **d.** not given

5.
   0.495
   0.03
 + 0.908

   a. 0.433
   b. 1.333
   c. 1.423
   d. not given

6.
   34.016
 − 32.125

   a. 1.891
   b. 2.891
   c. 2.991
   d. not given

7. Choose the best estimate: 10.975 + 9.86.

   a. less than 19   **b.** more than 20
   c. more than 21   **d.** less than 10

8. Write in standard form: 10 million, 40 thousand, eighteen.

   a. 1,040,018   **b.** 10,040,018
   c. 100,040,018   **d.** not given

9. $23.95 + $16.49

   a. $39.44   **b.** $40.34
   c. $40.44   **d.** not given

10.
   825,971
 − 735,872

   a. 90,099
   b. 90,109
   c. 90,199
   d. not given

11. $5 + n = 15$; find the missing number.

   a. 9   **b.** 10
   c. 11   **d.** not given

12. There are 718 girls and 673 boys who attend Parker Middle School. Which is the best estimate for the population of the school?

   a. 1,200   **b.** more than 1,300
   c. more than 1,500   **d.** not given

13. Susan, Dan, and Al went shopping. Susan spent $32. Dan spent $5 more than Susan. Al spent less than either Susan or Dan spent. How much money did they spend in all? Which phrase best describes this problem?

   a. not enough information
   b. too much information
   c. enough information

Your class has been asked to work on a project to clean up and beautify the area around the school. You have to decide what should be done and how the available money could best be used. How should the students in the class be organized? Which tasks will be assigned to each group?

4 DIVIDING WHOLE NUMBERS

Division Facts

A. John and Paul took 72 bottles to a recycling plant in Augusta, Maine. If they packed 9 bottles into each box, how many boxes did they fill?

You can divide to find the number of equal groups.

Divide $72 \div 9$.
Think: $n \times 9 = 72$.
    $8 \times 9 = 72$

So, $72 \div 9 = 8$.

They filled 8 boxes.

Jane and Lisa took 54 bottles to the same plant. They packed the bottles equally into 9 boxes. How many bottles did they pack into each box?

You can divide to find the number in each group.

Find the quotient of $9\overline{)54}$.
Think: $n \times 9 = 54$.
    $6 \times 9 = 54$

So, $9\overline{)54}$.
$\quad\quad^{6}$

They packed 6 bottles into each box.

B. Division can be shown in three ways.

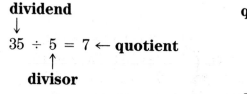
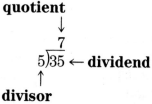
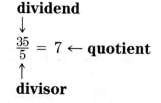

C. As you divide, remember:

Any number divided by 1 is that number.	$9 \div 1 = 9$
Any number, except 0, divided by itself is 1.	$6 \div 6 = 1$
0 divided by another number, except 0, is 0.	$0 \div 3 = 0$
A number is never divided by 0.	$8 \div 0 = n$
Think: $n \times 0 = 0$.	$n \times 0 = 8$
Any number is a solution.	No solution.

Divide.

1. $4\overline{)16}$ 2. $7\overline{)7}$ 3. $3\overline{)6}$ 4. $1\overline{)3}$ 5. $8\overline{)0}$

6. $1\overline{)6}$ 7. $3\overline{)9}$ 8. $5\overline{)5}$ 9. $9\overline{)18}$ 10. $2\overline{)14}$

11. $4\overline{)28}$ 12. $5\overline{)0}$ 13. $3\overline{)15}$ 14. $4\overline{)12}$ 15. $8\overline{)56}$

16. $9\overline{)72}$ 17. $9\overline{)45}$ 18. $3\overline{)24}$ 19. $5\overline{)15}$ 20. $8\overline{)48}$

21. $9\overline{)27}$ 22. $8\overline{)64}$ 23. $7\overline{)35}$ 24. $4\overline{)32}$ 25. $6\overline{)30}$

26. $81 \div 9$ 27. $35 \div 5$ 28. $63 \div 9$ 29. $40 \div 5$ 30. $36 \div 6$

31. $\frac{16}{2}$ 32. $\frac{25}{5}$ 33. $\frac{49}{7}$ 34. $\frac{32}{8}$ 35. $\frac{27}{3}$

Find n.

36. $5 \times n = 45$ 37. $42 \div 6 = n$ 38. $28 \div n = 4$ ★39. $n \div 3 = 8$

Solve.

40. Each of 9 students from a sixth-grade class searched the neighborhood for aluminum cans. They each collected the same number of cans. The total number collected was 81. How many cans did each student collect?

41. The students took the 81 cans to the local supermarket. They were paid 5¢ for each can. How much money did the students receive altogether for the cans?

42. Puldon Tire Company receives 24 tons of worn tires for recycling. Their plant melts 4 tons of tires per week in order to salvage oil from the rubber in the tires. How many weeks will it take to melt the 24 tons of tires?

43. Paper-recycling plants use machines called *pulpers*, which break down large amounts of paper into fibers. If one plant evenly divides 36 tons of paper among 9 pulpers, how many tons of paper will each pulper receive?

FOCUS: REASONING

Stack the cartons in three equal piles so that the sum of the numbers in each pile is the same.

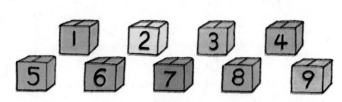

Order of Operations

A. Ms. Jones writes this example on the chalkboard.

$54 \div 9 - 3 = n$

Both Jack and Alice try to answer it. Who worked the example correctly?

Jack	*Alice*
$54 \div 9 - 3 = n$	$54 \div 9 - 3 = n$
$54 \div 6 = n$	$6 - 3 = n$
$9 = n$	$3 = n$
Jack subtracted and then divided.	Alice divided and then subtracted.

When an equation has two or more operations, use the following steps.

Multiply or divide from left to right. $54 \div 9 - 3 = n$
Add or subtract from left to right. $6 - 3 = n$
      $3 = n$

Alice worked the example correctly.

B. If an equation has parentheses or fraction bars, use the following steps.

Always do the operation in parentheses first.

$$(6 + 3) \times 5 = n \qquad 42 \div (7 - 2^2) = n$$
$$9 \times 5 = n \qquad 42 \div (7 - 4) = n$$
$$45 = n \qquad 42 \div 3 = n$$
$$14 = n$$

Always do the operations on either side of the fraction bar first.

$$\frac{8 + 4}{3} = n \qquad \frac{24}{6 \times 2} = n$$
$$\frac{12}{3} = n \qquad \frac{24}{12} = n$$
$$4 = n \qquad 2 = n$$

Checkpoint   Write the letter of the correct answer.

Compute.

1. $\dfrac{9 - 1}{4}$

a. 1
b. $1\frac{1}{4}$
c. 2
d. $8\frac{3}{4}$

2. $7 + 9 \times 7 - 1$

a. 61
b. 69
c. 96
d. 111

3. $(16 - 4) \div 2^2$

a. 0
b. 3
c. 6
d. 15

Compute.

1. $64 \div 8 - 7$
2. $7 + 36 \div 6$
3. $49 - 6 \div 3$
4. $48 \div 6 + 2$

5. $6 \times 8 - 12$
6. $50 - 5 \times 7$
7. $12 \times 3 + 8$
8. $4 + 11 \times 13$

9. $13 - 4 \times 3$
10. $16 - 4 \div 2$
11. $2 + 3 \times 8$
12. $24 \div 3 + 3$

13. $4 + 5 \times 9$
14. $16 - 2 \times 6$
15. $32 - 16 \div 16$
16. $18 \div 1 + 8$

17. $\frac{5^2 - 5}{5}$
18. $5 + 4 \times 3^2$
19. $\frac{29 - 25}{2^2}$
20. $5 + 2^3 \times 5$

21. $(11 - 6) \times 8$
22. $32 \div (4 + 12)$
23. $(42 \div 7) - 3$
24. $7 \times (3 + 5)$

25. $(1^4 + 3) \times 9$
26. $3 \times (6^2 - 31)$
27. $57 \div (4^2 + 3)$
28. $(9 \div 3^2) - 1$

29. $41 - (12 \times 3)$
30. $(41 - 12) \times 3$
31. $(14 - 4) \div 2$
32. $14 - (4 \div 2)$

★33. $82 - 8 \times (5 + 3)$
★34. $(76 + 8) \div (2 \times 3)$
★35. $\frac{8^2 - 4}{40 - 5^2}$

Solve.

36. To save water during a water shortage, one family switched from baths to showers. Baths for the entire family required a total of 216 gallons of water, but each of the 6 family members used only 10 gallons to shower. How many gallons of water did the family save each time it took showers instead of baths?

★37. The Rosmans's electric dishwasher uses 17 gallons of water each time it is run. In order to save water, the Rosmans cut down from 1 wash cycle per day to 1 wash cycle every other day. If they use the dishwasher on Monday, how much water will they have saved by the end of the next weekend?

FOCUS: REASONING

Solve

1. There are 8 people at a meeting. Each person shakes hands with every other person once. How many handshakes are there?

2. You have some pennies, nickels and dimes. Choose 21 coins that have a total value of $1.00.

Dividing with Remainders

Justin is going to plant 47 flowers as part of his contribution to Make Our Park Beautiful Day. He plans to plant them in groups of 5. How many full groups can he plant? How many plants will he have left?

Divide $5\overline{)47}$.

Think: $n \times 5$ is close to 47?

$8 \times 5 = 40$
$9 \times 5 = 45$
$10 \times 5 = 50$ Too great. So, use 9.

$$\begin{array}{r} 9 \text{ R2} \\ 5\overline{)47} \\ \underline{45} \\ 2 \end{array}$$

Multiply. $9 \times 5 = 45$
Subtract. $47 - 45 = 2$
Compare. $2 < 5$
Write the remainder.

Check. Multiply the quotient by the divisor and add the remainder. The answer should be the dividend.

$$\begin{array}{r} 9 \\ \times 5 \\ \hline 45 \\ + 2 \\ \hline 47 \end{array}$$

Justin can plant 9 full groups with 2 plants left.

Divide. Check your answer.

1. $9\overline{)83}$ 2. $7\overline{)51}$ 3. $8\overline{)57}$ 4. $6\overline{)32}$ 5. $9\overline{)48}$

6. $5\overline{)29}$ 7. $4\overline{)34}$ 8. $3\overline{)23}$ 9. $6\overline{)38}$ 10. $9\overline{)70}$

11. $7\overline{)45}$ 12. $8\overline{)26}$ 13. $4\overline{)27}$ 14. $8\overline{)63}$ 15. $8\overline{)47}$

16. $7\overline{)33}$ 17. $5\overline{)39}$ 18. $4\overline{)17}$ 19. $2\overline{)11}$ 20. $6\overline{)28}$

21. $17 \div 7$ 22. $48 \div 5$ 23. $35 \div 8$ 24. $34 \div 9$ 25. $14 \div 3$

26. $\frac{49}{6}$ 27. $\frac{75}{8}$ 28. $\frac{13}{2}$ 29. $\frac{8}{3}$ 30. $\frac{37}{6}$

What is the greatest remainder you can have when you divide

31. by 6?   32. by 8?   33. by 4?   34. by 9?   35. by 7?   36. by 1?

Divisibility

If a number can be divided by another number, with no remainder, then it is **divisible** by that number.

36 is divisible by 4.

37 is not divisible by 4.

$$4\overline{)36} \quad \begin{array}{r} 9 \\ \hline 36 \\ \hline 0 \end{array}$$

$$4\overline{)37} \quad \begin{array}{r} 9 \text{ R1} \\ \hline 36 \\ \hline 1 \end{array}$$

Here are some tests that you can use to find out if one number is divisible by another.

Divisor	Rule	Example
2	Any even number is divisible by 2. **Even numbers** end in 2, 4, 6, 8, or 0. Odd numbers are not divisible by 2. **Odd numbers** end in 1, 3, 5, 7, or 9.	8; 62; 766; and 1,054 are all divisible by 2.
3	The sum of the digits in the dividend must be divisible by 3.	615 is divisible by 3 since 6 + 1 + 5 = 12, and 12 is divisible by 3.
5	The digit in the ones place must be 0 or 5.	30; 75; 1,245; and 3,560 are all divisible by 5.
6	Any number that is divisible by both 2 and 3 is divisible by 6.	42; 132; 840; and 1,728 are all divisible by 6.
9	The sum of the digits in the dividend must be divisible by 9.	5,328 is divisible by 9 since 5 + 3 + 2 + 8 = 18 and 18 is divisible by 9.
10	The digit in the ones place must be 0.	50; 820; 970; and 1,270 are all divisible by 10.

Write 2, 3, 5, 6, 9, or 10 next to the numbers that are divisible by them.

1. 48

2. 53

3. 70

4. 226

5. 693

6. 2,481

7. 7,594

8. 9,783

9. 14,325

10. 97,326

11. 880,914

12. 1,506,999

Estimating Quotients

A. The Consolidated Power Company wants to find out its customers' views on solar energy. It sends 6 employees to conduct a survey in Carleton. They are to survey about 2,650 homes. About how many homes will each employee visit in the course of the survey?

Estimate $2,650 \div 6$.

Decide the number of digits in the quotient.

Divide the thousands. Think: $6\overline{)2}$. Not enough thousands.
Divide the hundreds. Think: $6\overline{)26}$.

So, the quotient begins in the hundreds place. It will have three digits.

$$6\overline{)2,650}$$

Think: $6 \times 4 = 24$.
$\qquad 6 \times 5 = 30$ Too great. So, use 4.

$$\begin{array}{r} 4 \\ 6\overline{)2,650} \end{array}$$

$\qquad$ Write zeros for the other digits.

$$\begin{array}{r} 400 \\ 6\overline{)2,650} \end{array}$$

400 is an underestimate. Each employee will need to visit more than 400 homes.

B. You can estimate the quotients of problems with larger dividends in the same way.

Estimate $24\overline{)56,413}$.

Decide the number of digits in the quotient.

$$24\overline{)56,413}$$

Divide to find the first digit.

$$\begin{array}{r} 2 \\ 24\overline{)56,413} \end{array}$$

Write zeros for the other digits.

$$\begin{array}{r} 2,000 \\ 24\overline{)56,413} \end{array}$$

2,000 is an underestimate. The estimate is more than 2,000.

Write the number of digits each quotient will contain,
not including remainders.

1. $9\overline{)285}$ **2.** $5\overline{)449}$ **3.** $6\overline{)676}$ **4.** $6\overline{)209}$ **5.** $38\overline{)264}$

6. $36\overline{)20,736}$ **7.** $77\overline{)154}$ **8.** $44\overline{)38,456}$ **9.** $5\overline{)314}$ **10.** $24\overline{)20,352}$

Write the letter of the best estimate.

11. $82\overline{)41,084}$ **a.** 5   **b.** 50   **c.** 500   **12.** $5\overline{)6,429}$ **a.** 10   **b.** 100   **c.** 1,000

13. $30\overline{)6,173}$ **a.** 20   **b.** 200   **c.** 2,000   **14.** $8\overline{)52,319}$ **a.** 6   **b.** 600   **c.** 6,000

Estimate the quotient.

15. $5\overline{)415}$ **16.** $7\overline{)22,340}$ **17.** $4\overline{)37,906}$ **18.** $3\overline{)15,748}$ **19.** $6\overline{)452}$

20. $34\overline{)349}$ **21.** $61\overline{)2,518}$ **22.** $11\overline{)999}$ **23.** $32\overline{)60,211}$ **24.** $54\overline{)443}$

25. $90\overline{)23,812}$ **26.** $4\overline{)301,452}$ **27.** $73\overline{)570}$ **28.** $21\overline{)7,925}$ **29.** $32\overline{)8,318}$

30. $9\overline{)46,399}$ **31.** $83\overline{)65,552}$ **32.** $19\overline{)533}$ **33.** $3\overline{)870}$ **34.** $91\overline{)2,109}$

Solve.

35. There is a total of 37,104 homes in Carleton County. The Consolidated Power Company has 4 power stations there. Each station provides power to about the same number of homes. About how many homes does each station serve?

★36. Consolidated Power Company employs 2,436 people. All the employees work at one of the company's 4 power plants. About the same number of people work at each one. About how many people work at 2 of the power plants?

FOCUS: ESTIMATION

Sunlight can be changed into electricity by solar cells. Solar cells are arranged on flat surfaces called *solar panels*. There are 160 solar cells on one solar panel. A bank of solar panels outside of Carleton consists of 3,360 solar cells. About how many solar panels are there in the bank?

Dividing by a 1-Digit Divisor

The lumber industry works to replant forests. One company in Alaska has 363 young trees to plant. It distributes them equally at 5 sites. How many trees are planted at each site? How many trees are left?

Divide $5\overline{)363}$.

Divide the hundreds.   Think: $5\overline{)3}$.   Not enough hundreds.

Divide the tens.   **Divide the ones.**
  Think: $5\overline{)36}$.   **Bring down the 3.**
  Write 7.   Think: $5\overline{)13}$.
              Write 2.

$$
\begin{array}{r}
7 \\
5\overline{)363} \\
35 \\
\hline
1
\end{array}
$$
Multiply.
Subtract.
Compare.

$$
\begin{array}{r}
72\ \text{R}3 \\
5\overline{)363} \\
35\downarrow \\
\hline
13 \\
10 \\
\hline
3
\end{array}
$$
Multiply.
Subtract and
compare.
Write the
remainder.

Check
$$
\begin{array}{r}
72 \\
\times\ 5 \\
\hline
360 \\
+\ 3 \\
\hline
363
\end{array}
$$

At each site, 72 trees are planted, and 3 trees are left.

Other examples:

$$
\begin{array}{r}
60 \\
6\overline{)360} \\
36 \\
\hline
00
\end{array}
\qquad
\begin{array}{r}
47\ \text{R}1 \\
2\overline{)95} \\
8 \\
\hline
15 \\
14 \\
\hline
1
\end{array}
\qquad
\begin{array}{r}
\$0.85 \\
4\overline{)\$3.40} \\
3\,2 \\
\hline
20 \\
20 \\
\hline
0
\end{array}
$$

> Divide money as if you were dividing whole numbers. Remember to write the dollar sign and the cents point in the quotient.

Checkpoint Write the letter of the correct answer.

Divide.

1. $2\overline{)87}$

2. $5\overline{)\$4.45}$

3. $\$7.36 \div 8$

a. 4
b. 34 R1
c. 43
d. 43 R1

a. 89
b. $0.89
c. 98
d. $0.98

a. $0.29
b. $0.90
c. $0.92
d. 92

Find the quotient and remainder.

1. $3\overline{)84}$ 2. $4\overline{)96}$ 3. $2\overline{)36}$ 4. $7\overline{)77}$ 5. $5\overline{)\$4.50}$

6. $4\overline{)53}$ 7. $3\overline{)74}$ 8. $6\overline{)81}$ 9. $2\overline{)29}$ 10. $2\overline{)175}$

11. $5\overline{)260}$ 12. $3\overline{)147}$ 13. $7\overline{)448}$ 14. $9\overline{)405}$ 15. $7\overline{)\$5.95}$

16. $731 \div 9$ 17. $335 \div 6$ 18. $109 \div 2$ 19. $618 \div 8$ 20. $500 \div 8$

21. $60 \div 5$ 22. $97 \div 5$ 23. $188 \div 2$ 24. $250 \div 7$ 25. $\$2.32 \div 4$

26. $\dfrac{87}{7}$ 27. $\dfrac{249}{4}$ 28. $\dfrac{569}{8}$ 29. $\dfrac{62}{3}$ 30. $\dfrac{314}{6}$

Solve.

31. A logger in Alaska earns $65 for 5 hours work. How much does he earn per hour?

32. One lumber yard logged 267 Sitka spruce trees in 3 days. If each day's tree count was the same, how many spruces were logged per day?

33. The Waskey family estimates that the lumber needed to build a new porch will cost $549. If the family saves $9 per week, for how many weeks must the family save in order to raise the money?

34. Maple trees in Maine produced 272 gallons of sap that were processed into 8 gallons of maple syrup. How many gallons of sap are needed for each gallon of maple syrup?

FOCUS: MENTAL MATH

How fast can you mentally compute half of a number?
Divide these numbers by two as quickly as you can.

1. 48   2. 36   3. 82   4. 54   5. 68   6. 112

7. 148   8. 236   9. 512   10. 846   11. 1,242   12. 3,848

Dividing Larger Numbers

A. One ranger at an African wildlife preserve travels for 9 days, inspecting an area of 1,845 acres. If the ranger inspects at a constant pace, how many acres does he <u>cover</u> each day?
Divide 9)1,845.

Divide the thousands.   Think: 9)1.   Not enough thousands.

Divide the hundreds.	Divide the tens.	Divide the ones.
Think: 9)18.	Bring down the 4.	Bring down the 5.
Multiply.	Think: 9)4.	Think: 9)45.
Subtract.	Not enough tens.	Multiply.
Compare.	Multiply.	Subtract.
	Subtract.	Compare.
	Compare.	

```
      2            20              205
  9)1,845       9)1,845        9)1,845
    1 8            1 8            1 8
                     4             4
                     0             0
                     4            45
                                  45
                                   0
```

Remember to write 0 in the quotient.

The ranger covers 205 acres each day.

Other examples:

```
    $8.27          6,095 R2         121 R2         1,434 R1
 8)$66.16       6)36,572        7)849          6)8,605
   64             36               7              6
    2 1            5              14              2 6
    1 6            0              14              2 4
     56           57               9              20
     56           54               7              18
      0           32               2              25
                  30                              24
                   2                               1
```

120

Divide.

1. $5\overline{)3,170}$ 2. $7\overline{)6,174}$ 3. $4\overline{)968}$ 4. $8\overline{)2,088}$ 5. $6\overline{)4,860}$

6. $9\overline{)4,929}$ 7. $8\overline{)6,758}$ 8. $6\overline{)5,936}$ 9. $4\overline{)559}$ 10. $5\overline{)1,537}$

11. $2\overline{)4,488}$ 12. $6\overline{)9,330}$ 13. $3\overline{)7,296}$ 14. $4\overline{)\$98.92}$ 15. $7\overline{)\$88.41}$

16. $6\overline{)8,276}$ 17. $3\overline{)9,809}$ 18. $2\overline{)3,261}$ 19. $9\overline{)9,127}$ 20. $7\overline{)7,353}$

21. $7\overline{)27,070}$ 22. $5\overline{)12,396}$ 23. $4\overline{)32,860}$ 24. $6\overline{)46,998}$ 25. $3\overline{)11,613}$

26. $4,622 \div 5$ 27. $2,785 \div 3$ 28. $5,216 \div 8$ 29. $\$95.20 \div 4$ 30. $\$8.49 \div 3$

31. $1,000 \div 9$ 32. $5,384 \div 6$ 33. $7,485 \div 5$ 34. $632 \div 4$ 35. $\$1.64 \div 2$

36. $\dfrac{8,154}{3}$ 37. $\dfrac{9,136}{4}$ 38. $\dfrac{811}{8}$ 39. $\dfrac{1,172}{5}$ 40. $\dfrac{2,655}{9}$

41. $\dfrac{5,868}{7}$ 42. $\dfrac{1,296}{2}$ 43. $\dfrac{6,875}{5}$ 44. $\dfrac{1,115}{6}$ 45. $\dfrac{2,052}{4}$

Solve.

46. A naturalist spent 4 years in Africa. During that time he spent a total of 1,728 hours observing lions. If he spent the same amount of time observing each year, how much time did he spend each year?

47. One pride of lions has 15 adult lions and 20 cubs in it. If each cub requires 3 gallons of water per day, how much water do all the cubs in the pride need per day?

48. The gnu, an African antelope, migrates 1,548 miles each year. A herd of gnu can complete this migration in 6 months. If the herd travels the same distance each month, how many miles do the gnu travel each month?

49. A naturalist tags gazelles. Every fifth gazelle is given a tag. The first year, the naturalist tags 1,486 gazelles, the second year, 1,722 gazelles and the third, 1,107 gazelles. How many gazelles are tagged during the 3 years?

MIDCHAPTER REVIEW

Compute.

1. $7\overline{)28}$ 2. $6\overline{)54}$ 3. $3\overline{)23}$ 4. $5\overline{)44}$ 5. $6\overline{)84}$

6. $8\overline{)97}$ 7. $5\overline{)1,307}$ 8. $9\overline{)\$27.18}$ 9. $12 - 6 \div 3$ 10. $63 \div 7 - 8$

PROBLEM SOLVING
Practice

JUNIOR MUSEUM GIFT SHOP

Posters	$4.85
Dinosaur model	$3.75
Shark model	$3.25
Wolf puzzle	$1.85
Energy data book	$1.95
Postcards	$0.50
Animal picture book	$3.95

This Week's Sale Items

Environment stamp book	$1.50
Kaleidoscope	$0.85

Use the price list to answer each question. Write the letter of the correct answer.

1. Sarah bought 2 postcards and an animal picture book. What was the total cost of the items?

   a. $4.45
   b. $4.95
   c. $5.45

2. Sam bought a shark model, an energy data book, and a picture book. He began with $10.00. How much did he have left?

   a. $0.85
   b. $3.30
   c. $9.15

Write the letter of the best estimate.

3. Lee wants to buy a dinosaur model and a wolf puzzle. About how much will she spend?

   a. $4.00–$5.00
   b. $5.00–$6.00
   c. $7.00–$8.00

4. In one day, the gift shop sold 97 postcards. About how much money was spent on postcards that day?

   a. $5.00
   b. $50.00
   c. $500.00

Write the letter of the information that either does not help you solve the problem or is missing.

5. Roberto bought a dinosaur model and 2 postcards. Carmen bought a poster and received $0.15 in change from her $5.00 bill. Who spent more?

   a. Roberto bought a dinosaur model and 2 postcards.
   b. Carmen bought a poster.
   c. Carmen received $0.15 in change.

6. Sigmund bought lunch at the cafeteria. He then bought the environment stamp book on sale. He also bought 7 postcards. How much did he spend in all?

   a. Sigmund bought 7 postcards.
   b. Sigmund spent $1.50 for lunch.
   c. The environment stamp book cost $1.50 on sale.

Write an equation, and solve.

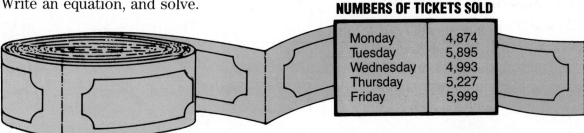

NUMBERS OF TICKETS SOLD

Monday	4,874
Tuesday	5,895
Wednesday	4,993
Thursday	5,227
Friday	5,999

7. The table shows the number of admission tickets sold by the Science Museum for one week. What was the total number of tickets sold?

8. Were more tickets sold on Wednesday or on Friday? How many more tickets were sold?

Write the operation needed to solve.

9. There are 96 people waiting in line to see the Planetarium Show. Each of 6 ticket lines contains the same number of people. How many people are there in each line?

10. Each ticket to the museum costs $1.55. How much money did the museum collect from the 96 ticket-buyers?

Read each problem. Without finding the exact answer, write the letter of the correct answer.

11. The sixth-grade class buys 26 admission tickets at $1.55 each. What is the total cost of admission for all the students?

a. $4.03   **b.** $40.30   **c.** $403.00

12. The Science Museum is visited by about 1,900 students a day. At that rate, about how many students will visit the museum during the month of April?

a. 5,700   **b.** 57,000   **c.** 570,000

Make a plan. Solve.

13. On Saturday, 1,975 students visited the Science Museum. On Sunday, there were 119 fewer visitors than on Saturday. If each student who visited the museum that Sunday spent $2.50 for souvenirs, how much in all did the students spend on souvenirs?

14. In the Museum Theater, there are 75 rows of seats. The first 25 rows of the theater have 12 seats per row, and the rest of the theater has 14 seats per row. If rows 1 through 50 are reserved for school groups, how many people can sit in the reserved section?

Short Division

A team of 7 scientists sets out to observe fish in the Mississippi River. They decide to station themselves evenly along the 1,344 miles of shoreline. How many miles of shoreline must each scientist cover?
Find the quotient: $7\overline{)1,344}$.
Short division can be used when the divisor is a one-digit number. Multiply and subtract mentally.

Divide the thousands.   Think: $7\overline{)1}$.   Not enough thousands.

Divide the hundreds.
Think: $7\overline{)13}$.
Write the remainder next to the tens.

$$\frac{1\quad\quad}{7\overline{)1,3^{6}44}}$$

Divide the tens.
Think: $7\overline{)64}$.
Write the remainder next to the ones.

$$\frac{1\;9\quad}{7\overline{)1,3^{6}4^{1}4}}$$

Divide the ones.
Think: $7\overline{)14}$.
Write the remainder, if necessary.

$$\frac{1\;9\;2}{7\overline{)1,3^{6}4^{1}4}}$$

Each scientist must cover 192 miles of shoreline.

Other examples:

$$\frac{1,2\;1\;6}{8\overline{)9,1^{7}2^{4}8}}$$

$$\frac{6\;9\;\text{R2}}{5\overline{)34^{4}7}}$$ Write the remainder.

$$\frac{\$1\;5.\;1\;9}{6\overline{)\$9^{3}1.^{1}5^{4}}}$$

Checkpoint   Write the letter of the correct answer.

Divide.

1. $6\overline{)324}$

a. 45
b. 50 R4
c. 53 R6
d. 54

2. $7\overline{)1,275}$

a. 110 R1
b. 182 R1
c. 281 R1
d. 1,821

3. $6\overline{)\$90.66}$

a. $10.11
b. $11.51
c. $15.11
d. 1,511

Use short division to divide.

1. $9\overline{)936}$ 2. $5\overline{)655}$ 3. $7\overline{)189}$ 4. $3\overline{)615}$ 5. $6\overline{)282}$

6. $2\overline{)209}$ 7. $3\overline{)434}$ 8. $9\overline{)861}$ 9. $4\overline{)710}$ 10. $8\overline{)372}$

11. $5\overline{)4,080}$ 12. $7\overline{)3,864}$ 13. $4\overline{)1,028}$ 14. $3\overline{)2,442}$ 15. $9\overline{)6,399}$

16. $4\overline{)3,250}$ 17. $8\overline{)6,647}$ 18. $5\overline{)4,751}$ 19. $7\overline{)2,150}$ 20. $6\overline{)5,054}$

21. $4\overline{)\$16.88}$ 22. $7\overline{)\$95.97}$ 23. $6\overline{)\$43.86}$ 24. $8\overline{)\$56.96}$ 25. $3\overline{)\$89.25}$

Solve.

26. During a 3-month period, an Environmental Protection Agency inspector visits 117 factories on the Clinton River. If she visits the same number each month, how many factories does she visit in a month?

27. The Clarksville town council divides a $1,056 grant among 3 environmental groups. Each group received the same amount of money. How much money did each of the groups receive?

28. For each pound of her weight, a female salmon will lay about 882 eggs. If she weighs 7 pounds, about how many eggs will a salmon lay?

29. A group of naturalists spent 144 hours during a 9-day period studying wildlife. If they spent the same number of hours each day, how many hours of each day did they spend studying wildlife?

ANOTHER LOOK

Multiply.

1. $\begin{array}{r} 453 \\ \times\ 26 \\ \hline \end{array}$ 2. $\begin{array}{r} 156 \\ \times\ 77 \\ \hline \end{array}$ 3. $\begin{array}{r} 205 \\ \times\ 73 \\ \hline \end{array}$ 4. $\begin{array}{r} 459 \\ \times\ 86 \\ \hline \end{array}$ 5. $\begin{array}{r} 344 \\ \times\ 54 \\ \hline \end{array}$

6. 333×107 7. 415×180 8. 63×101 9. 213×105 10. 592×47

More Practice, page 443

PROBLEM SOLVING
Estimation

When a problem can be solved by estimation, you often need to decide whether you should overestimate or underestimate.

> David is buying souvenirs at the Natural History Museum. He wants to buy dinosaur figures. They sell 8 for $3.39. David wants to buy 2. He has $1.38. Does he have enough money?

Since he wants to be sure that he has enough money, he decides to **overestimate** the cost.

Round up $3.39 $\longrightarrow$ $4.00
$4.00 \div 8 = 0.50 (cost of 1 dinosaur)
$0.50 \times 2 = 1.00 (cost of 2 dinosaurs)

Since $1.00 < $1.38, David has enough money.

Sally Rogers runs the movie theater in the Natural History Museum. She wants to determine whether the museum can afford to buy $2,500 worth of films. She looks at the list of ticket sales for that week to see if they add up to at least $2,500.

Tuesday: $592.15   Friday: $867.45
Wednesday: $428.75   Saturday: $865.00
Thursday: $234.25

Since Sally wants to make sure the museum has enough money, she decides to **underestimate** sales.

Round down
Tuesday: $592.15 $\longrightarrow$ $500.00
Wednesday: $428.75 $\longrightarrow$ 400.00
Thursday: $234.25 $\longrightarrow$ 200.00
Friday: $867.45 $\longrightarrow$ 800.00
Saturday: $865.00 $\longrightarrow$ 800.00
                              Total $2,700.00

Since $2,700.00 > $2,500.00, the museum has enough money to buy the films.

Write *underestimate* or *overestimate* to complete each sentence. Explain your answer.

Visitors to Gem Exhibit			
Tuesday	3,457	Friday	1,872
Wednesday	2,987	Saturday	4,118
Thursday	1,561	Sunday	3,422

1. A museum curator must decide whether to keep a gem exhibit open for another week. An exhibit will be kept open as long as it draws at least 12,500 people a week. She should ■ the number of people who visited the gem exhibit in the last week.

2. The curator has to order more brochures for the gem exhibit. She wants to order enough for the next week. The curator should ■ the number of people who visited the gem exhibit last week.

Solve. Estimate if possible.

Shell Price List	
Moon shell — — — — — — — — —	$0.29
Nautilus shell — — — — — — —	$4.25
Queen conch — — — — — — — —	$2.75
Cowrie shell — — — — — — — —	$0.39
Helmet shell — — — — — — — —	$3.29
Murex shell — — — — — — — —	$1.89

3. Russell wants to purchase shells from the museum gift shop. He can spend $4.56. Does Russell have enough money to buy 8 cowrie shells?

4. Gina has $6.79 to buy shells. If she buys 1 helmet shell, 3 cowrie shells, and 1 moon shell, how much money will she have left?

5. The planetarium director is planning the fall schedule. He knows that the Harvest Moon show takes exactly 47 minutes. He wants to find out if they can have 6 shows in 5 hours. (HINT: There are 60 minutes in an hour.)

6. Marvin has $5.50. What should he buy so that he has as many different kinds of shells as possible?

Dividing by Multiples of 10

A. A group of 70 sixth graders studied water-conservation practices in their town. They interviewed 630 familes to find out how they use and conserve water. Each sixth grader interviewed the same number of families. How many families did each student interview?

Divide 630 ÷ 70.

Think: 63 ÷ 7 = 9
        630 ÷ 70 = 9

Each student interviewed 9 families.

B. Patterns can help you divide by multiples of 10.

42 ÷ 7 = 6	28 ÷ 4 = 7
420 ÷ 7 = 60	280 ÷ 40 = 7
4,200 ÷ 70 = 60	2,800 ÷ 40 = 70
42,000 ÷ 700 = 60	28,000 ÷ 40 = 700

Checkpoint Write the letter of the correct answer.

Divide.

1. 2,700 ÷ 90

a. 3
b. 3 R1
c. 30
d. 300

2. 600)‾4,200

a. 7
b. 700
c. 7,000
d. 70,000

3. 48,000 ÷ 40

a. 12
b. 120
c. 1,200
d. 12,000

Divide.

1. $9\overline{)54}$ 2. $9\overline{)540}$ 3. $90\overline{)5,400}$ 4. $900\overline{)54,000}$

5. $7\overline{)35}$ 6. $70\overline{)350}$ 7. $70\overline{)3,500}$ 8. $700\overline{)35,000}$

9. $6\overline{)180}$ 10. $5\overline{)250}$ 11. $3\overline{)270}$ 12. $8\overline{)320}$

13. $70\overline{)490}$ 14. $80\overline{)560}$ 15. $90\overline{)720}$ 16. $600\overline{)3,600}$

17. $40\overline{)3,200}$ 18. $90\overline{)3,600}$ 19. $50\overline{)2,500}$ 20. $700\overline{)14,000}$

21. $60\overline{)48,000}$ 22. $30\overline{)27,000}$ 23. $40\overline{)20,000}$ 24. $80\overline{)24,000}$

25. $42,000 \div 60$ 26. $3,600 \div 40$ 27. $81,000 \div 90$ 28. $300 \div 50$

29. $2,800 \div 40$ 30. $2,200 \div 20$ 31. $240 \div 3$ 32. $64,000 \div 800$

Solve. For Problem 36, use the Infobank.

33. During a drought, people conserve water by using no more than 50 gallons per person per day. On one day, a family conserved and used 650 gallons of water. How many people are there in the family?

34. Edna researched the world's largest seawater-desalting plant in Kuwait. She found that it produced 540 million gallons of pure water in a 90-day period. If the plant produces the same amount each day, how many gallons of pure water does it produce in a day?

35. Clyde learns that the rainiest spot in the United States is Mt. Waialeale, Hawaii. About 600 inches of rain fell there during a 50-week period in 1948. About how many inches of rain fell there per week in 1948?

36. Use the information on page 432 to find how much water is used each hour for farming and manufacturing in the East and in the West. Then write two division problems of your own.

FOCUS: MENTAL MATH

To divide a number mentally by 5, use this method.
Since $10 = 2 \times 5$, divide by 10 and then multiply by 2.

Divide $5\overline{)700}$. | $700 \div 10 = 70$ $70 \times 2 = 140$ |

Compute mentally.

1. $5\overline{)800}$ 2. $5\overline{)900}$ 3. $5\overline{)12,000}$ 4. $5\overline{)21,000}$

Dividing by a 2-Digit Divisor

A. At 22 centers 199 people volunteer to study air pollution. Each center must have an equal number of volunteers. Any volunteers that are left will be coordinators between centers. How many volunteers are there at each center? How many become coordinators?

Find the quotient $22\overline{)199}$.

Divide the hundreds. Think: $22\overline{)1}$. Not enough hundreds.
Divide the tens. Think: $22\overline{)19}$. Not enough tens.

Divide the ones.
   Think: $22\overline{)199}$ or $2\overline{)19}$.   Estimate 9.

$$
\begin{array}{r}
9 \ \textbf{R1} \\
22\overline{)199} \\
\underline{198} \\
1
\end{array}
\quad
\begin{array}{l}
\text{Multiply.} \\
\text{Subtract.} \\
\text{Compare.}
\end{array}
\qquad
\begin{array}{r}
\text{Check.}\quad 22 \\
\times\ 9 \\
\hline
198 \\
+\ 1 \\
\hline
199
\end{array}
$$

There are 9 volunteers at each center, and 1 coordinator.

B. Divide $889 \div 37$.

Divide the hundreds. Think: $37\overline{)8}$. Not enough hundreds.

Divide the tens.
   Think: $37\overline{)88}$ or $3\overline{)8}$.
   Estimate 2.

$$
\begin{array}{r}
2 \\
37\overline{)889} \\
\underline{74} \\
14
\end{array}
\quad
\begin{array}{l}
\text{Multiply.} \\
\text{Subtract.} \\
\text{Compare.}
\end{array}
$$

Divide the ones.
   Think: $37\overline{)149}$ or $3\overline{)14}$.
   Estimate 4.

$$
\begin{array}{r}
24 \ \textbf{R1} \\
37\overline{)889} \\
\underline{74}\downarrow \\
149 \\
\underline{148} \\
1
\end{array}
\quad
\begin{array}{l}
\text{Multiply.} \\
\text{Subtract.} \\
\text{Compare.} \\
\text{Write the} \\
\text{remainder.}
\end{array}
\qquad
\begin{array}{r}
\text{Check.} \\
37 \\
\times\ 24 \\
\hline
888 \\
+\ 1 \\
\hline
889
\end{array}
$$

Other examples:

$$
\begin{array}{r}
\$0.13 \\
47\overline{)\$6.11} \\
\underline{4\,7} \\
1\,41 \\
\underline{1\,41} \\
0
\end{array}
\qquad
\frac{788}{63} \longrightarrow
\begin{array}{r}
12 \ \text{R32} \\
63\overline{)788} \\
\underline{63} \\
158 \\
\underline{126} \\
32
\end{array}
$$

Divide.

1. $32\overline{)96}$ 2. $47\overline{)96}$ 3. $11\overline{)99}$ 4. $21\overline{)71}$ 5. $25\overline{)75}$

6. $41\overline{)205}$ 7. $23\overline{)138}$ 8. $51\overline{)462}$ 9. $75\overline{)328}$ 10. $31\overline{)162}$

11. $34\overline{)829}$ 12. $61\overline{)673}$ 13. $13\overline{)286}$ 14. $46\overline{)644}$ 15. $29\overline{)\$3.19}$

16. $24\overline{)578}$ 17. $31\overline{)998}$ 18. $44\overline{)924}$ 19. $25\overline{)782}$ 20. $58\overline{)\$8.70}$

21. $69 \div 22$ 22. $78 \div 26$ 23. $229 \div 52$ 24. $696 \div 43$ 25. $\$8.06 \div 62$

26. $757 \div 24$ 27. $292 \div 11$ 28. $74 \div 37$ 29. $878 \div 61$ 30. $\$9.89 \div 23$

31. $64 \div 31$ 32. $882 \div 42$ 33. $94 \div 41$ 34. $475 \div 93$ 35. $\$5.44 \div 34$

36. $\frac{468}{36}$ 37. $\frac{999}{75}$ 38. $\frac{87}{29}$ 39. $\frac{315}{43}$ 40. $\frac{969}{57}$

Solve.

41. In one county, 72 small towns send 504 tons of solid waste per day to a disposal plant. On the average, how many tons of solid waste does each town send to the plant per day?

42. About 214 million tons of dangerous gases pollute the air each year. Of this, 90 million tons are from car exhausts. How many tons of gas are produced from other sources?

43. Many factories install scrubbers in their chimneys to remove dirt deposited by smoke. If a factory installs 114 scrubbers in 38 chimneys, how many scrubbers are installed in each chimney?

44. Of 437 commuters in one town, 260 ride in car pools. If there are 65 car pools, what is the average number of riders in each car pool?

CHALLENGE

The *unit price* is the price of one unit of a particular item. For example, the unit price for eggs would be the price of one egg. The unit price for milk would be the price per ounce. Calculate the unit price for each of the brands of laundry soap in the ad. Which would be the best buy?

Food-o-rama Soap Sale	
Bright (40 oz)	$3.20
Gone (16 oz)	$1.92
Gone (54 oz)	$4.86
All White (32 oz)	$2.88
All White (55 oz)	$3.85

Correcting Estimates

Mr. Herr owns a small orange grove. He packs his juice oranges in bags of 24. One day, he picks 857 juice oranges. How many bags can be filled? How many oranges will be left?

Divide $24\overline{)857}$.

Divide the hundreds. Think: $24\overline{)8}$. Not enough hundreds.
Divide the tens.
Think: $24\overline{)85}$ or $2\overline{)8}$.
Estimate 4.
Multiply. Too great.
You need to correct the estimate.

$$\begin{array}{r} 4 \\ 24\overline{)857} \\ 96 \\ \hline \end{array}$$

Try 3.
Multiply. Subtract and compare.

$$\begin{array}{r} 3 \\ 24\overline{)857} \\ 72 \\ \hline 13 \end{array}$$

Divide the ones.
Think: $24\overline{)137}$ or $2\overline{)13}$.
Estimate 6.
Multiply. Too great.
You need to correct the estimate.

$$\begin{array}{r} 36 \\ 24\overline{)857} \\ 72\downarrow \\ \hline 137 \\ 144 \end{array}$$

Try 5.
Multiply. Subtract.
Write the remainder.

$$\begin{array}{r} 35 \text{ R17} \\ 24\overline{)857} \\ 72\downarrow \\ \hline 137 \\ 120 \\ \hline 17 \end{array}$$

The juice oranges will fill 35 bags with 17 oranges left.

Checkpoint   Write the letter of the correct answer.

Divide.

1. $29\overline{)619}$ a. 2 R3   b. 20 R39   c. 21   d. 21 R10

2. $362 \div 73$ a. 4   b. 4 R7   c. 4 R70   d. 5 R12

3. $\dfrac{849}{47}$ a. 10 R28   b. 17 R50   c. 18   d. 18 R3

132

Find the quotient.

1. $39\overline{)234}$
2. $26\overline{)134}$
3. $89\overline{)799}$
4. $21\overline{)82}$
5. $25\overline{)65}$

6. $27\overline{)864}$
7. $33\overline{)627}$
8. $43\overline{)817}$
9. $28\overline{)898}$
10. $28\overline{)618}$

11. $21\overline{)690}$
12. $47\overline{)714}$
13. $32\overline{)858}$
14. $27\overline{)351}$
15. $65\overline{)890}$

16. $46\overline{)828}$
17. $47\overline{)864}$
18. $23\overline{)851}$
19. $38\overline{)950}$
20. $24\overline{)412}$

21. $790 \div 54$
22. $418 \div 22$
23. $259 \div 37$
24. $608 \div 32$
25. $242 \div 34$

26. $972 \div 67$
27. $595 \div 35$
28. $825 \div 89$
29. $827 \div 21$
30. $130 \div 26$

31. $\frac{918}{34}$
32. $\frac{961}{44}$
33. $\frac{285}{46}$
34. $\frac{846}{47}$
35. $\frac{810}{42}$

Solve.

36. An orange-juice company arranges to have 180 acres of swampland drained of excess water. The company estimates that the job will take 36 pumps. How many acres will each pump drain?

37. The average orange tree in Mr. Herr's grove produces 995 oranges per year. How many oranges do all 632 trees in the grove produce each year?

38. One day, Mr. Herr picks 620 navel oranges and packs them into wooden crates. Each crate holds 36 oranges. The extra oranges are placed in a plastic bag. How many crates are filled? How many oranges are placed in the plastic bag?

FOCUS: MENTAL MATH

To divide a number mentally by 25, use this method. Since $100 = 4 \times 25$, divide by 100 and then multiply by 4.

Divide $25\overline{)1,200}$.

$$1,200 \div 100 = 12 \qquad 12 \times 4 = 48$$

Compute mentally.

1. $25\overline{)800}$
2. $25\overline{)1,100}$
3. $25\overline{)9,000}$
4. $25\overline{)80,000}$

More Practice, page 444

Dividing Thousands

The Tennessee Valley Authority was created in 1933 to control flooding. Before 1933, floods wiped out some small towns. After the TVA built dams, populations of towns could increase in safety. Suppose a town with a population of 53 in 1933 has grown to a town of 6,837 today. How many times greater is today's population?

Divide $53\overline{)6,837}$.

Divide the thousands. Think: $53\overline{)6}$. Not enough thousands.

Divide the hundreds.
Think: $53\overline{)68}$, or $5\overline{)6}$.
Estimate 1.

$$\begin{array}{r} 1 \\ 53\overline{)6,837} \\ \underline{5\ 3} \\ 1\ 5 \end{array}$$

Divide the tens.
Think: $53\overline{)153}$, or $5\overline{)15}$.
Estimate 3.
Multiply.
Too great. Try 2.

$$\begin{array}{r} 12 \\ 53\overline{)6,837} \\ \underline{5\ 3} \\ 1\ 53 \\ \underline{1\ 06} \\ 47 \end{array}$$

Divide the ones.
Think: $53\overline{)477}$, or $5\overline{)47}$.
Estimate 9.

$$\begin{array}{r} 129 \\ 53\overline{)6,837} \\ \underline{5\ 3} \\ 1\ 53 \\ \underline{1\ 06} \\ 477 \\ \underline{477} \\ 0 \end{array}$$

Today's population is 129 times greater.

Other examples:

$$\begin{array}{r} 79 \\ 44\overline{)3,476} \\ \underline{3\ 08} \\ 396 \\ \underline{396} \\ 0 \end{array}$$

$$\begin{array}{r} 136\ \text{R}71 \\ 72\overline{)9,863} \\ \underline{7\ 2} \\ 2\ 66 \\ \underline{2\ 16} \\ 503 \\ \underline{432} \\ 71 \end{array}$$

$$\begin{array}{r} \$\ 0.18 \\ 77\overline{)\$13.86} \\ \underline{7\ 7} \\ 6\ 16 \\ \underline{6\ 16} \\ 0 \end{array}$$

Divide.

1. $77\overline{)1{,}386}$ 2. $53\overline{)5{,}247}$ 3. $62\overline{)4{,}898}$ 4. $56\overline{)1{,}736}$ 5. $84\overline{)\$14.28}$

6. $89\overline{)3{,}751}$ 7. $87\overline{)8{,}267}$ 8. $81\overline{)7{,}460}$ 9. $76\overline{)3{,}982}$ 10. $62\overline{)2{,}307}$

11. $17\overline{)6{,}579}$ 12. $32\overline{)9{,}536}$ 13. $46\overline{)7{,}590}$ 14. $15\overline{)2{,}940}$ 15. $69\overline{)\$91.77}$

16. $72\overline{)9{,}952}$ 17. $73\overline{)8{,}669}$ 18. $21\overline{)9{,}052}$ 19. $25\overline{)8{,}116}$ 20. $38\overline{)\$34.58}$

21. $5{,}904 \div 82$ 22. $4{,}586 \div 34$ 23. $9{,}510 \div 15$ 24. $1{,}652 \div 59$ 25. $\$98.64 \div 36$

26. $8{,}470 \div 35$ 27. $3{,}196 \div 68$ 28. $7{,}480 \div 85$ 29. $1{,}320 \div 58$ 30. $\$91.53 \div 81$

31. $2{,}249 \div 14$ 32. $9{,}660 \div 21$ 33. $8{,}291 \div 42$ 34. $5{,}432 \div 12$ 35. $\$55.44 \div 63$

Solve.

36. If a barge on the Tennessee River travels 81 miles each day, how long will the 1,296-mile round trip from Knoxville to New Johnsonville take?

37. The Chickamauga Lock can raise a barge 4.8 feet per minute. It takes 10 minutes to raise a barge from the bottom of the dam to the top. How high is the dam?

38. The TVA's Wilson Dam produces 7,560 megawatts of power every 12 hours. How many megawatts are produced each hour at the dam?

★39. Over the last 49 years, the TVA has replanted 1,862,000 acres in the Tennessee Valley. On the average, how many acres were replanted each year?

FOCUS: REASONING

Farmer Dylan has a problem. He is taking a fox, a chicken, and a bag of corn to the market. His problem is that he has to cross the river, but his boat can hold only one of the three items at a time. If he leaves the fox and the chicken alone together, the fox will eat the chicken. If he leaves the chicken and the corn alone together, the chicken will eat the corn. How can Farmer Dylan take all three safely across the river?

Dividing Larger Numbers

The *Clearwater* is a floating classroom that docks at towns along the Hudson River. Volunteers aboard the *Clearwater* teach people about conserving their environment. Last year, 30,624 people attended *Clearwater* events. On the average, how many people attended *Clearwater* events each month?

Divide 12)30,624.

Think: 12)3. Not enough ten thousands.
Think: 12)30. Place the first digit of the quotient in the thousands place. Divide.

```
      2,552
12)30,624
   24
    6 6
    6 0
      62
      60
       24
       24
        0
```

Check.
```
   2,552
×     12
  30,624
```

Each month, an average of 2,552 people attended *Clearwater* events.

Other examples:

```
      31,562
31)978,422
   93
   48
   31
   17 4
   15 5
    1 92
    1 86
      62
      62
       0
```

```
      2,537 R13
26)65,975
   52
   13 9
   13 0
      97
      78
     195
     182
      13
```

Divide.

1. 21)76,041   **2.** 12)75,040   **3.** 36)85,035   **4.** 15)$537.30

5. 42)56,785   **6.** 30)84,569   **7.** 34)88,298   **8.** 29)$768.79

9. 23)298,287   **10.** 53)664,991   **11.** 53)182,553   **12.** 57)$2,635.11

13. 60)706,620   **14.** 36)475,876   **15.** 12)443,328   **16.** 32)$7,793.28

17. 72,864 ÷ 49   **18.** 182,336 ÷ 56   **19.** 492,534 ÷ 99   **20.** $1,619.42 ÷ 17

21. 533,711 ÷ 16   **22.** 894,546 ÷ 28   **23.** 98,050 ÷ 39   **24.** $7,305.00 ÷ 20

Solve.

25. The *Clearwater* depends on volunteers to help carry out its many programs. Over a three-year period, 96 volunteer crew members worked a total of 49,344 hours. How many hours did each volunteer crew member work?

★26. Every June, the *Clearwater* hosts the Hudson River Revival. Last year, the revival earned $102,640 on one-day tickets that cost $10 each. It earned $52,972 on two-day tickets that cost $17 each. How many people attended the revival last year?

CHALLENGE

The density of a gas is a relative measure of how much the gas weighs in relation to other gases. To calculate density in grams per cubic meter, divide a mass in grams by a volume in cubic meters.

Solve.

1. If 25 cubic meters of methane weigh 17,925 grams, what is methane's density?

2. If hydrogen's density is 90 grams per cubic meter, how many cubic meters would 471,060 grams of hydrogen take up?

Zeros in the Quotient

Scientists are concerned about the loss of rain forests. Due to farming, logging, and mining, some areas are losing 21,744 acres every 24 hours. How many acres are being lost every hour?

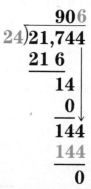

Divide 24)21,744.

Think: 24)2.   Not enough ten thousands.
Think: 24)21.   Not enough thousands.

Divide the hundreds.
  Think: 24)217.
  Estimate: 9

$$\begin{array}{r} 9 \\ 24\overline{)21{,}744} \\ 21\ 6 \\ \hline 1 \end{array}$$

Divide the tens.
  Think: 24)14.
  Not enough tens.
  Write 0.

$$\begin{array}{r} 90 \\ 24\overline{)21{,}744} \\ 21\ 6\downarrow \\ \hline 14 \\ 0 \\ \hline 14 \end{array}$$

Divide the ones.
  Think: 24)144.
  Estimate: 7
  Multiply. Too great.
  Try 6.

$$\begin{array}{r} 906 \\ 24\overline{)21{,}744} \\ 21\ 6\ \ \\ \hline 14\ \ \\ 0\downarrow \\ \hline 144 \\ 144 \\ \hline 0 \end{array}$$

Every hour, 906 acres of rain forest are being lost.

Other examples:

$$\begin{array}{r} 300 \text{ R5} \\ 31\overline{)9{,}305} \\ 9\ 3\ \ \\ \hline 0\ \ \\ 0\ \ \\ \hline 5 \\ 0 \\ \hline 5 \end{array}$$

$$\begin{array}{r} 30 \\ 28\overline{)840} \\ 84 \\ \hline 0 \\ 0 \\ \hline 0 \end{array}$$

$$\begin{array}{r} \$440.21 \\ 17\overline{)\$7{,}483.57} \\ 6\ 8\ \ \\ \hline 68 \\ 68 \\ \hline 3 \\ 0 \\ \hline 3\ 5 \\ 3\ 4 \\ \hline 17 \\ 17 \\ \hline 0 \end{array}$$

Divide.

1. $17\overline{)6{,}841}$ 2. $34\overline{)7{,}049}$ 3. $21\overline{)2{,}115}$ 4. $55\overline{)5{,}705}$ 5. $43\overline{)\$89.01}$

6. $47\overline{)42{,}665}$ 7. $40\overline{)36{,}031}$ 8. $79\overline{)40{,}160}$ 9. $72\overline{)14{,}928}$ 10. $82\overline{)\$508.40}$

11. $22\overline{)80{,}960}$ 12. $75\overline{)97{,}875}$ 13. $23\overline{)37{,}720}$ 14. $30\overline{)45{,}003}$ 15. $14\overline{)\$140.56}$

16. $77\overline{)462{,}924}$ 17. $28\overline{)197{,}800}$ 18. $70\overline{)630{,}300}$ 19. $13\overline{)899{,}600}$ 20. $15\overline{)\$5{,}350.35}$

21. $45\overline{)7{,}658}$ 22. $28\overline{)10{,}360}$ 23. $40\overline{)25{,}205}$ 24. $31\overline{)124{,}230}$ 25. $46\overline{)\$667.00}$

26. $67{,}725 \div 75$ 27. $59{,}470 \div 66$ 28. $7{,}435 \div 37$ 29. $\$3{,}621.76 \div 32$

30. $392{,}588 \div 98$ 31. $13{,}165 \div 26$ 32. $6{,}185 \div 60$ 33. $\$1{,}321.10 \div 22$

Solve.

34. In Malaysia 401,526 acres of rain forest were cleared to make room for 18 townships. Each township was given an equal area of land. How many acres did each township receive?

35. A large paper plant on the Amazon River processes wood from the surrounding rain forest. In 26 months, workers clear and process wood from 313,482 acres. If they clear the same number of acres each month, how many acres of rain forest do they clear each month?

36. A factory in New Guinea makes chopsticks. During a typical 12-hour day, 130,956 chopsticks are made. If the factory sells each chopstick for 3 cents, how many dollars' worth of chopsticks does the factory produce in one hour?

ANOTHER LOOK

Write the product.

1. 8^3 2. 4^5 3. 1^9 4. 10^4 5. 6^2 6. 5^4

7. 3^2 8. 2^6 9. 10^2 10. 9^5 11. 4^4 12. 7^7

More Practice, page 444   **139**

Dividing by a 3-Digit Divisor

People visit Redwood National Park to see the ancient redwoods, which are the world's tallest trees. One year, 984,093 people visited the park. If the park is open 363 days a year, how many people visited the park during an average day?

Divide $363\overline{)984,093}$.

Think: $363\overline{)9}$. Not enough hundred thousands.
Think: $363\overline{)98}$. Not enough ten thousands.
Think: $363\overline{)984}$. Place the first digit of the quotient in the thousands place. Divide.

```
          2,711
   363)984,093
        726
        258 0
        254 1
            3 99
            3 63
              363
              363
                0
```

Check.

```
    2,711
  ×   363
  984,093
```

During an average day, 2,711 people visited Redwood National Park.

Other examples:

```
        1,556 R20
   603)938,288
       603
       335 2
       301 5
        33 78
        30 15
         3 638
         3 618
            20
```

```
        3,000 R17
   268)804,017
       804
         0
         0
         1
         0
        17
         0
        17
```

```
          $32.74
   179)$5,860.46
        5 37
        490
        358
        132 4
        125 3
          7 16
          7 16
             0
```

Divide.

1. $340\overline{)125{,}460}$
2. $673\overline{)162{,}822}$
3. $732\overline{)574{,}217}$
4. $176\overline{)79{,}552}$

5. $463\overline{)660{,}238}$
6. $146\overline{)175{,}492}$
7. $278\overline{)551{,}836}$
8. $253\overline{)\$7{,}605.18}$

9. $759\overline{)719{,}532}$
10. $260\overline{)164{,}065}$
11. $323\overline{)871{,}577}$
12. $220\overline{)\$7{,}095.00}$

13. $899\overline{)793{,}817}$
14. $521\overline{)270{,}532}$
15. $471\overline{)960{,}840}$
16. $333\overline{)\$1{,}248.75}$

17. $121\overline{)761{,}090}$
18. $129\overline{)57{,}898}$
19. $790\overline{)500{,}000}$
20. $881\overline{)\$2{,}026.30}$

21. $486\overline{)155{,}520}$
22. $806\overline{)624{,}598}$
23. $639\overline{)618{,}570}$
24. $795\overline{)\$1{,}566.15}$

25. $251{,}356 \div 700$
26. $782{,}920 \div 460$
27. $311{,}955 \div 531$
28. $\$1{,}409.80 \div 371$

29. $382{,}501 \div 887$
30. $248{,}248 \div 200$
31. $148{,}996 \div 196$
32. $\$9{,}112.96 \div 928$

Solve.

33. A survey was conducted of 135 visitors to Yellowstone National Park. The survey showed that the visitors spent $115,425 on their trips. What was the average amount spent by each person?

★34. For 80 years, the Old Faithful geyser has attracted visitors to Yellowstone. During that period, it has erupted about 642,000 times. About how many eruptions per day is that?

CALCULATOR

Here is a way of finding the whole-number remainder when using a calculator to divide.

Calculate	Display
Enter 2,375,907 ÷ 4,538.	523.55817
Multiply 523 × 4,538.	2,373,374
Subtract 2,375,907 − 2,373,374.	2,533

The difference is the remainder.
The quotient would be 523 R2,533.
Check. $(4{,}538 \times 523) + 2{,}533 = 2{,}375{,}907$

Use a calculator to divide. Find the quotient and whole-number remainder.

1. $7{,}824{,}832 \div 3{,}513$
2. $603{,}987 \div 2{,}719$
3. $983{,}654 \div 9{,}504$

Equations

A. Division and multiplication are related.

Recall:
$$8 \times 7 = 56 \qquad 56 \div 7 = 8$$
$$7 \times 8 = 56 \qquad 56 \div 8 = 7$$

You can divide to find a missing factor.

$7 \times n = 490$ Think: What number multiplied by 7 equals 490?

$n = 490 \div 7$ Write a related division sentence.

$n = 70$ Find n.

B. You can multiply to find a missing dividend.

$n \div 5 = 50$ Think: What number divided by 5 equals 50?

$5 \times 50 = n$ Write a related multiplication sentence.

$n = 250$ Find n.

C. You can divide to find a missing divisor.

$360 \div n = 4$ Think: 360 divided by what number equals 4?

$360 \div 4 = n$ Write another division sentence.

$n = 90$ Find n.

Find n.

1. $n \times 30 = 150$ **2.** $n \times 70 = 420$ **3.** $n \times 20 = 180$ **4.** $n \times 90 = 270$

5. $7 \times n = 210$ **6.** $4 \times n = 240$ **7.** $5 \times n = 250$ **8.** $3 \times n = 180$

9. $n \div 5 = 60$ **10.** $n \div 4 = 70$ **11.** $n \div 8 = 50$ **12.** $n \div 9 = 40$

13. $n \div 8 = 46$ **14.** $n \div 3 = 57$ **15.** $n \div 9 = 67$ **16.** $n \div 6 = 97$

17. $360 \div n = 40$ **18.** $5 \times n = 350$ **19.** $n \div 9 = 90$ **20.** $n \times 50 = 500$

21. $n \div 7 = 82$ **22.** $8 \times n = 720$ **23.** $n \div 5 = 76$ **24.** $n \div 6 = 70$

Write an equation to find the answer.

25. The dividend is 350. The divisor is 70. What is the quotient?

26. The product is 720. One factor is 80. What is the missing factor?

27. The quotient is 6. The divisor is 50. What is the dividend?

28. The product is 132. One factor is 22. What is the missing factor?

29. The quotient is 36. The dividend is 288. What is the divisor?

★30. The dividend is 162. The sum of the quotient and the divisor is 27. Write a division equation with the correct quotient and divisor.

CHALLENGE

Replace each ● with $\times$ or $\div$ and $=$ to make each equation true.

1. 36 ● 9 ● 324 **2.** 312 ● 6 ● 52 **3.** 7 ● 98 ● 686

4. 23 ● 33 ● 759 **5.** 195 ● 5 ● 39 **6.** 4 ● 62 ● 248

★7. 6 ● 330 ● 55 **★8.** 12 ● 156 ● 13 **9.** 49 ● 3,234 ● 66

PROBLEM SOLVING
Interpreting the Quotient and the Remainder

Sometimes when you divide to solve a problem, the answer is not a whole number. If the answer is a quotient with a remainder, read the question again. Be sure that the answer you write really answers the question. You may need to drop the remainder, round the quotient to the next-greater whole number, or use only the remainder.

The sixth graders had a cleanup campaign to raise money for a class trip. They collected 1,255 bottles to take to the recycling center. The bottles are stored in cartons that hold 8 bottles each.

Divide.

$$
\begin{array}{r}
156 \text{ R7} \\
8\overline{)1{,}255} \\
\underline{8} \\
45 \\
\underline{40} \\
55 \\
\underline{48} \\
7
\end{array}
$$

Read each question. Think about how the answers differ for each question.

1. How many cartons will be completely filled?
   Drop the remainder.
   156 cartons will be completely filled.

2. How many cartons will be needed to hold all the bottles?
   Round the quotient to the next-greater whole number.
   157 cartons will be needed. One carton will be needed for the bottles left after the 156 cartons have been filled.)

3. How many bottles will there be in the unfilled carton?
   Use only the remainder.
   There will be 7 bottles in the unfilled carton.

Write the letter of the correct answer.

1. The conservation center printed 1,950 brochures for its "Day to Conserve" campaign. It divided the brochures evenly among the 9 school groups that visited that day and kept the rest. How many brochures did the center keep?

   a. 6
   b. 216
   c. 216 R6

2. The conservation center evenly distributes 143 posters to the 4 schools in its area. The remaining posters are given to the local library. How many posters does each school receive?

   a. 3
   b. 35
   c. 35 R3

Solve.

3. A group of 41 students will visit a wildlife sanctuary. They plan to travel by minibus. Each minibus can carry 7 students. How many minibuses will be needed to carry all the students at one time?

4. There are 317 bales of recycled landfill material. A truck will transport 8 bales at a time. How many round trips must the truck make to transport all the material?

5. The newspaper club collects 221 bundles of newspaper. The students use a wagon to take the bundles to the recycling plant. The wagon can hold 6 bundles at a time. How many full loads will the students take to the plant?

6. Martha is selling recycled paper. The paper is packed in boxes of 250 sheets. She sells 9 boxes of paper. How many sheets of recycled paper did she sell?

7. There are 78 aluminum cans to be recycled. Write a division problem that uses this information and has 9 as its answer.

8. Members of the sixth-grade class plan to raise money for the wildlife sanctuary. How many lawns, at $6 per lawn, will they have to mow to earn at least $400?

9. Mrs. Reise has 28 students in her class. She divides them into 3 equal teams to clean the school yard. The students who are not on a team will be in charge of the cleaning equipment. How many students will there be on each team?

10. Mr. Jacobs had 237 ecology buttons to give to the 5 classes who were part of the recycling drive. If he distributes the buttons equally and keeps the extras, how many buttons will each class receive? How many buttons will Mr. Jacobs keep?

CALCULATOR

You can use a calculator to solve equations with more than one operation, such as $(13 \times 25) + 37 = n$.

To solve for n on a calculator, you should follow the rules for order of operations. Find the product in the parentheses; then add.

Press: $\boxed{1}\ \boxed{3}\ \boxed{\times}\ \boxed{2}\ \boxed{5}\ \boxed{+}\ \boxed{3}\ \boxed{7}\ \boxed{=}$

The display should show 362. Press the $\boxed{=}$ only after the last step. When you press another operation key, the calculator remembers the total to that point.

Use the calculator to solve for n.

1. $(9 \times 22) + 6 - 8 = n$

2. $(16 \times 27) - 51 + 14 = n$

3. $(7 \times 18) - 16 + 49 = n$

4. $(16 \times 5) + 8 - 37 = n$

5. $(29 + 126) \times 24 = n$

6. $[(65 \times 18) + 22] \div 4 = n$

For some equations, you have to do part of the sentence, press the equal sign, write the result, and use it later. Try this example.

$(24 + 93) + (15 \times 28) = n$

Press: $\boxed{2}\ \boxed{4}\ \boxed{+}\ \boxed{9}\ \boxed{3}\ \boxed{=}$. Write the sum of 117.

Now press: $\boxed{1}\ \boxed{5}\ \boxed{\times}\ \boxed{2}\ \boxed{8}\ \boxed{+}\ \boxed{1}\ \boxed{1}\ \boxed{7}\ \boxed{=}$

The answer is 537.

Use a calculator to solve for n.
Write the intermediate results.

7. $14,352 \div (23 \times 16) = n$

$14,352 \div \blacksquare$

8. $4,671 + (892 \times 21) = n$

$4,671 + \blacksquare$

9. $(7,914 - 3,824) + (9,036 \div 36) = n$

$\blacksquare + \blacksquare$

10. $(2,183 \div 59) \times (4,352 \div 128) = n$

$\blacksquare \times \blacksquare$

GROUP PROJECT

The Great Debate

The problem: Your class is going to form the two teams described below to debate whether a factory should be built in your town. Use the information that follows to plan your strategy and present your argument. Try to predict the points that the other team will make. Your teacher will represent the City Planning Board and will judge which team has presented the more persuasive argument.

Key Facts

FOR THE FACTORY

- The factory will provide 1,500 much-needed jobs.
- Other businesses would grow, since more people would be working and would have more money to spend.
- An estimated 400 factory workers will use the local bus system to travel to work. Increased ridership could bring in as much as $200,000 per year. Much of this money would go toward improving bus service and maintaining equipment.

AGAINST THE FACTORY

- Waste from the factory might pollute the air and the water.
- The factory would mar the natural landscape, and its construction would destroy 15 acres of trees.
- The factory could add as many as 1,000 cars to local rush-hour traffic.
- Extra road maintenance would have to be funded from taxes collected by the town.

Key Questions

- What methods could the factory employ to prevent pollution?
- Could the factory be designed so that it would blend in with the landscape?
- What could the town do with the increased tax revenues from the growth of business?

- How would pollution affect the environment?
- Where would the factory be built?
- Is the land being used now? If so, how is it being used?
- Is the town prepared for the many changes that the factory would cause?

CHAPTER TEST

Compute. (page 112)

1. $6 + 12 \div 3$ **2.** $(14 - 7) \times 24$ **3.** $24 \div 4 + 5$

Write 2, 3, 5, 6, 9, or 10 next to the numbers that are evenly divisible by them. (page 115)

4. 54   **5.** 720   **6.** 16,200

Write the number of digits each quotient will contain, not including the remainder. (page 116)

7. $8\overline{)872}$ **8.** $37\overline{)3,291}$ **9.** $34\overline{)1,972}$ **10.** $6\overline{)4,580}$

Divide. (pages 114, 118, and 120)

11. $7\overline{)63}$ **12.** $2\overline{)59}$ **13.** $4\overline{)312}$ **14.** $4\overline{)2,824}$ **15.** $4\overline{)\$31.60}$

Use short division to find the quotient. (page 124)

16. $7\overline{)2,856}$ **17.** $2\overline{)802}$ **18.** $4\overline{)1,352}$ **19.** $9\overline{)\$64.89}$

Divide (pages 128, 130, 132, 134, 136, 138, and 140)

20. $420 \div 70$ **21.** $8,100 \div 90$ **22.** $\$504 \div 56$ **23.** $425 \div 85$

24. $78\overline{)702}$ **25.** $36\overline{)212}$ **26.** $68\overline{)475}$ **27.** $37\overline{)3,291}$ **28.** $41\overline{)1,393}$

29. $33\overline{)13,704}$ **30.** $100\overline{)90,000}$ **31.** $61\overline{)24,888}$ **32.** $109\overline{)123,388}$

Find n. (page 142)

33. $n \times 7 = 609$

34. $n \times 8 = 328$

35. $n \div 4 = 37$

36. $392 \div n = 49$

Solve. (pages 126 and 144)

37. Mrs. Carter's class is planting 43 trees as part of Ecology Week. They want to plant 5 trees in each row. How many full rows of 5 trees will they plant?

38. Last May, the state gave out 1,470 fishing licenses. About how many licenses per day were given out during the month?

39. The residents of Willow Avenue are cleaning up their block. There are 27 people. Dan suggests they split up into teams of 4 people each. How many people would be left?

40. The recycling center received 30,850 pounds of newspaper on Saturday. The papers were tied in bundles weighing 50 pounds each. About how many bundles of newspaper were there?

BONUS

Find n.

1. $6,471 \div n = 719$

2. $n \div 7 = 446$

3. $2,368 \div n = 592$

4. $n \div 5 = 632$

5. $3,908 \div n = 977$

6. $1,644 \div n = 274$

RETEACHING

Sometimes you <u>need to</u> correct your estimate when you divide. Divide 27)8,239.

Think: 27)8. Not enough thousands.

Divide the hundreds.
Think: 27)82, or 2)8.
Estimate 4. Multiply. Too great.
You need to correct the estimate.

$$\begin{array}{r} 4 \\ 27\overline{)8{,}239} \\ 1\ 08 \end{array}$$

Try 3. Multiply.
Subtract and compare.

$$\begin{array}{r} 3 \\ 27\overline{)8{,}239} \\ \underline{8\ 1} \\ 1 \end{array}$$

Divide the tens.
Think: 27)13. Not enough tens.
Write 0 in the quotient.
Multiply. Subtract and compare.

$$\begin{array}{r} 30 \\ 27\overline{)8{,}239} \\ 8\ 1\downarrow \\ \overline{13} \\ \underline{0} \\ 13 \end{array}$$

Divide the ones.
Think: 27)139, or 2)13.
Estimate 6. Multiply. Too great.

Try 5. Multiply.

Subtract and compare.
Write the remainder.

$$\begin{array}{r} 305\text{R}4 \\ 27\overline{)8{,}239} \\ 8\ 1\downarrow \\ \overline{13}\quad \\ 0\downarrow \\ \overline{139} \\ \underline{135} \\ 4 \end{array}$$

Find the quotient.

1. 18)756　　**2.** 21)174　　**3.** 45)540　　**4.** 32)999　　**5.** 16)$8.96

6. 18)6,426　　**7.** 49)7,663　　**8.** 36)8,928　　**9.** 97)9,889　　**10.** 52)$63.96

11. 42)84,630　　**12.** 89)92,150　　**13.** 43)939,949　　**14.** 88)$1,313.84

15. 880 ÷ 16　　**16.** 9,849 ÷ 23　　**17.** 99,759 ÷ 14　　**18.** $7,671 ÷ 53

19. 14,035 ÷ 35　　**20.** 25,536 ÷ 42　　**21.** 129,785 ÷ 63　　**22.** $356,633 ÷ 71

ENRICHMENT

Tangrams

Copy this figure on a piece of graph paper. Cut out the pieces. You've made a tangram.

The object of this ancient Chinese puzzle is to rearrange the pieces into different shapes.

1. First, rearrange the pieces back into the original square.

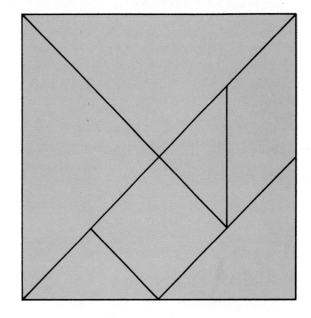

Now that you've had practice, see if you can make these shapes.

2.
bullfrog
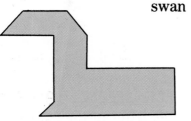

3.
space shuttle
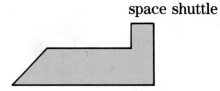

4.
swan
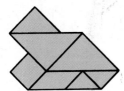

5.
spaceship

★6. Arrange the pieces into a rectangle. (**Hint:** Make two squares.)

CUMULATIVE REVIEW

Write the letter of the correct answer.

1. $8.27
   $\times$ 4

   a. $32.08
   b. $32.88
   c. $33.08
   d. not given

2. 700 × 40

   a. 2,800
   b. 28,000
   c. 280,000
   d. not given

3. 5.326
   × 1,000

   a. 53.26
   b. 532.6
   c. 53,260
   d. not given

4. $82.64 × 9

   a. $743.76
   b. $743.96
   c. $74,376.00
   d. not given

5. 7.5
   × 0.24

   a. 0.18
   b. 1.8
   c. 1,800
   d. not given

6. Find the product: 3^4.

   a. 12
   b. 34
   c. 81
   d. not given

7. Identify the property shown:
   $4 \times (6 + 3) = (4 \times 6) + (4 \times 3)$.

   a. Associative
   b. Distributive
   c. Commutative
   d. not given

8. Round 324,578 to the nearest ten thousand.

   a. 300,000
   b. 320,000
   c. 325,000
   d. not given

9. $376.65
    0.98
   +   53.19

   a. $329.82
   b. $429.82
   c. $430.62
   d. not given

10. Order from the least to the greatest: 0.09; 0.089; 0.0091.

   a. 0.089; 0.09; 0.0091
   b. 0.09; 0.089; 0.0091
   c. 0.0091; 0.089; 0.09
   d. not given

11. 9.24 − 6.3627

   a. 2.8773
   b. 2.8783
   c. 3.8873
   d. not given

12. Choose the best estimate: 18.902 + 16.287.

   a. more than 24
   b. less than 34
   c. more than 34
   d. less than 24

13. Nancy, Steve, and Sid ran a total of 5 miles. Nancy ran 2.5 miles. Steve ran 1.75 miles. How far did Sid run?

   a. 0.75 miles
   b. 0.85 miles
   c. 4.25 miles
   d. not given

14. The Weiss family drove 55 miles on the first day and 75 miles on the second day of their vacation. How many miles did they drive in all? Without finding the exact answer, write the letter of the correct answer.

   a. 20
   b. 130
   c. 230

Congratulations! You have won a trip to France to see a famous bicycle race, the *Tour de France.* In addition to your transportation, you have been given $1,000 to spend on the trip. What is the current value of dollars in French francs? Where and how will you spend your money?

5 DIVIDING WITH DECIMALS
Metric Measurement

Dividing Decimals by Whole Numbers

A. The Wilsons left Los Angeles with a full tank of gas. The drive to the Mexican border was 142.2 miles. At the border, the Wilsons filled the tank with 6 gallons. How many miles per gallon did the Wilsons' car get?

Divide 142.2 ÷ 6.

First, estimate the quotient.   150 ÷ 6 = 25

Place the decimal point. Divide the tens. **Divide the ones.** **Divide the tenths.**

$$
\begin{array}{r}
2\ . \\
6\overline{)142.2} \\
\underline{12} \\
2
\end{array}
\qquad
\begin{array}{r}
23. \\
6\overline{)142.2} \\
\underline{12}\downarrow \\
22 \\
\underline{18} \\
4
\end{array}
\qquad
\begin{array}{r}
23.7 \\
6\overline{)142.2} \\
\underline{12} \\
22 \\
\underline{18}\downarrow \\
4\,2 \\
\underline{4\,2} \\
0
\end{array}
$$

The Wilsons' car got 23.7 miles per gallon. The answer is reasonably close to the estimate.

B. Sometimes you need to write a zero in the quotient.

$$
\begin{array}{r}
1.09 \\
3\overline{)3.27} \\
\underline{3} \\
2 \\
\underline{0} \\
27 \\
\underline{27} \\
0
\end{array}
$$

> If the quotient is less than 1, place a 0 before the decimal point.

$$
\begin{array}{r}
0.015 \\
13\overline{)0.195} \\
\underline{13} \\
65 \\
\underline{65} \\
0
\end{array}
$$

Checkpoint Write the letter of the correct answer.

Divide.

1. 22)87.34   **a.** 3.95   **b.** 3.97   **c.** 39.7   **d.** 397

2. 0.945 ÷ 15   **a.** 0.0063   **b.** 0.063   **c.** 0.630   **d.** 63

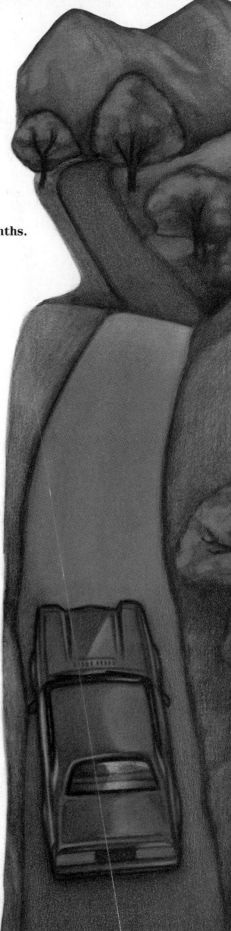

Divide.

1. $9\overline{)77.4}$ 2. $3\overline{)59.1}$ 3. $8\overline{)49.6}$ 4. $7\overline{)58.8}$

5. $8\overline{)34.16}$ 6. $5\overline{)15.05}$ 7. $4\overline{)24.32}$ 8. $6\overline{)\$17.94}$

9. $59\overline{)0.236}$ 10. $11\overline{)0.088}$ 11. $92\overline{)0.552}$ 12. $98\overline{)90.454}$

13. $48\overline{)5.9232}$ 14. $33\overline{)31.8582}$ 15. $88\overline{)52.8352}$ 16. $21\overline{)2.6019}$

17. $70.3 \div 19$ 18. $46.775 \div 5$ 19. $35.36 \div 68$ 20. $\$88.55 \div 7$

21. $31.5009 \div 9$ 22. $2.7012 \div 6$ 23. $41.4 \div 46$ 24. $\$31.05 \div 23$

Solve.

25. During three days of the trip, Mrs. Wilson drove 1,051.44 km in 12 hours. How many kilometers did she drive in 1 hour?

26. In Mexico City, the Wilsons ate a traditional Mexican meal. The bill was $48.25 for the 5 family members. How much did the meal cost per person?

27. The elevation of Mexico City is 27.5 times greater than the elevation of Los Angeles. Los Angeles is 0.084 km above sea level. How far above sea level is Mexico City?

28. Mexico City is the largest city in the Western Hemisphere. Its population of 14.5 million is 5 times greater than the population of Los Angeles. What is the population of Los Angeles?

CHALLENGE

Fluorine is one of the gaseous elements. 45 atoms of fluorine weigh 1,595.385 atomic mass units (amu). 9 molecules of fluorine weigh 638.154 amu. How many amu does 1 atom of fluorine weigh? 1 molecule? How many atoms of fluorine are there in a molecule of fluorine?

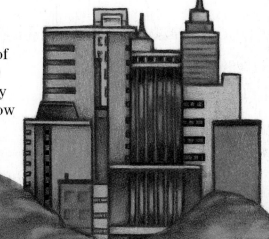

More Dividing by Whole Numbers

While visiting the Andes Mountains, Lucien saw a basket that was made by a native of Peru. The basket consisted of 16 coils, each of equal thickness. It measured exactly 24.8 cm high. How thick was each coil?

Divide 24.8 ÷ 16.

Place the decimal point. Divide the whole number.

```
    1.
16)24.8
   16
   ‾‾
    8
```

Divide the tenths.

```
    1.5
16)24.8
   16 ↓
   ‾‾
    8 8
    8 0
    ‾‾‾
      8
```

Write a 0 in the dividend. Divide the hundredths.

```
    1.55
16)24.80
   16 |
   ‾‾
    8 8 |
    8 0 ↓
    ‾‾‾
      80
      80
      ‾‾
       0
```

Each coil was 1.55 cm thick.

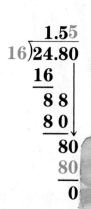

Another example: 1 ÷ 16 ⟶

```
      0.0625
16)1.0000
   96
   ‾‾
    40
    32
    ‾‾
     80
     80
     ‾‾
      0
```

Remember to write this 0.

Checkpoint Write the letter of the correct answer.

Divide.

1. 5)$160.15

a. $3.23
b. $32.03
c. $32.30
d. 3,203

2. 3.42 ÷ 12

a. 0.28
b. 0.285
c. 2.8
d. 4

3. 8 ÷ 32

a. 0.25
b. 2.5
c. 4
d. 25

Divide.

1. $4\overline{)2.16}$ 2. $4\overline{)44.02}$ 3. $8\overline{)8.2}$ 4. $4\overline{)38}$ 5. $5\overline{)\$41.65}$

6. $5\overline{)3.2}$ 7. $5\overline{)2.66}$ 8. $5\overline{)0.002}$ 9. $2\overline{)83}$ 10. $8\overline{)\$1.76}$

11. $7\overline{)21.693}$ 12. $36\overline{)645.3}$ 13. $96\overline{)290.88}$ 14. $80\overline{)404}$ 15. $31\overline{)\$56.42}$

16. $92\overline{)4.6}$ 17. $76\overline{)1.9}$ 18. $95\overline{)3.8}$ 19. $25\overline{)23}$ 20. $35\overline{)\$1.05}$

21. $4\overline{)37.98}$ 22. $5\overline{)0.2}$ 23. $5\overline{)0.737}$ 24. $35\overline{)14}$ 25. $4\overline{)\$2.16}$

26. $2\overline{)14.33}$ 27. $6\overline{)0.357}$ 28. $75\overline{)4.95}$ 29. $6\overline{)33}$ 30. $5\overline{)\$61.90}$

31. $4.4 \div 8$ 32. $0.29 \div 58$ 33. $25 \div 8$ 34. $\$3.06 \div 6$

35. $0.42 \div 84$ 36. $0.045 \div 75$ 37. $79 \div 20$ 38. $\$55.60 \div 8$

Solve.

39. A group of Peruvians used llamas to help carry their packs. The packs weighed a total of 165 kilograms. The weight was evenly distributed among 4 llamas. How much weight did each llama carry?

★40. The Andes Mountains are rich in copper. Lucien buys 5 copper medallions as souvenirs. They weigh a total of 125.35 grams. The largest one weighs 39.87 grams. The other 4 all have the same weight. What is the weight of each of the other 4 medallions?

ANOTHER LOOK

Compute.

1. $8 + 32 \div 8$ 2. $86 - 44 \div 11$ 3. $9 \times 6 - 5$ 4. $43 \times 4 + 96$

5. $(60 - 33) \div 9$ 6. $(15 + 8) \times 9$ 7. $63 \div (3 \times 7)$ 8. $(63 \div 3) \times 7$

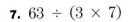
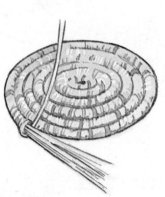

More Practice, page 445

Dividing Decimals by 10; 100; or 1,000

Charlie and Daniel are hiking in the
Himalayas on a tour sponsored by their
hiking club. They carry pedometers to
gauge their walking speed. After 10
hours, they check their pedometers and
find that they have walked 32.5 miles.
On the average, how far did Charlie and
Daniel walk each hour?

Divide 32.5 ÷ 10.

You can use a shortcut when you divide by 10; 100; or
1,000. Move the decimal point one place to the left for
each zero in the divisor. Write zeros as needed to place
the decimal point in the quotient.

Look at the pattern.
32.5 ÷ 10 = 3.25   one place to the left
32.5 ÷ 100 = 0.325   two places to the left
32.5 ÷ 1,000 = 0.0325   three places to the left

Charlie and Daniel walked an average of 3.25 miles
each hour.

Other examples:

Dividing by 10	Dividing by 100	Dividing by 1,000
456 ÷ 10 = 45.6	3,268 ÷ 100 = 32.68	78,913 ÷ 1,000 = 78.913
45.6 ÷ 10 = 4.56	32.68 ÷ 100 = 0.3268	78.913 ÷ 1,000 = 0.078913
4.56 ÷ 10 = 0.456	0.3268 ÷ 100 = 0.003268	

Checkpoint Write the letter of the correct answer.

Divide.

1. 154.3 ÷ 10

a. 1.543
b. 15.43
c. 154.3
d. 1,543

2. 100)0.09

a. 0.0009
b. 0.009
c. 0.09
d. 9.0

3. 65.7 ÷ 1,000

a. 0.00657
b. 0.0657
c. 0.657
d. 65,700

4. 1,000)$4,520.00

a. 4.52
b. $4.52
c. $452,000
d. $4,520,000

Divide.

1. $10\overline{)0.01}$ 2. $10\overline{)7.92}$ 3. $10\overline{)0.87}$ 4. $10\overline{)\$47.80}$

5. $100\overline{)942.9}$ 6. $100\overline{)36.29}$ 7. $100\overline{)890.35}$ 8. $100\overline{)\$88.00}$

9. $1{,}000\overline{)7.57}$ 10. $1{,}000\overline{)22.85}$ 11. $1{,}000\overline{)0.69}$ 12. $1{,}000\overline{)\$81{,}980.00}$

13. $10\overline{)725.6}$ 14. $1{,}000\overline{)4.7}$ 15. $100\overline{)0.7}$ 16. $10\overline{)\$188.10}$

17. $0.17 \div 10$ 18. $276.6 \div 10$ 19. $71.3 \div 1{,}000$ 20. $\$6{,}280 \div 1{,}000$

21. $448.7 \div 100$ 22. $2.51 \div 1{,}000$ 23. $84.75 \div 10$ 24. $\$2{,}697.80 \div 10$

25. $83.8 \div 100$ 26. $60.9 \div 100$ 27. $490.79 \div 10$ 28. $\$46.00 \div 100$

Solve.

29. Charlie, Daniel, and the 8 other club members share the cost of a van rental. The rent is $252.30 per week. How much does each person give?

30. Daniel calculates that he will need 1.7 pounds of food per day for a hike. How many pounds of food will he need for a 10-day hike?

31. Charlie wants to exchange his plane ticket from Nepal to China for one from Nepal to Japan. The airline charges Charlie $270 more because the flight to Japan is 1,000 miles longer. How much does the airline charge for each additional mile?

★32. Daniel visits a Tibetan lodge. Its 14-meter walls are built of stones stacked 100 stones high. One wall has a doorway 14 stones high. Daniel is 1.83 meters tall. Can he walk through the door way without bending down?

CHALLENGE

Mike works in Zyger, which is 7,856 meters from his home. Mike's drive to work is 100 blocks long. 11 traffic lights are evenly spaced along the route, including one outside Mike's home and another by his office.

1. How far is the third traffic light from the fourth?

2. How long is an average block?

3. Mike's round trip takes 16 minutes 40 seconds. How fast, in meters per second, does he drive?

Dividing by a Decimal

In Switzerland, Alice watches a craftsman make an *alpenhorn*. It is 3.445 meters long and is made of pieces of wood that are 0.53 meters long. How many wooden sections does the alpenhorn have?

Divide 3.445 ÷ 0.53.

Before you divide, multiply both the divisor and the dividend by a power of 10 to make the divisor a whole number.

Multiply the divisor and the dividend by 100.

$$0.53\overline{)3.44.5}$$

Place the decimal point in the quotient.

$$0.53\overline{)3.44.5}$$

Divide.

$$
\begin{array}{r}
6.5 \\
053\overline{)344.5} \\
318 \\
\hline
26\,5 \\
26\,5 \\
\hline
0
\end{array}
$$

The alpenhorn has 6.5 wooden sections.

Other examples:

$$
\begin{array}{r}
\$\,5\,25. \\
0.03\overline{)\$15.75.} \\
15 \\
\hline
7 \\
6 \\
\hline
15 \\
15 \\
\hline
0
\end{array}
$$

Multiply the divisor and the dividend by 100.

$$
\begin{array}{r}
0.18 \\
0.641\overline{)0.115.38} \\
64\,1 \\
\hline
51\,28 \\
51\,28 \\
\hline
0
\end{array}
$$

Multiply the divisor and the dividend by 1,000.

Checkpoint Write the letter of the correct answer.

Divide.

1. $0.5\overline{)0.65}$

a. 0.013
b. 0.13
c. 1.3
d. 13

2. $7.3\overline{)83.95}$

a. 0.115
b. 1.15
c. 11.5
d. 111.5

3. $5.44 \div 3.2$

a. 0.17
b. 1.7
c. 17
d. 170

4. $0.06608 \div 1.12$

a. 0.00059
b. 0.059
c. 0.59
d. 59

Divide.

1. $0.8\overline{)0.08}$
2. $0.6\overline{)0.54}$
3. $0.4\overline{)2.4}$
4. $0.3\overline{)0.51}$

5. $0.9\overline{)0.378}$
6. $0.4\overline{)0.124}$
7. $0.8\overline{)709.6}$
8. $0.2\overline{)0.918}$

9. $7.7\overline{)200.2}$
10. $1.8\overline{)\$14.85}$
11. $1.7\overline{)991.1}$
12. $1.2\overline{)0.912}$

13. $5.3\overline{)0.0371}$
14. $7.8\overline{)0.702}$
15. $0.6\overline{)0.018}$
16. $0.7\overline{)0.0056}$

17. $7.2\overline{)\$71.64}$
18. $0.1\overline{)0.0027}$
19. $0.5\overline{)\$129.32}$
20. $0.3\overline{)25.5}$

21. $3.65\overline{)\$25.55}$
22. $2.43\overline{)167.67}$
23. $0.123\overline{)0.83394}$
24. $85.7\overline{)89.128}$

25. $\$166.94 \div 0.4$
26. $28.572 \div 0.6$
27. $3.296 \div 0.8$
28. $1.76 \div 0.8$

29. $0.448 \div 0.7$
30. $2.9181 \div 0.137$
31. $23.82 \div 0.3$
32. $11.6 \div 0.4$

Solve.

33. Alice went skiing while in Switzerland. During her best run, she raced down the final 127.4 m of the hill at a rate of 9.8 meters per second. How many seconds did it take for Alice to ski that distance?

34. Alice saw a bicycle race while she visited Switzerland. The race was 102.2 km long and was held on a 14.6-km circuit through the streets of Basel. How many times did the racers have to complete the circuit to finish the race?

FOCUS: ESTIMATION

Dividing a number by 1 is easy. $n \div 1 = n$
Dividing by a number whose value is close to 1 is almost as easy.

Estimate $27 \div 0.98$.

$27 \div 0.98$ is about $27 \div 1$, or 27. Since $0.98 < 1$, $27 \div 0.98$ is a little more than 27.

Estimate whether the quotient will be greater than or less than the dividend.

1. $36 \div 0.943$ 2. $316 \div 0.89$ 3. $416 \div 1.03$ 4. $45 \div 1.004$ 5. $37.8 \div 0.93$

More Dividing by a Decimal

A. A DC-10 airplane travels 0.24 miles per gallon of aviation fuel. It has a cruising range of 5,076 miles. How many gallons of fuel can the tanks of a DC-10 hold?

Divide 5,076 ÷ 0.24.

Multiply the divisor and the dividend by 100.

$$0.24 \overline{)5,076.00}$$

Write zeros as needed.

Place the decimal point in the quotient.

$$0.24 \overline{)5076.00.}$$

Divide.

$$
\begin{array}{r}
21,150. \\
0.24 \overline{)5076.00.} \\
48 \\
\overline{27} \\
24 \\
\overline{3\ 6} \\
2\ 4 \\
\overline{1\ 20} \\
1\ 20 \\
\overline{0}
\end{array}
$$

The tanks of a DC-10 can hold 21,150 gallons of fuel.

B. Sometimes you need to write zeros in the dividend *and* in the quotient.

Divide 0.1845 ÷ 7.5.

Multiply the divisor and the dividend by 10.

$$7.5 \overline{)0.1845}$$

Place the decimal point in the quotient.

$$75 \overline{)01.845}$$

Divide.

$$
\begin{array}{r}
0.0246 \\
75 \overline{)01.8450} \\
1\ 50 \\
\overline{345} \\
300 \\
\overline{450} \\
450 \\
\overline{0}
\end{array}
$$

Write zeros in both the dividend and the quotient.

Divide.

1. $2.8\overline{)23.8}$ 2. $4.2\overline{)27.3}$ 3. $2.6\overline{)11.7}$ 4. $3.4\overline{)18.7}$

5. $2.2\overline{)0.11}$ 6. $3.8\overline{)1.33}$ 7. $6.4\overline{)2.88}$ 8. $8.2\overline{)\$1.23}$

9. $3.5\overline{)46.2}$ 10. $8.8\overline{)21.56}$ 11. $1.6\overline{)13.944}$ 12. $9.2\overline{)37.858}$

13. $1.5\overline{)1.302}$ 14. $3.6\overline{)0.018}$ 15. $7.5\overline{)0.045}$ 16. $1.4\overline{)0.091}$

17. $0.42\overline{)3.15}$ 18. $0.44\overline{)3.102}$ 19. $0.28\overline{)0.602}$ 20. $0.42\overline{)3.381}$

21. $0.35\overline{)2.0419}$ 22. $0.18\overline{)13.905}$ 23. $0.95\overline{)0.038}$ 24. $0.78\overline{)4.017}$

25. $15.246 \div 2.8$ 26. $1.265 \div 2.2$ 27. $0.31 \div 6.2$ 28. $\$4.95 \div 0.75$

29. $\$22.78 \div 6.8$ 30. $0.143 \div 2.6$ 31. $\$1.19 \div 0.35$ 32. $0.252 \div 0.35$

Solve. For Problem 35, use the Infobank.

33. Jet fuel capacity is measured in pounds. A 767 jet, which uses 47.35 pounds of fuel per mile, can carry 248,114 pounds of fuel. What is its cruising range?

34. In 1979, it cost $12,859 to fuel a DC-10. In 1984, it cost $18,515. How much more did it cost to fuel a DC-10 in 1984?

35. Use the information on page 433 to solve. Refer to the distance chart to plan two trips between two cities. Use 16.11 kilometers per minute as an average air speed, and find the flying time for each trip.

★36. A DC-9 cruising at 510 miles per hour flies over a section of the English Channel that is 32.3 miles wide. How many minutes does it take the plane to fly over the channel?

FOCUS: MENTAL MATH

Dividing by 0.5 is the same as multiplying by 2.

Example: $0.5\overline{)22.0}$ → $44.$ $22 \times 2 = 44$

Divide mentally.

1. $34 \div 0.5$ 2. $26 \div 0.5$ 3. $123 \div 0.5$ 4. $42.1 \div 0.5$

PROBLEM SOLVING
Choosing the Operation

You can discover hints in a problem by reading it carefully. You can use these hints to choose the best operation to use to solve the problem.

A travel agency offered free car transportation to the airport for a special group of travelers. There were 32 full carloads. Each car held 5 travelers. How many people went on the trip?

Hints:

If you know	and you want to find	you can
• that the number in each set is the same • how many there are in each set • how many sets there are	how many there are in all	multiply.
• that the number in each set is the same • how many there are in all • how many there are in each set	how many sets there are	divide.
• that the number in each set is the same • how many there are in all • how many sets there are	how many there are in each set	divide.

You could add to find the total, but it would be easier to multiply. Once you have chosen the operation, you can solve the problem.

how many in each set   how many sets   how many in all
$$5 \times 32 = 160$$

160 people went on the trip.

Decide whether you would choose addition, subtraction, multiplication, or division to solve each problem. Write the letter of the correct answer.

1. Andrew is going on a 12-day trip to Europe. He plans to split his time evenly between London and Paris. How many days will he spend in each city?

   a. addition
   b. subtraction
   c. multiplication
   d. division

2. Andrew is working up a budget for his European trip. He figures he will spend about $20 a day on food. How much should he budget for food on his 12-day trip?

   a. addition
   b. subtraction
   c. multiplication
   d. division

Solve.

3. Andrew spent weeks looking for an inexpensive flight from the United States to Europe. He found a flight for $149 one way. How much is the round-trip fare?

4. During his first day in London, Andrew visited the Houses of Parliament. He learned that the House of Commons has 635 members; the House of Lords, 1,170. How many members are there in both houses?

5. Andrew also saw the famous clock Big Ben. Big Ben started to chime in 1859. It was wound by hand until 1913 when an electric motor took over. For how many years did the English wind Big Ben by hand?

6. While in England, Andrew went to the Wimbledon Tennis Tournament. On Monday 91,983 people watched the matches. On Tuesday 92,035 fans were in attendance. Which day's crowd was larger?

7. A few days later, Andrew had lunch at an outdoor cafe in Paris. The bill was 47 francs. Andrew gave the waiter a 100-franc note. How many francs did he receive as change?

8. Andrew took 12 photos of the Eiffel Tower, 7 photos of Notre Dame cathedral, and 4 photos of the Arc de Triomphe. How many photos in all did he take?

9. Andrew sent 5 air mail postcards to his friends and family. The total postage for the cards was 15.75 francs. How much per card did Andrew pay for postage?

★10. Andrew bought 2 miniature Eiffel Towers for 25 francs each and 3 Eiffel Tower keychains for 15 francs each. How much in all did he spend on the souvenirs?

Rounding Decimal Quotients

At the London airport's duty-free shop, Andrea sees a purse that costs 6 pounds sterling, or $7.75. At what rate of exchange, in dollars per pound, does the shop calculate its prices?

Divide 7.75 ÷ 6. Round to the nearest cent.

Divide to one place beyond the place to which you are rounding.

Round the quotient to the nearest cent.

$$1.291 \longrightarrow \$1.29$$

```
     1.291
  6)7.750
     6
     1 7
     1 2
       55
       54
       10
        6
        4
```

The rate of exchange is $1.29 per pound sterling. Rounded to the nearest ten cents, $1.29 is $1.30. To the nearest dollar, $1.29 is $1.00.

Another example:

Divide 10 ÷ 3.4. Round to the nearest thousandth.

```
        2.9411
  3.4)10.0,0000
        6 8
        3 2 0
        3 0 6
          1 40
          1 36
            40
            34
            60
            34
            26
```

2.9411 rounds to 2.941

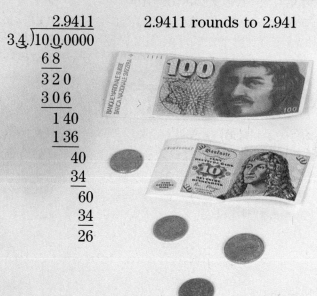

Round to the nearest tenth or the nearest ten cents.

1. 7)0.522

2. 0.18)3.448

3. 0.09)0.354

4. 11)$35.25

5. 3.7)7

6. 0.07)3

7. 2.4)0.78

8. 4)$8.50

Round to the nearest hundredth or the nearest cent.

9. 8)0.62

10. 0.08)3.83

11. 0.09)0.07

12. 1.19)$2.52

13. 0.46)0.094

14. 4)0.052

15. 0.4)0.822

16. 0.70)$5.00

Round to the nearest thousandth.

17. 0.62)0.03

18. 0.35)0.6

19. 0.29)3.91

20. 6)4.357

21. 4.3)0.08

22. 0.82)0.425

23. 0.76)0.46

24. 0.71)1

Round to the nearest whole number or the nearest dollar.

25. 0.002)0.009

26. 0.01)0.1494

27. 0.5)0.49

28. 7.14)$5.25

29. 1.2)6.78

30. 0.88)1.76

31. 8.3)16.22

32. 1.40)$50.15

Solve.

33. While Diana was in Switzerland, a Swiss franc was worth $0.42. How many Swiss francs would Diana have received in exchange for $100? Round your answer to the nearest franc.

34. Andrea traveled to Ireland, where she exchanged 46 British pounds for 55 Irish pounds. If the British pound was still worth $1.29, how many dollars was the Irish pound worth? Round your answer to the nearest cent.

MIDCHAPTER REVIEW

Find the quotient.

1. 4)33.2

2. 13)83.2

3. 6)42.3

4. 25)31.5

5. 67)161.47

6. 1.3)1.69

7. 6.8)1.768

8. 1.2)1.5

9. 0.8)26

10. 5.6)22.12

PROBLEM SOLVING
Writing an Equation

It is sometimes helpful to write an equation to solve a word problem. An equation can help you see the relationship between the numbers you know and the number you need to find.

> The Greenbergs are taking a motorbike tour through England. The first weekend, the family cycled a total of 225 miles at about 45 miles per hour. For how many hours did they ride their motorbikes that weekend?

1. List what you know and what you want to find.

The bikes were ridden 225 miles at 45 miles per hour. For how many hours were the bikes ridden?

2. Think about how to use this information to solve the problem.

You know how many miles in all the bikes were ridden. You also know the speed at which the bikes were ridden. So, you divide to find how many hours the bike was ridden.

3. Write an equation. Use n to stand for the number you want to find.

$$\frac{\text{total}}{\text{miles}} \div \frac{\text{miles}}{\text{per hour}} = \frac{\text{total}}{\text{hours}}$$
$$225 \div 45 = n$$

4. Solve. Write the answer.

$$225 \div 45 = n$$
$$5 = n$$

The motorbikes were ridden for 5 hours that weekend.

168

Read the problem. Write the letter of the correct equation.

1. The Greenbergs spent $23.32 per day for meals. How much did they spend for meals in one week?

   a. $23.32 × 7 = n
   b. $23.32 ÷ 7 = n
   c. $23.32 + 7 = n

2. The Greenbergs cycle from Windsor to Oxford, 77.2 kilometers away, in 3 hours. How many kilometers did they cycle in 1 hour?

   a. 77.2 + 3 = n
   b. 77.2 ÷ 3 = n
   c. 77.2 × 3 = n

Write an equation. Solve.

3. The price for a gallon of gasoline at a self-service station is $1.08. How much does it cost to buy 15 gallons?

4. Each of the Greenbergs' motorbikes costs $0.14 per mile to drive. How much will it cost to drive one motorbike 1,400 miles?

5. The Greenbergs budgeted $1,625 for the month of August for traveling expenses. How much can they spend per week?

6. Mrs. Greenberg bought 3 magazines for $1.75 each. How much did she pay in all?

★7. The cyclometer on Mr. Greenberg's bike read 3,948.6 kilometers when he started cycling this morning. After 5 hours, it read 4,033.6 kilometers. How fast did Mr. Greenberg cycle today?

★8. The Greenbergs and 3 other members of the tour take a car trip to Lancaster Castle. Before leaving, they buy $23.50 in gas to fill the tank. The admission to the castle costs $20 in all. On the way back, they spend $35.45 on dinner. The gas gauge reads $\frac{1}{2}$ when they get back to the hotel. How much did the trip cost per person?

Metric Units of Length

A. When Margot travels, she usually brings her backpack.

The backpack's fabric is about 1 millimeter thick.
The zippers are about 1 centimeter wide.
The side pockets are about 1 decimeter long.
The backpack is about 1 meter long.
Margot can walk 1 kilometer in about 10 minutes.

Millimeters, centimeters, decimeters, meters, and **kilometers** are all metric units of length.

10 millimeters (mm) = 1 centimeter (cm)
10 centimeters (cm) = 1 decimeter (dm)
10 decimeters (dm) = 1 meter (m)
1,000 meters (m) = 1 kilometer (km)

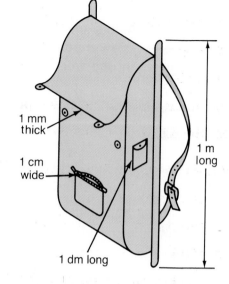

1 mm thick
1 cm wide
1 dm long
1 m long

B. Measure the pencil to the nearest centimeter, and then to the nearest millimeter. Which is the more precise measurement?

The smaller the unit, the more precise the measurement.

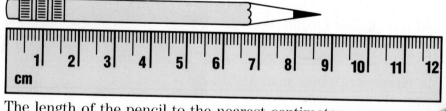

The length of the pencil to the nearest centimeter is 9 cm.

The length of the pencil to the nearest millimeter is 87 mm.

The more precise measurement is 87 mm.

You can write 87 mm as 8 cm 7 mm, or 8.7 cm.

Which unit would you use to measure? Write *cm*, *m*, or *km*.

1. a sheet of paper
2. an airplane
3. the width of your wrist
4. a pencil
5. a space voyage
6. a swimming race
7. a bicycle race
8. a baseball
9. the distance from home plate to first base
10. the distance from Chicago to Los Angeles

Write the letter of the correct measurement.

11. the height of a tulip   a. 6.1 cm   b. 6.1 dm   c. 6.1 m
12. the height of a kangaroo   a. 1.8 dm   b. 1.8 m   c. 1.8 km
13. the length of a marathon   a. 42,220 cm   b. 42,220 m   c. 42,220 km
14. the height of a basketball hoop   a. 0.003 cm   b. 0.003 m   c. 0.003 km

Measure to the nearest centimeter and to the nearest millimeter.

15.    16.

FOCUS: ESTIMATION

Copy the table. Estimate the length of each object. Then measure each object, and compare the actual measurement to your estimate.

Object	Estimation	Actual measurement
Your desk	■	■
Your textbook	■	■
The chalkboard	■	■
A window	■	■

Equal Metric Units of Length

A. Fiona measures the distance she hikes by counting her strides. She knows that her stride is 0.75 meters long. What is the length of her stride in centimeters?

You can use this chart to help you rename one metric unit with another.

km kilometer 1 km = 1,000 m	hm hectometer 1 hm = 100 m	dam dekameter 1 dam = 10 m	m meter	dm decimeter 10 dm = 1 m	cm centimeter 100 cm = 1 m	mm millimeter 1,000 mm = 1 m

To rename larger units with smaller units, multiply.

0.75 m = ■ cm
0.75 × 100 = 75
0.75 m = 75 cm

Think: To multiply by 100, move the decimal point two places to the right.
0.75 = 75

Fiona's stride measures 75 cm.

B. To rename smaller units with larger units, divide.

2,800 m = ■ km
2,800 ÷ 1,000 = 2.8
2,800 m = 2.8 km

Think: To divide by 1,000, move the decimal point three places to the left.
2.800. = 2.8

Other examples:

123 cm = ■ mm

123 × 10 = 1,230

123.0. = 1,230
123 cm = 1,230 mm

256 cm = ■ m

256 ÷ 100 = 2.56

2.56. = 2.56
256 cm = 2.56 m

0.00372 km = ■ m

0.00372 × 1,000 = 3.72

0.003.72 = 3.72
0.00372 km = 3.72 m

Checkpoint Write the letter of the correct answer.

1. 400 mm = ■ m

a. 0 m
b. 0.4 m
c. 4.0 m
d. 400,000 m

2. 2 km = ■ cm

a. 0.00002 cm
b. 2,000 cm
c. 200,000 cm
d. 2,000,000 cm

3. 3 hm = ■ km

a. 0.03 km
b. 0.3 km
c. 30 km
d. 300 km

Complete.

1. 0.9 km = 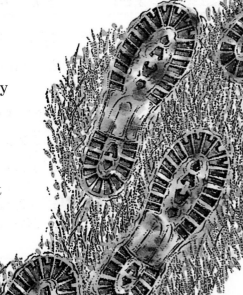 m

2. 17 m = ▧ cm

3. 6 m = ▧ cm

4. 31 km = ▧ m

5. 49 m = ▧ mm

6. 69.4 cm = ▧ mm

7. 0.819 m = ▧ cm

8. 7.07 km = ▧ cm

9. 680 mm = ▧ cm

10. 460 mm = ▧ cm

11. 52,000 mm = ▧ m

12. 855.1 cm = ▧ m

13. 8,739 hm = ▧ km

14. 790.9 dm = ▧ m

15. 61 km = ▧ m

16. 7,100 mm = ▧ cm

17. 8.44 m = ▧ mm

18. 25.5 m = ▧ cm

★19. 4.816 dm = ▧ m

★20. 9,387 m = ▧ dam

★21. 32 km = ▧ dam

Which measurement is greater?

22. 6 km or 6,500 m

23. 76.5 cm or 7.78 mm

24. 51 cm or 5.1 m

25. 6.5 dam or 6,500 dm

26. 3.3 hm or 303 m

★27. 34.3 cm or 3.43 dm

Solve.

28. Diana took a 10.25-kilometer bus ride through Helsinki, Finland. The next day, she took a 9,985-meter boat ride. Which trip was longer?

★29. To reach her hotel room, Diana had to walk up three different sets of stairs. The first was 8.3 meters high. The second was 830 centimeters high. The third was 8,300 millimeters high. How high in meters were the three sets of stairs altogether?

CHALLENGE

Mercury barometers, which meteorologists use to measure air pressure, consist of a column of mercury inside a long glass tube. The column of mercury is normally 760 millimeters high. A falling column of mercury signals a low-pressure weather system. A rising column signals a high-pressure system.

If a mercury barometer reads 77.5 centimeters, what kind of weather system is developing? What if the barometer reads 7.54 decimeters?

PROBLEM SOLVING
Practice

The Curtz family is taking a trip to South America this summer.
Write the letter of the operation you would use to solve each problem.

1. A round-trip plane ticket from Chicago to Lima, Peru, costs $1,240. There are 5 people in the Curtz family. What is the total cost of the plane tickets?

   a. addition   **c.** multiplication
   b. subtraction   **d.** division

2. In all, the 5 Curtzes carried 15 pieces of luggage onto the plane. The airline wouldn't allow them to carry any more. How many bags per person does the airline allow on its planes?

   a. addition   **c.** multiplication
   b. subtraction   **d.** division

Choose whether to estimate or to find the exact answer. Write either *estimate* or *exact*.

3. The plane to Lima has 355 seats. Of them, 135 seats have been reserved for a tour. How many seats are still available?

4. In Peru, the distance from Lima to Cuzco is 350 miles. At an average speed of 55 miles per hour, about how long would the trip take?

Write the letter of the best estimate.

5. The Curtzes spent $65.80 for souvenirs and $185.75 for meals on a 3-day trip into the Andes. The amount they spent for meals is about how many times the amount they spent on souvenirs?

   a. 2 times   **b.** 3 times   **c.** 4 times

6. The family plans to drive 485 miles in one day. If they drive at about 50 miles per hour, about how many hours will the trip take?

   a. 8 hours
   b. 10 hours
   c. 12 hours

Make a plan, and solve each problem.

7. The Curtzes traveled 1,978 miles by train and 965 miles by car on their trip in South America. If they averaged 327 miles per day, how many days did they spend traveling?

8. The amount spent for lodging was $1,785.00 for 30 days. An additional $750.00 was spent for food. If there are 5 people in the family, what was the average amount spent for food per person each day?

Harold's	
tweed overcoat	$156.00
lambs-wool sweater	$28.40
leather travel bag	$39.80
raincoat	$129.50
Irish-wool sweater	$38.75
Shipping to the United States:	
$5 for up to 10 lb	
Handling: $2.85 per order	

Son Ridges	
Irish-wool scarf	$19.15
cashmere scarf	$39.25
cashmere sweater	$68.50
suits: women's	$58.50
men's	$98.25
Shipping to the United States:	
$4 for up to 12 lb.	
Handling: Free	

Write an equation, and solve. Use the price list if you need to.

9. Last week, Harold's store sold 7 lambs-wool sweaters. How much money did it take in from the sales of lambs-wool sweaters last week?

10. Janet makes a list of what she'd like to buy at Son Ridges. It includes a cashmere sweater, and a woman's suit. How much will she spend, not including shipping or handling?

Solve.

11. If Janet buys only the cashmere scarf and a woman's suit, about how much will she spend, not including shipping and handling?

12. James bought a traveling bag at Harold's. The bag weighs 4 pounds. If he has the bag shipped to the United States, how much will it cost?

13. Sarah bought an Irish-wool sweater at Harold's. The sweater weighs 1 pound. What is the final cost if she has it shipped to the United States?

14. One packing box holds 3 scarves. Jonathan buys 10 scarves. Write the letter of the number of packing boxes he will need.

   a. 3   b. 4   c. 5

★15. Mr. Johnson bought 3 suits at Son Ridges. Mrs. Johnson bought 4 suits. Together, the suits weigh 15 pounds. What is the final cost, including shipping and handling?

★16. You have $125. How much change will you receive if you buy 2 Irish-wool sweaters that weigh 2 lb each from Harold's and an Irish-wool scarf that weighs 1.5 lb from Son Ridges and you have your purchases shipped to the United States?

Metric Units of Capacity and Mass

A. Michelle visited the Roquefort area of southern France. There she saw some of the sheep that, each year, produce the 48,000,000 liters of milk used to make Roquefort cheese.

Milliliters, liters, and **kiloliters** are metric units of capacity.

$$1,000 \text{ mL} = 1 \text{ L} \qquad 1 \text{ kL} = 1,000 \text{ L}$$

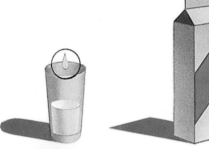

milliliter (mL)   liter (L)   kiloliter (kL)

B. Milligrams, grams, and **kilograms** are metric units of mass.

$$1,000 \text{ mg} = 1 \text{ g} \qquad 1 \text{ kg} = 1,000 \text{ g}$$

milligram (mg)   gram (g)   kilogram (kg)

C. To rename a larger unit of mass or capacity with a smaller unit, multiply.

6.4 kL = ▧ L
6.400. = 6,400
6.4 kL = 6,400 L

$$6.4 \times 1,000 = 6,400$$

To rename a smaller unit of mass or capacity with a larger unit, divide.

800 mg = ▧ g
.800 = 0.800
800 mg = 0.8 g

$$800 \div 1,000 = 0.800$$

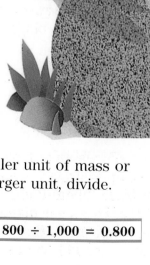

176

Write the better measurement.

1.    **2.**    **3.**    **4.**

1 L   1 kL   2 L   2 mL   50 mg   50 g   500 mg   0.5 kg

Copy and complete each table.

	g	kg
5.	500	▦
6.	25,000	▦
7.	2	▦

	mL	L
8.	2,500	▦
9.	620	▦
10.	13,000	▦

	kL	L
11.	6	▦
12.	0.3	▦
13.	48,000	▦

Complete.

14. 6.2 mL = ▦ L

15. 735 L = ▦ kL

16. 450 mg = ▦ g

17. 0.035 g = ▦ mg

18. 3.25 kg = ▦ g

19. 0.009 kL = ▦ L

20. 990 mg = ▦ g

21. 99 L = ▦ kL

22. 45 mL = ▦ L

23. 1 kL = ▦ mL

24. 1,200 mg = ▦ kg

25. 0.8 kg = ▦ mg

Solve.

26. Michelle bought 6 postcards. Each postcard weighed 500 mg. How many grams did the postcards weigh?

★27. Michelle visits a restaurant that keeps a 0.25-kL pot of onion soup on the stove. How many 0.5-L bowls of soup does the pot hold?

CALCULATOR

Michelle wants to have her photos of France developed. Joe's Camera Shop will develop 24 photos for $6.75. Photo-Rama will develop 72 photos for $19.05. Use a calculator to determine which shop offers the lower price. How much will Michelle save by having her 144 photos developed there?

PROBLEM SOLVING
Using a Map

Many maps serve special purposes. This map shows distance and direction, and it tells a story as well.

Many years ago, Robert Louis Stevenson wrote an adventure book about his travels with a donkey through southern France. Carolyn B. Patterson decided to retrace his journey 99 years later. This is a map of her trip.

Like Stevenson, Patterson traveled from Le Monastier to Le Bouchet St. Nicholas on the first day of her trip. But unlike Stevenson, Patterson could not travel the main roads with her donkey because those roads are now too busy for pedestrians. Instead, she walked along country roads and paths. How long was her walk?

On the edge of a piece of paper, mark the length of each section of her route.

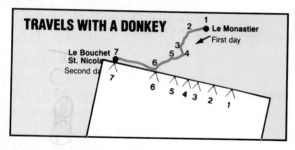

Then, compare the total route to the distance scale.

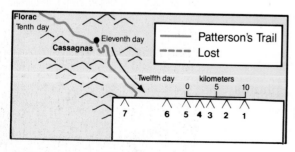

Patterson walked about 22 kilometers.

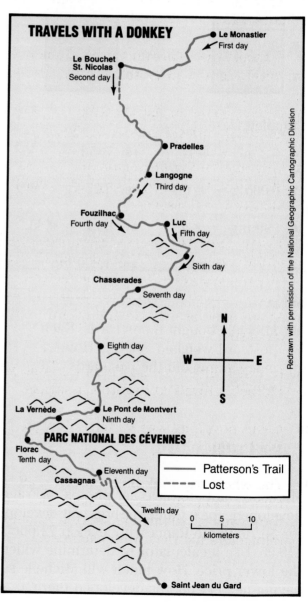

Solve.

1. On the second day of her trip, Patterson has 29 kilometers to go. She loses her way early in the day and reaches Pradelles 2 hours before sunset. If she averages 3 kilometers per hour, can she reach Langogne before sunset?

2. Describe Patterson's third day on the trail.

3. After Luc, Patterson's path becomes steeper. How does this affect her progress?

4. Estimate the total number of kilometers Patterson walked on the eleventh and twelfth days.

5. Is the statement, "La Vernède is east of Le Pont de Montvert." true or false?

6. Why did Carolyn Patterson and Robert Louis Stevenson take such a long route from Le Pont de Montvert to Cassagnas?

7. Which pair of towns is closer together—Langogne and Fouzilhac or La Vernede and Florac? Is the difference greater than 10 kilometers?

8. About how far is St. Jean du Gard from Le Monastier?

9. In which direction did Patterson walk when she left Florac and walked toward Cassagnas?

★10. About how long was Patterson's route for the whole trip?

★11. The whole trip took both Carolyn Patterson and Robert Louis Stevenson 12 days. But Stevenson's route was 32 kilometers shorter. About how many kilometers did they walk each day?

READING MATH

Symbols

Write the meaning of each symbol.

1. $+$

2. $-$

3. $>$

4. $<$

5. $\%$

6. $\times$

7. $\div$

8. $=$

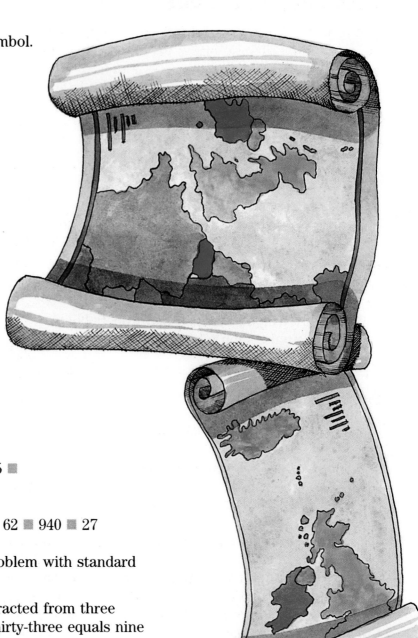

Fill in each missing symbol.

9. 425 ▦ 36 ▦ 389

10. 6,276 ▦ 8,475

11. 1 ▦ 321 ▦ 100 ▦ 132.1

12. 452 ▦ 352

13. 756 ▦ 2 ▦ 10 ▦ 7,562

14. 735 ▦ 1,000 ▦ 0.735 ▦ 73.5 ▦

15. 845 ▦ 75 ▦ 63 ▦ 375

16. 46 ▦ 25 ▦ 862 ▦ 4 ▦ 31 ▦ 62 ▦ 940 ▦ 27

Use symbols to write each problem with standard numerals.

17. Twenty-five hundred subtracted from three thousand, four hundred thirty-three equals nine hundred thirty-three.

18. One million, six hundred two thousand, four hundred twenty is greater than one million, six hundred thousand, three hundred ten.

GROUP PROJECT

Which Way Do You Go?

The problem: Your class has raised enough money to go on a summer trip to either Peru or France. How do you decide which country to visit? You have raised $625 for each student. The trip costs listed below cover travel, food, and accommodations. Consider the following factors, and decide how you would make a decision.

Peru

- Trip costs $475 per student for 2 weeks.
- Three people in your class speak Spanish.
- Your class has studied the Inca Empire.
- For 5 nights, you would stay with Peruvian families.
- Three days of the trip would be spent camping in the Andes.
- Your travel package includes a choice of 2 of the following:
  a. dinner at the beautiful *El Gato Restaurant*, a $50 value
  b. a full-day tour of Lima, Peru's capital, a $35 value
  c. a $25 gift certificate for the Turista Souvenir Shop.

France

- Trip costs $525 per student for 3 weeks.
- Your entire class has been learning French.
- Your class has studied European architecture.
- You would stay in hotels and youth hostels.
- The trip would include 4 days in West Germany.
- Your travel package includes a choice of 2 of the following:
  a. Dinner at the luxurious *Le Chat Restaurant*, a $40 value
  b. a half-day tour of Paris, a $20 value
  c. a $15 gift certificate for the Seine Souvenir Shop.

CHAPTER TEST

Find the quotient. (pages 154 and 156)

1. $7\overline{)41.3}$ **2.** $9\overline{)78.12}$ **3.** $14\overline{)0.616}$

4. $42.4 \div 8$ **5.** $\$81.13 \div 19$ **6.** $4.998 \div 42$

Find the quotient. (page 158)

7. $10\overline{)0.5}$ **8.** $10\overline{)56.39}$ **9.** $100\overline{)729.52}$ **10.** $1,000\overline{)\$84,760.00}$

Find the quotient. (pages 160 and 162)

11. $0.6\overline{)0.06}$ **12.** $0.4\overline{)0.868}$ **13.** $1.9\overline{)\$734.16}$

14. $24.92 \div 0.8$ **15.** $0.534 \div 0.6$ **16.** $3.2745 \div 0.15$

Round to the nearest tenth or to the nearest ten cents. (page 166)

17. $0.25\overline{)0.459}$ **18.** $6\overline{)4.578}$ **19.** $0.3\overline{)\$8.00}$

Round to the nearest thousandth. (page 166)

20. $0.86\overline{)0.05}$ **21.** $0.37\overline{)6.54}$ **22.** $3\overline{)8.462}$

Choose the unit you would most likely use to measure each. (page 170)

23. the length of a football   **a.** mm   **b.** cm   **c.** m

24. the length of a football field   **a.** cm   **b.** m   **c.** km

25. the weight of a bus   **a.** mg   **b.** g   **c.** kg

26. the weight of a feather   **a.** mg   **b.** g   **c.** kg

27. the capacity of a drop of water   **a.** mL   **b.** L   **c.** kL

28. the capacity of a jug of apple juice   **a.** mL   **b.** L   **c.** kL

Complete. (pages 172 and 176)

29. $65 \text{ cm} = \blacksquare \text{ mm}$ **30.** $37 \text{ km} = \blacksquare \text{ m}$ **31.** $840 \text{ cm} = \blacksquare \text{ m}$

32. $5.7 \text{ kL} = \blacksquare \text{ L}$ **33.** $1,000,000 \text{ mL} = \blacksquare \text{ kL}$ **34.** $9.2 \text{ mL} = \blacksquare \text{ L}$

35. $400 \text{ mg} = \blacksquare \text{ g}$ **36.** $2,000 \text{ g} = \blacksquare \text{ kg}$ **37.** $0.0009 \text{ kg} = \blacksquare \text{ mg}$

Write whether you need to multiply or divide to solve
the problem. Then solve. (page 164)

38. Mike mows lawns on Saturdays. For one job, he
pushed his lawn mower 0.54 km to the Johnson
house. It took him 9 min to reach there. How far,
on the average, did he travel in 1 min?

Write an equation to solve the problem. Then solve. (page 168)

39. For the past 12 weeks, Mike has been saving up for
a trip. Every Saturday, he deposits $11 into his
savings account. How much money has Mike
saved?

Solve. (page 178)

40. On the map on page 178, about how far is it
from Le Bouchet St. Nicolas to Pradelles?

BONUS

Type of person/object	Height (to the nearest meter)
A small child (A)	1 m
A pro basketball player (B)	2 m
A giant redwood tree (C)	84 m
The Empire State Building (D)	381 m
Mount McKinley (E)	6,194 m

Write the correct letter or letters from the chart for
each question below.

1. Which of the items in the chart are more than 9,000 cm tall?

2. Which are less than 100,000 mm tall?

3. Which is closest in height to 0.4 km?

4. Which is just over 6 km tall?

5. Which is taller than 100 cm but shorter than 300 cm?

6. Which are taller than 1,000 mm but shorter than 1,000,000 mm?

RETEACHING

To divide by a decimal, multiply both the divisor and the dividend by a power of 10 to make the divisor a whole number. Then divide as you would whole numbers.

You must sometimes write zeros in the dividend and in the quotient.

Divide $0.03 \div 7.5$.

Multiply the divisor and the dividend by 10.

$7.5\overline{)0.0.3}$

Place the decimal point in the quotient.

$7.5\overline{)0.0.3}$

Divide.

$$7.5\overline{)0.0.300} \quad \begin{array}{r} 0.004 \\ \hline \end{array}$$

$$\begin{array}{r} 0.004 \\ 7.5\overline{)0.0.300} \\ 0\downarrow \\ \hline 30 \\ 0\downarrow \\ \hline 300 \\ 300 \\ \hline 0 \end{array}$$

| Write zeros as needed. |

Divide.

1. $0.3\overline{)51}$ **2.** $0.75\overline{)6}$ **3.** $3.6\overline{)18}$ **4.** $3.7\overline{)296}$ **5.** $0.06\overline{)42}$

6. $2.2\overline{)0.11}$ **7.** $6.4\overline{)3.2}$ **8.** $1.5\overline{)1.302}$ **9.** $2.8\overline{)23.8}$ **10.** $2.6\overline{)0.13}$

11. $3.5\overline{)46.2}$ **12.** $4.2\overline{)27.3}$ **13.** $3.6\overline{)0.018}$ **14.** $3.8\overline{)1.33}$ **15.** $8.8\overline{)21.56}$

16. $13.944 \div 1.6$ **17.** $2.88 \div 6.4$ **18.** $1.23 \div 8.2$ **19.** $17.69 \div 5.8$

20. $12.033 \div 4.5$ **21.** $3.57 \div 7.14$ **22.** $0.324 \div 4.05$ **23.** $19.0485 \div 3.06$

24. $8.648 \div 2.3$ **25.** $12.597 \div 1.7$ **26.** $43.12 \div 8.8$ **27.** $38.097 \div 6.12$

ENRICHMENT

Reading 24-Hour Time

The 24-hour time schedule is used to number the hours of the day from 1 to 24. Unlike standard time, it does not use A.M. or P.M. to divide the day into two periods. For example, the hours from 1:00 to 4:00 P.M. standard time are written in 24-hour time as 13:00, 14:00, 15:00, 16:00. For all times earlier than 1:00 P.M., 24-hour time is the same as standard time.

To convert the hours of 13:00 to 24:00 to standard time, subtract 12 from the number.

Example: 18:00 = 18 − 12, or 6:00 P.M. standard time.

Look at the chart at the right to see how standard time is written in 24-hour time. Then study the train schedule below.

Standard time	24-hour time
1:00 P.M.	13:00
2:00 P.M.	14:00
3:00 P.M.	15:00
4:00 P.M.	16:00
5:00 P.M.	17:00
6:00 P.M.	18:00
7:00 P.M.	19:00
8:00 P.M.	20:00
9:00 P.M.	21:00
10:00 P.M.	22:00
11:00 P.M.	23:00
12:00 midnight	24:00

TRAINS FROM SPRING RIVER TO WOODRIDGE

	Train Number					
	160A	160B	160C	170A	170B	170C
Spring River	5:41	7:25	9:45	13:00	15:35	18:15
Westwood	7:51	9:35	11:55	15:10	17:45	19:25
Andersonville	8:45	10:38	12:58	16:13	18:48	20:28
Kingston	11:00	. . .	15:04	18:19	. . .	22:34
Monroe	14:07	. . .	18:11	21:26	. . .	1:41
Woodridge	15:14	16:00	19:20	22:35	24:00	2:48

Use the schedule to answer each question.

1. What is the number of the first train to arrive in Westwood in the afternoon?

2. In standard time, at what time does the 160C train arrive in Kingston?

3. Nancy left Andersonville on the 160A train. In standard time, at what time did she arrive in Monroe?

4. Tim takes the 170B train from Spring River. In standard time, at what time does he arrive in Woodridge?

TECHNOLOGY

Here's a BASIC program that uses an INPUT statement.

```
10   PRINT "TYPE A NUMBER"
20   INPUT N
30   LET T = 2 * N
40   PRINT "TWICE YOUR NUMBER IS" T
```

When you RUN this program, your screen might look like this.

```
RUN
TYPE A NUMBER
?  16
TWICE YOUR NUMBER IS 32
```

Whatever number you type is stored in the variable N.

If you RUN this program again and type in a different number, that new number will be stored in N.

Here is a problem.

Assume that sales tax is 5%. Compute the amount of tax you would pay on several items. They cost $25.00, $13.00, and $9.00.

This program will compute the sales tax on the first item.

```
10   LET IT = 25.00
20   LET TX = .05
30   LET TP = IT * TX
40   PRINT "THE TAX IS $" TP
```

Notice that the dollar sign is included inside the quotation marks. When you RUN this program, it will print this.

THE TAX IS $1.25

1. Change this program so that it asks you for the price of the item. You should change one line and add one line.

2. What does the computer print on the screen when you RUN the program and give the answer 13.00?

3. What does the computer print when you answer 9.00?

4. Write a program that asks you for a number and lets you type it in. The program should compute the product of 3 times that number, and print out the new number with a message.

Look at this program. There are two INPUT statements in this program. The INPUT statement in line 20 stores the first number you type in the variable A. The INPUT statement in line 40 stores the second number you type in B.

```
10   PRINT "TYPE A NUMBER"
20   INPUT A
30   PRINT "TYPE ANOTHER NUMBER"
40   INPUT B
50   LET C = A + B
60   PRINT A "PLUS" B "IS" C
```

When you RUN this program, your screen might look like this.

```
TYPE A NUMBER
?  5
TYPE ANOTHER NUMBER
?  10
5 PLUS 10 IS 15
```

5. Change two lines of the program so that it prints the product of the two numbers.

6. Write a program that will print this on the screen.

```
TYPE IN A NUMBER OF WEEKS
?  3
3 WEEKS ARE 21 DAYS
```

7. Write a program that asks how many boxes are on the shelf, and how much each box weighs. The program should compute and print the weight of all the boxes. Your screen might look like this.

```
HOW MANY BOXES ARE ON THE SHELF
?  10
HOW MUCH DOES EACH BOX WEIGH (IN POUNDS)
?  6.5
THE BOXES WEIGH 65 POUNDS ALTOGETHER
```

CUMULATIVE REVIEW

Write the letter of the correct answer.

1. $9\overline{)7218}$

   a. 92   **b.** 702

   c. 802   **d.** not given

2. $148\overline{)\$793.28}$

   a. $5.36   **b.** $5.41

   c. $6.02   **d.** not given

3. Solve for n: $8 \times n = 720$.

   a. 80   **b.** 85

   c. 90   **d.** not given

4. 132 is divisible by 2 and 3. It can also be divided by ■.

   a. 5   **b.** 6

   c. 9   **d.** not given

5. $6 \times 6 - 5$

   a. 6   **b.** 31

   c. 37   **d.** not given

6. $560 \div 70$

   a. 8   **b.** 80

   c. 800   **d.** not given

7. Write how many digits this quotient will contain: $5\overline{)1,600}$.

   a. 1   **b.** 2

   c. 3   **d.** not given

8. $\$35$
   $\times\ 21$

   a. $70.35   **b.** $73.05

   c. $105.00   **d.** not given

9. Write the value of the blue digit: 140,830.

   a. 4,000   **b.** 40,000

   c. 400,000   **d.** not given

10. $\$43.08$
   $+\ \ 26.13$

   a. $16.95   **b.** $23.21

   c. $69.21   **d.** not given

11. Round 0.0756 to the nearest hundredth.

   a. 0.07   **b.** 0.075

   c. 0.08   **d.** not given

12. 6.345
   $\times\ \ 2.7$

   a. 1.71315   **b.** 13.1345

   c. 17.1315   **d.** not given

13. Choose the best estimate: $12.93 - 6.4$.

   a. less than 5   **b.** less than 7

   c. more than 8   **d.** not given

14. Which decimal is equal to $\frac{21}{100}$?

   a. 2.1   **b.** 0.21

   c. 0.021   **d.** not given

15. Twenty-eight preschool children were snacking. 7 apples were to be divided equally among them. Into how many pieces should each apple be cut?

   a. 3   **b.** 4

   c. 196   **d.** not given

You have just received a check for $200 from a long-lost aunt. Your aunt wants you to invest in the stock market. You can buy only 1 share of stock in any company in which you invest. Should you buy 1 share of stock for $200 or 10 shares from 10 different companies for $20 per share? How will you decide which companies to invest in? How will you keep track of how your stock is doing?

6 NUMBER THEORY, FRACTIONS

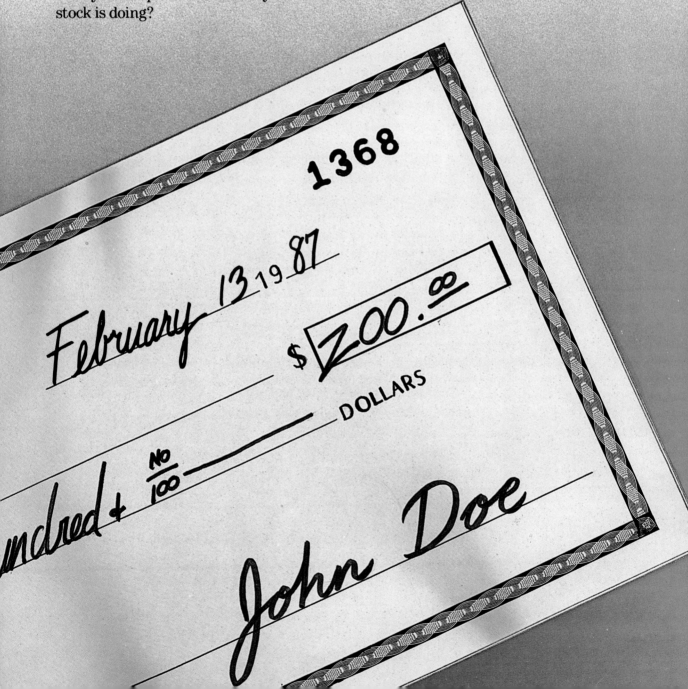

Least Common Multiple

A. The product of any number and 2 is a **multiple** of 2.

Think: $2 \times 0 = 0$ $2 \times 4 = 8$

$2 \times 1 = 2$ $2 \times 5 = 10$

$2 \times 2 = 4$ $2 \times 6 = 12$

$2 \times 3 = 6$

0, 2, 4, 6, 8, 10, and 12 are some multiples of 2.

B. To find the common multiples of 2 and 3:

List the multiples of 2: 0, 2, 4, 6, 8, 10, 12, . . .
List the multiples of 3: 0, 3, 6, 9, 12, 15, . . .

The common multiples of 2 and 3 are 0, 6, 12, . . .

C. The **least common multiple** of two or more numbers is the smallest number other than 0 that is a common multiple.

To find the least common multiple of 4 and 6:

List the multiples of 4: 0, 4, 8, 12, 16, 20, 24, . . .
List the multiples of 6: 0, 6, 12, 18, 24, 30, . . .

The common multiples of 4 and 6 are 0, 12, 24, . . .
The least common multiple of 4 and 6 is 12.

Other examples:

Find the least common multiple of 2, 4, and 5.

Multiples of 2: 0, 2, 4, 6, 8, 10, 12, 14, 16, 18, 20, . . .
Multiples of 4: 0, 4, 8, 12, 16, 20, . . .
Multiples of 5: 0, 5, 10, 15, 20, . . .

The common multiples of 2, 4, and 5 are 0, 20, . . .
The least common multiple of 2, 4, and 5 is 20.

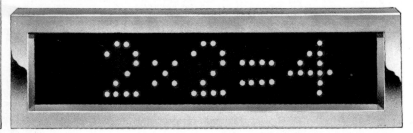

List the first six multiples of each number.

1. 2 **2.** 4 **3.** 5 **4.** 6 **5.** 8 **6.** 9

7. 10 **8.** 12 **9.** 14 **10.** 15 **11.** 20 **12.** 27

Copy and complete the table. Circle the common multiples.

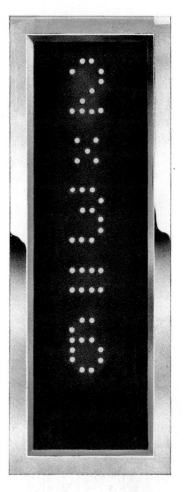

	Number	First seven multiples	Least common multiple
13.	3 5	0, 3, 6, 9, 12, 15, 18 0, 5, 10, 15, 20, 25, 30	▪
14.	6 8	▪, ▪, ▪, ▪, ▪, ▪, ▪ ▪, ▪, ▪, ▪, ▪, ▪, ▪	▪
15.	5 6	▪, ▪, ▪, ▪, ▪, ▪, ▪ ▪, ▪, ▪, ▪, ▪, ▪, ▪	▪
16.	2 3 4	▪, ▪, ▪, ▪, ▪, ▪, ▪ ▪, ▪, ▪, ▪, ▪, ▪, ▪ ▪, ▪, ▪, ▪, ▪, ▪, ▪	▪

Find the least common multiple.

17. 2 and 6 **18.** 4 and 7 **19.** 6 and 9 **20.** 8 and 12

21. 8 and 20 **22.** 10 and 20 **23.** 20 and 30 **24.** 20 and 25

25. 5, 6, and 7 **26.** 3, 6, and 8 **27.** 8, 9, and 10 **★28.** 4, 10, 12, and 15

CALCULATOR

Tell whether you would use mental math, pencil and paper, or a calculator to solve each. Tell why, then solve.

1. 527 + 999

2. 685 × 29

3. 400 × 70

4. 9,257 × 100

5. 0.5 × 240

6. 4,800 ÷ 80

Greatest Common Factor

A. Any number used in multiplication to form a product is called a **factor** of that product.

Find the factors of 8.

$8 \times 1 = 8$ $4 \times 2 = 8$ $2 \times 4 = 8$ $1 \times 8 = 8$

1, 2, 4, and 8 are the factors of 8.

B. To find the common factors of 4 and 12:

List the factors of 4: 1, 2, 4.
List the factors of 12: 1, 2, 3, 4, 6, and 12.

The common factors of 4 and 12 are 1, 2, and 4.

C. The **greatest common factor** of two or more numbers is the greatest number that is a factor of each number.

To find the greatest common factor of 30 and 40:

List the factors of 30: 1, 2, 3, 5, 6, 10, 15, and 30.
List the factors of 40: 1, 2, 4, 5, 8, 10, 20, and 40.
List the common factors: 1, 2, 5, and 10.

The greatest common factor of 30 and 40 is 10.

Other examples:

Find the greatest common factor of 24, 60, and 84.

The factors of 24 are 1, 2, 3, 4, 6, 8, 12, and 24.
The factors of 60 are 1, 2, 3, 4, 5, 6, 10, 12, 15, 20, 30, and 60.
The factors of 84 are 1, 2, 3, 4, 6, 7, 12, 14, 21, 28, 42, and 84.
The common factors are 1, 2, 3, 4, 6, and 12.

The greatest common factor of 24, 60, and 84 is 12.

List the factors of the number.

1. 1   **2.** 5   **3.** 10   **4.** 12   **5.** 18   **6.** 20

7. 24   **8.** 26   **9.** 36   **10.** 45   **11.** 66   **12.** 80

List the common factors.

13. 3 and 6   **14.** 8 and 10   **15.** 6 and 15   **16.** 12 and 30

17. 4, 8, and 10   **18.** 6, 9, and 18   **19.** 10, 20, and 45   **20.** 30, 36, and 42

Find the greatest common factor.

21. 4 and 12   **22.** 6 and 9   **23.** 16 and 24   **24.** 20 and 50

25. 3, 6, and 12   **26.** 4, 8, and 18   **27.** 12, 30, and 60   **28.** 25, 50, and 75

Solve.

29. Steve owns $48.00 worth of stock in the Bryant Company. Perry owns $56.00 worth of stock in Shopfast, Inc. Sharon owns $64.00 worth of stock in Eliot Industries. A share in each of these companies sells for the same price. What is the greatest possible price for one share?

30. Arthur goes to the bank and withdraws $100. The teller gives Arthur $100 in bills that are all of the same denomination. List all the possible combinations that the teller could have used.

ANOTHER LOOK

Divide.

1. $2.6\overline{)0.13}$ **2.** $1.4\overline{)308.56}$ **3.** $0.71\overline{)0.639}$ **4.** $5.2\overline{)23.66}$

5. $24.156 \div 0.03$ **6.** $0.018 \div 3.6$ **7.** $3.782 \div 0.61$ **8.** $19.822 \div 2.2$

Primes, Composites, and Prime Factors

A. A **prime number** has exactly two different factors: itself and 1.

List all the factors of 29: 1 and 29.
29 is a prime number.

Some other prime numbers are 2, 3, 5, 17, 19, 61, 83, and 89.

B. A **composite number** has more than two factors.

List all the factors of 24: 1, 2, 3, 4, 6, 8, 12, and 24.
24 is a composite number.

> Since it has only one factor, 1 is neither composite nor prime.

C. A composite number can be shown as the product of prime factors. This is called the **prime factorization** of the number.

You can use a factor tree to help you find the prime factorization of 54.

Begin by choosing any two factors of 54.

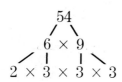
```
        54
       /  \
      6  ×  9
     / |    | \
    2 × 3 × 3 × 3
```

The prime factorization of 54 is 2 × 3 × 3 × 3.

Here are two more factor trees for 54.

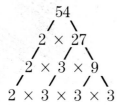
```
        54
       /  \
      2  × 27
     /   /  \
    2 × 3  × 9
   /   /   / \
  2 × 3 × 3 × 3
```

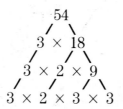
```
        54
       /  \
      3  × 18
     /   /  \
    3 × 2  × 9
   /   /   / \
  3 × 2 × 3 × 3
```

Note that the prime factors of 54 are always the same.

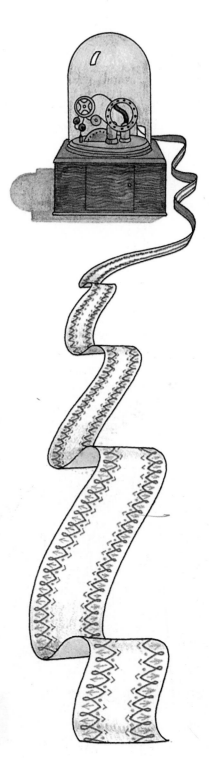

194

List the factors of each number. Then write whether
the number is *prime* or *composite*.

1. 3 **2.** 6 **3.** 8 **4.** 14 **5.** 15 **6.** 16

7. 19 **8.** 20 **9.** 23 **10.** 27 **11.** 35 **12.** 39

13. 51 **14.** 53 **15.** 66 **16.** 81 **17.** 91 **18.** 99

Copy and complete each factor tree.

19.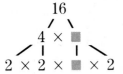

20.

21.

22.

23.

24.

Draw a factor tree to find the prime factorization of
each number.

25. 18 **26.** 24 **27.** 40 **28.** 60 **29.** 72 **30.** 100

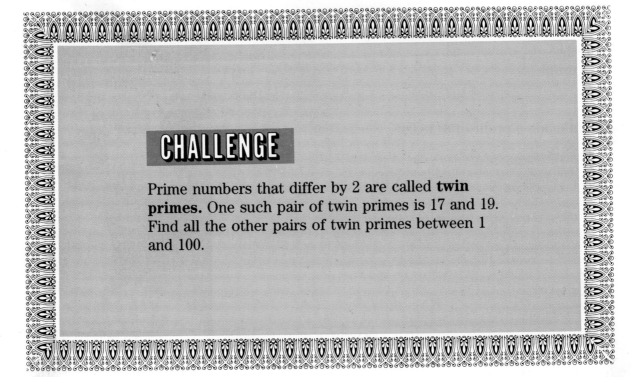

CHALLENGE

Prime numbers that differ by 2 are called **twin
primes.** One such pair of twin primes is 17 and 19.
Find all the other pairs of twin primes between 1
and 100.

PROBLEM SOLVING
Writing a Simpler Problem

A problem sometimes looks harder to solve than it really is because it contains large numbers, decimals, or fractions. Substituting simpler numbers for the actual numbers can help you decide how to solve the problem. After you have solved the problem this way, use the actual numbers to solve it.

> Benita Marconi bought $6,499.52 worth of municipal stock at $42.76 per share. When the stock rose to $46.25 per share, she sold 34 shares. How much profit did Benita make?

Make a plan, and substitute simpler numbers.

— 1.

| Find the amount of profit on each share. | $46
− 43
$ 3 | Now use the same plan with the actual numbers. | $46.25
− 42.76
$ 3.49 |

— 2.

| Find the total profit. | 34
× 3
$102 | | $3.49
× 34
$118.66 |

Benita made a profit of $118.66.

Write the letter of the correct plan.

1. Mrs. Henderson purchased 80 shares of Bronson Oil stock at $4.50 per share. She paid a stockbroker's fee of $25.75. How much did she pay in all?

   a. $80 \times \$4 = \$320$
   $\$320 + \$25 = \$345$

   b. $\$4 + \$25 = \$29$
   $\$29 \times 80 = \$2,320$

2. Stan bought 35 shares of stock in the Burton Company for $21.50 per share. Because the stock fell in value, Stan decided to sell all his shares on Friday for $16.75 per share. How much money did Stan lose?

   a. $\$35 \times \$22 = \$770$
   $\$770 - \$17 = \$753$

   b. $\$22 - \$17 = \$5$
   $\$5 \times 35 = \$175$

Solve. Simplify the problem if necessary.

3. Cara bought 45 shares of Cameo Gas stock at $6.35 per share. The following year, she sold the stock at $7.25 per share. How much profit did she make?

4. Hernando wants to invest $1,200. He can buy stock in Peterson Foods at $12.50 per share or in Riker's Machine Tools at $14.40 per share. How many shares of Peterson stock can he buy for $1,200? How many shares of Riker's stock?

5. Paolo bought 46 shares of Boko stock at $43.25 per share. Three weeks later, he sold all the shares at $39.50 per share. How much money did he lose?

6. Sally bought 90 shares of Allen stock at $7.50 per share. She could have sold it at $10.25 per share, but she waited until it fell to $9.25 per share. She then sold all 90 shares. How much more money would she have earned if she had sold it at $10.25?

7. The price of APR stock closed at $30.25 per share on Monday and at $29.25 on Tuesday. On Wednesday, it rose to $31.75 per share. Marcia bought 45 shares on Monday and sold all 45 shares on Wednesday. What was her profit?

8. Larry owns 24 shares of Winds stock. This year, he received a dividend of $6.24 per share. Last year, he received $5.25 per share. How much more did he receive in dividends this year on his 24 shares of Winds stock?

Fractions and Equivalent Fractions

A. The Cooper Company occupies 1 floor of a building. The floor is divided into 4 sections: 1 for storage space and 3 for office space. What fraction of the floor is used for office space?

Fractions can be used to name parts of a whole.

numerator ⟶ 3 ⟵ number of office sections
denominator ⟶ 4 ⟵ total number of sections

office space

$\frac{3}{4}$ of the floor is used for office space.

B. Fractions can also name parts of a group. What fraction of this set of circles is shaded?

$\frac{3}{5}$ of the circles are red.

C. Two or more fractions that name the same number are called **equivalent fractions**.

To find an equivalent fraction, multiply the numerator and the denominator by any number but zero.

$$\frac{3}{4} = \frac{6}{8}$$

$$\frac{1}{2} = \frac{1 \times 2}{2 \times 2} = \frac{2}{4} \qquad \frac{1}{2} = \frac{1 \times 3}{2 \times 3} = \frac{3}{6} \qquad \frac{1}{2} = \frac{1 \times 4}{2 \times 4} = \frac{4}{8} \qquad \frac{1}{2} = \frac{1 \times 5}{2 \times 5} = \frac{5}{10}$$

$\frac{1}{2}, \frac{2}{4}, \frac{3}{6}, \frac{4}{8}$, and $\frac{5}{10}$ are all equivalent fractions.

D. You can use what you know about equivalent fractions to find missing numerators and denominators.

$\frac{2}{3} = \frac{\blacksquare}{12}$ **Think:** $3 \times \blacksquare = 12$.

$3 \times 4 = 12$ So, $\frac{2}{3} = \frac{2 \times 4}{3 \times 4} = \frac{8}{12}$.

$\frac{2}{3} = \frac{8}{12}$.

You can also use cross-products to find missing numerators and denominators.

$\frac{2}{5} = \frac{6}{\blacksquare}$ $\qquad \frac{2}{5} \diagdown\!\!\!\diagup \frac{6}{\blacksquare}$

$2 \times \blacksquare = 5 \times 6$
$2 \times \blacksquare = 30$
$\blacksquare = 30 \div 2 = 15$

$\frac{2}{5} = \frac{6}{15}$

Write a fraction for the part that is shaded.

1.   **2.** 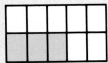 **3.** ○○○○ ○○○○ **4.** ▢▢▢ ▢▢ ▢▢▢

Write the next three equivalent fractions.

5. $\frac{1}{2}, \frac{2}{4}, \frac{3}{6}, \blacksquare, \blacksquare, \blacksquare$
6. $\frac{3}{8}, \frac{6}{16}, \frac{9}{24}, \blacksquare, \blacksquare, \blacksquare$
7. $\frac{4}{5}, \frac{8}{10}, \frac{12}{15}, \blacksquare, \blacksquare, \blacksquare$
8. $\frac{5}{12}, \frac{10}{24}, \frac{15}{36}, \blacksquare, \blacksquare, \blacksquare$

Complete.

9. $\frac{1}{5} = \frac{\blacksquare}{10}$
10. $\frac{2}{3} = \frac{\blacksquare}{9}$
11. $\frac{3}{4} = \frac{6}{\blacksquare}$
12. $\frac{2}{5} = \frac{8}{\blacksquare}$

13. $\frac{5}{9} = \frac{\blacksquare}{27}$
14. $\frac{5}{7} = \frac{\blacksquare}{35}$
15. $\frac{1}{6} = \frac{6}{\blacksquare}$
16. $\frac{6}{7} = \frac{18}{\blacksquare}$

17. $\frac{3}{5} = \frac{\blacksquare}{20}$
18. $\frac{7}{10} = \frac{\blacksquare}{100}$
19. $\frac{5}{12} = \frac{\blacksquare}{36}$
20. $\frac{2}{7} = \frac{\blacksquare}{21}$

21. $\frac{1}{4} = \frac{6}{\blacksquare}$
22. $\frac{2}{3} = \frac{30}{\blacksquare}$
23. $\frac{5}{6} = \frac{35}{\blacksquare}$
★24. $\frac{21}{24} = \frac{7}{\blacksquare}$

Compare. Write = or ≠ for each ●.

25. $\frac{4}{9} \bullet \frac{8}{18}$
26. $\frac{3}{10} \bullet \frac{12}{30}$
27. $\frac{5}{7} \bullet \frac{10}{35}$
28. $\frac{1}{3} \bullet \frac{9}{27}$

Solve.

29. The Harper Company manufactures cassette tapes that are $\frac{1}{3}$ foot long. Will they fit into 3-inch-long boxes? HINT: 1 foot = 12 inches

30. One week, the Harper Company spent $\frac{1}{6}$ of its factory time making cassettes. If the factory operated for 54 hours that week, how many hours were spent making cassettes?

FOCUS: REASONING

Solve.

1. When Paul counted the sections on one floor by fours, he had 2 left over. When he counted them by fives, he had 1 left over. How many sections were there?

2. Tanya has two United States coins in her hand. Together they total 55 cents. If one is not a nickel, what are the two coins?

More Practice, page 447

Simplifying Fractions

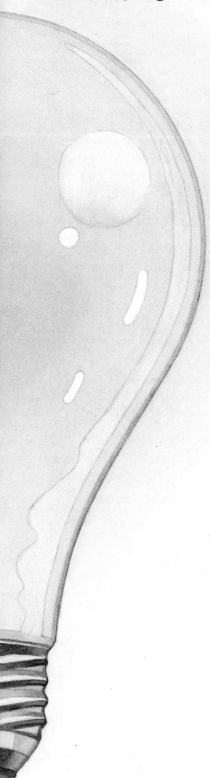

A. At closing time on Friday, Precision Light Company's stock was up $\frac{4}{8}$. Write this fraction in **simplest form.**

A fraction is in simplest form when the numerator and the denominator have no common factors other than 1.

Divide the numerator and the denominator by a common factor.

$\frac{4}{8} = \frac{4 \div 2}{8 \div 2} = \frac{2}{4}$ The fraction is not in simplest form. Divide by a common factor again.

$\frac{2}{4} = \frac{2 \div 2}{4 \div 2} = \frac{1}{2}$ 1 and 2 have no common factors other than 1.

The simplest form of $\frac{4}{8}$ is $\frac{1}{2}$.

B. An easier way to write a fraction in simplest form is to divide the numerator and the denominator by their greatest common factor.

Write $\frac{20}{25}$ in simplest form.

Find the greatest common factor of 20 and 25. The greatest common factor of 20 and 25 is 5. Divide.

$\frac{20 \div 5}{25 \div 5} = \frac{4}{5}$

The simplest form of $\frac{20}{25}$ is $\frac{4}{5}$.

Checkpoint Write the letter of the correct answer.

Write the fraction in simplest form.

1. $\frac{2}{4}$

a. $\frac{1}{4}$

b. $\frac{2}{8}$

c. $\frac{1}{3}$

d. $\frac{1}{2}$

2. $\frac{8}{12}$

a. $\frac{1}{12}$

b. $\frac{1}{6}$

c. $\frac{2}{3}$

d. $\frac{4}{6}$

3. $\frac{12}{36}$

a. $\frac{1}{6}$

b. $\frac{1}{3}$

c. $\frac{4}{12}$

d. 3

4. $\frac{18}{72}$

a. $\frac{2}{9}$

b. $\frac{2}{8}$

c. $\frac{1}{4}$

d. $\frac{1}{18}$

Complete.

1. $\frac{2}{4} = \frac{\blacksquare}{2}$ **2.** $\frac{6}{8} = \frac{\blacksquare}{4}$ **3.** $\frac{3}{9} = \frac{\blacksquare}{3}$ **4.** $\frac{10}{14} = \frac{\blacksquare}{7}$ **5.** $\frac{14}{16} = \frac{\blacksquare}{8}$

6. $\frac{8}{12} = \frac{2}{\blacksquare}$ **7.** $\frac{10}{20} = \frac{1}{\blacksquare}$ **8.** $\frac{12}{30} = \frac{2}{\blacksquare}$ **9.** $\frac{32}{40} = \frac{4}{\blacksquare}$ **10.** $\frac{33}{39} = \frac{11}{\blacksquare}$

11. $\frac{2}{8} = \frac{\blacksquare}{4}$ **12.** $\frac{6}{9} = \frac{\blacksquare}{3}$ **13.** $\frac{8}{10} = \frac{\blacksquare}{5}$ **14.** $\frac{3}{12} = \frac{\blacksquare}{4}$ **15.** $\frac{30}{36} = \frac{\blacksquare}{6}$

16. $\frac{10}{12} = \frac{5}{\blacksquare}$ **17.** $\frac{15}{20} = \frac{3}{\blacksquare}$ **18.** $\frac{20}{28} = \frac{5}{\blacksquare}$ **19.** $\frac{30}{45} = \frac{2}{\blacksquare}$ **20.** $\frac{40}{60} = \frac{2}{\blacksquare}$

Write the fraction in simplest form.

21. $\frac{4}{8}$ **22.** $\frac{2}{3}$ **23.** $\frac{6}{9}$ **24.** $\frac{8}{10}$ **25.** $\frac{9}{12}$

26. $\frac{8}{20}$ **27.** $\frac{9}{18}$ **28.** $\frac{5}{30}$ **29.** $\frac{15}{25}$ **30.** $\frac{10}{35}$

31. $\frac{20}{24}$ **32.** $\frac{45}{50}$ **33.** $\frac{24}{27}$ **34.** $\frac{35}{49}$ **35.** $\frac{60}{80}$

Solve. Write the answer in simplest form.

36. A broker tells his client that stock in Precision Light Company is expected to go up $\frac{6}{8}$. How many fourths will the stock rise?

37. Dori owns 16 shares of stock in Precision Light Company. She plans to sell 3 of her shares to Theo, and another 5 of her shares to George. What fraction of her shares does Dori plan to sell?

ANOTHER LOOK

Compute.

1. $(9 + 10) \times 4$ **2.** $(6 + 3) \times 7$ **3.** $11 \times (5 + 12)$ **4.** $8 \times (21 + 5)$

5. $3 \times (9 + 9)$ **6.** $(12 + 5) \times 4$ **7.** $30 \times (3 + 2)$ **8.** $(7 + 6) \times 8$

Writing Decimals for Fractions

A. Lin Chung works for 10 hours each day at the New York Stock Exchange. He spends 3 hours during each day, or $\frac{3}{10}$ of his time, talking on the telephone with his clients. How is $\frac{3}{10}$ written as a decimal?

$$\frac{3}{10} = \begin{array}{|c|c|} \hline \text{Ones} & \text{Tenths} \\ \hline 0 & 3 \\ \hline \end{array} = 0.3$$

B. You can also write a decimal for a fraction that has a denominator other than 10.

If the denominator is a factor of 10, write an equivalent fraction that has 10 as the denominator.

$$\frac{3}{5} = \frac{6}{10} = 0.6$$

If the denominator is not a factor of 10, divide the numerator by the denominator.

$$\frac{3}{4} = \begin{array}{r} 0.75 \\ 4\overline{)3.00} \\ \underline{2\ 8} \\ 20 \\ \underline{20} \end{array}$$

Sometimes you may want to round the quotient.

$$\frac{1}{8} = \begin{array}{r} 0.125 \\ 8\overline{)1.000} \\ \underline{8} \\ 20 \\ \underline{16} \\ 40 \\ \underline{40} \end{array}$$

The decimal 0.125 rounded to the nearest hundredth is 0.13.

Checkpoint Write the letter of the correct answer.

Choose the decimal equivalent of each fraction.

1. $\frac{9}{10}$

a. 0.9
b. 0.910
c. 9.1
d. 90

2. $\frac{1}{2}$

a. 0.1
b. 0.5
c. 5
d. 50

3. $\frac{1}{4}$

a. 0.01
b. 0.2
c. 0.25
d. 2.5

4. $\frac{3}{8}$

a. 0.03
b. 0.3
c. 0.375
d. 0.38

Write each as a decimal.

1. $\frac{2}{10}$ 2. $\frac{5}{10}$ 3. $\frac{4}{10}$ 4. $\frac{9}{10}$ 5. $\frac{6}{10}$ 6. $\frac{10}{10}$

Write each as a fraction that has a denominator of 10. Then write the correct decimal for each fraction.

7. $\frac{1}{2}$ 8. $\frac{1}{5}$ 9. $\frac{1}{1}$ 10. $\frac{2}{5}$ 11. $\frac{4}{5}$ 12. $\frac{2}{2}$

Divide to find a decimal for each. Round your answer to the nearest hundredth.

13. $\frac{1}{4}$ 14. $\frac{3}{5}$ 15. $\frac{4}{8}$ 16. $\frac{2}{8}$ 17. $\frac{1}{20}$ 18. $\frac{1}{25}$

19. $\frac{3}{16}$ 20. $\frac{2}{7}$ 21. $\frac{4}{14}$ 22. $\frac{1}{7}$ 23. $\frac{5}{13}$ 24. $\frac{7}{8}$

25. $\frac{5}{7}$ 26. $\frac{7}{13}$ 27. $\frac{1}{14}$ 28. $\frac{11}{17}$ 29. $\frac{19}{21}$ 30. $\frac{23}{34}$

Solve.

31. In one week, 97 of the 357 letters received by the Cortez Stock Brokerage Company were orders to buy. Write this as a decimal to the nearest hundredth.

32. Mrs. O'Brien is a secretary at the Cortez Company. She spends $\frac{1}{4}$ of her day typing and $\frac{5}{8}$ of her day answering the phone. Another $\frac{1}{10}$ of her day is spent filing. Write a decimal to show the amount of time Mrs. O'Brien spends on each activity.

CALCULATOR

Sometimes when you divide to write a fraction as a decimal, the quotient is a **repeating decimal.** The bar above the 3 in 0.3 tells you that the digit repeats.

$$\begin{array}{r} 0.33 \\ 3\overline{)1.00} \\ \underline{9} \\ 10 \\ \underline{9} \end{array} = 0.\overline{3}$$

Use your calculator to change these fractions into repeating decimals. Do you notice a pattern?

1. $\frac{1}{11}$ 2. $\frac{2}{11}$ 3. $\frac{3}{11}$ 4. $\frac{4}{11}$ 5. $\frac{5}{11}$

Use the pattern to write each of these fractions as a repeating decimal.

6. $\frac{6}{11}$ 7. $\frac{7}{11}$ 8. $\frac{8}{11}$ 9. $\frac{9}{11}$ 10. $\frac{10}{11}$

Mixed Numbers and Fractions

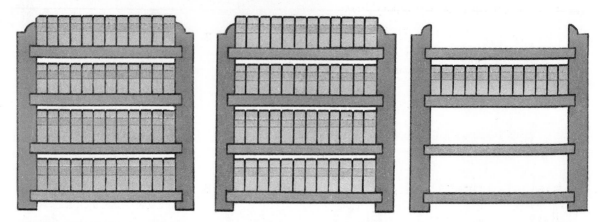

A. The Sullivan Company stores its business records in 3 bookcases. The bookcases are divided into fourths by shelves. How many fourths are full?

Nine fourths are full. Write $\frac{9}{4}$.

The records fill 2 whole bookcases and $\frac{1}{4}$ of the other bookcase. Write $2\frac{1}{4}$.

$\frac{9}{4} = 2\frac{1}{4}$

$2\frac{1}{4}$ is a **mixed number.**

B. You can divide to rename some fractions as mixed numbers.

Divide the numerator by the denominator.	Write the quotient as a whole number.	Write the remainder as a fraction.

$$\frac{9}{4} \longrightarrow 4\overline{)9} \;\begin{array}{c} 2 \\ \underline{8} \\ 1 \end{array} \qquad\qquad 2 \qquad\qquad 2\frac{1}{4} \begin{array}{l}\longleftarrow \text{remainder} \\ \longleftarrow \text{divisor}\end{array}$$

Some fractions can also be written as whole numbers. $\frac{10}{2} \to 5$

C. You can also write a mixed number as a fraction.

Multiply the whole number by the denominator.	Add the product and the numerator.	Write the sum over the denominator.

$$4\frac{1}{3} \longrightarrow 4 \times 3 = 12 \qquad 12 + 1 = 13 \qquad \frac{13}{3}$$

A whole number can also be written as a fraction. $6 \to \frac{6}{1}, \frac{12}{2}, \frac{18}{3}, \dots$

Write a fraction and either a mixed number or a whole
number to describe the shaded regions.

1.

2.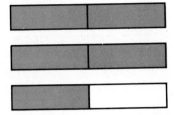

3.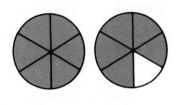

4.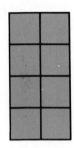

5.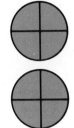

6.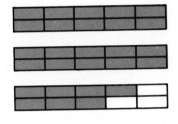

Write each as a whole number or as a mixed number.

7. $\frac{4}{2}$ **8.** $\frac{6}{3}$ **9.** $\frac{16}{4}$ **10.** $\frac{7}{3}$ **11.** $\frac{11}{2}$ **12.** $\frac{17}{5}$

13. $\frac{18}{3}$ **14.** $\frac{22}{4}$ **15.** $\frac{42}{6}$ **16.** $\frac{26}{8}$ **17.** $\frac{52}{7}$ **18.** $\frac{99}{9}$

19. $\frac{37}{13}$ **20.** $\frac{46}{22}$ **21.** $\frac{61}{55}$ **22.** $\frac{81}{27}$ **23.** $\frac{87}{29}$ **24.** $\frac{95}{35}$

Write each as a fraction.

25. 2   **26.** 5   **27.** $4\frac{1}{2}$ **28.** $6\frac{2}{3}$ **29.** 8   **30.** $3\frac{5}{6}$

31. $6\frac{1}{5}$ **32.** 7   **33.** $9\frac{5}{8}$ **34.** $8\frac{3}{10}$ **35.** $12\frac{1}{6}$ **36.** $10\frac{2}{3}$

37. $12\frac{3}{4}$ **38.** 14   **39.** $17\frac{12}{20}$ **40.** $15\frac{9}{15}$ **41.** $19\frac{1}{5}$ **42.** $20\frac{3}{5}$

MIDCHAPTER REVIEW

Find the missing numerator or denominator.

1. $\frac{3}{4} = \frac{\blacksquare}{20}$ **2.** $\frac{5}{6} = \frac{\blacksquare}{48}$ **3.** $\frac{11}{15} = \frac{33}{\blacksquare}$ **4.** $\frac{9}{10} = \frac{108}{\blacksquare}$

Write each fraction in simplest form.

5. $\frac{3}{15}$ **6.** $\frac{12}{36}$ **7.** $\frac{8}{26}$ **8.** $\frac{35}{105}$ **9.** $\frac{16}{24}$ **10.** $\frac{14}{58}$

More Practice, page 447

Comparing and Ordering Fractions and Mixed Numbers

A. Compare $\frac{1}{4}$ and $\frac{3}{4}$.

You can use a number line.

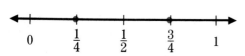

$\frac{3}{4}$ is to the right of $\frac{1}{4}$. So, $\frac{3}{4} > \frac{1}{4}$.

OR If the denominators are the same, you can compare the numerators.

$\frac{3}{4}$ $\frac{1}{4}$ $3 > 1$ So, $\frac{3}{4} > \frac{1}{4}$.

B. Compare $\frac{5}{6}$ and $\frac{3}{5}$.

The denominators are not the same. Write equivalent fractions for $\frac{5}{6}$ and $\frac{3}{5}$ that have common denominators.

Write equivalent fractions. The least common multiple of 5 and 6 is 30.

$\frac{5}{6} = \frac{25}{30}$ $\frac{3}{5} = \frac{18}{30}$

Compare the numerators.

$\frac{25}{30} > \frac{18}{30}$ So, $\frac{5}{6} > \frac{3}{5}$.

C. Compare $2\frac{2}{5}$ and $2\frac{3}{7}$.

Compare the whole numbers.

$2 = 2$

Write equivalent fractions that have a common denominator.

$\frac{2}{5} = \frac{14}{35}$ $\frac{3}{7} = \frac{15}{35}$

Compare the numerators.

$\frac{14}{35} < \frac{15}{35}$ So, $\frac{2}{5} < \frac{3}{7}$.

D. Order $3\frac{1}{6}$, $3\frac{2}{9}$, and $3\frac{1}{3}$ from the least to the greatest.

Write each mixed number as a fraction.

$3\frac{1}{6} = \frac{19}{6}$

$3\frac{2}{9} = \frac{29}{9}$

$3\frac{1}{3} = \frac{10}{3}$

Write equivalent fractions that have a common denominator.

$\frac{19}{6} = \frac{57}{18}$

$\frac{29}{9} = \frac{58}{18}$

$\frac{10}{3} = \frac{60}{18}$

Compare.

$\frac{57}{18} < \frac{58}{18} < \frac{60}{18}$

The order from the least to the greatest is: $3\frac{1}{6}$, $3\frac{2}{9}$, $3\frac{1}{3}$.

The order from the greatest to the least is: $3\frac{1}{3}$, $3\frac{2}{9}$, $3\frac{1}{6}$.

Compare. Write >, <, or = for each ⬤.

1. $\frac{5}{8}$ ⬤ $\frac{3}{8}$

2. $\frac{31}{50}$ ⬤ $\frac{32}{50}$

3. $5\frac{1}{8}$ ⬤ $5\frac{2}{8}$

4. $8\frac{3}{6}$ ⬤ $8\frac{5}{6}$

5. $3\frac{15}{16}$ ⬤ $4\frac{13}{16}$

6. $\frac{1}{4}$ ⬤ $\frac{1}{2}$

7. $\frac{1}{2}$ ⬤ $\frac{5}{8}$

8. $\frac{3}{4}$ ⬤ $\frac{7}{8}$

9. $\frac{2}{3}$ ⬤ $\frac{7}{12}$

10. $\frac{4}{20}$ ⬤ $\frac{1}{5}$

11. $3\frac{2}{9}$ ⬤ $3\frac{1}{3}$

12. $9\frac{1}{8}$ ⬤ $9\frac{1}{4}$

13. $4\frac{1}{2}$ ⬤ $4\frac{1}{8}$

14. $7\frac{5}{8}$ ⬤ $7\frac{2}{4}$

15. $5\frac{9}{16}$ ⬤ $5\frac{7}{8}$

★16. $\frac{4}{3}$ ⬤ $1\frac{2}{3}$

★17. $2\frac{1}{2}$ ⬤ $\frac{6}{2}$

★18. $3\frac{1}{4}$ ⬤ $\frac{15}{4}$

★19. $\frac{9}{4}$ ⬤ $1\frac{1}{8}$

★20. $\frac{16}{5}$ ⬤ $3\frac{2}{10}$

Order from the greatest to the least.

21. $\frac{3}{4}, \frac{7}{8}, \frac{5}{6}$

22. $5\frac{3}{8}, 5\frac{1}{2}, 4\frac{7}{8}$

23. $6\frac{1}{2}, \frac{21}{24}, 3$

24. $\frac{21}{8}, 2\frac{1}{2}, \frac{11}{4}$

Order from the least to the greatest.

25. $\frac{33}{8}, \frac{15}{4}, 5\frac{1}{4}$

26. $\frac{19}{12}, 1\frac{1}{2}, \frac{4}{3}$

27. $\frac{35}{8}, 3\frac{7}{8}, \frac{51}{12}$

28. $\frac{17}{9}, \frac{7}{3}, 2\frac{1}{6}$

Solve. For Problem 30, use the Infobank.

29. After studying stock reports, $\frac{2}{3}$ of Mr. Norbet's class think that oil company stocks will go up in price next year. Another $\frac{1}{8}$ think prices will go down. In which direction do more students think oil company stock prices will go?

30. Use the information on page 433 to answer these questions: Which is the least expensive stock? Which is the most expensive?

FOCUS: ESTIMATION

Each fraction has a specific value. The fraction $\frac{1}{2}$ is a good reference point for comparing fractions.

If the numerator of a fraction is less than half the value of the denominator, the fraction is less than $\frac{1}{2}$.

If the numerator of a fraction is more than half the value of the denominator, the fraction is greater than $\frac{1}{2}$.

$\frac{7}{10}$	$\frac{3}{5}$	$\frac{2}{7}$
$\frac{5}{8}$	$\frac{4}{9}$	$\frac{7}{16}$
$\frac{1}{3}$	$\frac{2}{5}$	$\frac{5}{12}$

Sort the fractions listed in the box. Which fractions are greater than $\frac{1}{2}$? less than $\frac{1}{2}$?

Estimating Fraction Sums

A. It is often helpful to estimate fraction sums before finding an exact sum. To estimate the sum of fractions, first round each of the addends.

Compare the numerator and denominator of a fraction to round it to 0, $\frac{1}{2}$, or 1.

Fractions near 0 $\rightarrow$ $\frac{1}{9}$ $\frac{7}{100}$ $\frac{2}{25}$ $\frac{4}{75}$ $\rightarrow$ The numerator is very small compared to the denominator.

Fractions near $\frac{1}{2}$ $\rightarrow$ $\frac{4}{7}$ $\frac{3}{8}$ $\frac{5}{12}$ $\frac{23}{40}$ $\rightarrow$ The denominator is almost twice the numerator.

Fractions near 1 $\rightarrow$ $\frac{8}{9}$ $\frac{9}{10}$ $\frac{15}{16}$ $\frac{17}{20}$ $\rightarrow$ The numerator is about the same as the denominator.

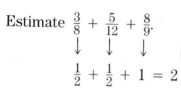

Estimate $\frac{3}{8} + \frac{5}{12} + \frac{8}{9}$.

$$\frac{1}{2} + \frac{1}{2} + 1 = 2$$

The sum is about 2.

B. You can estimate the sum of mixed numbers in a similar way.

Estimate $3\frac{1}{9} + 4\frac{4}{5} + 2\frac{7}{15}$.

Find the sum of the whole numbers.

$$3 + 4 + 2 = 9$$

Round the fractions and estimate their sum.

$$\frac{1}{9} + \frac{4}{5} + \frac{7}{15}$$

$$0 + 1 + \frac{1}{2} = 1\frac{1}{2}$$

Add.

$$9 + 1\frac{1}{2} = 10\frac{1}{2}$$

The sum is about $10\frac{1}{2}$.

Choose two fractions that are

1. close to 0.

2. close to $\frac{1}{2}$. $\frac{19}{23}$ $\frac{7}{9}$ $\frac{2}{27}$ $\frac{15}{31}$ $\frac{1}{10}$ $\frac{7}{12}$

3. close to 1.

Estimate. Write $>$ or $<$ for each ●.

4. $\frac{3}{7} + \frac{4}{9}$ ● 2

5. $\frac{8}{9} + \frac{4}{7}$ ● 2

6. $\frac{4}{5} + \frac{7}{8}$ ● 2

7. $\frac{1}{9} + \frac{8}{15}$ ● 1

8. $\frac{4}{9} + \frac{5}{8} + \frac{2}{5}$ ● 1

9. $\frac{4}{5} + \frac{5}{6} + \frac{7}{8}$ ● 2

10. $3\frac{1}{9} + 2\frac{1}{5}$ ● 6

11. $2\frac{2}{3} + 3\frac{4}{5}$ ● 6

12. $3\frac{7}{9} + 2\frac{2}{10}$ ● 7

13. $7\frac{8}{10} + 4\frac{5}{6}$ ● 12

14. $1\frac{1}{4} + 2\frac{3}{5} + 1\frac{1}{8}$ ● 5

15. $2\frac{7}{8} + 1\frac{5}{9} + 2\frac{1}{5}$ ● 7

Estimate.

16. $\frac{3}{8} + \frac{5}{9}$

17. $\frac{8}{15} + \frac{4}{5}$

18. $\frac{8}{9} + \frac{1}{8}$

19. $\frac{7}{8} + \frac{9}{11}$

20. $9\frac{6}{13} + 1\frac{4}{7}$

21. $5\frac{2}{19} + 7\frac{8}{9}$

22. $3\frac{2}{13} + 2\frac{4}{7} + \frac{7}{15}$

23. $10\frac{4}{5} + 5\frac{1}{9} + 4\frac{6}{7}$

24. $23\frac{3}{5} + 3\frac{11}{14} + 2\frac{3}{17}$

25. $3\frac{1}{4} + 2\frac{2}{3} + \frac{7}{9}$

26. $1\frac{7}{8} + 2\frac{4}{5} + 3\frac{4}{9}$

27. $30\frac{4}{5} + 6\frac{8}{10} + 2\frac{5}{6}$

Solve.

Claude takes inventory of the office supplies at Biggles' Brokerage Firm. He needs to have an approximate idea of his inventory. Estimate the total for each item.

28. Paper: Typing — $20\frac{4}{5}$ packs

Legal-sized — $9\frac{3}{7}$ packs

Memo — $42\frac{2}{9}$ packs

Total packs: _____

★29. Pens: Blue — $3\frac{1}{8}$ boxes

Red — $10\frac{3}{5}$ boxes

Green — $9\frac{7}{9}$ boxes

Brown — $12\frac{4}{5}$ boxes

Total boxes: _____

Adding Fractions

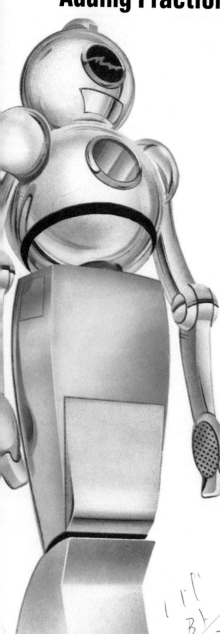

A. Megan plans to invest $\frac{1}{8}$ of her money in a robot-manufacturing company and $\frac{3}{8}$ of her money in the solar-energy industry. What fraction of her money will Megan invest in these two industries?

Find $\frac{1}{8} + \frac{3}{8}$.

To add fractions that have like denominators, add the numerators. Use the same denominator.

$$\frac{1}{8} + \frac{3}{8} = \frac{1+3}{8} = \frac{4}{8}, \text{ or } \frac{1}{2}$$

Megan will invest $\frac{1}{2}$ of her money.

B. To add fractions that have different denominators, you can write the fractions as equivalent fractions that have like denominators.

Find $\frac{7}{8} + \frac{2}{3}$.

$$\begin{aligned}
\frac{7}{8} &= \frac{7 \times 3}{8 \times 3} = \frac{21}{24} \\
+\frac{2}{3} &= \frac{2 \times 8}{3 \times 8} = \frac{16}{24} \\
\hline
& \qquad\qquad \frac{37}{24} = 1\frac{13}{24}
\end{aligned}$$

Other examples:

$$\frac{5}{12} + \frac{7}{12} = \frac{5+7}{12} = \frac{12}{12}, \text{ or } 1 \qquad \begin{array}{ccc} \frac{1}{2} & + \frac{1}{4} & + \frac{1}{8} \\ \downarrow & \downarrow & \downarrow \\ \frac{4}{8} & + \frac{2}{8} & + \frac{1}{8} = \frac{4+2+1}{8} = \frac{7}{8} \end{array}$$

Checkpoint Write the letter of the correct answer.

Add. The answer must be in simplest form.

1. $\frac{2}{5} + \frac{1}{5}$

2. $\frac{3}{8} + \frac{1}{2}$

3. $\frac{2}{3} + \frac{1}{5}$

4. $\frac{5}{14} + \frac{6}{7}$

a. $\frac{1}{5}$

a. $\frac{3}{16}$

a. $\frac{2}{15}$

a. $\frac{30}{98}$

b. $\frac{3}{10}$

b. $\frac{2}{6}$

b. $\frac{3}{15}$

b. $\frac{11}{21}$

c. $\frac{3}{5}$

c. $\frac{4}{10}$

c. $\frac{3}{8}$

c. $1\frac{3}{14}$

d. 3

d. $\frac{7}{8}$

d. $\frac{13}{15}$

d. $1\frac{4}{7}$

Add. Write the answer in simplest form.

1. $\frac{1}{3} + \frac{2}{3}$ 2. $\frac{2}{9} + \frac{5}{9}$ 3. $\frac{5}{12} + \frac{11}{12}$ 4. $\frac{7}{16} + \frac{9}{16}$ 5. $\frac{3}{20} + \frac{7}{20}$

6. $\frac{2}{5} + \frac{5}{7}$ 7. $\frac{3}{4} + \frac{3}{8}$ 8. $\frac{3}{9} + \frac{1}{3}$ 9. $\frac{1}{4} + \frac{1}{6}$ 10. $\frac{1}{8} + \frac{7}{10}$

11. $\frac{1}{7} + \frac{2}{7} + \frac{3}{7}$ 12. $\frac{1}{10} + \frac{3}{10} + \frac{9}{10}$ 13. $\frac{2}{5} + \frac{1}{10} + \frac{4}{15}$ 14. $\frac{2}{6} + \frac{1}{3} + \frac{1}{12}$

15. $\begin{array}{r} \frac{7}{9} \\ + \frac{5}{9} \\ \hline \end{array}$ 16. $\begin{array}{r} \frac{5}{8} \\ + \frac{3}{8} \\ \hline \end{array}$ 17. $\begin{array}{r} \frac{3}{35} \\ + \frac{4}{35} \\ \hline \end{array}$ 18. $\begin{array}{r} \frac{1}{4} \\ + \frac{7}{16} \\ \hline \end{array}$ 19. $\begin{array}{r} \frac{1}{3} \\ + \frac{2}{5} \\ \hline \end{array}$

20. $\begin{array}{r} \frac{5}{10} \\ + \frac{2}{10} \\ \hline \end{array}$ 21. $\begin{array}{r} \frac{2}{15} \\ + \frac{3}{5} \\ \hline \end{array}$ 22. $\begin{array}{r} \frac{1}{6} \\ + \frac{3}{8} \\ \hline \end{array}$ 23. $\begin{array}{r} \frac{1}{20} \\ \frac{11}{20} \\ + \frac{13}{20} \\ \hline \end{array}$ 24. $\begin{array}{r} \frac{1}{3} \\ \frac{1}{6} \\ + \frac{4}{9} \\ \hline \end{array}$

Solve.

25. Last week, $\frac{2}{3}$ of Mr. Mason's client list bought stock in Data Base Company, and $\frac{1}{6}$ bought stock in Techno-Skill Company. What fraction of Mr. Mason's client list bought stock in either of the two companies?

26. An investment firm advises one of its clients to buy stock in the Sunspot Energy Company. The client invests $\frac{1}{8}$ of his money one year, $\frac{1}{4}$ of his money the next year, and $\frac{1}{16}$ of his money the following year. How much of his money did the client invest during those three years?

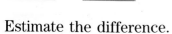

FOCUS: ESTIMATION

You can estimate the difference between fractions by rounding each fraction to 0, $\frac{1}{2}$, or 1.

$\frac{7}{8} \quad - \quad \frac{2}{5}$
$\downarrow \qquad \downarrow$
$\boxed{\text{about 1}} - \boxed{\text{about } \frac{1}{2}} \longrightarrow 1 - \frac{1}{2} = \frac{1}{2}$

Estimate the difference.

1. $\frac{8}{9} - \frac{4}{5}$ 2. $\frac{3}{5} - \frac{1}{8}$ 3. $\frac{5}{9} - \frac{3}{8}$ 4. $\frac{7}{8} - \frac{4}{9}$ 5. $\frac{9}{16} - \frac{1}{10}$ 6. $\frac{9}{10} - \frac{1}{12}$

Subtracting Fractions

A. Sally and Joe are stockbrokers. Sally spends $\frac{4}{5}$ of her day working on the stock-exchange floor. Joe spends $\frac{1}{5}$ of his day working there. How much longer does Sally stay on the floor than Joe?

Find $\frac{4}{5} - \frac{1}{5}$.

To subtract fractions that have like denominators, subtract the numerators. Use the same denominator.

$$\frac{4}{5} - \frac{1}{5} = \frac{4-1}{5} = \frac{3}{5}$$

The difference between Sally's exchange-floor time and Joe's exchange-floor time is $\frac{3}{5}$ of a day.

B. Find $\frac{2}{5} - \frac{1}{6}$.

To subtract fractions that have different denominators, write equivalent fractions that have like denominators.

$$\begin{aligned}
\frac{2}{5} &= \frac{2 \times 6}{5 \times 6} = \frac{12}{30} \\
-\frac{1}{6} &= \frac{1 \times 5}{6 \times 5} = \frac{5}{30} \\
\hline
& \qquad\qquad\quad \frac{7}{30}
\end{aligned}$$

Another example:

$$\frac{5}{6} - \frac{1}{3}$$
$$\downarrow \qquad \downarrow$$
$$\frac{5}{6} - \frac{2}{6} = \frac{3}{6} = \frac{1}{2}$$

Checkpoint Write the letter of the correct answer.

Subtract. The answer must be in simplest form.

1. $\frac{3}{4} - \frac{2}{4}$

a. $\frac{1}{4}$

b. $\frac{5}{8}$

c. $\frac{5}{4}$

d. $\frac{1}{0}$

2. $\frac{5}{8} - \frac{1}{4}$

a. $\frac{3}{8}$

b. $\frac{6}{12}$

c. $\frac{7}{8}$

d. $\frac{8}{4}$

3. $\frac{3}{5} - \frac{1}{2}$

a. $\frac{1}{10}$

b. $\frac{4}{7}$

c. $\frac{2}{3}$

d. $\frac{11}{10}$

Subtract. Write the difference in simplest form.

1. $\frac{2}{3} - \frac{1}{3}$ 2. $\frac{5}{6} - \frac{1}{6}$ 3. $\frac{7}{8} - \frac{3}{8}$ 4. $\frac{9}{10} - \frac{8}{10}$ 5. $\frac{5}{20} - \frac{1}{20}$

6. $\frac{3}{8} - \frac{1}{4}$ 7. $\frac{5}{6} - \frac{1}{2}$ 8. $\frac{1}{2} - \frac{1}{8}$ 9. $\frac{7}{12} - \frac{1}{4}$ 10. $\frac{2}{3} - \frac{2}{9}$

11. $\frac{1}{2} - \frac{1}{3}$ 12. $\frac{2}{3} - \frac{1}{4}$ 13. $\frac{4}{5} - \frac{1}{3}$ 14. $\frac{5}{6} - \frac{3}{4}$ 15. $\frac{5}{8} - \frac{1}{6}$

16. $\begin{array}{r} \frac{9}{10} \\ -\frac{3}{10} \\ \hline \end{array}$ 17. $\begin{array}{r} \frac{11}{12} \\ -\frac{5}{12} \\ \hline \end{array}$ 18. $\begin{array}{r} \frac{5}{6} \\ -\frac{1}{3} \\ \hline \end{array}$ 19. $\begin{array}{r} \frac{2}{3} \\ -\frac{7}{15} \\ \hline \end{array}$ 20. $\begin{array}{r} \frac{4}{5} \\ -\frac{1}{4} \\ \hline \end{array}$

21. $\begin{array}{r} \frac{5}{6} \\ -\frac{3}{10} \\ \hline \end{array}$ 22. $\begin{array}{r} \frac{8}{9} \\ -\frac{5}{9} \\ \hline \end{array}$ 23. $\begin{array}{r} \frac{8}{9} \\ -\frac{1}{3} \\ \hline \end{array}$ 24. $\begin{array}{r} \frac{8}{9} \\ -\frac{1}{2} \\ \hline \end{array}$ 25. $\begin{array}{r} \frac{5}{7} \\ -\frac{3}{14} \\ \hline \end{array}$

★26. $\frac{n}{3} - \frac{1}{3} = \frac{1}{3}$ ★27. $\frac{7}{8} - \frac{n}{8} = \frac{1}{4}$ ★28. $\frac{1}{6} - \frac{n}{12} = \frac{1}{12}$ ★29. $\frac{n}{12} - \frac{5}{9} = \frac{1}{36}$

Solve.

30. The Ace Investment Company wants to own $\frac{5}{6}$ of the stock of Michaelson Home Appliances. The Ace Company already owns $\frac{1}{3}$ of the Michaelson stock. How much more Michaelson stock must Ace buy?

★31. On Monday, stock in Peterson, Inc., went down $\frac{1}{4}$. On Tuesday, it went up $\frac{3}{8}$. On Wednesday, it dropped $\frac{1}{8}$. Was the value of Peterson stock on Wednesday greater than, less than, or equal to its value on Monday?

ANOTHER LOOK

Multiply.

1. 0.5×31.5

2. 8.25×4.3

3. 6.7×9.2

4. 54.3×7.9

5. 27.4×3.7

6. 9.72×5.8

More Practice, page 448

213

Adding Mixed Numbers

A. Felipe and Renee write a report together on the stock market. Felipe spends $3\frac{1}{4}$ hours on his research. Renee spends $4\frac{1}{4}$ hours on her research. How long does it take them to conduct the research for their report?

Find $3\frac{1}{4} + 4\frac{1}{4}$.

Add the fractions.	Add the whole numbers.	Write the sum in simplest form.
$\begin{array}{r} 3\frac{1}{4} \\ + 4\frac{1}{4} \\ \hline \frac{2}{4} \end{array}$	$\begin{array}{r} 3\frac{1}{4} \\ + 4\frac{1}{4} \\ \hline 7\frac{2}{4} \end{array}$	$7\frac{2}{4} = 7\frac{1}{2}$

Their research takes $7\frac{1}{2}$ hours.

B. Find $2\frac{1}{5} + 3\frac{1}{2} + 1\frac{1}{10}$.

Find fractions that have like denominators.	Add.	Write the sum in simplest form.
$\begin{array}{rcl} 2\frac{1}{5} &=& 2\frac{2}{10} \\ 3\frac{1}{2} &=& 3\frac{5}{10} \\ + 1\frac{1}{10} &=& 1\frac{1}{10} \\ \hline & & \end{array}$	$\begin{array}{rcl} 2\frac{1}{5} &=& 2\frac{2}{10} \\ 3\frac{1}{2} &=& 3\frac{5}{10} \\ + 1\frac{1}{10} &=& 1\frac{1}{10} \\ \hline & & 6\frac{8}{10} \end{array}$	$6\frac{8}{10} = 6\frac{4}{5}$

Checkpoint Write the letter of the correct answer.

Add. The answer must be in simplest form.

1. $4\frac{1}{8} + 2\frac{1}{8}$

a. $6\frac{1}{4}$

b. $6\frac{4}{16}$

c. $6\frac{1}{2}$

d. $6\frac{4}{8}$

2. $5\frac{2}{3} + 2\frac{1}{4}$

a. $7\frac{1}{4}$

b. $7\frac{3}{12}$

c. $7\frac{3}{7}$

d. $7\frac{11}{12}$

3. $2\frac{3}{8} + 4\frac{1}{8} + 3\frac{1}{4}$

a. $9\frac{5}{16}$

b. $9\frac{5}{8}$

c. $9\frac{3}{4}$

d. $10\frac{5}{8}$

Add. Write the sum in simplest form.

1. $5\frac{1}{4} + 2\frac{2}{4}$

2. $3\frac{1}{5} + 4\frac{3}{5}$

3. $8\frac{3}{10} + 3\frac{3}{10}$

4. $6\frac{1}{12} + 5\frac{9}{12}$

5. $3\frac{1}{4} + 2\frac{1}{2}$

6. $6\frac{1}{2} + 4\frac{1}{3}$

7. $9\frac{2}{5} + 2\frac{1}{4}$

8. $4\frac{1}{3} + 5\frac{5}{12}$

9. $3\frac{2}{7} + 2\frac{1}{2}$

10. $6\frac{1}{2} + 3\frac{3}{8}$

11. $9\frac{7}{12} + 3\frac{1}{6}$

12. $2\frac{3}{10} + 8\frac{1}{2}$

13. $\begin{array}{r} 8\frac{1}{3} \\ + 2\frac{1}{3} \\ \hline \end{array}$

14. $\begin{array}{r} 3\frac{1}{6} \\ + 2\frac{2}{3} \\ \hline \end{array}$

15. $\begin{array}{r} 5\frac{1}{8} \\ + 4\frac{3}{8} \\ \hline \end{array}$

16. $\begin{array}{r} 6\frac{2}{3} \\ + 5\frac{1}{4} \\ \hline \end{array}$

17. $\begin{array}{r} 8\frac{1}{5} \\ + 2\frac{3}{4} \\ \hline \end{array}$

18. $\begin{array}{r} 5\frac{1}{6} \\ + 2\frac{5}{8} \\ \hline \end{array}$

19. $\begin{array}{r} 4\frac{1}{8} \\ 3\frac{5}{8} \\ + 7\frac{1}{8} \\ \hline \end{array}$

20. $\begin{array}{r} 2\frac{1}{3} \\ 3\frac{1}{6} \\ + 2\frac{1}{6} \\ \hline \end{array}$

21. $\begin{array}{r} 1\frac{1}{4} \\ 2\frac{1}{3} \\ + 3\frac{1}{12} \\ \hline \end{array}$

22. $\begin{array}{r} 4\frac{1}{2} \\ 3\frac{1}{4} \\ + 1\frac{1}{6} \\ \hline \end{array}$

23. $\begin{array}{r} 6\frac{3}{8} \\ 8\frac{1}{6} \\ + 4\frac{1}{4} \\ \hline \end{array}$

24. $\begin{array}{r} 7\frac{3}{8} \\ 2\frac{1}{5} \\ + 2\frac{3}{10} \\ \hline \end{array}$

Solve.

25. Felipe and Renee present their report to their class in two sections. Renee reads "A History of Wall Street" in $8\frac{1}{4}$ minutes. Felipe reads "Close-Up: Life of a Firm" in $7\frac{1}{4}$ minutes. How long does it take for them to read their reports?

26. Renee takes $3\frac{1}{2}$ hours to type a rough draft of her section of the report. Felipe's rough draft takes $4\frac{1}{4}$ hours to type. Their final draft takes a total of $5\frac{1}{6}$ hours to type. How many hours do they spend typing the report?

FOCUS: MENTAL MATH

Before you add a list of fractions, see if there are pairs of fractions that total 1. Then add.

$$\frac{1}{4} + \frac{1}{2} + \frac{3}{4} + \frac{1}{2} + \frac{1}{4}$$
$$1 \qquad 1$$
$$1 + 1 \qquad + \frac{1}{4} = 2\frac{1}{4}$$

Compute mentally.

1. $\frac{1}{5} + \frac{3}{4} + \frac{4}{5}$

2. $\frac{3}{7} + \frac{4}{9} + \frac{8}{14}$

3. $1 + \frac{1}{4} + \frac{1}{2} + \frac{3}{4} + \frac{1}{4} + \frac{1}{2}$

Subtracting Mixed Numbers

A. Wall Street in New York City is the financial center of the United States. Sandy commutes to Wall Street by train. Her average commuting time is $3\frac{1}{4}$ hours per day. Last Friday, train delays extended her commute to $5\frac{3}{4}$ hours. How much more time than usual did Sandy spend commuting on Friday?

Find $5\frac{3}{4} - 3\frac{1}{4}$.

Subtract the fractions.	Subtract the whole numbers.	Write the difference in simplest form.
$\begin{array}{r} 5\frac{3}{4} \\ -\,3\frac{1}{4} \\ \hline \frac{2}{4} \end{array}$	$\begin{array}{r} 5\frac{3}{4} \\ -\,3\frac{1}{4} \\ \hline 2\frac{2}{4} \end{array}$	$2\frac{2}{4} = 2\frac{1}{2}$

Sandy spent $2\frac{1}{2}$ more hours than usual commuting on Friday.

B. Find $4\frac{2}{3} - 3\frac{1}{6}$.

Find fractions that have like denominators.	Subtract.	Write the difference in simplest form.
$\begin{array}{r} 4\frac{2}{3} = 4\frac{4}{6} \\ -\,3\frac{1}{6} = 3\frac{1}{6} \\ \hline \end{array}$	$\begin{array}{r} 4\frac{2}{3} = 4\frac{4}{6} \\ -\,3\frac{1}{6} = 3\frac{1}{6} \\ \hline 1\frac{3}{6} \end{array}$	$1\frac{3}{6} = 1\frac{1}{2}$

Another example:

$$\begin{array}{r} 6\frac{7}{8} \\ -\,4 \\ \hline 2\frac{7}{8} \end{array}$$

Checkpoint Write the letter of the correct answer.

Subtract. The answer must be in simplest form.

1. $7\frac{3}{6} - 3\frac{1}{6}$ **a.** $4\frac{1}{6}$ **b.** $4\frac{1}{3}$ **c.** $10\frac{1}{3}$ **d.** $10\frac{2}{3}$

2. $8\frac{5}{12} - 6\frac{1}{4}$ **a.** $2\frac{1}{6}$ **b.** $2\frac{2}{12}$ **c.** $2\frac{1}{2}$ **d.** $2\frac{4}{8}$

Subtract. Write the answer in simplest form.

1. $5\frac{2}{3}$
$-\ 3\frac{1}{3}$

2. $6\frac{5}{6}$
$-\ 2\frac{1}{6}$

3. $7\frac{7}{8}$
$-\ 1\frac{1}{8}$

4. $5\frac{9}{10}$
$-\ 2\frac{3}{10}$

5. $8\frac{5}{12}$
$-\ 6\frac{1}{12}$

6. $7\frac{1}{2}$
$-\ 5\frac{1}{4}$

7. $8\frac{1}{3}$
$-\ 3\frac{1}{6}$

8. $9\frac{3}{10}$
$-\ 6\frac{1}{5}$

9. $10\frac{2}{3}$
$-\ 4\frac{7}{12}$

10. $4\frac{1}{5}$
$-\ 3\frac{2}{15}$

11. $8\frac{2}{5} - 4\frac{1}{5}$

12. $9\frac{7}{8} - 6$

13. $5\frac{5}{8} - 3\frac{3}{8}$

14. $10\frac{3}{4} - 5\frac{2}{5}$

15. $9\frac{7}{8} - 4$

16. $8\frac{7}{12} - 2$

17. $7\frac{9}{10} - 3\frac{1}{2}$

18. $9\frac{7}{9} - 3\frac{2}{6}$

Solve.

19. Jimmy Lau drives to Wall Street. His old car traveled $19\frac{3}{8}$ miles per gallon. His new car travels $27\frac{1}{2}$ miles per gallon. How many more miles per gallon can Jimmy travel in his new car?

★20. It used to take Lynn about $21\frac{1}{2}$ minutes to bicycle to Wall Street. This week, a new bicycle lane was opened, and Lynn's riding time dropped to $17\frac{1}{4}$ minutes. How much time does the new bicycle lane save her?

FOCUS: ESTIMATION

Estimate $6\frac{7}{10} - 4\frac{3}{5}$.
Subtract the whole numbers. $6 - 4 = 2$
Compare the fractions. Adjust $\frac{7}{10} \bullet \frac{3}{5}$ $\frac{7}{10} > \frac{6}{10}$ Adjust up.

So, $6\frac{7}{10} - 4\frac{3}{5}$ is 2^+ or slightly more than 2.

Estimate.
Example: $10\frac{4}{9} - 4\frac{3}{4}$ $10 - 4 = 6$ $\frac{4}{9} < \frac{3}{4}$ Estimate 6^-.

1. $7\frac{7}{8} - 2\frac{4}{5}$

2. $9\frac{2}{3} - 4\frac{3}{5}$

3. $5\frac{1}{3} - 2\frac{7}{12}$

4. $10\frac{9}{10} - 8$

5. $6\frac{6}{14} - 3\frac{5}{7}$

6. $8\frac{7}{9} - 4\frac{5}{6}$

Adding and Subtracting with Renaming

A. The workers at Samson Brothers, Inc., threw shredded paper out of the office windows during the ticker-tape parade. They used $4\frac{3}{4}$ pounds of shredded computer paper and $5\frac{5}{8}$ pounds of shredded newspaper. How many pounds of paper did they use?

Find $4\frac{3}{4} + 5\frac{5}{8}$.

Find fractions that have like denominators.

$$4\frac{3}{4} = 4\frac{6}{8}$$
$$+ 5\frac{5}{8} = 5\frac{5}{8}$$

Add.

$$4\frac{3}{4} = 4\frac{6}{8}$$
$$+ 5\frac{5}{8} = 5\frac{5}{8}$$
$$9\frac{11}{8}$$

Write the sum in simplest form.

$$9\frac{11}{8} = 9 + 1\frac{3}{8} = 10\frac{3}{8}$$

The workers used a total of $10\frac{3}{8}$ pounds of paper.

B. Sometimes you need to rename when you subtract.

Find $6\frac{1}{3} - 4\frac{3}{4}$.

Find fractions that have like denominators.

$$6\frac{1}{3} = 6\frac{4}{12}$$
$$- 4\frac{3}{4} = 4\frac{9}{12}$$

Compare fractions. Rename if necessary.

$$\frac{9}{12} > \frac{4}{12}$$
$$6\frac{4}{12} = 5 + 1\frac{4}{12} = 5\frac{16}{12}$$

Subtract.

$$6\frac{4}{12} = 5\frac{16}{12}$$
$$- 4\frac{9}{12} = 4\frac{9}{12}$$
$$1\frac{7}{12}$$

Another example:

$$7 = 6\frac{3}{3}$$
$$- 4\frac{1}{3} = 4\frac{1}{3}$$
$$2\frac{2}{3}$$

218

Add. Write the answer in simplest form.

1. $3\frac{1}{4} + 2\frac{3}{4}$ **2.** $5\frac{3}{8} + 4\frac{7}{8}$ **3.** $7\frac{5}{6} + 2\frac{1}{6}$ **4.** $8\frac{5}{7} + 3\frac{6}{7}$ **5.** $6\frac{2}{5} + 3\frac{1}{5}$

6. $\begin{array}{r} 4\frac{5}{6} \\ + 6\frac{1}{8} \\ \hline \end{array}$ **7.** $\begin{array}{r} 1\frac{2}{3} \\ + 9\frac{5}{9} \\ \hline \end{array}$ **8.** $\begin{array}{r} 8\frac{3}{4} \\ + 4\frac{4}{5} \\ \hline \end{array}$ **9.** $\begin{array}{r} 7\frac{10}{12} \\ + 3\frac{5}{6} \\ \hline \end{array}$ **10.** $\begin{array}{r} 6\frac{3}{5} \\ + 2\frac{2}{3} \\ \hline \end{array}$

Subtract. Write the answer in simplest form.

11. $6\frac{5}{11} - 4\frac{3}{11}$ **12.** $5\frac{1}{5} - 3\frac{2}{5}$ **13.** $9\frac{2}{6} - 6\frac{4}{6}$ **14.** $5\frac{1}{8} - 2\frac{2}{8}$ **15.** $12\frac{2}{3} - 8\frac{5}{6}$

16. $\begin{array}{r} 8\frac{1}{4} \\ - 3\frac{1}{2} \\ \hline \end{array}$ **17.** $\begin{array}{r} 9\frac{6}{10} \\ - 5\frac{2}{5} \\ \hline \end{array}$ **18.** $\begin{array}{r} 7\frac{3}{7} \\ - 3\frac{1}{2} \\ \hline \end{array}$ **19.** $\begin{array}{r} 9 \\ - 6\frac{3}{8} \\ \hline \end{array}$ **20.** $\begin{array}{r} 14 \\ - 7\frac{7}{8} \\ \hline \end{array}$

Add or subtract. Write the answer in simplest form.

21. $4\frac{1}{2} + 3\frac{1}{2}$ **22.** $7\frac{7}{12} + 2\frac{4}{6}$ **23.** $8\frac{3}{4} - 7\frac{1}{8}$ **24.** $6 - 4\frac{3}{5}$

25. $10\frac{4}{7} - 7\frac{1}{7}$ **26.** $9 - 3\frac{1}{3}$ **27.** $10\frac{1}{2} + 2\frac{5}{6}$ **28.** $9\frac{2}{3} + 3\frac{4}{9}$

Solve.

29. During the ticker-tape parade down Broadway, the astronauts rode for $3\frac{2}{3}$ blocks, and then walked $5\frac{3}{4}$ blocks. How many blocks did they travel in all?

30. In preparation for the parade, the workers at Samson Brothers, Inc. filled each of 5 bags with 15 pounds of shredded paper. What was the total weight of all 5 bags?

CHALLENGE

Here is a list of the opening and closing prices of the most active stocks at the National Exchange. Find the net change in each. Gains should be marked with a +, and losses with a −. Copy and complete the table.

NATIONAL EXCHANGE'S MOST ACTIVE STOCKS

Stock	Open	Close	Net change
Sun Energy	$23\frac{1}{4}$	$22\frac{3}{8}$	▪
BGC Construction	$18\frac{7}{8}$	20	▪
Speedline Phones	$6\frac{3}{4}$	$7\frac{3}{8}$	▪
Global Air	$129\frac{3}{4}$	$126\frac{1}{4}$	▪

PROBLEM SOLVING
Solving Multistep Problems/Making a Plan

Many problems cannot be solved in one step. Before you can answer the question in the problem, you should make a plan. Decide how to obtain the data you need.

Betty has $75. Flint Company stock sells for $5.50 per share. Shares in Dyno Industries sell for $3.75 each. Does Betty have enough money to buy 8 shares of stock in each company?

Needed Data:

how much 8 shares of Flint Company stock will cost

how much 8 shares of Dyno Industries stock will cost

Plan
Step 1: Find the cost of the Flint Company stock.
Step 2: Find the cost of the Dyno Industries stock.
Step 3: Find the total cost of the stocks.
Step 4: Compare the total cost of the stocks to the amount of money that Betty has.

Step 1:

$$\text{cost of Flint Company stock} = \text{cost per share} \times \text{number of shares}$$
$$n = \$5.50 \times 8$$
$$n = \$44.00$$

Step 2:

$$\text{cost of Dyno Industries stock} = \text{cost per share} \times \text{number of shares}$$
$$x = \$3.75 \times 8$$
$$x = \$30.00$$

Step 3:

$$\text{total cost of the stocks} = \text{cost of Flint Company stock} + \text{cost of Dyno Industries stock}$$
$$y = \$44.00 + \$30.00$$
$$y = \$74.00$$

Step 4:

$$\begin{array}{ccc} \text{total cost of the stocks} & & \text{amount of money Betty has} \\ \$74.00 & < & \$75.00 \end{array}$$

Betty has enough money to buy the stock she wants.

Write the steps to complete each plan.

1. Johnson Company stock is currently selling at $32 per share. Stock in the Smith Company sells for $24. Mark owns 5 shares of each company's stock. How much is all his stock worth?

    Step 1:
    Step 2:
    Step 3:

2. Last week, Kim bought 12 shares of Miller, Inc., stock at $81 a share. Yesterday, she sold all 12 shares at $102 a share. How much profit did she make on the stock (before the broker's fee)?

    Step 1:
    Step 2:
    Step 3:

Make a plan for each problem. Solve.

3. Matthew, a stock broker, worked a 7-hour day today. He met with a different client every half hour. Each client asked Matthew to conduct exactly three "buy" or "sell" transactions. How many transactions did Matthew conduct for his clients today?

4. One of Matthew's clients, Mrs. Stevens, owns $728.00 worth of stock in Jupiter Oil and $883.50 worth of stock in Saturn Oil. She asks Matthew to sell exactly half of her stock in each company. What is the total value of the stock Mrs. Stevens wants to keep?

5. Nancy bought 10 shares of Happy Hat Company stock at $12.50 per share. She then sold 5 shares of her stock at $17.00 per share. Later, she sold the other 5 shares at $14.50 per share. How much profit did Nancy make on the Happy Hat stock (before the broker's fee)?

CALCULATOR

Many calculators have special command keys that allow you to use the calculator's memory.

M+   Adds the number in the display to the number in the memory.

M−   Subtracts the number in the display from the number in the memory.

RM   Recalls the number in the memory and displays it.

CM   Clears the memory.

The keys for these commands may be different in different calculators.

You can use these keys to help you add and subtract fractions. More than one method is possible.

Add $\frac{3}{8} + \frac{2}{5}$. Write the sum as a decimal.

Method 1: [CM] [3] [×] [5] [M+] [2] [×] [8] [+] [RM] [÷] [8] [÷] [5] [=]

Method 2: [CM] [3] [÷] [8] [M+] [2] [÷] [5] [+] [RM] [=]

Using either method you would get the sum 0.775.

If your calculator does not have memory keys, then you will need to write the result of each step.

Subtract $\frac{2}{5} - \frac{1}{16}$. Write the difference as a decimal.

Method 1: [CM] [2] [×] [1] [6] [M+] [1] [×] [5] [M−] [RM] [÷] [1] [6] [÷] [5] [=]

Method 2: [CM] [2] [÷] [5] [M+] [1] [÷] [1] [6] [M−] [RM]

Using either method you would get the difference 0.3375.

Add or subtract. Write your answers as decimals.

1. $\frac{5}{8} + \frac{3}{4}$ **2.** $\frac{7}{16} + \frac{3}{5}$ **3.** $\frac{3}{8} + \frac{2}{5}$

4. $\frac{3}{5} - \frac{3}{16}$ **5.** $\frac{2}{5} - \frac{3}{8}$ **6.** $\frac{25}{32} - \frac{9}{16}$

7. Can you devise a shorter method for adding fractions on a calculator? (Hint: Remember what the M+ key does.)

GROUP PROJECT

A Musical Business

The problem: You and your classmates have been given the opportunity by a group of wealthy citizens to open your own record store. You have to plan how you will run your business. Consider the following information before making your plan.

Key Facts

- 10–25-year-old people buy the most records.
- Today, many different kinds of music are popular.
- Tastes in rock-and-roll music change more quickly than they do in jazz or in classical music.
- You will have space for only a limited number of records.

Key Questions

- What kinds of music do 10–25-year-old people in your area prefer: jazz, classical, blues, country and western, rock and roll, or show tunes? Take a random survey to find out.
- Can you afford to stock less-popular kinds of music, or will you have to please the majority of buyers?
- During what hours will your store be open? Which nights will your store stay open late?
- Who will work at the store?
- How will you advertise? Will you spend much money on advertising?
- How much money do you think you can earn?
- What will you do with the profits?

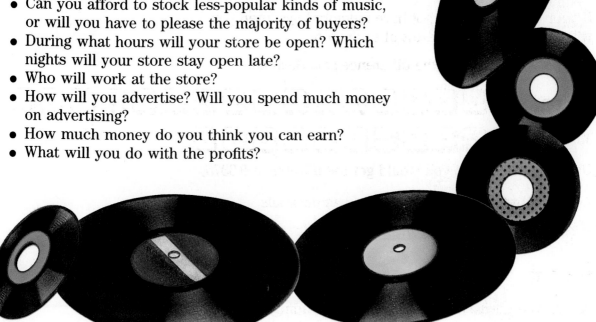

CHAPTER TEST

Find the least common multiple. (page 190)

1. 4 and 10

2. 4, 5, and 6

Find the greatest common factor. (page 192)

3. 8 and 12

4. 12, 24, and 42

List the factors of each number. Then write whether it is *prime* or *composite*. (page 194)

5. 13

6. 14

Copy and complete the factor tree. (page 194)

7.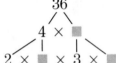

Complete. (page 198)

8. $\frac{4}{5} = \frac{\blacksquare}{20}$

9. $\frac{3}{4} = \frac{21}{\blacksquare}$

Write each fraction in simplest form. (page 200)

10. $\frac{12}{24}$

11. $\frac{60}{75}$

Write each as a decimal. Round your answer to the nearest hundredth. (page 202)

12. $\frac{3}{8}$

13. $\frac{2}{5}$

Write each as a whole number or as a mixed number. (page 204)

14. $\frac{9}{4}$

15. $\frac{40}{8}$

Write each as a fraction. (page 204)

16. $3\frac{1}{2}$

17. $4\frac{4}{5}$

Order from the least to the greatest. (page 206)

18. $\frac{2}{3}, \frac{5}{6}, \frac{7}{9}$

Order from the greatest to least. (page 206)

19. $3\frac{1}{2}, \frac{14}{3}, 4$

Estimate. (page 208)

20. $\frac{1}{3} + \frac{3}{4}$ **21.** $\frac{9}{10} + 2\frac{5}{6}$ **22.** $\frac{7}{8} + \frac{7}{12}$ **23.** $\frac{1}{8} + 2\frac{3}{4} + 5\frac{1}{7}$

Add. Write the sum in simplest form. (page 210)

24. $\frac{3}{4} + \frac{1}{4}$ **25.** $\frac{7}{8} + \frac{1}{2}$ **26.** $\frac{1}{3} + \frac{1}{6} + \frac{3}{5}$

Subtract. Write the difference in simplest form. (page 212)

27. $\frac{4}{5} - \frac{1}{5}$ **28.** $\frac{7}{10} - \frac{1}{2}$ **29.** $\frac{2}{3} - \frac{5}{8}$

Add. Write the sum in simplest form. (page 214)

30. $5\frac{1}{4} + 3\frac{2}{4}$ **31.** $2\frac{1}{8} + 4\frac{3}{8}$ **32.** $6\frac{1}{3} + 5\frac{1}{2}$

Subtract. Write the difference in simplest form. (page 216)

33. $4\frac{4}{5} - 3\frac{3}{5}$ **34.** $5\frac{5}{8} - 2\frac{1}{8}$ **35.** $9\frac{3}{4} - 7\frac{2}{3}$

Add or subtract. Write the answer in simplest form. (page 218)

36. $2\frac{1}{3} + 3\frac{2}{3}$ **37.** $6\frac{1}{4} - 2\frac{1}{2}$ **38.** $1\frac{5}{6} + 5\frac{1}{4}$

Make a plan for each problem. Solve. (page 220)

39. Ken has $150. Anderson Industries stock sells for $8.50 per share. Shares in the Robertson Company sell for $6.25. Does Ken have enough money to buy 10 shares of stock in each company?

40. Last week, Maura bought 20 shares of Allen Company stock at $7\frac{1}{2}$ points per share. Yesterday, she sold all 20 shares at $9\frac{1}{4}$ points per share. How much profit did she make on the stock (before the broker's fees)?

BONUS

Solve.

1. $6\frac{2}{3} + 5\frac{1}{2} + 5\frac{3}{4}$ **2.** $8\frac{1}{2} + \frac{5}{6} - 6\frac{3}{4}$

3. $\frac{3}{8} + \frac{5}{9} + \frac{11}{12} + \frac{1}{6}$ **4.** $\frac{5}{3} - \frac{5}{6} + \frac{5}{2} - \frac{5}{4}$

RETEACHING

A. Before you can add mixed-numbers, you must make sure their fractions have like denominators.

Find $3\frac{2}{3} + 4\frac{5}{6}$.

Find fractions that have like denominators.

$$3\frac{2}{3} = \quad 3\frac{4}{6}$$
$$+ 4\frac{5}{6} = +4\frac{5}{6}$$

Add.

$$3\frac{2}{3} = \quad 3\frac{4}{6}$$
$$+ 4\frac{5}{6} = +4\frac{5}{6}$$
$$\overline{\qquad 7\frac{9}{6}}$$

Write the sum in simplest form.

$$7\frac{9}{6} = 7 + 1\frac{3}{6}$$
$$= 8\frac{3}{6}$$
$$= 8\frac{1}{2}$$

B. Sometimes you need to rename when you subtract.

Find $7\frac{1}{4} - 5\frac{1}{3}$.

Find fractions that have like denominators.

$$7\frac{1}{4} = \quad 7\frac{3}{12}$$
$$- 5\frac{1}{3} = -5\frac{4}{12}$$

Compare fractions. Rename if necessary.

$$\boxed{\frac{3}{12} < \frac{4}{12}}$$

$$7\frac{3}{12} = 6 + 1\frac{3}{12}$$
$$= 6\frac{15}{12}$$

Subtract.

$$7\frac{3}{12} = \quad 6\frac{15}{12}$$
$$- 5\frac{4}{12} = -5\frac{4}{12}$$
$$\overline{\qquad 1\frac{11}{12}}$$

Compute. Write the answer in simplest form.

1. $\quad 1\frac{3}{4}$
$\quad + 2\frac{1}{2}$

2. $\quad 5\frac{1}{2}$
$\quad + 3\frac{5}{8}$

3. $\quad 6\frac{1}{6}$
$\quad + 3\frac{11}{12}$

4. $\quad 10\frac{3}{5}$
$\quad + 2\frac{13}{15}$

5. $\quad 7\frac{2}{3}$
$\quad + 6\frac{3}{4}$

6. $\quad 4\frac{1}{2}$
$\quad - 3\frac{3}{4}$

7. $\quad 5\frac{1}{3}$
$\quad - 2\frac{5}{6}$

8. $\quad 8\frac{3}{10}$
$\quad - 6\frac{1}{2}$

9. $\quad 7\frac{2}{3}$
$\quad - 4\frac{4}{5}$

10. $\quad 9\frac{1}{6}$
$\quad - 8\frac{1}{4}$

11. $6\frac{1}{6} - 2\frac{5}{6}$

12. $3\frac{7}{10} + 4\frac{9}{10}$

13. $8\frac{1}{12} - 1\frac{1}{3}$

14. $5\frac{3}{4} + 3\frac{4}{5}$

15. $7\frac{5}{6} - 6\frac{6}{7}$

ENRICHMENT

Scientific Notation

To make working with large numbers easier, scientists use scientific notation. To show a number in scientific notation, write the number as the product of a number between 1 and 10 multiplied by a power of 10.

<u>Standard Notation</u>
$60{,}000 = 6 \times 10{,}000 \ (10{,}000 = 10^4)$

<u>Scientific Notation</u>
6×10^4

To write a number in scientific notation, move the decimal point left until there is only one digit to its left. The number of places the decimal point is moved equals the number of the exponent showing the power of 10.

To change a number from scientific notation to standard form, move the decimal point right the number of places indicated by the exponent.

$5{,}700{,}000.0 = 5.7 \times 10^6$

$4.33 \times 10^5 = 4.33000. = 433{,}000$

> Decimal point moved 6 places.
> The exponent is 6.

> The exponent is 5.
> Move the decimal point 5 places.

Copy and complete the table.

Fact	Standard form	Scientific notation
1. the number of hairs on an average person's head	▧	10×10^4
2. the number of miles light travels in a year	▧	5.88×10^{12}
3. the number of minutes the average American will live	39,000,000	▧
4. the number of years since the last dinosaur lived	▧	6.3×10^7
5. the temperature of the sun (in degrees Fahrenheit)	▧	10×10^3
6. the population of the United States	227,000,000	▧
7. the weight of Earth (in tons)	▧	6.588×10^{21}

CUMULATIVE REVIEW

Write the letter of the correct answer.

1. 0.32401 ÷ 100

   a. 0.0032401   **b.** 0.032401
   c. 32.401   **d.** not given

2. 6.72 ÷ 4

   a. 1.13   **b.** 1.68
   c. 26.88   **d.** not given

3. Measure to the nearest millimeter.

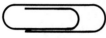

   a. 1.28   **b.** 2.8
   c. 28   **d.** not given

4. 305 cm = ■ m

   a. 0.03   **b.** 0.305
   c. 30.5   **d.** not given

5. Round the quotient to the nearest tenth.

$$3.2876 \div 4.1$$

   a. 0.8   **b.** 0.82
   c. 0.9   **d.** not given

6. Which would you use to measure the distance from Michigan to Florida?

   a. kilograms   **b.** meters
   c. kilometers   **d.** not given

7. 10 + 6 ÷ 2

   a. 8   **b.** 12
   c. 13   **d.** not given

8. Write as a decimal. $14\frac{56}{100}$

   a. 1.456   **b.** 14.56
   c. 145.6   **d.** not given

9. Thirteen thousand, six = ■.

   a. 136   **b.** 1,306
   c. 13,006   **d.** not given

10. Choose the best estimate.
$$\begin{array}{r} 1.35 \\ \times\ 3.5 \\ \hline \end{array}$$

   a. less than 3   **b.** more than 3.5
   c. more than 4   **d.** not given

11.
$$\begin{array}{r} 25.681 \\ +\ 7.032 \\ \hline \end{array}$$

   a. 32.613   **b.** 32.653
   c. 32.713   **d.** not given

12. Alan took a quiz and scored 62.5 points. Each question was worth 12.5 points. How many questions did he answer correctly? Which operation would you use to solve?

   a. addition   **b.** subtraction
   c. division   **d.** not given

13. The principal gave Mrs. Chu 120 graduation tickets to distribute to her sixth-grade students. There are 30 children in her class. Which equation would you write to find how many tickets each student would receive?

   a. $120 \times 3 = n$ **b.** $120 - 3 = n$
   c. $30 + 120 = n$ **d.** not given

Have you ever created an original outfit? Have you ever designed your own costume? Choose to design either an article of clothing or an entire costume. Decide which materials you will use. Take measurements, and decide how much of each item to buy.

7 MULTIPLYING AND DIVIDING FRACTIONS
Customary Measurement

Multiplying Fractions by Fractions

A. Mr. Asher made collars for shirts in the Cut-Rate Shirt Factory. First he cut $\frac{2}{3}$ yard of material. Then he used $\frac{3}{4}$ of the material he had cut for collars. How much material did Mr. Asher use for collars?

Find $\frac{3}{4}$ of $\frac{2}{3}$.

You can draw pictures to find the answer.
Mr. Asher used $\frac{6}{12}$ or $\frac{1}{2}$ yard of material for collars.

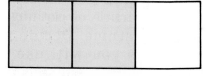
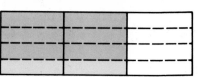

B. You can also multiply to find the answer.
Multiply $\frac{3}{4} \times \frac{2}{3}$.

Multiply the numerators.	Multiply the denominators.	Write the product in simplest form.
$\frac{3}{4} \times \frac{2}{3} = \frac{6}{}$	$\frac{3}{4} \times \frac{2}{3} = \frac{6}{12}$	$\frac{6}{12} = \frac{1}{2}$

C. If the numerator of one fraction and the denominator of the other have a common factor, you can use a shortcut to multiply the fractions.

Multiply $\frac{5}{6} \times \frac{3}{4}$.

3 is a common factor of 3 and 6. Divide by 3; then multiply.

$$\frac{5}{\overset{2}{\cancel{6}}} \times \frac{\overset{1}{\cancel{3}}}{4} = \frac{5}{2} \times \frac{1}{4} = \frac{5}{8}$$

Other examples:

$$\frac{\overset{1}{\cancel{2}}}{\underset{1}{\cancel{3}}} \times \frac{\overset{3}{\cancel{9}}}{\underset{5}{\cancel{10}}} = \frac{3}{5} \qquad \frac{\overset{1}{\cancel{2}}}{3} \times \frac{\overset{1}{\cancel{5}}}{\underset{3}{\cancel{6}}} \times \frac{7}{\underset{2}{\cancel{10}}} = \frac{7}{18}$$

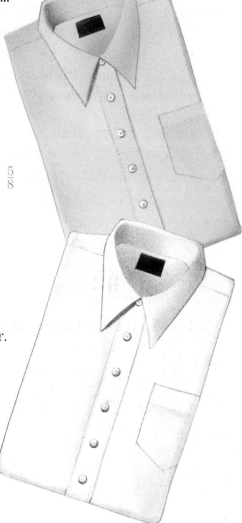

Checkpoint Write the letter of the correct answer.

Multiply. The answer must be in simplest form.

1. $\frac{1}{3} \times \frac{1}{4}$ **a.** $\frac{1}{12}$ **b.** $\frac{2}{7}$ **c.** $\frac{7}{12}$ **d.** $\frac{4}{3}$

2. $\frac{1}{6} \times \frac{3}{4}$ **a.** $\frac{1}{24}$ **b.** $\frac{1}{8}$ **c.** $\frac{3}{24}$ **d.** $\frac{11}{12}$

3. $\frac{3}{10} \times \frac{5}{6}$ **a.** $\frac{8}{60}$ **b.** $\frac{15}{60}$ **c.** $\frac{1}{4}$ **d.** $\frac{1}{2}$

Multiply. Write the answer in simplest form.

1. $\frac{1}{3} \times \frac{1}{8}$
2. $\frac{1}{2} \times \frac{1}{5}$
3. $\frac{1}{4} \times \frac{1}{9}$
4. $\frac{1}{3} \times \frac{1}{7}$
5. $\frac{1}{6} \times \frac{1}{5}$

6. $\frac{3}{8} \times \frac{5}{7}$
7. $\frac{5}{12} \times \frac{7}{8}$
8. $\frac{2}{3} \times \frac{4}{5}$
9. $\frac{3}{10} \times \frac{3}{5}$
10. $\frac{7}{11} \times \frac{3}{4}$

11. $\frac{3}{11} \times \frac{5}{6}$
12. $\frac{3}{10} \times \frac{4}{7}$
13. $\frac{5}{6} \times \frac{2}{3}$
14. $\frac{1}{10} \times \frac{5}{12}$
15. $\frac{5}{6} \times \frac{3}{4}$

16. $\frac{5}{6} \times \frac{1}{10}$
17. $\frac{4}{7} \times \frac{7}{9}$
18. $\frac{1}{4} \times \frac{2}{5}$
19. $\frac{1}{8} \times \frac{4}{5}$
20. $\frac{1}{2} \times \frac{4}{7}$

21. $\frac{3}{8} \times \frac{2}{9}$
22. $\frac{3}{4} \times \frac{8}{9}$
23. $\frac{5}{6} \times \frac{3}{10}$
24. $\frac{2}{3} \times \frac{9}{16}$
25. $\frac{5}{8} \times \frac{12}{25}$

26. $\frac{4}{5} \times \frac{3}{10} \times \frac{5}{6}$
27. $\frac{3}{7} \times \frac{5}{9} \times \frac{21}{25}$
28. $\frac{4}{5} \times \frac{1}{10} \times \frac{5}{6}$

Solve.

29. Of the shirts made by the Super Shirt Co., $\frac{1}{2}$ are white. Of those white shirts, $\frac{2}{3}$ are short sleeved. What fraction of the shirts are white and short sleeved?

30. Mr. Lewis spent $\frac{1}{2}$ of Monday sewing shirtsleeves. For $\frac{3}{4}$ of that time, he sewed long sleeves. What part of his day was spent sewing long sleeves?

31. Of all the shirts made by the Look Sharp Shirt Co., $\frac{1}{3}$ are blue. Another $\frac{1}{5}$ are pink. What fraction of all the shirts are either blue or pink?

★32. Ms. Hall had a card filled with buttons. She used $\frac{2}{3}$ of the buttons and gave away $\frac{3}{4}$ of the buttons that remained. What part of the buttons was left?

CHALLENGE

Find the next two numbers in each sequence.

1. $1, \frac{1}{3}, \frac{1}{9}, \ldots$

2. $1, \frac{3}{7}, \frac{9}{49}, \ldots$

3. $6, \frac{5}{2}, \frac{25}{24}, \ldots$

4. $9, 4, \frac{16}{9}, \ldots$

Multiplying Fractions and Whole Numbers

A. Andy works in a shop that sells sports equipment. During the beginning of the football season, about $\frac{1}{3}$ of Andy's workday is spent outfitting the local football team. If the workday is 8 hours long, how many hours of the day does Andy spend outfitting the football team?

Find $\frac{1}{3}$ of 8.

Write the whole number as a fraction.	Multiply the fractions.	Write the product in simplest form.
$\frac{1}{3} \times \frac{8}{1}$	$\frac{1}{3} \times \frac{8}{1} = \frac{8}{3}$	$\frac{8}{3} = 2\frac{2}{3}$

Andy spends $2\frac{2}{3}$ hours outfitting the football team.

B. You can also use the shortcut when multiplying whole numbers and fractions.

Multiply $\frac{3}{4} \times 6$.

Long way

$$\frac{3}{4} \times \frac{6}{1} = \frac{18}{4} = \frac{9}{2} = 4\frac{1}{2}$$

Shortcut

$$\frac{3}{\overset{}{\underset{2}{4}}} \times \frac{\overset{3}{6}}{1} = \frac{9}{2} = 4\frac{1}{2}$$

Other examples:

$$10 \times \frac{2}{5} = \frac{\overset{2}{10}}{1} \times \frac{2}{\underset{1}{5}} = 4$$

$$\frac{2}{3} \times \frac{1}{2} \times 7 = \frac{\overset{1}{2}}{3} \times \frac{1}{\underset{1}{2}} \times \frac{7}{1} = \frac{7}{3} = 2\frac{1}{3}$$

Checkpoint Write the letter of the correct answer.

Multiply. The answer must be in simplest form.

1. $12 \times \frac{5}{6}$ **a.** $\frac{5}{72}$ **b.** $\frac{5}{6}$ **c.** $\frac{60}{6}$ **d.** 10

2. $\frac{3}{4} \times 5$ **a.** $\frac{3}{20}$ **b.** $\frac{15}{4}$ **c.** $3\frac{3}{4}$ **d.** $5\frac{3}{4}$

Multiply. Write the answer in simplest form.
Use the shortcut if you can.

1. $4 \times \frac{1}{12}$ **2.** $8 \times \frac{1}{4}$ **3.** $3 \times \frac{1}{9}$ **4.** $9 \times \frac{1}{18}$ **5.** $10 \times \frac{1}{15}$

6. $\frac{1}{2} \times 6$ **7.** $\frac{1}{15} \times 15$ **8.** $\frac{3}{5} \times 10$ **9.** $\frac{2}{5} \times 2$ **10.** $\frac{2}{7} \times 3$

11. $3 \times \frac{2}{5}$ **12.** $6 \times \frac{7}{12}$ **13.** $\frac{2}{3} \times 14$ **14.** $5 \times \frac{11}{12}$ **15.** $7 \times \frac{1}{6}$

16. $7 \times \frac{2}{7}$ **17.** $15 \times \frac{1}{20}$ **18.** $\frac{3}{18} \times 8$ **19.** $\frac{1}{8} \times 40$ **20.** $12 \times \frac{5}{9}$

21. $6 \times \frac{3}{4}$ **22.** $\frac{5}{6} \times 9$ **23.** $\frac{1}{2} \times 27$ **24.** $9 \times \frac{2}{3}$ **25.** $50 \times \frac{1}{4}$

26. $\frac{1}{6} \times 18 \times \frac{7}{9}$ **27.** $12 \times \frac{1}{2} \times \frac{3}{4}$ **28.** $\frac{2}{3} \times \frac{1}{8} \times 16$

★29. $\frac{2}{3} \times n = 1$ **★30.** $n \times 9 = 1$ **★31.** $\frac{3}{5} \times n = 1$ **★32.** $n \times 6 = 1$

Solve.

33. Andy's sports shop sells shoelaces for all types of shoes. The laces for basketball shoes are 36 inches long. The laces for football shoes are $\frac{2}{3}$ as long. How long are the laces for the football shoes?

★34. Andy has just received a shipment of 60 specialty baseball caps. Of the caps, $\frac{1}{2}$ have fake antlers attached, $\frac{1}{4}$ have fuzzy ears, and $\frac{1}{4}$ have plastic propellers. How many caps have antlers or ears?

FOCUS: MENTAL MATH

Fractions that have 1 as a numerator are called *unit fractions*.

To multiply a unit fraction by a number, divide the number by the denominator.

$\frac{1}{3}$ of $12 = \frac{1}{3} \times 12 = \frac{12}{3} = 12 \div 3 = 4$

To find $\frac{2}{3}$ of 12, think:

| $\frac{2}{3}$ is $2 \times \frac{1}{3}$. | $\frac{1}{3}$ of 12 is 4. |

$\frac{2}{3}$ of $12 \longrightarrow 2 \times 4 = 8$

Compute mentally.

1. $\frac{3}{4}$ of 8 is ▩ .   **2.** $\frac{2}{3}$ of 24 is ▩ .   **3.** $\frac{4}{5}$ of 20 is ▩ .

More Practice, page 449

Estimating a Fraction of a Number

A. About one-fourth of the Grant Elementary School students own Ace running shoes. There are 379 students enrolled. About how many students own Ace running shoes?

Estimate $\frac{1}{4}$ of 379.

Round 379 to a number that is easily divisible by 4.

$379 \rightarrow 360$ OR $379 \rightarrow 400$

$\frac{1}{4}$ of $360 = 90$ $\frac{1}{4}$ of $400 = 100$

Both 90 and 100 are good estimates.

Other examples:

$\frac{1}{5}$ of 373 $\frac{1}{8}$ of 1,416

$\frac{1}{5}$ of $400 = 80$ $\frac{1}{8}$ of $1,600 = 200$

$\frac{1}{5}$ of $350 = 70$ $\frac{1}{8}$ of $1,200 = 150$

B. You can also estimate when the fraction is not a unit fraction.

Estimate $\frac{2}{3}$ of 253.

Estimate $\frac{1}{3}$ of 253.

Round to a number easily divisible by 3.

$\frac{1}{3}$ of $240 = 80$

Multiply by 2.

$80 \times 2 = 160$

$\frac{2}{3}$ of 253 is about 160.

Other examples:

$\frac{3}{4}$ of 169 $\frac{2}{5}$ of 4,165

$\frac{1}{4}$ of $160 = 40$ $\frac{1}{5}$ of $4,000 = 800$

$\frac{3}{4}$ of $160 = 3 \times 40 = 120$ $\frac{2}{5}$ of $4,000 = 2 \times 800 = 1,600$

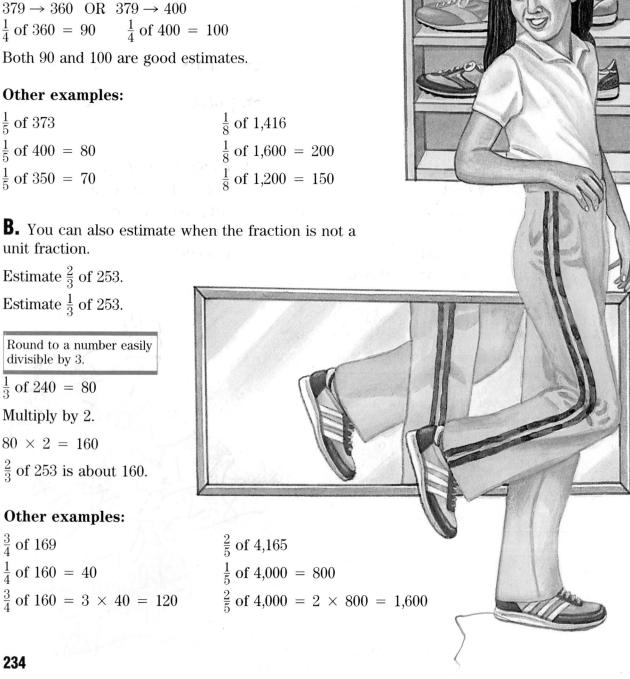

Mentally compute.

1. $\frac{1}{6}$ of 24

2. $\frac{1}{3}$ of 150

3. $\frac{1}{4}$ of 100

4. $\frac{1}{5}$ of 450

5. $\frac{1}{4}$ of 800

6. $\frac{1}{8}$ of 160

7. $\frac{1}{3}$ of 300

8. $\frac{1}{10}$ of 270

Estimate.

9. $\frac{1}{2}$ of 499

10. $\frac{1}{3}$ of 118

11. $\frac{1}{4}$ of 78

12. $\frac{1}{10}$ of 987

13. $\frac{1}{6}$ of 62

14. $\frac{1}{8}$ of 647

15. $\frac{1}{5}$ of 488

16. $\frac{1}{4}$ of 235

17. $\frac{2}{3}$ of 297

18. $\frac{2}{5}$ of 348

19. $\frac{3}{10}$ of 792

20. $\frac{3}{8}$ of 242

21. $\frac{3}{4}$ of 398

22. $\frac{5}{8}$ of 638

23. $\frac{3}{5}$ of 548

24. $\frac{5}{6}$ of 312

25. $\frac{2}{3}$ of 20,975

26. $\frac{3}{4}$ of 371

27. $\frac{5}{6}$ of 539

28. $\frac{8}{9}$ of 809

Solve.

29. The Ace Shoe Company is sponsoring a contest. Of the winners selected, $\frac{2}{3}$ are third-prize winners, who receive fancy socks. There are 357 winners chosen. About how many of the winners will receive fancy socks?

★30. Jason filled out 170 entry blanks for the contest. He could only afford postage for about $\frac{3}{8}$ of them. About how many of the entry blanks could he afford to send?

CHALLENGE

Find the mystery number.

The mystery number is $\frac{1}{4}$ of $\frac{3}{5}$ of $\frac{1}{2}$ of 1,000.
HINT: Work backward.

PROBLEM SOLVING
Estimation

Sometimes, in order to solve a problem, you can find an estimated answer.

> Marla's class has earned $143.71. They want to use the money to visit a sneaker factory 32 miles away. Bus rental costs $35 per hour. Has the class earned enough money to rent a bus to visit the factory?

To answer this problem, you need to estimate the time the bus trip will take to and from the factory and how long the factory tour will last.

First, you need to provide a reasonable estimate of how long it would take a bus to travel 32 miles. You have to consider speed limits, traffic, and other possible delays.

- The speed limit is 55 miles per hour. So, the bus can travel no faster than that speed.
- There might be traffic along the route to the factory.

Marla's class decides to allow 1 hour each way for the bus ride.

Next, you need to decide how much time to allow for the tour itself. Here is some information about other class trips.

- Marla's class visited a paper mill. The tour lasted 1 hour 15 minutes.
- A class trip to an art museum lasted $1\frac{1}{2}$ hours.
- A trip to a zoo lasted 2 hours 20 minutes.

Marla's class realizes that a factory tour will probably not last as long as a trip to the zoo. They decide to estimate $1\frac{1}{2}$ hours for the tour.

$$
\begin{array}{l}
\quad\ \$35 \quad \leftarrow \text{ bus rental fee per hour} \\
\underline{\times\ 3.5} \quad \leftarrow \text{ estimated total time (in hours)} \\
\$122.50 \quad \leftarrow \text{ estimated total cost of renting a bus}
\end{array}
$$

Marla's class has earned enough money to rent a bus to visit the factory.

After their trip to the sneaker factory, Marla and her classmates decide to start their own business. They plan to knit striped mittens in their school colors. They have to decide how many mittens to make and what to charge for each pair.

Decide whether each question needs to be answered. If it does, decide whether the exact answer or only an estimate should be found. Write *need not answer, exact answer,* or *estimate only.*

1. How much yarn is needed for 1 pair of mittens?

2. How much will the yarn cost for each pair of mittens?

3. How much will the needles cost?

4. How many pairs of mittens can the students make in a week?

5. How much money will they need for start-up costs?

6. How many pairs of mittens can they sell?

7. Who should be the treasurer?

8. How much will they need to charge to make a profit of $125?

Use the information in the box to answer the question.

9. Marla's classmates are planning a dinner to celebrate the success of their business. They want to serve a chicken dinner at 6:30 P.M. At what time should they begin to prepare the meal?

- They can't start their preparations before 3:00 P.M.
- They have to go to a market and buy the food.
- They will have to clean and cut the vegetables and prepare the chicken.
- Their chicken recipe calls for a cooking time of 40 to 50 minutes.
- Vegetables cook more quickly than chicken.

Multiplying Mixed Numbers

A. Angel tests new running shoes for the Gazelle Shoes Company. This morning, he ran $\frac{3}{4}$ mile, testing the company's new Rocket shoe. In the afternoon, he ran $3\frac{1}{2}$ times as far, testing the Cruiser model. How far did Angel run this afternoon?

Find $3\frac{1}{2} \times \frac{3}{4}$.

Rename the mixed number.	**Multiply the fractions.**	**Write the product in simplest form.**
$3\frac{1}{2} = \frac{7}{2}$	$\frac{7}{2} \times \frac{3}{4} = \frac{21}{8}$	$\frac{21}{8} = 2\frac{5}{8}$

Angel ran $2\frac{5}{8}$ miles this afternoon.

B. Sometimes both factors need to be renamed as fractions.

$$2\frac{1}{4} \times 6 = \frac{9}{\overset{}{\underset{2}{4}}} \times \overset{3}{\frac{6}{1}} = \frac{27}{2} = 13\frac{1}{2}$$

$$4\frac{2}{3} \times 1\frac{5}{7} = \frac{\overset{2}{14}}{\underset{1}{3}} \times \frac{\overset{4}{12}}{\underset{1}{7}} = \frac{8}{1} = 8$$

Checkpoint Write the letter of the correct answer.

Multiply. The answer must be in simplest form.

1. $5 \times 3\frac{1}{10}$

2. $4\frac{1}{3} \times \frac{5}{6}$

3. $2\frac{1}{2} \times 3\frac{2}{3}$

a. $6\frac{1}{2}$

b. $15\frac{1}{10}$

c. $15\frac{1}{2}$

d. $15\frac{5}{10}$

a. $2\frac{2}{9}$

b. $3\frac{1}{3}$

c. $3\frac{11}{18}$

d. $5\frac{1}{6}$

a. $6\frac{1}{3}$

b. $7\frac{1}{3}$

c. 8

d. $9\frac{1}{6}$

Multiply. Write the answer in simplest form.

1. $\frac{2}{3} \times 1\frac{1}{8}$ **2.** $2\frac{2}{5} \times \frac{3}{5}$ **3.** $2\frac{1}{3} \times \frac{4}{5}$ **4.** $\frac{1}{2} \times 8\frac{2}{9}$ **5.** $\frac{4}{9} \times 5\frac{3}{4}$

6. $6 \times 1\frac{2}{3}$ **7.** $4 \times 4\frac{3}{4}$ **8.** $4 \times 2\frac{3}{8}$ **9.** $9 \times 3\frac{1}{3}$ **10.** $8 \times 5\frac{1}{2}$

11. $3\frac{2}{5} \times 4\frac{4}{5}$ **12.** $6\frac{1}{2} \times 5\frac{1}{2}$ **13.** $1\frac{2}{3} \times 1\frac{5}{6}$ **14.** $4\frac{2}{3} \times 1\frac{1}{3}$ **15.** $1\frac{7}{8} \times 4\frac{1}{3}$

16. $\frac{1}{2} \times 3\frac{1}{7}$ **17.** $\frac{3}{4} \times 3\frac{1}{3}$ **18.** $6\frac{1}{6} \times 7\frac{1}{2}$ **19.** $1\frac{1}{6} \times 18$ **20.** $9\frac{5}{7} \times 9\frac{1}{4}$

21. $10\frac{2}{5} \times 8\frac{1}{3}$ **22.** $\frac{4}{5} \times 10\frac{1}{2}$ **23.** $\frac{3}{5} \times 2\frac{1}{7}$ **24.** $7\frac{1}{3} \times 9\frac{7}{8}$ **25.** $12 \times 1\frac{3}{4}$

26. $1\frac{5}{9} \times 1\frac{4}{5}$ **27.** $\frac{1}{8} \times 3\frac{1}{3}$ **28.** $\frac{7}{8} \times 7\frac{3}{7}$ **29.** $4 \times 6\frac{1}{4}$ **30.** $3\frac{1}{6} \times 4\frac{4}{5}$

Solve.

31. One week Angel tested 6 pairs of shoes. The next week, he tested $1\frac{1}{2}$ times as many pairs. How many pairs of shoes did Angel test during the second week?

★32. Pat works with Angel. One day she ran $3\frac{1}{3}$ miles in the morning, and $\frac{3}{4}$ of that distance in the afternoon. Angel ran $2\frac{1}{4}$ miles in the morning, and $1\frac{1}{3}$ times as far in the afternoon. Who ran farther that day, Pat or Angel?

FOCUS: MENTAL MATH

You can use the Distributive Property to help you multiply a whole number and a mixed number.

Multiply $9 \times 4\frac{1}{3}$.

Think: $9 \times 4\frac{1}{3} = (9 \times 4) + (9 \times \frac{1}{3}) = 36 + 3 = 39$.

Multiply. Use the Distributive Property.

1. $6 \times 2\frac{1}{2}$ **2.** $15 \times 2\frac{1}{3}$ **3.** $12 \times 3\frac{1}{4}$ **4.** $4 \times 5\frac{1}{4}$

5. $28 \times 2\frac{1}{7}$ **6.** $32 \times 3\frac{1}{4}$ **★7.** $6 \times 2\frac{2}{3}$ **★8.** $12 \times 2\frac{3}{5}$

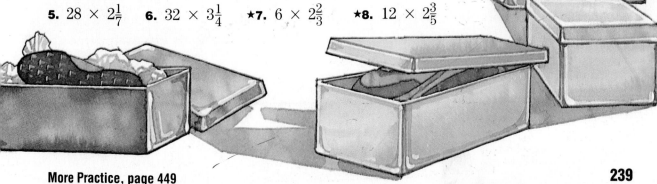

More Practice, page 449

Dividing Whole Numbers and Fractions

A. Willy is dyeing T-shirts for the Oakwood School softball team. He has 12 cups of dye. It takes $\frac{3}{4}$ cup to dye 1 shirt. How many T-shirts can he dye?

Divide $12 \div \frac{3}{4}$.

To divide by a fraction, you multiply by the reciprocal of the fraction.

Reciprocals are numbers whose product is 1.

Fraction   Reciprocal

$\frac{3}{4} \times \frac{4}{3} = 1$

To find the reciprocal of a mixed number or a whole number, first write the number as a fraction.

$5\frac{2}{3} \longrightarrow \frac{17}{3} \times \frac{3}{17}$ $\frac{17}{3} \times \frac{3}{17} = 1$

$18 \longrightarrow \frac{18}{1} \times \frac{1}{18}$ $\frac{18}{1} \times \frac{1}{18} = 1$

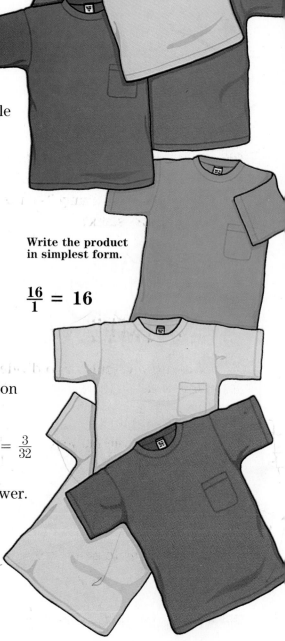

Write the whole number as a fraction.	Multiply by the reciprocal of the fraction.	Write the product in simplest form.
$12 \div \frac{3}{4} = \frac{12}{1} \div \frac{3}{4}$	$\overset{4}{\underset{1}{\cancel{12}}}{1} \times \frac{4}{\cancel{3}} = \frac{16}{1}$	$\frac{16}{1} = 16$

Willy can dye 16 T-shirts.

B. You can follow the same steps to divide a fraction by another fraction or by a whole number.

$\frac{1}{2} \div \frac{3}{8} = \frac{1}{\cancel{2}} \times \frac{\overset{4}{\cancel{8}}}{3} = \frac{4}{3} = 1\frac{1}{3}$ $\frac{3}{4} \div 8 = \frac{3}{4} \times \frac{1}{8} = \frac{3}{32}$

Checkpoint   Write the letter of the correct answer.

Divide. The answer must be in simplest form.

1. $8 \div \frac{2}{3}$ **a.** $\frac{16}{3}$ **b.** $7\frac{1}{3}$ **c.** $\frac{24}{2}$ **d.** 12

2. $\frac{3}{4} \div \frac{1}{8}$ **a.** $\frac{3}{32}$ **b.** $\frac{1}{6}$ **c.** 6   **d.** 24

3. $\frac{4}{5} \div 6$ **a.** $\frac{2}{15}$ **b.** $\frac{4}{5}$ **c.** $4\frac{4}{5}$ **d.** $7\frac{1}{2}$

Write the recipocal of each number.

1. $\frac{1}{8}$ **2.** 16   **3.** $\frac{3}{4}$ **4.** $2\frac{1}{2}$ **5.** $3\frac{3}{8}$ **6.** 8   **7.** $\frac{3}{5}$

8. $10\frac{1}{2}$ **9.** $1\frac{2}{5}$ **10.** $\frac{5}{9}$ **11.** 2   **12.** $4\frac{5}{8}$ **13.** $7\frac{1}{2}$ **14.** $5\frac{5}{6}$

Divide. Write the answer in simplest form.

15. $7 \div \frac{2}{3}$ **16.** $15 \div \frac{7}{10}$ **17.** $30 \div \frac{1}{4}$ **18.** $43 \div \frac{3}{4}$ **19.** $27 \div \frac{1}{2}$

20. $\frac{1}{4} \div \frac{2}{3}$ **21.** $\frac{5}{12} \div \frac{5}{12}$ **22.** $\frac{1}{7} \div \frac{8}{11}$ **23.** $\frac{1}{2} \div \frac{1}{6}$ **24.** $\frac{7}{8} \div \frac{5}{7}$

25. $\frac{1}{10} \div 24$ **26.** $\frac{2}{9} \div 18$ **27.** $\frac{5}{6} \div 40$ **28.** $\frac{1}{5} \div 1$ **29.** $\frac{4}{7} \div 34$

30. $\frac{1}{7} \div \frac{9}{10}$ **31.** $15 \div \frac{3}{4}$ **32.** $\frac{1}{2} \div \frac{4}{5}$ **33.** $\frac{2}{3} \div 29$ **34.** $\frac{5}{6} \div 36$

35. $\frac{3}{4} \div 50$ **36.** $\frac{6}{7} \div 11$ **37.** $\frac{1}{5} \div 36$ **38.** $14 \div \frac{5}{8}$ **39.** $15 \div \frac{4}{7}$

Solve.

40. A stack of folded T-shirts is 4 inches high. Each folded shirt is $\frac{1}{4}$ inch thick. How many T-shirts are there in the stack?

★41. Willy also made some jerseys for the team. The $\frac{3}{4}$ cup of dye that was enough for a T-shirt was only $\frac{2}{3}$ of what was needed to dye a jersey. How much dye was needed for 16 jerseys?

CALCULATOR

You can use a calculator to divide a whole number by a fraction.

Divide $26 \div \frac{2}{3}$.

Multiply the whole number by the denominator.

$26 \times 3 = 78$

$26 \div \frac{2}{3} = 39$

Divide the product by the numerator.

$78 \div 2 = 39$

Use a calculator to compute.

1. $100 \div \frac{4}{5}$ **2.** $36 \div \frac{2}{3}$ **3.** $81 \div \frac{3}{7}$ **4.** $65 \div \frac{5}{6}$ **5.** $27 \div \frac{3}{5}$

6. $520 \div \frac{4}{9}$ **7.** $1,040 \div \frac{2}{3}$ **8.** $25 \div \frac{5}{7}$ **9.** $99 \div \frac{99}{100}$ **10.** $52 \div \frac{26}{12}$

Dividing Fractions and Mixed Numbers

Mr. Amato makes the costumes that he sells in his costume shop. Today, Mr. Amato used $7\frac{1}{2}$ yards of cloth to make 5 capes for superhero costumes. How much cloth did he need for each cape?

Divide $7\frac{1}{2} \div 5$.

Rename both numbers as fractions.	Multiply by the reciprocal of the divisor.	Write the product in simplest form.
$7\frac{1}{2} \div 5 = \frac{15}{2} \div \frac{5}{1}$	$\frac{\overset{3}{\cancel{15}}}{2} \times \frac{1}{\cancel{5}} = \frac{3}{2}$	$\frac{3}{2} = 1\frac{1}{2}$

He needed $1\frac{1}{2}$ yards of cloth for each cape.

Other examples:

$$2\frac{1}{2} \div \frac{1}{2} = \frac{5}{\underset{1}{\cancel{2}}} \times \frac{\overset{1}{\cancel{2}}}{1} = 5$$

$$4\frac{1}{6} \div 2\frac{2}{3} = \frac{25}{\underset{2}{\cancel{6}}} \times \frac{\overset{1}{\cancel{3}}}{8} = \frac{25}{16} = 1\frac{9}{16}$$

$$\frac{5}{8} \div 2\frac{2}{3} = \frac{5}{8} \times \frac{3}{8} = \frac{15}{64}$$

Checkpoint Write the letter of the correct answer.

Divide. The answer must be in simplest form.

1. $2\frac{1}{2} \div \frac{3}{4}$

2. $2\frac{1}{3} \div 4$

3. $1\frac{3}{4} \div 1\frac{1}{8}$

4. $\frac{7}{8} \div 4\frac{1}{2}$

a. $\frac{3}{10}$

a. $\frac{1}{2}$

a. $1\frac{3}{32}$

a. $\frac{7}{32}$

b. $1\frac{7}{8}$

b. $\frac{7}{12}$

b. $1\frac{3}{5}$

b. $\frac{7}{36}$

c. $3\frac{1}{5}$

c. $1\frac{5}{7}$

c. $1\frac{5}{9}$

c. $3\frac{15}{16}$

d. $3\frac{1}{3}$

d. 9

d. $1\frac{31}{32}$

d. $5\frac{1}{7}$

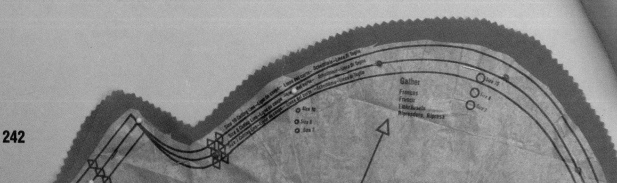

Divide. Write the answer in simplest form.

1. $6\frac{1}{2} \div \frac{3}{4}$

2. $8\frac{2}{3} \div \frac{1}{3}$

3. $8\frac{4}{5} \div \frac{3}{4}$

4. $1\frac{1}{10} \div \frac{7}{10}$

5. $4\frac{5}{8} \div \frac{1}{4}$

6. $8\frac{1}{2} \div 6$

7. $6\frac{1}{3} \div 2$

8. $2\frac{1}{2} \div 6$

9. $2\frac{1}{2} \div 4$

10. $7\frac{1}{3} \div 2$

11. $4\frac{2}{3} \div 1\frac{1}{2}$

12. $9\frac{1}{2} \div 4\frac{1}{2}$

13. $9\frac{1}{9} \div 2\frac{1}{2}$

14. $3\frac{1}{2} \div 2\frac{3}{4}$

15. $4\frac{9}{10} \div 3\frac{1}{2}$

16. $\frac{3}{4} \div 6\frac{1}{2}$

17. $\frac{7}{9} \div 2\frac{1}{2}$

18. $\frac{1}{4} \div 10\frac{2}{9}$

19. $\frac{2}{9} \div 6\frac{1}{2}$

20. $\frac{1}{8} \div 4\frac{1}{10}$

21. $4\frac{1}{4} \div 3$

22. $1\frac{3}{4} \div 3$

23. $6\frac{1}{2} \div 4\frac{1}{4}$

24. $4\frac{1}{3} \div \frac{1}{3}$

25. $7\frac{3}{4} \div 2\frac{3}{4}$

26. $8\frac{4}{7} \div 6\frac{2}{3}$

27. $1\frac{1}{3} \div \frac{1}{3}$

28. $10\frac{2}{3} \div \frac{1}{2}$

29. $3\frac{2}{3} \div \frac{2}{7}$

30. $6\frac{5}{7} \div 1\frac{5}{7}$

Solve.

31. Mr. Amato uses a piece of elastic $2\frac{1}{2}$ yards long to make eye patches for pirate costumes. He uses $\frac{1}{2}$ yard for each eye patch. How many eye patches can he make?

32. Mr. Amato used all of his polka-dot fabric to make 12 clown outfits. He started out with $52\frac{1}{2}$ yards of fabric. For each outfit, he used the same amount of fabric. How much fabric was used for each outfit?

33. Mr. Amato used $29\frac{3}{4}$ yards of silver metallic fabric for alien costumes. He needed $4\frac{1}{4}$ yards for each costume. How many costumes did he make?

MIDCHAPTER REVIEW

Compute. Write the answer in simplest form.

1. $\frac{4}{7} \times \frac{2}{5}$

2. $\frac{2}{3} \times \frac{7}{8}$

3. $6 \times \frac{4}{5}$

4. $9 \times \frac{3}{7}$

5. $5 \times 3\frac{1}{3}$

6. $4\frac{1}{2} \times 3\frac{2}{3}$

7. $4 \div \frac{5}{6}$

8. $\frac{1}{4} \div \frac{8}{9}$

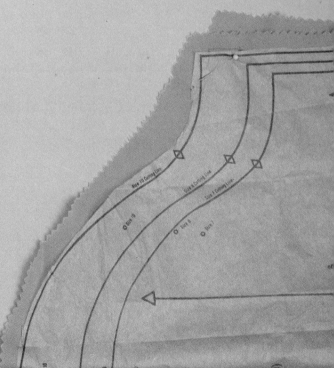

PROBLEM SOLVING
Interpreting the Quotient and the Remainder

Often, the answer to a division problem has a remainder. You have to understand the question and think about the quotient and the remainder in order to answer the question correctly.

Marco works for the Wear-Well Clothing Company. He needs to pack 20 pounds of buttons into boxes for the sewing-machine operators. Marco knows that $\frac{3}{4}$ lb of buttons fills one box.

Divide: $20 \div \frac{3}{4} = \frac{20}{1} \times \frac{4}{3} = \frac{80}{3} = 26\frac{2}{3}$.

Read each question. Think about how to interpret the remainder to answer each question.

1. How many boxes does Marco fill with buttons? Drop the remainder.
   Marco fills 26 boxes with buttons.

2. How many boxes does Marco need to pack all the buttons?
   Round the quotient up to the nearest whole number.
   Marco needs 27 boxes to pack all the buttons.

3. What part of the last box is full of buttons? Use only the remainder.
   The last box is $\frac{2}{3}$ full of buttons.

Write the letter of the correct answer.

1. Ken is packing shirts into boxes that are 14 inches high. Each folded shirt is $\frac{3}{4}$ of an inch thick. How many shirts can Ken fit into one box?

   a. $\frac{2}{3}$ b. 18 c. 19

2. Marcia has 25 yards of trim. She uses $\frac{2}{3}$ of a yard to trim one vest. How many vests can she trim?

   a. 37 b. $37\frac{1}{2}$ c. 38

Solve.

3. Carol has $10\frac{1}{2}$ oz of dye. It takes $\frac{3}{4}$ of an ounce to dye one batch of material. How many batches can Carol dye?

4. Tom is packing 66 lb of safety pins into boxes. He can fit $2\frac{1}{4}$ lb of pins into one box. How many boxes does Tom need to pack all the pins?

5. Sandra is packing 42 oz of sequins into plastic bags. She knows that $\frac{7}{8}$ oz of sequins fills each bag. After all the bags are completely filled, how full will the last bag be?

6. Janice has 56 yards of silk. She needs $3\frac{1}{2}$ yards of fabric to make one dress. How many dresses can she make?

7. David is packing 29 lb of felt into bundles. Each bundle weighs $1\frac{3}{4}$ lb. How full is the last bundle after all the others are completed?

8. Liza knows that 1 yard of material produces $7\frac{1}{2}$ ties. How many yards of material does she need to make 80 ties? (She can buy the material she needs only by the whole yard.)

Measuring Customary Lengths

A. **Inches (in.), feet (ft), yards (yd),** and **miles (mi)** are all customary units of length.

The length of a baby's finger is about 1 inch. A football is about 1 foot long. The height of a drinking fountain is about 1 yard. You can ride a bicycle 1 mile in about 5 minutes.

B. Maura works in a dressmaking factory. It is her job to make sure that the hem on each dress is at least $1\frac{1}{4}$ inches wide. Is this hem wide enough?

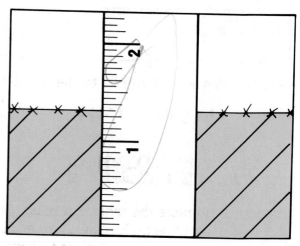

The width of the hem is

* 1 in. to the nearest in.
* $1\frac{1}{2}$ in. to the nearest $\frac{1}{2}$ in.
* $1\frac{1}{4}$ in. to the nearest $\frac{1}{4}$ in.
* $1\frac{3}{8}$ in. to the nearest $\frac{1}{8}$ in.
* $1\frac{5}{16}$ in. to the nearest $\frac{1}{16}$ in.

The smaller the unit, the more precise the measurement. The hem is $1\frac{5}{16}$ in. wide.

It is wide enough.

Choose the most appropriate unit of measure.
Write *in.*, *ft*, *yd*, or *mi*.

1. length of a baseball bat

2. length of a football field

3. amount of yarn in a spool

4. length of knitting needles

5. length of a car

6. distance from Denver to Houston

7. length of a shoelace

8. length of a jump rope

Choose the best estimate.

9. height of a man   **a.** 6 ft   **b.** 6 yd   **c.** 60 ft

10. distance a ball is thrown   **a.** 30 in.   **b.** 3 ft   **c.** 30 yd

11. height of a doll   **a.** 12 in.   **b.** 12 ft   **c.** 12 yd

★12. height of a skyscraper   **a.** 1,000 in.   **b.** 1,000 ft   **c.** 1,000 yd

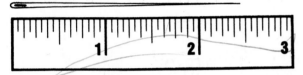

Measure this sewing needle to the nearest

13. in.   14. $\frac{1}{2}$ in.   15. $\frac{1}{4}$ in.   16. $\frac{1}{8}$ in.   17. $\frac{1}{16}$ in.

FOCUS: ESTIMATION

Copy and complete the table. Estimate the customary length of each object. Then measure each object and compare the actual measurement to your estimate.

Object	Estimation	Measurement
One shoe	▦	▦
One jacket sleeve	▦	▦
A glove	▦	▦
A shoelace	▦	▦
Your belt	▦	▦
A scarf	▦	▦

Customary Units of Length

A. You can use this table to help you rename one customary unit of length with another.

12 inches (in.) = 1 foot (ft)	
3 feet = 1 yard (yd)	5,280 feet = 1 mile (mi)
36 inches = 1 yard	1,760 yards = 1 mile

To rename larger units with smaller units, you can multiply.

2 ft = ■ in.
2 × 12 = 24   **1 ft = 12 in.**
2 ft = 24 in.

To rename smaller units with larger units, you can divide.

63 ft = ■ yd
63 ÷ 3 = 21   **3 ft = 1 yd**
63 ft = 21 yd

Other examples:

4 ft 10 in. = ■ in.
(4 × 12) + 10 = 58
4 ft 10 in. = 58 in.

7,480 yd = ■ mi
7,480 ÷ 1,760 = $4\frac{1}{4}$
7,480 yd = $4\frac{1}{4}$ mi

B. You can add and subtract with customary units of length.

Add.

$$\begin{array}{r} 1 \text{ mi } 1{,}435 \text{ yd} \\ + 3 \text{ mi } \phantom{1{,}}767 \text{ yd} \\ \hline 4 \text{ mi } 2{,}202 \text{ yd} = 5 \text{ mi } 442 \text{ yd} \end{array}$$

Rename 2,202 yd as 1 mi 442 yd.

Subtract.

$$\begin{array}{r} \overset{12}{\cancel{13}} \text{ ft } \overset{19}{\cancel{7}} \text{ in.} \\ - 6 \text{ ft } 8 \text{ in.} \\ \hline 6 \text{ ft } 11 \text{ in.} \end{array}$$

Rename 13 ft 7 in. as 12 ft 19 in.

Checkpoint Write the letter of the correct answer.

Compute.

1. 6,600 yd = ■

a. 3 mi
b. $183\frac{1}{3}$ in.
c. 2,200 ft
d. 3 mi 1,320 yd

2. 2 ft 8 in.
     + 5 ft 6 in.

a. 7 ft 2 in.
b. 7 ft 4 in.
c. 8 ft 2 in.
d. 8 ft 4 in.

3. 9 yd 5 ft
     − 2 yd 8 ft

a. 6 yd
b. 6 yd 7 ft
c. 6 yd 9 ft
d. 15 yd 1 ft

248

Complete.

1. 12 yd = ▦ ft
2. 5 mi = ▦ yd
3. 4 ft = ▦ in.

4. 72 in. = ▦ ft
5. 27 ft = ▦ yd
6. 14,080 yd = ▦ mi

7. 7 ft 2 in. = ▦ in.
8. 13 yd 2 ft = ▦ ft
9. 3 mi 690 yd = ▦ yd

10. 76 ft = ▦ yd ▦ ft
11. 726 in. = ▦ ft ▦ in.
12. 8,780 yd = ▦ mi ▦ yd

13. $2\frac{1}{3}$ yd = ▦ in.
14. $3\frac{1}{8}$ mi = ▦ ft
15. 4 yd $2\frac{5}{6}$ ft = ▦ in.

16. ▦ yd = 8 ft = ▦ in.
17. ▦ mi = 2,640 yd = ▦ ft

Compute.

18.　　3 ft 4 in.
　　+ 3 ft 7 in.

19.　　14 yd 1 ft
　　+ 5 yd 2 ft
　　30 2

20.　　2 mi 1,625 yd
　　+ 1 mi 1,205 yd
　　3 00 0

21.　　40 ft 9 in.
　　− 32 ft 8 in.

22.　　2 yd 1 ft
　　− 1 yd 2 ft
　　4 3

23.　　6 mi 200 yd
　　− 4 mi 1,350 yd
　　2 00

24.　　6 yd 2 ft
　　+ 9 yd 2 ft

25.　　4 mi 500 yd
　　− 2 mi 800 yd
　　1 0 3

26.　　3 mi 7 in.
　　+ 2 mi 8 in.
　　1 1 1

27.　　14 yd
　　− 5 yd 1 ft

★28.　　29 yd 1 ft 11 in.
　　+ 14 yd 2 ft 10 in.
　　1 0 0

★29.　　13 yd 1 ft 2 in.
　　− 9 yd 2 ft 11 in.
　　2 0 0 0

Solve.

30. Fabric is measured in units called *bolts*. One bolt is equal to 40 yards of cloth. How many feet of cloth are there in a bolt? How many inches?

★31. A rack of clothes at a factory holds 12 skirts and 8 blouses. Each skirt contains 5 feet of fabric. Each blouse contains 4 feet. How many yards of fabric were used to make the clothes?

ANOTHER LOOK

Find the prime factorization of each number.

1. 28
2. 60
3. 69
4. 100

5. 56
6. 72
7. 125
8. 248

More Practice, page 450

Customary Units of Capacity and Weight

A. **Fluid ounces (fl oz), cups (c), pints (pt), quarts (qt),** and **gallons (gal)** are customary units of capacity.

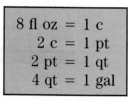

8 fl oz = 1 c
2 c = 1 pt
2 pt = 1 qt
4 qt = 1 gal

 1 cup

 1 pint

 1 quart

 1 gallon

To rename larger units with smaller units, multiply.

8 c = ▨ fl oz
8 × 8 = 64
8 c = 64 fl oz

| **1 c = 8 fl oz** |

To rename smaller units with larger units, divide.

16 qt = ▨ gal
16 ÷ 4 = 4
16 qt = 4 gal

| **4 qt = 1 gal** |

B. **Ounces (oz), pounds (lb),** and **tons (T)** are customary units of weight.

 1 ounce

 1 pound

 1 ton

16 oz = 1 lb
2,000 lb = 1 T

8 T = ▨ lb
8 × 2,000 = 16,000
8 T = 16,000 lb

| **1 T = 2,000 lb** |

80 oz = ▨ lb
80 ÷ 16 = 5
80 oz = 5 lb

| **16 oz = 1 lb** |

Choose the best measurement.

1. water in a washing machine   **a.** 10 fl oz   **b.** 10 qt   **c.** 10 gal

2. bottle of liquid detergent   **a.** 16 fl oz   **b.** 16 pt   **c.** 16 qt

Which unit would you use to measure? Write *oz*, *lb*, or *T*.

3. a spool of thread   **4.** a winter coat

5. a coat hanger   **6.** a pickup truck

Complete.

7. 20 c = ■ pt   **8.** 4 pt = ■ qt   **9.** 592 oz = ■ lb   **10.** 24 qt = ■ gal

11. 24 pt = ■ c   **12.** 11 qt = ■ pt   **13.** 197 lb = ■ oz   **14.** 3 T = ■ lb

15. 12 c = ■ pt   **16.** 19 pt = ■ c   **17.** 192 oz = ■ lb   **18.** 221 lb = ■ oz

19. 8,000 lb = ■ T   **20.** 21 pt = ■ c   **21.** 32 pt = ■ qt   **22.** 92 qt = ■ gal

23. 1,000 lb = ■ T   **24.** 1,000 lb = ■ oz   **25.** 12 c = ■ pt   **26.** 5 qt = ■ pt

★**27.** 4 gal 3 qt = ■ qt   ★**28.** $2\frac{1}{4}$ qt = ■ c   ★**29.** 87 oz = ■ lb ■ oz

Solve.

30. A vat of dye at a textile mill holds 550 gallons of dye. How many quarts does it hold?

31. A modern loom weighs 6,000 pounds. How many tons does it weigh?

32. Modern looms need oil to continue running. One loom uses 6 quarts of oil in one day. Another uses 14 pints of oil a day. Does the first loom or the second loom use more oil in one day?

★**33.** A loom can produce 50 bolts of fabric in one day. Each bolt weighs 60 pounds. How many tons of fabric does a loom produce in one day?

ANOTHER LOOK

Divide.

1. $2 \div 1.6$ **2.** $6 \div 1.2$ **3.** $24 \div 6.4$ **4.** $3 \div 0.6$

5. $9.9 \div 5.5$ **6.** $4.4 \div 2.2$ **7.** $10.25 \div 5$ **8.** $9.36 \div 6.4$

Units of Time: Addition and Subtraction

A. The Wear-Right Jeans Factory produces 1 pair of blue jeans each minute. How many pairs of jeans does it produce in 3 hours?

The table below shows equivalent measures of time.

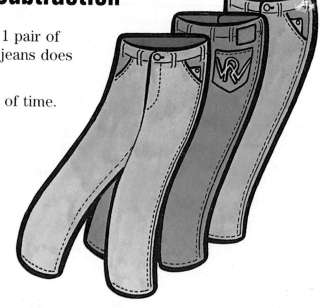

60 seconds (s)	=	1 minute (min)
60 minutes (min)	=	1 hour (h)
24 hours (h)	=	1 day (d)
7 days (d)	=	1 week (wk)
365 days	=	1 year (y)
52 weeks	=	1 year
12 months (mo)	=	1 year
100 years	=	1 century (c)

To rename larger units with smaller units, multiply.

3 h = ■ min
3 × 60 = 180   **1 h = 60 min**
3 h = 180 min

To rename smaller units with larger units, divide.

63 d = ■ wk
63 ÷ 7 = 9   **7 d = 1 wk**
63 d = 9 wk

The factory produces 180 pairs of jeans in 3 hours.

B. When you add or subtract units of time, remember to regroup as needed.

$$\begin{array}{r} 1\ \text{h}\ 50\ \text{min} \\ +\ 3\ \text{h}\ 25\ \text{min} \\ \hline 4\ \text{h}\ 75\ \text{min} = 5\ \text{h}\ 15\ \text{min} \end{array}$$

Rename 75 min as 1 h 15 min.

$$\begin{array}{r} \overset{17}{\cancel{18}}\ \text{min}\ \overset{87}{\cancel{27}}\ \text{s} \\ -\ \ 8\ \text{min}\ 34\ \text{s} \\ \hline 9\ \text{min}\ 53\ \text{s} \end{array}$$

Rename 18 min 27 s as 17 min 87 s.

Checkpoint Write the letter of the correct answer.

Compute.

1. 3 h 25 min = ■ min

a. 28
b. 180
c. 205
d. 1,503

2.
$$\begin{array}{r} 5\ \text{d}\ 15\ \text{h} \\ +\ 3\ \text{d}\ 10\ \text{h} \end{array}$$

a. 2 d 5 h
b. 8 d 1 h
c. 8 d 25 h
d. 9 d 1 h

3.
$$\begin{array}{r} 9\ \text{y}\ \ 8\ \text{mo} \\ -\ 7\ \text{y}\ 11\ \text{mo} \end{array}$$

a. 1 y 9 mo
b. 2 y 3 mo
c. 2 y 9 mo
d. 17 y 7 mo

Complete.

1. 300 s = ▨ min **2.** 600 min = ▨ h **3.** 48 h = ▨ d

4. 180 min = ▨ h **5.** 144 h = ▨ d **6.** 480 s = ▨ min

7. 3 d = ▨ h **8.** 8 y = ▨ mo **9.** 11 h = ▨ min

10. 36 h = ▨ d **11.** 16 mo = ▨ y **12.** 150 s = ▨ min

13. 4 wk 4 d = 3 wk ▨ d **14.** 1 y 1 mo = ▨ mo **15.** 3 min 32 s = 2 min ▨ s

16. 11 wk 5 d = ▨ wk 12 d **17.** 9 y = 8 y ▨ mo **18.** 12 min 55 s = 11 min ▨ s

Compute.

19. 6 min 28 s
     + 3 min 16 s

20. 2 h 2 min
     + 10 h 35 min

21. 8 h 30 min
     + 11 h 49 min

22. 1 h 34 min
     + 6 h 28 min

23. 22 h 30 min
     − 15 h 6 min

24. 23 h 23 min
     − 15 h 20 min

25. 13 min 8 s
     − 8 min 13 s

26. 16 h 16 min
     − 6 h 44 min

27. 6 min 59 s
     + 2 min 25 s

★28. 8 h 34 min 52 s
      + 3 h 26 min 15 s

★29. 3 c 26 y 5 mo
      − 2 c 73 y 7 mo

Solve. For Problem 31, use the Infobank.

30. The Wear-Right Jeans Factory has been making Free-Style designer jeans for 1 year 10 months. They have made Ranch-Hand jeans for 10 years 3 months. For how much longer have they been making Ranch-Hand jeans?

31. Use the information on page 434 to solve. If a regular work week is 35 hours, how much overtime did Brenda work this week?

CHALLENGE

At the right is the daily time record for the employees of the Wear-Right Factory. Each employee has a $7\frac{1}{2}$-hour workday. Copy and complete the table.

EMPLOYEE TIME RECORD

Employee	Arrive (A.M.)	Depart (P.M.)
Mike Richards	9:00	4:30
Susan Tilson	9:30	▨
John Danton	9:15	▨
Hal Sorenson	▨	4:50
Tina Goldman	▨	5:20

Temperature: Fahrenheit

A. Temperature can be measured on the Fahrenheit scale. It is measured in **degrees Fahrenheit (°F).**

The thermometer at the right shows a temperature of 40 degrees above zero, or 40°F.

If the thermometer read 40 degrees below zero, you would write ⁻40°F.

B. If the temperature falls from 40°F to ⁻40°F, by how many degrees has the temperature fallen?

Think: From 40° to 0° is 40°.
From 0° to ⁻40° is 40°.
40° + 40° = 80°

The temperature has fallen 80°F.

Write the temperature.

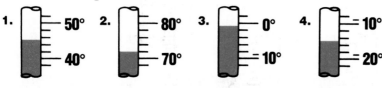

1. 50° / 40°
2. 80° / 70°
3. 0° / 10°
4. 10° / 20°

The thermometer on the right shows:

220° — water boils at 212°F
210°
200°
190°
130°
120°
110°
100° — 98.6°F is normal body temperature
90°
80°
70° — a warm day
60°
50°
40° — water freezes at 32°F
30°
20° — a cold day
10°
0°
⁻10°
⁻20°
⁻30°
⁻40°

Copy and complete the chart.

	Reading	Change	New reading
5.	20°F	rose 18°F	▦
6.	0°F	▦	⁻10°F
7.	42°F	fell 49°F	▦
8.	▦	rose 6°F	1°F

Solve.

9. In her chemistry class, Fran is studying the three physical states of water: gas, liquid, and solid. What is the smallest number of degrees Fran would have to cool steam to turn it into ice?

★10. Miguel buys a new refrigerator. According to the manual, it can cool itself down 5 degrees per minute. If the room temperature is 77 degrees when Miguel first plugs it in, how long will it be before he can make ice?

Temperature: Celsius

A. Temperature can also be measured on the Celsius scale. It is measured in **degrees Celsius (°C)**.

The thermometer at the right shows a temperature of 25 degrees above zero, or 25°C.

If the thermometer read 25 degrees below zero, you would write ⁻25°C.

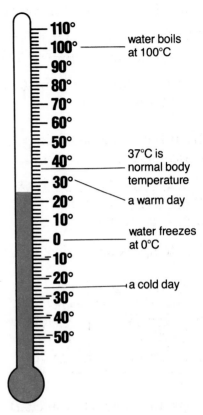

water boils at 100°C

37°C is normal body temperature

a warm day

water freezes at 0°C

a cold day

B. If the temperature rises from ⁻25°C to 25°C, by how many degrees has the temperature risen?

Think: From ⁻25° to 0° is 25°.
From 0° to 25° is 25°.
25° + 25° = 50°

The temperature has risen 50°C.

Write the temperature.

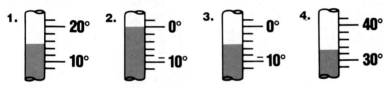

1. 20° 10° **2.** 0° 10° **3.** 0° 10° **4.** 40° 30°

Copy and complete the chart.

	Reading	Change	New reading
5.	28°C	rose 8°C	▨
6.	⁻4°C	▨	11°C
7.	10°C	fell 26°C	▨
8.	▨	fell 17°C	0°C

Solve.

9. Marjorie hears on the weather report that the temperature is 39°C outside. Should she wear a heavy jacket or a bathing suit?

10. The lowest temperature ever recorded in Canada was ⁻63°C. The highest temperature was 45°C. What is the difference in the temperature extremes in that country?

PROBLEM SOLVING
Using a Schedule/Time-Zone Map

A schedule is useful when you are planning a trip. A time-zone map is also helpful. You can use it to find what the time is in different sections of the country or world.

Beth is planning a plane flight from San Francisco, Calif., to Newark, N.J.

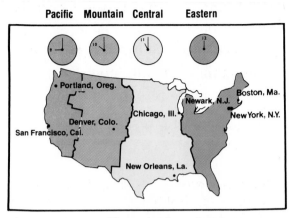

Here is the information you should study on this kind of schedule.

- The main heading tells you where the plane leaves from.
- The capital letters (PST) show the time zone of the city of departure (Pacific Standard Time).
- The subheadings tell you where the plane is flying to.
- The columns show you the time at which each plane leaves, the time at which it arrives, and the flight number.
- The *a* or the *p* after the time shows you whether the time is morning (A.M.) or afternoon (P.M.).

Use the schedule and the time-zone map to answer this question.

Beth decides to take the 12:30 P.M. flight to Newark. At what time will she arrive, and how long will the flight take?

Here is the plane schedule she will use.

Leave	Arrive	Flight
San Francisco, Cal. (PST)		
To		
Newark, N.J.		
6:40a	4:36p	154/210
7:00a	4:36p	674/210
7:00a	6:05p	110/114
7:01a	6:35p	462/210
7:11a	8:11p	122
7:32a	8:11p	708/122
10:05a	8:18p	126/104
10:10a	8:18p	206/104
12:04p	9:55p	488/174
12:05p	9:55p	980/174
12:30p	8:45p	34
1:10p	11:14p	128/220
1:10p	11:14p	128/308
1:20a	11:14p	676/220
1:20a	11:14p	676/308
1:20a	11:14p	300/220
1:20a	11:14p	300/308
10:35p	9:42a	214/256
11:45p	9:42a	574/256
11:55p	9:42a	132/256
12:41a	11:27a	136/258
New Orleans, La.		
7:01a	3:39p	482/616
7:55a	3:49p	748/616

Look at the schedule. The departure time is 12:30 P.M. from San Francisco. The flight arrives in Newark at 8:45 P.M. Now look at the time-zone map. San Francisco is in the Pacific time zone, and Newark is in the Eastern time zone. Eastern time is 3 hours ahead of Pacific time.

You need to convert the arrival time to agree with the time zone of the place of departure. Then subtract to find the difference. When it is 8:45 P.M. in Newark, it is 5:45 P.M. in San Francisco. The flight will begin at 12:30 P.M., Pacific time, and will arrive at 5:45 P.M. Pacific time. The flight will take 5 hours and 15 minutes.

Use the time-zone map to verify each statement. Write either *true* or *false*.

1. Denver, Colo. and New Orleans, La. are in the same time zone.

2. It is 1 hour earlier in Boston than it is in New Orleans.

3. The Mountain time zone and the Eastern time zone are 2 hours apart.

4. As you travel west, each time zone will be 1 hour earlier than the previous one.

Use the time-zone map and the schedules at the right to solve each problem.

5. Beth decides to change her travel plans. She calls her friend Rachael who lives in New York City to arrange to meet her in Chicago, Ill. If it is 11:30 A.M. in San Francisco when Beth calls, what time is it in New York City?

6. Before flying to Chicago, Beth flies to Portland, Oreg. to visit her grandparents. If she wants to arrive in Portland before 7:00 P.M., what is the latest flight she can take from San Francisco?

7. How long is the 5:16 P.M. flight from San Francisco to Portland? Will Beth need to reset her watch when she reaches Portland?

8. In order to fly from Portland, Oreg., to Chicago, Ill., Beth has to change planes in Denver, Colo. She takes the 12:00 noon flight from Portland to Denver. She wants to allow at least 45 minutes between flights. What is the earliest flight she can take from Denver to Chicago?

★9. The 12:00 noon flight from Portland to Denver arrives 21 minutes late. Beth's watch still shows Portland time. What time does it read?

★10. Beth arrives on time in Chicago, Ill., after taking the 5:35 P.M. flight from Denver. If her watch is set to Denver time, what time does it show? How long was the entire trip from Portland to Chicago, including the stopover in Denver?

Leave	Arrive	Flight
San Francisco, Calif. (PST)		
To		
Portland, Me.		
7:32a	8:26p	708/852
8:23a	8:26p	438/376/652
10:05a	8:26p	126/552
Portland, Oreg.		
6:55a	8:27a	184
8:46a	10:20a	1212
12:50p	2:24p	1134
4:05p	5:39p	1278
5:16p	6:48p	1158
6:00p	11:18p	295/1232

Leave	Arrive	Flight
Portland, Oreg. (PST)		
To		
Dallas/ Fort Worth, Texas		
8:10a	3:07p	850/438
11:00a	6:17p	1260/336
12:00n	7:02p	434/340
2:59p	9:44p	298
Denver, Colo.		
6:45a	10:07a	680
8:10a	11:28a	850
12:00n	3:18p	494
2:59p	6:17p	298

Leave	Arrive	Flight
Denver, Colo. (MST)		
To		
Chicago, Ill.		
10:12a	1:28p	26
10:54a	3:08p	576
11:01a	2:15p	916
11:01a	3:50a	482/584
11:04a	2:15p	670
12:55p	4:05p	376
4:00p	7:18p	296
4:09p	8:52p	328
5:35p	8:47p	276
6:57p	11:01p	636
7:15p	10:19p	254
8:35p	11:39p	278

CALCULATOR

Calculators are useful when you have to make many repetitious calculations.

Compute the average for each item for each group of students. Round averages to the nearest whole unit.

GROUP A

Student	Height (in.)	Weight (lb)	Waist (in.)	Sleeve Length (in.)
Sally	58	98	$25\frac{1}{2}$	$23\frac{1}{2}$
Sidney	62	101	26	25
Pat	60	110	26	26
Henry	64	120	29	$27\frac{1}{2}$
Elisha	54	90	$21\frac{1}{2}$	23
Average	▓	▓	▓	▓

GROUP B

Student	Height (in.)	Weight (lb)	Waist (in.)	Sleeve Length (in.)
Paulo	63	100	25	27
Moira	59	94	$23\frac{1}{2}$	23
Claude	66	115	28	$25\frac{1}{2}$
Bette	62	101	$23\frac{1}{2}$	24
Bob	60	105	24	$24\frac{1}{2}$
Average	▓	▓	▓	▓

Which group has the greater average height?
Which group has the greater average weight?
Which group has the wider average waist?
Which group has the greater average sleeve length?

GROUP PROJECT

The Look You Like

The problem: Your classmates are tired of spending too much money on clothes. You decide to hold a contest to come up with a design for inexpensive after-school outfits. Form groups of 4 or 5, and think about a style you would like to create. Use the key facts below to help you decide on a design. To enter the contest, submit a drawing of your design as seen from the front, the back, and the side.

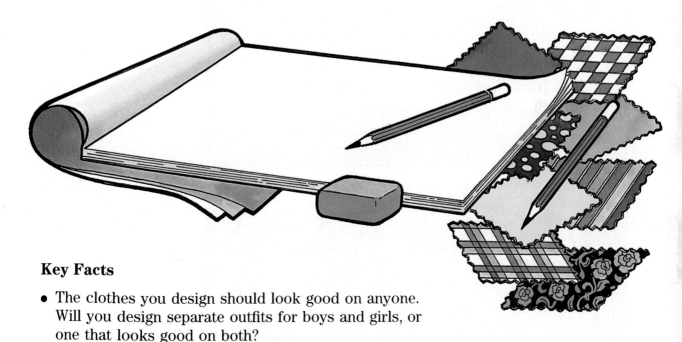

Key Facts

- The clothes you design should look good on anyone. Will you design separate outfits for boys and girls, or one that looks good on both?
- The clothes should look good in many sizes.
- You need to decide how much you will charge for the outfit. Should you charge less for smaller sizes?
- Compare the costs of several kinds of material. Many fabrics are too expensive to use for an economical line of clothing.
- Will a complicated design cost more to produce?
- You'll want to use goods that are made in the United States.
- You may want to design accessories (hats, belts, and ties) as well.
- The entries will be judged on appeal and low cost.

CHAPTER TEST

Multiply. (pages 230, 232, and 238)

1. $\frac{3}{7} \times \frac{2}{3}$ **2.** $\frac{2}{5} \times \frac{1}{4}$ **3.** $\frac{1}{9} \times \frac{9}{10}$ **4.** $\frac{2}{5} \times 100$

5. $63 \times \frac{1}{9}$ **6.** $\frac{1}{6} \times 5\frac{1}{3}$ **7.** $\frac{3}{8} \times 8\frac{2}{3}$ **8.** $4\frac{1}{2} \times 5\frac{1}{3}$

Estimate. (page 234)

9. $\frac{1}{4}$ of 362   **10.** $\frac{2}{3}$ of 597

Divide. (pages 240 and 242)

11. $\frac{1}{4} \div \frac{2}{3}$ **12.** $\frac{5}{12} \div \frac{5}{12}$ **13.** $7\frac{1}{2} \div 3$ **14.** $10\frac{2}{3} \div 4$

15. $\frac{1}{4} \div 1\frac{1}{6}$ **16.** $\frac{3}{4} \div 1\frac{1}{8}$ **17.** $7\frac{1}{8} \div 5\frac{7}{10}$ **18.** $9\frac{5}{8} \div 5\frac{1}{4}$

Measure to the nearest $\frac{1}{16}$ inch. (page 246)

19.

20.

Choose the best estimate. (pages 246 and 250)

21. height of a giraffe   **a.** 17 in.   **b.** 17 ft   **c.** 17 yd

22. length of a scarf   **a.** 4 ft   **b.** 4 yd   **c.** 4 mi

23. a carton of milk   **a.** 1 fl oz   **b.** 1 c   **c.** 1 qt

Complete. (pages 248, 250, and 252)

24. $6\frac{2}{3}$ yd = ▧ ft

25. ▧ in. = $7\frac{5}{6}$ ft

26. ▧ qt = 15 pt

27. 7 gal = ▧ c

28. ▧ oz = $1\frac{1}{2}$ lb

29. 5,000 lb = ▧ T

30. ▧ h = 5 d

31. ▧ d 12 h = 60 h

Compute. (page 252)

32.   11 h 53 min
        $+$ 5 h 16 min

33.   19 min 27 s
        $-$ 4 min 10 s

Copy and complete the temperature chart below.
(pages 254–255)

	Reading	Change	New Reading
34.	13° F	rose 14°	▨
35.	▨	fell 6°	5°C
36.	0°C	▨	⁻8°C
37.	⁻2°C	rose 25°	▨

Solve. (pages 236, 244, and 256)

38. A piece of red velvet measures 380 yards long. A piece of blue satin is $\frac{3}{5}$ as long. Estimate how many yards long the piece of blue satin is.

39. Carla has 67 yards of dress fabric. She needs $4\frac{1}{2}$ yards of fabric to make one dress. How many dresses can Carla make?

40. Pablo, a salesman for the Apex Shirt Company, is flying from New York to Denver on business. His plane takes off from New York at 7:00 A.M. Eastern time. If the flight takes $3\frac{1}{2}$ hours, at what time does the plane land in Denver? (Denver is on Mountain time, which is 2 hours earlier than Eastern time.)

BONUS

Solve.

There is a three-hour time difference between Detroit and Los Angeles. (When it is 1 o'clock in Los Angeles, it is 4 o'clock in Detroit.) Jill lives in Detroit. She called her grandfather in Los Angeles at 4:47 P.M. Detroit time. They talked for 28 minutes. Exactly 3 hours 58 minutes later, Jill's grandfather left for the supermarket. What time was it in Los Angeles when he went to the market?

RETEACHING

To divide with mixed numbers, first write the dividend and the divisor as fractions.

Divide $5\frac{1}{2} \div 1\frac{1}{3}$.

Write fractions for both numbers.	**Multiply by the reciprocal of the divisor.**	**Write the product in simplest form.**
$5\frac{1}{2} \div 1\frac{1}{3} = \frac{11}{2} \div \frac{4}{3}$	$\frac{11}{2} \times \frac{3}{4} = \frac{33}{8}$	$\frac{33}{8} = 4\frac{1}{8}$

Other examples:

$6\frac{1}{5} \div 2 = \frac{31}{5} \div \frac{2}{1} = \frac{31}{5} \times \frac{1}{2} = \frac{31}{10} = 3\frac{1}{10}$

$7\frac{1}{3} \div \frac{3}{4} = \frac{22}{3} \div \frac{3}{4} = \frac{22}{3} \times \frac{4}{3} = \frac{88}{9} = 9\frac{7}{9}$

Divide.

1. $10\frac{1}{3} \div \frac{3}{7}$ **2.** $8 \div 4\frac{1}{2}$ **3.** $8\frac{1}{2} \div 2\frac{3}{7}$ **4.** $5\frac{1}{6} \div \frac{1}{5}$ **5.** $5\frac{2}{3} \div 1\frac{3}{4}$

6. $4\frac{1}{2} \div 5$ **7.** $10\frac{1}{6} \div \frac{5}{6}$ **8.** $1\frac{5}{8} \div \frac{2}{5}$ **9.** $9\frac{3}{5} \div 2\frac{4}{5}$ **10.** $6\frac{8}{9} \div 2\frac{2}{3}$

11. $3\frac{1}{2} \div 1\frac{3}{5}$ **12.** $9\frac{9}{10} \div \frac{3}{5}$ **13.** $3\frac{2}{3} \div 3$ **14.** $4\frac{2}{3} \div 1\frac{3}{5}$ **15.** $7\frac{1}{3} \div \frac{1}{2}$

16. $11\frac{3}{7} \div 6\frac{2}{3}$ **17.** $9\frac{1}{6} \div 1\frac{1}{4}$ **18.** $8\frac{2}{7} \div \frac{7}{8}$

19. $12\frac{5}{9} \div 4\frac{1}{6}$ **20.** $5 \div 2\frac{3}{8}$ **21.** $17\frac{1}{2} \div 6\frac{2}{3}$

22. $5\frac{2}{5} \div 2\frac{1}{10}$ **23.** $4\frac{2}{7} \div 6$ **24.** $8\frac{1}{8} \div 1\frac{2}{3}$

25. $6\frac{1}{3} \div \frac{1}{5}$ **26.** $12\frac{3}{8} \div 1\frac{1}{5}$ **27.** $8\frac{9}{10} \div 1\frac{1}{2}$

28. $18 \div 4\frac{1}{6}$ **29.** $4\frac{2}{3} \div 2\frac{4}{5}$ **30.** $4\frac{1}{10} \div \frac{3}{8}$

ENRICHMENT

Latitude and Longitude

The surface of the globe is divided into measurements called *latitude* and *longitude*. Latitude runs east and west on a map. Longitude runs north and south. When describing a location on a map, latitude is given first, longitude second.

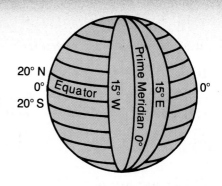

The equator divides Earth into the Northern Hemisphere and the Southern Hemisphere. Latitude is measured in degrees north (*N. lat.*) and degrees south (*S. lat.*) of the equator.

Example: Cairo, Egypt, is located at about 30° north latitude, and 30° east longitude (30°N, 30°E).

The prime meridian begins at the North Pole and ends at the South Pole. It runs through Greenwich, England. Longitude is measured in degrees east (E. long.) and degrees west (W. long.) of the prime meridian.

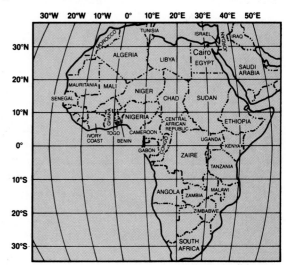

Look at the map of Africa to answer Questions 1–4.

1. Is Chad north or south of the equator?

2. In which country does 10°N intersect 10°E?

3. In which country does 20°N intersect 30°E?

4. In which country does the equator intersect 20°E?

Use an atlas or a globe to find the latitude and longitude of

5. your hometown. ▨° lat. ▨° long.

6. Cleveland, Ohio. ▨° lat. ▨° long.

★7. Auckland, New Zealand.

★8. Quito, Ecuador.

263

CUMULATIVE REVIEW

Write the letter of the correct answer.

1. What is the least common multiple of 3 and 6?

   a. 6   b. 9
   c. 18   d. not given

2. Find the greatest common factor of 24, 36, and 54.

   a. 3   b. 6
   c. 12   d. not given

3. What is the prime factorization of 63?

   a. 63×1 b. $7 \times 3 \times 3$
   c. 7×9 d. not given

4. $\frac{4}{5} = \frac{\blacksquare}{25}$

   a. 5   b. 15
   c. 24   d. not given

5. Choose the simplest form for $\frac{48}{66}$.

   a. $\frac{4}{11}$ b. $\frac{8}{11}$
   c. $\frac{24}{33}$ d. not given

6. Choose the decimal that is equal to $\frac{4}{5}$.

   a. 0.08   b. 0.8
   c. 0.4   d. not given

7. $\frac{2}{5} + \frac{1}{3}$

   a. $\frac{3}{8}$ b. $\frac{11}{15}$
   c. $\frac{11}{20}$ d. not given

8. $0.06\overline{)0.0084}$

   a. 0.0014   b. 0.014
   c. 0.14   d. not given

9. $\$96.60 \div 46$

   a. $2.10   b. $21
   c. 210   d. not given

10. $3.981 \times 1,000$

    a. 39.81   b. 398.1
    c. 3,981   d. not given

11. Round 0.6842 to the nearest hundredth.

    a. 0.68   b. 0.69
    c. 0.7   d. not given

12. $\$57.08 - 38.98$

    a. $18.10   b. $18.96
    c. $21.90   d. not given

13. $1,690 \text{ g} = \blacksquare \text{ kg}$

    a. 0.169   b. 1.69
    c. 16.9   d. not given

14. Miss Jones is making copies of a test she will give her two classes. One class consists of 29 students. There are 34 students in the other class. The test is 2 pages long. How many pages will Miss Jones copy?

    a. 31.5   b. 63
    c. 126   d. not given

15. Greg's recipe calls for $1\frac{1}{3}$ cups flour for each dozen muffins. Greg is making 4 dozen muffins. Is 5 cups of flour enough?

    a. yes   b. no

264

Suppose you wanted to buy a new camera. How much money would a camera that suits your needs cost? How would you earn the money to pay for the camera? Do you walk neighbors' dogs, baby-sit, do yard work, or deliver newspapers?

8 RATIO, PROPORTION, PERCENT

Ratios

A. The *News-Herald* is often called a picture newspaper because it features so many photographs. Alongside a recent article about a senator, the newspaper printed 5 photographs. Of these, 3 were of the senator himself. How does the number of photos of the senator compare to the total number of photos run with the article?

You can use a **ratio** to compare two related numbers. You can express a ratio in different ways.

The ratio of photos of the senator to the total number of photos is $\frac{3}{5}$, or 3 to 5, or 3:5.

Because you are comparing a *part* to the *whole* or *total*, you can also express this ratio as 3 of 5. When you compare numbers in a ratio, be careful to write them in the correct order. If you needed to compare the total number of photos to the photos of the senator, you would write $\frac{5}{3}$, or 5 to 3, or 5:3.

B. You can also use ratio to express a **rate.** The words *per*, *for*, and *each* usually indicate that the comparison being made is a rate.

24 photos *per* roll of film means $\frac{24}{1}$, or 24 to 1, or 24:1.

8 rolls of film developed *for* every 2 hours means $\frac{8}{2}$, or 8 to 2, or 8:2.

192 photos developed *each* 120 minutes means $\frac{192}{120}$, or 192 to 120, or 192:120.

Compare the number of photos used for each article. Write each ratio in two different ways.

PHOTOS IN THE *NEWS-HERALD* JUNE 15

Article title	Number of photos
"Mayor's Press Conference"	2
"New Office Tower"	9
"Wedding Announcements"	3
"Public School System: End of the Year Review"	6
"Flag Day Celebration" (Four-page pullout)	18
"Sports Section"	24

1. "Wedding Announcements" to "Mayor's Press Conference"

2. "New Office Tower" to "Sports Section"

3. "Public School System" to "Flag Day Celebration"

4. "Sports Section" to "New Office Tower"

★5. "Mayor's Press Conference" to total number of photos listed.

Write as a fraction.

6. 2 to 5

7. 12:25

8. 35 miles per hour

9. 10 for $2

Solve.

10. The photography department of the *News-Herald* employs 23 photographers and 5 editors. Write a fraction for the ratio of editors to photographers.

11. The *News-Herald* agrees to pay one photographer $550 for 11 photos from his trip to China. At what rate does the *News-Herald* pay the photographer?

12. Two *News-Herald* staff members photograph a sand-sculpture competition. They take a combined total of 144 shots. Of these, 6 are printed in the paper. Write the ratio of photos taken to photos that appear in the paper.

ANOTHER LOOK

Multiply.

1. $5 \times 3\frac{2}{5}$

2. $8 \times 4\frac{3}{4}$

3. $1\frac{5}{8} \times 7\frac{1}{2}$

4. $3\frac{1}{2} \times 5\frac{3}{4}$

5. $10\frac{1}{4} \times 2\frac{1}{5}$

6. $3\frac{2}{3} \times 3\frac{5}{6}$

7. $10 \times 4\frac{3}{5}$

8. $\frac{3}{8} \times 4$

Equal Ratios

A. As a member of the movie club at the Mr. Video store, Miguel can borrow 1 movie for free every time he rents 3 movies. At the end of the week, he has rented 9 movies. How many movies can he borrow for free?

You can use **equal ratios** to find how many movies he can borrow. Two ratios are equal if they can be written as equivalent fractions.

Write the ratios of borrowed movies to rented ones.

Find equivalent fractions.

borrowed $\longrightarrow$
rented $\longrightarrow$ $\dfrac{1}{3} = \dfrac{n}{9}$ | **Think:** $3 \times 3 = 9.$ | $\dfrac{1}{3} = \dfrac{1 \times 3}{3 \times 3} = \dfrac{3}{9}$

Miguel can borrow 3 movies for free.

B. To help their customers, the staff of the Mr. Video store posts a sign. How many movies does Miguel have to rent to borrow 4 free movies?

Borrow	1	2	3	4
Rent	3	6	9	

$\dfrac{1}{3} = \dfrac{4}{n}$ | **Think:** $1 \times 4 = 4.$ | $\dfrac{1}{3} = \dfrac{1 \times 4}{3 \times 4} = \dfrac{4}{12}$

Miguel has to rent 12 movies.
$\dfrac{1}{3}, \dfrac{2}{6}, \dfrac{3}{9},$ and $\dfrac{4}{12}$ are equal ratios.

C. You can also compare **cross products** to see whether two ratios are equal.

Are $\dfrac{6}{9}$ and $\dfrac{10}{15}$ equal ratios?

Multiply 6×15 and 9×10.

$\dfrac{6}{9} \diagup\!\!\!\!\diagdown \dfrac{10}{15}$ $6 \times 15 = 90$
           $9 \times 10 = 90$

The cross products are equal; so, $\dfrac{6}{9}$ and $\dfrac{10}{15}$ are equal ratios.

Are $\dfrac{7}{8}$ and $\dfrac{4}{12}$ equal ratios?

Multiply 7×12 and 8×4.

$\dfrac{7}{8} \diagup\!\!\!\!\diagdown \dfrac{4}{12}$ $7 \times 12 = 84$
           $8 \times 4 = 32$

The cross products are not equal; so, $\dfrac{7}{8}$ and $\dfrac{4}{12}$ are not equal ratios.

Write the next two equal ratios.

1. $\frac{5}{6}, \frac{10}{12}$ **2.** $\frac{3}{7}, \frac{6}{14}$ **3.** $\frac{9}{12}, \frac{18}{24}$ **4.** $\frac{4}{9}, \frac{8}{18}$

Find the missing value.

5. $\frac{3}{7} = \frac{15}{n}$ **6.** $\frac{1}{n} = \frac{4}{32}$ **7.** $\frac{n}{5} = \frac{32}{40}$ **8.** $\frac{4}{9} = \frac{n}{27}$

Copy and complete.

9.

1	2	4	6	8	10
24	▨	▨	▨	▨	▨

10.

1	4	▨	8	▨	25
▨	12	18	▨	51	▨

Use cross products to see whether the ratios are equal.
Write = or ≠ for ●.

11. $\frac{5}{7} ● \frac{20}{28}$ **12.** $\frac{4}{9} ● \frac{8}{18}$ **13.** $\frac{12}{5} ● \frac{24}{15}$ **14.** $\frac{9}{10} ● \frac{27}{40}$

15. $\frac{3}{13} ● \frac{12}{52}$ **16.** $\frac{8}{14} ● \frac{20}{28}$ **17.** $\frac{6}{8} ● \frac{15}{48}$ **18.** $\frac{18}{24} ● \frac{3}{4}$

Solve.

19. On one Saturday morning, 3 of every 4 movies rented by Mr. Video were cartoons. If Mr. Video rented 24 movies that morning, how many were cartoons?

★20. 1 page of a movie script equals 2 minutes in a movie. Joe's movie script is 87 pages long. How long would the movie made from Joe's script be? To shorten the movie to $2\frac{1}{2}$ hours, how many pages would he have to cut?

FOCUS: REASONING

Help a movie sleuth find clues using this map. She can move along the lines in 4 directions, north (N), east (E), south (S), and west (W). She starts at A and returns to A. Two of the routes are EW and ESWN. Find five more.

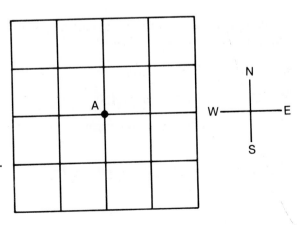

269

PROBLEM SOLVING
Working Backward

If a problem gives you a final result and asks for the original number, you can solve the problem by working backward.

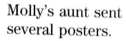

> Molly's aunt sent her several movie posters. She donated half of them to a film club. Molly divided the rest equally among herself and her two friends, Felix and Hector. If Molly's share was 6 posters, how many did her aunt send?

1. Arrange the information given in the problem into ordered steps.

2. Write an equation for each step. Use a different letter for each number you are looking for.

Molly's aunt sent several posters.	Molly gave half to a film club.	She divided half equally among herself and her friends.	She had 6 posters.
n	$n \times \frac{1}{2} = x$	$x \div 3 = y$	$y = 6$

3. Work the problem backward. You can use related sentences to solve each equation.

How many posters did Molly divide equally?
Since $y = 6$
and $x \div 3 = y$,
then $x \div 3 = 6$.
Think: $6 \times 3 = x$.
$18 = x$

How many posters did her aunt send?
Since $x = 18$
and $n \times \frac{1}{2} = x$,
then $n \times \frac{1}{2} = 18$.
Think: $18 \div \frac{1}{2} = n$.
$36 = n$

Molly's aunt sent 36 posters.

Check your answer.

number of posters	that number divided in half	the half divided among three
36	$36 \times \frac{1}{2} = 18$	$18 \div 3 = 6$

The answer is correct.

Work backward. Then, write the letter of the correct answer.

1. The results of the "What's your favorite movie?" poll were printed in the film club's newsletter. *The Empire Strikes Back* received half the votes. *Superman III* received half the remaining votes, and *E.T.* received the remaining 60 votes. How many people answered the poll?

   a. 120   **b.** 240   **c.** 360

2. The entire film club wanted to see a new movie. Two members went to the first show. Of the remaining members, $\frac{1}{2}$ went to the afternoon show. The last 8 members went to the evening show. How many people belong to the film club?

   a. 14   **b.** 16   **c.** 18

Work backward to solve.

3. One afternoon, several members of the film club saw a movie that they liked very much. Each member who saw the movie told 4 other people about it. The next morning, 6 additional people were told about it. That evening, everyone who knew about the film told 1 more person, making a total of 36 people who knew about the film. How many club members originally saw the movie?

4. Felix received some complimentary movie tickets. He gave $\frac{1}{2}$ of them to Hector to give away, plus 2 for Hector to use himself. Felix then gave $\frac{1}{2}$ of what was left to Molly, plus 2 for her own use. Felix then gave 2 tickets to Rita and kept the last 2 for himself. How many complimentary tickets did Felix receive?

★5. In one year, Molly saw twice as many movies as Hector. Hector saw 8 more than Rita. Felix saw 10 fewer than Molly. Rita saw 19 movies. How many movies did each of them see?

★6. Rita, Carlos, Felix, and Molly passed out fliers for the club's film party. Rita passed out $\frac{1}{4}$ of the fliers. Carlos passed out $\frac{1}{2}$ of those left. Felix passed out 8 fliers, and Molly passed out the remaining 4 fliers. How many fliers were there originally?

   a. 24   **b.** 32   **c.** 36

Proportions

A. A television crew used 120 feet of videotape to prepare a 3-minute introduction for an old horror movie. They have 400 feet left with which to prepare a 10-minute preview of the movies to be shown next week. Do they have enough tape?

You can use equal ratios to write a proportion to find the answer.

A **proportion** is an equation that states that two ratios are equal. You can use cross products to determine whether two ratios are equal.

Write ratios. Determine whether they are equal.

$$\text{feet of tape} \longrightarrow \dfrac{120}{3} \diagdown\diagup \dfrac{400}{10} \qquad 120 \times 10 = 1{,}200$$
$$\text{minutes} \longrightarrow \qquad\qquad\qquad 3 \times 400 = 1{,}200$$

The ratios are equal.

So, $\dfrac{120}{3} = \dfrac{400}{10}$ is a proportion.

The television crew has enough tape.

B. You can use cross products to find the missing term in a proportion.

Find n.

$$\dfrac{n}{13} = \dfrac{12}{39}$$
$$n \times 39 = 13 \times 12$$
$$n \times 39 = 156$$
$$n = 156 \div 39$$
$$n = 4$$

Find n.

$$\dfrac{12}{n} = \dfrac{20}{25}$$
$$12 \times 25 = n \times 20$$
$$300 = n \times 20$$
$$300 \div 20 = n$$
$$15 = n$$

Checkpoint Write the letter of the correct answer.

Find the missing term.

1. $\dfrac{1}{4} = \dfrac{n}{48}$ **a.** 4   **b.** 12   **c.** $12\frac{1}{4}$ **d.** 192

2. $\dfrac{3}{5} = \dfrac{6}{n}$ **a.** $2\frac{1}{2}$ **b.** $3\frac{3}{5}$ **c.** 10   **d.** 30

3. $\dfrac{6}{n} = \dfrac{8}{480}$ **a.** 10   **b.** 360   **c.** 640   **d.** 2,880

Is the equation a proportion? Write *yes* or *no*.

1. $\frac{16}{5} = \frac{32}{10}$
2. $\frac{7}{20} = \frac{21}{60}$
3. $\frac{5}{4} = \frac{18}{12}$
4. $\frac{14}{15} = \frac{3}{5}$
5. $\frac{10}{8} = \frac{5}{4}$

6. $\frac{1}{4} = \frac{2}{8}$
7. $\frac{19}{16} = \frac{18}{5}$
8. $\frac{15}{4} = \frac{75}{20}$
9. $\frac{10}{19} = \frac{36}{76}$
10. $\frac{16}{3} = \frac{21}{5}$

11. $\frac{4}{15} = \frac{2}{8}$
12. $\frac{8}{3} = \frac{4}{10}$
13. $\frac{11}{12} = \frac{33}{36}$
14. $\frac{4}{5} = \frac{20}{25}$
15. $\frac{9}{13} = \frac{2}{4}$

16. $\frac{6}{3} = \frac{30}{15}$
17. $\frac{20}{2} = \frac{100}{10}$
18. $\frac{20}{18} = \frac{80}{64}$
19. $\frac{6}{16} = \frac{5}{12}$
20. $\frac{45}{3} = \frac{75}{5}$

Find the missing term.

21. $\frac{2}{3} = \frac{n}{27}$
22. $\frac{8}{72} = \frac{1}{n}$
23. $\frac{2}{6} = \frac{n}{51}$
24. $\frac{n}{3} = \frac{18}{27}$

25. $\frac{4}{7} = \frac{40}{n}$
26. $\frac{5}{3} = \frac{n}{30}$
27. $\frac{13}{6} = \frac{52}{n}$
28. $\frac{4}{n} = \frac{92}{23}$

29. $\frac{2}{3} = \frac{48}{n}$
30. $\frac{25}{n} = \frac{20}{12}$
31. $\frac{10}{n} = \frac{45}{63}$
32. $\frac{40}{n} = \frac{8}{28}$

Solve.

33. A camera crew will often shoot 6 minutes of tape to obtain enough tape for a 30-second commercial. At that rate, how many minutes of tape will it take to shoot a 45-second commercial?

34. A weekly movie program is 150 minutes long. There are 2 minutes of commercials for each 30 minutes of movie. How many minutes of commercials are shown in each broadcast?

35. Copy and complete the table at the right.

TV BROADCAST SCHEDULE

Hours on the air	19	▨	589	6,935
Days	1	7	▨	▨

FOCUS: REASONING

Although some of my friends own bikes, not all of them own ten-speeds. Which of the following statements is false?

a. Not all my friends own bikes.

b. Some of my friends own ten-speeds.

c. All my friends own bikes.

PROBLEM SOLVING
Writing a Proportion

Sometimes you can use a proportion to solve a problem. Peter is a set designer for a local television studio. He wanted to paint the rear stairway of the studio with a special mixture of paint and sand so that people would not slip on the stairs.

Peter created this mixture for his special paint.

4 gallons brown paint   2 pounds sand

2 gallons black paint $\frac{1}{2}$ cup paint thinner

> Peter's mixture yielded 6 gallons. After he had painted the stairway, however, he decided to paint the hallways and steps in other parts of the studio. To do this, Peter will need 9 gallons of paint mixture. To increase the quantity, how much sand should he use?

Peter wants the amount of sand in the new mixture to be in proportion to the amount in the original mixture. To find out how much sand he needs to use, set up a proportion.

Let n = the amount of sand in the new mixture.

amount of sand in
the original mixture $\longrightarrow \dfrac{2}{6} = \dfrac{n}{9} \longleftarrow$ the new mixture
number of gallons $\longrightarrow$ amount of sand in
in the original mixture   number of gallons
in the new mixture

Write the fractions in simplest form.

$$\frac{\overset{1}{\cancel{2}}}{\underset{3}{\cancel{6}}} = \frac{n}{9}$$

Cross multiply. $3n = 9 \times 1$

Solve for n. $3n = 9$

$n = 9 \div 3$

$n = 3$

Peter should use 3 pounds of sand in the new mixture.

Write each percent as a fraction in simplest form.

1. 30%
2. 14%
3. 75%
4. 80%
5. 5%

6. 11%
7. 21%
8. 67%
9. 3%
10. 91%

11. 18%
12. 31%
13. 25%
14. 7%
★15. 119%

Write each percent as a decimal.

16. 18%
17. 37%
18. 24%
19. 68%
20. 94%

21. 2%
22. 8%
23. 6%
24. 9%
25. 1%

26. 86%
27. 7%
28. 19%
29. 4%
★30. 252%

Solve.

31. Jacob enlarges a photo of his dog and ends up with a print 65% larger than the original. Write this as a fraction in simplest form.

32. In his photo lab, Jacob has a work table, 25% of which is taken up by his enlarger. Write a fraction for the part of his work table *not* taken up by the enlarger.

33. Photographs are printed on special, coated paper. A package of 20 sheets of photographic paper costs $6.00. How much does each sheet of paper cost?

★34. One of Jacob's favorite photos is an enlargement of a photo of his father. The enlargement is 150% larger than the original snapshot. Write this as a decimal.

FOCUS: MENTAL MATH

Finding 1%, 10%, or 100% of a number can be done mentally.

Find 1% of 360.

Since 1% = $\frac{1}{100}$, divide by 100.

$360 \div 100 = 3.6$

Find 10% of 360.

Since 10% = $\frac{10}{100} = \frac{1}{10}$, divide by 10.

$360 \div 10 = 36$

Find 100% of 360.

Since 100% = $\frac{100}{100} = 1$, divide by 1.

$360 \div 1 = 360$

Compute mentally.

1. 1% of 420
2. 10% of 420
3. 100% of 420
4. 1% of 387

5. 10% of 387
6. 100% of 387
7. 1% of 46.5
8. 10% of 46.5

Percents for Fractions

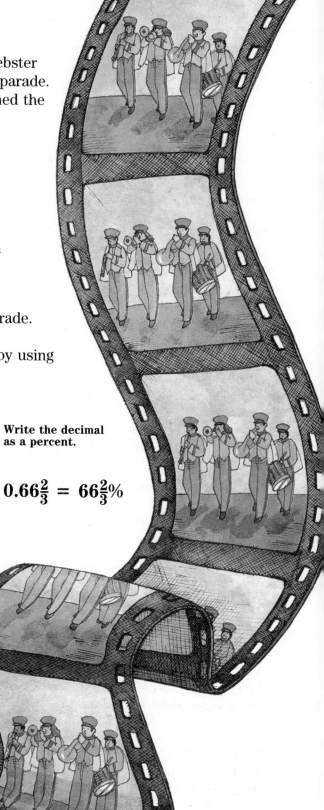

A. On Friday, 12 of the 20 members of the Webster School's photo club took pictures of the local parade. What percent of the club members photographed the parade?

Write the ratio as a fraction.

photographed the parade ⟶ $\dfrac{12}{20}$
all the club members ⟶

Write the fraction as a percent.

Find an equivalent fraction that has a denominator of 100.

$$\frac{12}{20} = \frac{12 \times 5}{20 \times 5} = \frac{60}{100}$$

Write the fraction as a percent.

$$\frac{60}{100} = 60\%$$

60% of the club members photographed the parade.

B. You can also write a fraction as a percent by using division.

Write $\frac{2}{3}$ as a percent.

Divide the numerator by the denominator.

$$\begin{array}{r} 0.66 \\ 3\overline{)2.00} \\ \underline{1\ 8} \\ 20 \\ \underline{18} \\ 2 \end{array}$$

Write the remainder as a fraction.

$$\begin{array}{r} 0.66\frac{2}{3} \\ 3\overline{)2.00} \\ \underline{1\ 8} \\ 20 \\ \underline{18} \\ 2 \end{array}$$

Write the decimal as a percent.

$$0.66\tfrac{2}{3} = 66\tfrac{2}{3}\%$$

$\frac{2}{3}$ is equal to $66\frac{2}{3}\%$.

Another example:

Write $\frac{8}{10}$ as a percent.

$$\begin{array}{r} 0.8 \\ 10\overline{)8.0} \\ \underline{8\ 0} \\ 0 \end{array}$$

$$0.8 = 0.80 = 80\%$$

Write a percent for each fraction.

1. $\frac{2}{25}$ 2. $\frac{8}{10}$ 3. $\frac{6}{20}$ 4. $\frac{7}{50}$ 5. $\frac{9}{36}$ 6. $\frac{7}{35}$

7. $\frac{16}{40}$ 8. $\frac{32}{80}$ 9. $\frac{9}{50}$ 10. $\frac{60}{75}$ 11. $\frac{4}{5}$ 12. $\frac{4}{25}$

13. $\frac{12}{36}$ 14. $\frac{21}{40}$ 15. $\frac{5}{45}$ 16. $\frac{3}{8}$ 17. $\frac{6}{18}$ 18. $\frac{1}{24}$

19. $\frac{4}{32}$ 20. $\frac{6}{13}$ 21. $\frac{7}{8}$ 22. $\frac{45}{80}$ 23. $\frac{5}{35}$ 24. $\frac{42}{80}$

25. $\frac{9}{20}$ 26. $\frac{14}{32}$ 27. $\frac{10}{22}$ 28. $\frac{36}{48}$ 29. $\frac{25}{65}$ 30. $\frac{13}{25}$

31. $\frac{8}{64}$ 32. $\frac{3}{20}$ 33. $\frac{6}{36}$ 34. $\frac{12}{20}$ 35. $\frac{19}{90}$ 36. $\frac{13}{20}$

★37. $\frac{50}{25}$ ★38. $\frac{4}{3}$ ★39. $\frac{60}{24}$ ★40. $\frac{75}{20}$ ★41. $\frac{90}{42}$ ★42. $\frac{25}{5}$

Solve.

43. There were 6 members of the 20-member photo club who could not photograph the parade because they were marching with the school band. What percent of the photo club is also in the school band?

44. At the parade, Jo-Jo photographed an 80-piece marching band. There were 16 trumpet players in the band. What percent of the band is composed of trumpet players?

45. Russ's film has 36 pictures per roll. He used 3 rolls of film at the parade. How many pictures did Russ take?

★46. Abe took 24 pictures of the parade, including 6 pictures of floats. What percent of Abe's pictures do *not* show floats?

CHALLENGE

A baseball player's batting average is really a percent. You can find this percent by dividing the number of hits by the number of times at bat and rounding to the thousandths place.

Times at bat → $84\overline{)28.000}$ ← Batting average ↑ Hits ← 0.333

Before tonight's game, Morris is leading the league with a 0.333 average (28 hits in 84 times at bat). Wolf is second at 0.328 (22 for 67). Tonight, Morris hits 1 for 6, while Wolf hits 1 for 4. What are Morris and Wolf's updated averages? Is Morris still leading the league?

More Practice, page 451

Percent of a Number

A. The Camera Shop received a shipment of 80 cameras. The manager put 50% of them on sale. How many cameras were on sale?

50% of 80 = n

To find the percent of a number, change the percent to a fraction or a decimal. Then multiply.

Rename as a fraction.

$50\% = \frac{50}{100} = \frac{1}{2}$

Rename as a decimal.

$50\% = 0.50$

Multiply.

$\frac{1}{2} \times 80 = 40$

Multiply.

$$\begin{array}{r} 80 \\ \times\, 0.50 \\ \hline 40.00 \end{array}$$

There were 40 cameras on sale.

B. If you know how to find a percent of a number, you can find discounts.

A camera that usually sells for $65 is on sale at a 20% discount. What is the sale price?

Multiply to find the amount of the discount.

$$\begin{array}{r} \$65.00 \\ \times\quad 0.20 \\ \hline \$13.00 \end{array}$$

Subtract the discount from the original price.

$$\begin{array}{r} \$65.00 \\ -\quad 13.00 \\ \hline \$52.00 \end{array}$$

The sale price of the camera is $52.00.

C. To raise money, many cities and states charge consumers a sales tax on items they purchase.

If the sales tax on the camera is 5%, find the total cost.

Multiply to find the sales tax.

$$\begin{array}{r} \$52.00 \\ \times\quad 0.05 \\ \hline \$2.60 \end{array}$$

Add the sales tax to the sale price.

$$\begin{array}{r} \$52.00 \\ +\quad 2.60 \\ \hline \$54.60 \end{array}$$

The total cost of the camera is $54.60.

Find the percent of each number.

1. 5% of 80   **2.** 12% of 16   **3.** 15% of 60   **4.** 35% of 75

5. 70% of 152   **6.** 56% of 130   **7.** 85% of 250   **8.** 98% of 320

Find the amount of each discount.
Then find each sale price.

9. Price: $10.50
Discount: 20%

10. Price: $17.80
Discount: 10%

11. Price: $36
Discount: 15%

12. Price: $84.50
Discount: 40%

13. Price: $375
Discount: 12%

14. Price: $1,150
Discount: 25%

Find the amount of each discount.
Then find each sale price.

15. Price: $3.00
Tax: 4%

16. Price: $4.80
Tax: 5%

17. Price: $16.50
Tax: 6%

18. Price: $35.00
Tax: 7%

19. Price: $76.25
Tax: 8%

20. Price: $110
Tax: 4%

Solve.

21. The Camera Shop had 15 telephoto lenses in stock at the beginning of the month. 12 were sold. What percent of the lenses were sold?

★22. Tom bought a $100 camera at a 10% discount and paid 10% sales tax. Did he spend more than $100 or less than $100?

FOCUS: MENTAL MATH

You can use subtraction to find percents close to 100%.

Find 90% of 160.

Think: 100% of 160 = 160.
        10% of 160 = 16.

| Move the decimal point one place to the left. |

Subtract.

$$\begin{array}{rcl} 100\% &\longrightarrow& 160 \\ -\ \ 10\% &\longrightarrow& 16 \\ \hline 90\% &\longrightarrow& 144 \end{array}$$

90% of 160 is 144.

Compute mentally.

1. 90% of 600   **2.** 90% of 250   **3.** 80% of 380   **★4.** 95% of 460

Finding Percents

A. The Video Salon is having a sale on videocassette recorders (VCRs). The store has 85 VCRs in stock, of which 51 are on sale. What percent of the VCRs are on sale?

What percent of 85 is 51?

Write an equation. Then solve it.

$$n \times 85 = 51$$
$$n = 51 \div 85$$
$$n = 0.6 = 60\%$$

$$\begin{array}{r} 0.6 \\ 85\overline{)51.0} \\ \underline{51\,0} \end{array}$$

60% of the VCRs are on sale.

B. One brand of VCR is sale priced at $360. The original price was $480. What is the percent, or rate, of discount?

Find the amount of discount.

$$\$480 - \$360 = \$120$$

What percent of 480 is 120?

Write an equation. Then solve it.

$$n \times 480 = 120$$
$$n = 120 \div 480$$
$$n = \frac{120}{480} = \frac{1}{4}$$
$$n = 0.25 = 25\%$$

$$\begin{array}{r} 0.25 \\ 4\overline{)1.00} \\ \underline{8} \\ 20 \\ \underline{20} \end{array}$$

Check.

$480	$\times \frac{1}{4} =$	$120
↑	↑	↑
Original price	Rate of discount	Amount of discount

The rate of discount is 25%.

Checkpoint Write the letter of the correct answer.

Find the percent.

1. What percent of 80 is 68?

a. 8.5%
b. 12%
c. 85%
d. 117%

Find the rate of discount.

2. Original price: $60; sale price: $36

a. 4%
b. 6%
c. 40%
d. 60%

Find the percent.

1. What percent of 37 is 3.7?
2. What percent of 55 is 16.5?
3. What percent of 175 is 87.5?
4. What percent of 60 is 9?
5. What percent of 150 is 52.5?
6. What percent of 210 is 88.2?
7. 11.4 is what percent of 19?
8. 20.4 is what percent of 24?
9. 14.52 is what percent of 132?
10. 49.92 is what percent of 52?
★11. 378 is what percent of 315?
★12. 107.5 is what percent of 86?

Find the rate of discount.

13. Sale price: $99
    Original price: $110
14. Sale price $18.99
    Original price: $37.98
15. Sale price: $27
    Original price: $36
16. Sale price: $94.50
    Original price: $135
17. Sale price: $48.75
    Original price: $75
18. Sale price: $135
    Original price: $225
19. Sale price: $47.60
    Original price: $56
20. Sale price: $116.64
    Original price: $162

Solve. For Problem 23, use the Infobank.

21. The Video Salon has a sale. Of the 580 people who attend, 377 make purchases. What percent of all the customers make purchases?

22. The Video Salon offers VCR Model 1330 on an installment plan of $24.95 a month for 16 months. What will its final cost be?

23. Use the information on page 434 to solve. Find the rate of discount for each model. What is the greatest discount? What is the least discount?

★24. T-120 VCR tapes usually sell for $5.00 each. The Video Salon offers packages of 5 for $23.95. At what rate of discount are the tapes in the packages of 5 sold?

ANOTHER LOOK

Find the difference. Write the answer in simplest form.

1. $2\frac{3}{4} - 2\frac{1}{4}$
2. $6\frac{5}{7} - 3\frac{1}{7}$
3. $4\frac{9}{10} - 2\frac{2}{10}$
4. $1\frac{2}{6} - 1\frac{1}{6}$
5. $3\frac{5}{7} - 1\frac{6}{14}$
6. $3\frac{3}{4} - 1\frac{1}{5}$
7. $11\frac{3}{5} - 9\frac{17}{20}$
8. $12 - 8\frac{1}{6}$

More Practice, page 452

Finding the Total Number

The Webster School puts together an exhibition of photographs taken by students in its photo club. 42 of the photographs are photos of wildlife. This is 30% of all the photos in the exhibition. How many photographs are there in the exhibition?

30% of what number is 42?

Write the equation.	$30\% \times n = 42$
Write 30% as a decimal.	$0.30 \times n = 42$
Solve.	$n = 42 \div 0.30$
	$n = 140$

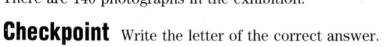

There are 140 photographs in the exhibition.

Checkpoint Write the letter of the correct answer.

1. 20% of what number is 13?

a. 2.6
b. 6.5
c. 65
d. 260

2. 32 is 80% of what number?

a. 4
b. 25.6
c. 40
d. 400

Complete.

1. 10% of what number is 35?
2. 50% of what number is 16?
3. 90% of what number is 117?
4. 70% of what number is 112?
5. 39% of what number is 312?
6. 66% of what number is 66?
7. 90% of what number is 81?
8. 45% of what number is 36?
9. 47% of what number is 235?
10. 26% of what number is 143?
11. 55% of what number is 11?
12. 6% of what number is 9?
13. 5% of what number is 6?
14. 75% of what number is 57?
15. 60% of what number is 150?
16. 20% of what number is 15?
17. 12 is 24% of what number?
18. 12 is 6% of what number?
19. 51 is 34% of what number?
20. 58 is 10% of what number?
21. 7 is 10% of what number?
22. 21 is 28% of what number?
23. 30 is 40% of what number?
24. 24 is 25% of what number?
25. 72 is 48% of what number?
26. 68 is 68% of what number?
★27. $\frac{3}{4}$ is 25% of what number?
★28. $\frac{1}{2}$ is 40% of what number?
★29. 550 is 110% of what number?
★30. 357 is 204% of what number?

Solve.

31. A total of 540 students visit the Webster School's photo club exhibition. This is 72% of all the students in the school. How many students attend the school?

32. There are 140 photos in the exhibition. Ribbons of merit are awarded to 5% of them. How many photos are awarded ribbons?

CALCULATOR

Paul is shopping for a new turntable for his stereo. He finds the model he wants for $109 in New Jersey, where the sales tax is 6%. He sees the same model on sale for $100 in New York, where the sales tax is $8\frac{1}{4}$%. Paul could also have the turntable shipped from New York to New Jersey with a $4.50 charge for shipping and handling but no sales tax. What is the cheapest way for Paul to buy a new turntable?

More Practice, page 452

PROBLEM SOLVING
Using a Circle Graph

A circle graph is a useful way to show data given in percents. Each section of the graph represents a part of the whole (100%). The larger the percent, the larger the section. This circle graph shows the budget for a rock video that the Ringlets are producing.

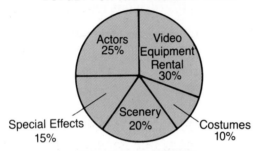

BUDGET FOR THE RINGLETS' VIDEO

Actors 25%
Video Equipment Rental 30%
Special Effects 15%
Scenery 20%
Costumes 10%

Total Budget: $48,000

The size of each section of the graph shows the size of its percent of the whole. Find the part labeled *Special Effects*.

The graph tells you that 15% of the $48,000 budget will be spent for special effects.

Find 15% of $48,000.
Rename 15% as a decimal.
$$15\% = 0.15$$

$$
\begin{array}{r}
\$48{,}000 \\
\times \quad 0.15 \\
\hline
240000 \\
48000 \\
\hline
\$7{,}200.00
\end{array}
$$

The Ringlets plan to spend $7,200 for special effects.

Use the graph to answer each question. Write the letter of the correct answer.

1. Which will cost the most money?

   a. actors   **b.** scenery   **c.** video-equipment rental

2. How much will the video-equipment rental cost?

   a. $1,440   **b.** $14,400   **c.** $144,000

Use the circle graph to answer Questions 3–8.

START-UP COSTS FOR TED'S PHOTOGRAPHY HOBBY

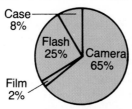

Case 8%
Flash 25%
Camera 65%
Film 2%

Total Cost: $200

3. Which item was Ted's greatest start-up expense?

4. What percent of his start-up costs did Ted use to buy the flash?

5. What percent did Ted use for the camera and the case combined?

6. How much did the film cost?

7. How much more did the flash cost than the case?

8. How much money in all did Ted spend for items other than the camera?

Circle graphs can be used to compare information. Use the three circle graphs below to answer Questions 9–14.

TYPES OF PHOTOS TAKEN BY PHOTOGRAPHY CLUB MEMBERS

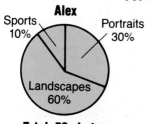

Alex
Sports 10%
Portraits 30%
Landscapes 60%
Total: 50 photos

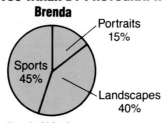

Brenda
Portraits 15%
Sports 45%
Landscapes 40%
Total: 100 photos

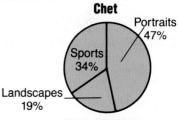

Chet
Portraits 47%
Sports 34%
Landscapes 19%
Total: 200 photos

9. What percent of Brenda's photos were landscape shots?

10. Who took more landscape shots than sports photos and portraits combined?

11. How many landscape shots did Alex take?

12. Who took the greatest percent of portrait photos?

13. Who took the most landscape shots?

14. How many more sports photos did Chet take than Brenda?

PROBLEM SOLVING
Using a Recipe

Dave has a gourmet cooking show. One of his most popular recipes is his chicken recipe.

Lotte and Len watch Dave's cooking show. They decide to use Dave's chicken recipe. They want to make 6 servings. The recipe provides for only 4 servings. How much chicken should Lotte and Len use?

DAVE'S CHICKEN

2 eggs   1½ cup bread crumbs

¼ cup milk   2 tablespoons oil

2 pounds chicken   2 lemons

1 tablespoon basil

Preheat oven to 350°.
Beat eggs and add milk. Dip the chicken into the egg-and-milk mixture.
Mix the basil and bread crumbs. Coat the chicken with bread crumbs.
Place oil in baking dish. Place chicken in dish and bake for 45 minutes
–1 hour, or until tender. Garnish with lemons and serve.

Makes 4 servings. About 250 calories per serving.

You can write a proportion to find the answer. You can use cross products to find the missing term in a proportion.

$$\frac{\text{servings needed} \longrightarrow 6}{\text{servings in recipe} \longrightarrow 4} \underset{\nearrow}{\overset{\searrow}{\times}} \frac{n \longleftarrow \text{amount of chicken needed}}{2 \longleftarrow \text{pounds of chicken in recipe}}$$

$4 \times n = 6 \times 2$
$4 \times n = 12$
$ n = 12 \div 4$
$ n = 3$

Lotte and Len should use 3 pounds of chicken.

Use information from Dave's recipe to solve.

1. Lotte and Len decide to make Dave's chicken again. This time, they want to make enough to serve 10 people. How many eggs will they need?

2. Will increasing the size of the recipe in order to feed 10 people also increase the preparation and cooking time?

3. If the recipe is increased to 12 servings, how many calories will there be per serving?

4. If 18 people are coming to dinner, how much chicken should Lotte and Len use?

5. If Lotte makes 6 servings of Dave's chicken, how much oil will she need?

6. Len buys 5 pounds of chicken. If he wants to make 3 batches of the chicken recipe, will he have enough chicken?

7. Boneless chicken costs $2.38 per pound. If Lotte and Len want to serve Dave's chicken to 12 people, how much will they spend on chicken? How much will they spend if they serve only 6 people?

8. Two slices of bread make about 1 cup of bread crumbs. How many slices of bread would be needed to make bread crumbs for 2 servings of Dave's chicken? for 8 servings?

9. Lotte and Len want to serve Dave's chicken to 16 people. They have only 8 eggs. Will this number be enough to make 16 servings of Dave's chicken?

10. Lotte has 6 lemons. She wants to make 14 servings of Dave's chicken. Will she have enough lemons?

LOGICAL REASONING

Sometimes you can use two statements to reach a new conclusion. But be careful to consider all cases before you reach a conclusion. Drawing a diagram may also help you.

> STATEMENTS: Mariano belongs to the hobby club. Every member of the stamp club belongs to the hobby club.
> CONCLUSION: Mariano belongs to the stamp club.

Think: Could the conclusion be **incorrect?**

1. If so, Mariano belongs to the hobby club, but *not* to the stamp club.

2. The statements do *not* say that every member of the hobby club is a member of the stamp club.

So, the conclusion is incorrect.

Write which conclusions are *correct* and which are *incorrect.*

1. STATEMENTS: All seventh graders take a foreign language. Jan and Ramon are seventh graders.
CONCLUSION: Jan and Ramon take a foreign language.

2. STATEMENTS: There was rain every Saturday in April. It rained on April 8.
CONCLUSION: April 8 was a Saturday.

3. STATEMENTS: Every train that left after 8:00 was late. Mr. Avery's train left at 7:30.
CONCLUSION: Mr. Avery's train was not late.

4. STATEMENTS: Every bouquet of flowers had carnations. Every red flower was a rose. Every bouquet had a red flower.
CONCLUSIONS: Every carnation was red. Every bouquet had a rose.

GROUP PROJECT

The Case of the Disappearing Diamond

Read the mystery below. Form teams of detectives in your class. See which team can crack the code, read the clues, and solve the case first.

Rikkie Smythe held a birthday party for her daughter, Alberta, and invited Alberta's friends, Paula, Jack, Carey, and Jamie. Alberta received many presents. Rikkie gave her a diamond pin, and Alberta put it on her sweater. Alberta's dog Bruno jumped up and gave her a sloppy kiss.

The party was fun for all. They ate pizza and drank fruit punch. Then they played charades. Paula took pictures with her instant camera. Paula was taking a picture of Jamie and Alberta near the punch bowl when Alberta suddenly screamed. Her diamond pin was missing!

They searched the house but couldn't find the pin. Rikkie called the police. Detective Christopher Wise arrived and questioned everyone carefully. Then he noticed the last picture that Paula had taken. In the excitement, everyone had forgotten it. He studied the photo and then announced: "I know where the diamond pin is."

How did he know, and where was the diamond pin?

Code

The first 17 letters of the alphabet have been replaced by 2-digit numbers. The other 9 letters are 1-digit numbers.

(HINT: Disappearing Diamond = 23-18-8-26-11-11-22-26-9-18-13-20   23-18-26-14-12-13-23)

Clues

- 26-15-25-22-9-7-26   8-7-18-15-15   19-26-23 7-19-22   11-18-13   26-21-7-22-9 24-19-26-9-26-23-22-8.
- 25-9-5-13-12   13-22-5-22-9   7-12-6-24-19-22-23 7-19-22   11-18-13.
- 7-19-22   11-19-12-7-12   4-26-8   12-21 17-26-14-18-22   13-22-26-9   7-19-22 11-6-13-24-19   25-12-4-15.

CHAPTER TEST

Write each ratio in two different ways. (page 266)

1. 1 to 3

2. 2:7

3. $\frac{9}{4}$

4. 14 out of 15

Write the next two equal ratios. (page 268)

5. $\frac{8}{7}, \frac{16}{14}$

6. $\frac{9}{5}, \frac{18}{10}$

7. $\frac{5}{3}, \frac{10}{6}$

8. $\frac{7}{2}, \frac{14}{4}$

Find the missing term. (page 272)

9. $\frac{5}{19} = \frac{10}{n}$

10. $\frac{7}{4} = \frac{n}{40}$

11. $\frac{23}{3} = \frac{92}{n}$

12. $\frac{n}{2} = \frac{70}{28}$

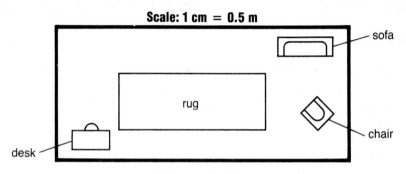

Scale: 1 cm = 0.5 m

Measure the above drawing and find the actual dimensions of the following. (page 276)

13. the sofa

14. the desk

15. the rug

Write as a percent. (page 280)

16.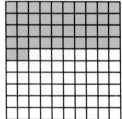

17. 62:100

18. $\frac{34}{100}$

19. 0.9

Write as a fraction in simplest form. (page 282)

20. 97%

21. 60%

22. 36%

Write as a decimal. (page 282)

23. 16%

24. 64%

25. 61%

Write as a percent. (page 284)

26. $\frac{13}{50}$ **27.** $\frac{36}{80}$ **28.** $\frac{5}{24}$ **29.** $\frac{21}{75}$

Find the percent of each number. (page 286)

30. 40% of 250   **31.** 64% of 50   **32.** 14% of 350   **33.** 25% of 60

Complete. (pages 288 and 290)

34. What percent of 70 is 28?

35. What percent of 56 is 42?

36. 35% of what number is 7?

37. 12% of what number is 39?

Solve. (pages 274, 292, and 294)

38. Caroline directs a weekly TV show. The proportion of advertising time to regular air time is 3:16. If the show is 60 minutes long, how much time is devoted to advertising?

39. Jim uses 2 cups chopped vegetables to make vegetable soup for 3 people. How much chopped vegetables should he use to make soup for 7 people?

40. How much money does the Sumino High video club spend on film? on equipment? on rental fees?

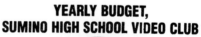

**YEARLY BUDGET,
SUMINO HIGH SCHOOL VIDEO CLUB**

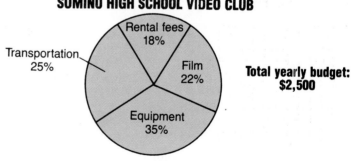

Total yearly budget:
$2,500

BONUS

Solve.

The weather service in Patterson reported that 40% of the 365 days last year were cloudy. Of that 40%, 50% of the days had rain. How many days in Patterson last year were cloudy and without rain?

RETEACHING

A. Find 20% of 60.

To find the percent of a number, write the percent as a fraction or as a decimal. Then multiply.

Write as a fraction.

$20\% = \frac{20}{100} = \frac{1}{5}$

$\frac{1}{5} \times 60 = 12$

20% of 60 is 12.

Write as a decimal.

$20\% = 0.20$

$$\begin{array}{r} 60 \\ \times\, 0.20 \\ \hline 12.00 \end{array}$$

B. What percent of 75 is 30?

Write an equation. Then solve it.

$n \times 75 = 30$

$\qquad n = 30 \div 75$

$\qquad n = 0.4 = 40\%$

40% of 75 is 30.

Find the percent of each number.

1. 10% of 90
2. 20% of 80
3. 50% of 30
4. 25% of 76

5. 75% of 48
6. 5% of 60
7. 16% of 50
8. 34% of 200

9. 10% of 65
10. 9% of 10
11. 44% of 20
12. 99% of 50

13. 58% of 25
14. 32% of 85
15. 15% of 92
16. 1% of 5

Find the percent.

17. What percent of 50 is 45?
18. What percent of 40 is 10?

19. What percent of 25 is 15?
20. What percent of 100 is 5?

21. What percent of 60 is 18?
22. What percent of 96 is 24?

23. What percent of 75 is 30?
24. What percent of 60 is 54?

25. 28.8 is what percent of 36?
26. 11.5 is what percent of 46?

27. 54.6 is what percent of 84?
28. 38.4 is what percent of 96?

29. 25 is what percent of 62.5?
30. 38 is what percent of 47.5?

31. 45 is what percent of 150?
32. 75 is what percent of 60?

ENRICHMENT

Computing With Commission

The Millburn Camera Club is raising money to buy new equipment. They are selling cards for $4.50 per box. The company that makes the cards offers two methods of payment. They will pay each person who sells the cards $3.65 per hour, or they will pay the camera club a commission of 30% for each box of cards sold. A **commission** is a percent of the money earned, paid to the seller for each item that is sold.

The club decides to sell the cards over a trial weekend to see which method earns the most money.

Use this information to answer each question.

1. Billie and Jake sell the cards at the Oak-Grove shopping mall. Billie is paid $3.65 an hour and works for 5 hours. Jake is paid 30% of the price of each box of cards he sells. He sells 20 boxes in 5 hours.

   Who earned more money, Billie or Jake?
   Who earned more per hour?

2. Twelve camera club members worked over the weekend at the hourly rate. They each worked 7 hours. Twelve other club members sold the cards for the 30% commission. They sold 214 boxes of cards in a combined total of 84 hours.

   Which group earned more money—the hourly rate group or the commission group?
   Which group earned more money per hours worked?

   If you were in the camera club, which method of payment would you choose?
   Why?

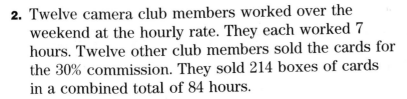

TECHNOLOGY

This LOGO procedure draws a triangle.

TO TRIANGLE
REPEAT 3 [FD 40   RT 120]
END

The REPEAT 3 command causes the turtle to repeat
the commands shown in the brackets 3 times.
The FD 40 command causes the turtle to move forward
40 steps. The RT 120 command tells the turtle to turn
120° to the right.

You can use more than one REPEAT statement in a
LOGO procedure. This procedure draws a row of
triangles.

TO TRIANGLEROW
REPEAT 4 [REPEAT 3 [FD40   RT 120] PU RT 90 FD 40 LT 90 PD]
END

The second REPEAT statement is inside the brackets
that enclose the first REPEAT statements. The second
REPEAT statement is the one that actually draws the
triangles. The turtle carries out that statement. Then it
obeys the commands that follow the second REPEAT
statement. It performs this entire procedure 4 times.

1. Write a procedure that will draw one large square
   divided into 4 equal parts. Use the REPEAT
   statement.

2. Follow the procedure to finish this picture.

TO SQUAREAROUND
REPEAT 8 [REPEAT 4 [FD 40   RT 90] RT 45]
END

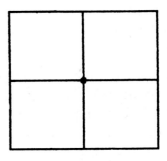

3. This procedure draws a line of triangles.
Draw them.

TO ROW
RT 30
REPEAT 6 [REPEAT 3 [FD 40   RT 120] RT 60   FD 40   LT 60]
END

4. Rewrite the procedure from Problem 3 so that it
draws this figure instead.

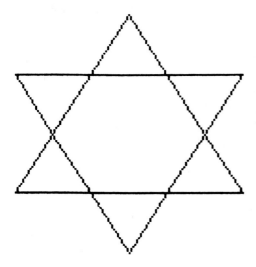

CUMULATIVE REVIEW

Write the letter of the correct answer.

1. $\frac{4}{9} \times \frac{3}{5}$

  a. $\frac{4}{15}$ **b.** $\frac{7}{14}$

  c. $\frac{12}{15}$ **d.** not given

2. $1\frac{1}{4} \div \frac{1}{4}$

  a. $\frac{5}{16}$ **b.** $\frac{5}{4}$

  c. 5   **d.** not given

3. Which unit would you use to weigh a letter?

  a. ounce   **b.** pound

  c. ton   **d.** not given

4. 15 qt = ■ pt

  a. 3   **b.** $7\frac{1}{2}$

  c. 60   **d.** not given

5. Measure to the nearest $\frac{1}{16}$ in.

  ————————

  a. $\frac{3}{16}$ in.   **b.** $1\frac{3}{16}$ in.

  c. $1\frac{4}{16}$ in.   **d.** not given

6. 8 y 6 mo − 4 y 10 mo

  a. 3 y 8 mo   **b.** 4 y 4 mo

  c. 4 y 8 mo   **d.** not given

7. $1\frac{4}{5} - \frac{2}{3}$

  a. $\frac{7}{8}$ **b.** $1\frac{2}{15}$

  c. 2   **d.** not given

8. $\frac{6}{10} + \frac{2}{5}$

  a. $\frac{8}{10}$ **b.** 1

  c. $1\frac{2}{10}$ **d.** not given

9. 73.6 ÷ 100

  a. 0.0736   **b.** 0.736

  c. 7.36   **d.** not given

10. Choose the best unit of measure for weighing a toothbrush.

  a. milligrams   **b.** grams

  c. kilograms   **d.** not given

11. Use short division: $6\overline{)354}$.

  a. 59   **b.** 62 R2

  c. 590   **d.** not given

12. What is the product of 5^4?

  a. 20   **b.** 125

  c. 625   **d.** not given

13.   36.72
    − 17.05

  a. 18.77   **b.** 19.67

  c. 53.77   **d.** not given

14. At the start of the school year, Jerry was 64 cm tall. At the end of the year, he was 72 cm tall. How many centimeters did he grow? To solve this problem, you must

  a. add.   **b.** subtract.

  c. multiply.   **d.** not given.

15. Rose is 5 feet tall. She wants to find out her height in inches. There are 12 inches in 1 foot. Which operation should Rose use?

  a. addition   **b.** multiplication

  c. division   **d.** not given

The Great Pyramid of Khufu is outside Cairo, Egypt. It is the only one of the Seven Wonders of the Ancient World still standing. One of the reasons for this is the triangular shapes of its sides. Triangular structures are often used in buildings because they add strength and stability. Find examples of triangular shapes in buildings or structures in your area.

9 GEOMETRY

Basic Ideas Of Geometry

The word **geometry** comes from ancient words that mean "earth" and "to measure." In studying geometry, an understanding of these ideas will be helpful:

A **point** is an exact location in space. It is named by a capital letter.	**Point** P, or P •P
A **line** is a straight path of points that continues infinitely in two directions. A line is named by any two points on it.	**Line** AB, or $\overleftrightarrow{AB}$
A **ray** is a part of a line that begins at an **endpoint** and continues infinitely in one direction. It is named by its endpoint and any other point on it.	**Ray** CD, or $\overrightarrow{CD}$
A **line segment** is part of a line that begins at one point and ends at another point. It is named by its two endpoints. Two line segments of equal length are **congruent.**	**Line segment** EF, or $\overline{EF}$
An **angle** is a figure formed by two different rays that have the same endpoint. Each ray is called a **side** of the angle. The endpoint for both rays is called the **vertex.** An angle is named by its vertex or by three points with the vertex in the middle. Two angles with the same measurement are congruent.	**Angle** Y, **angle** XYZ, **angle** ZYX, or $\angle Y$, $\angle XYZ$, $\angle ZYX$
A **plane** is a flat surface. It continues infinitely in all directions. It is usually named by a small letter.	**Plane** m

Refer to the figure at the right to answer Exercises 1–6.

1. Name five points on the same line.
2. Name three rays with endpoint *D*.
3. Name five line segments with endpoint *F*.
4. Name one line.
5. Name six angles with vertex *B*.
6. Name three line segments on $\overrightarrow{FE}$.

Draw and label a figure for each.

7. $\overleftrightarrow{PQ}$ 8. $\overline{MN}$ 9. $\overrightarrow{AB}$ 10. $\angle CAB$ 11. plane *s*

12. $\overleftrightarrow{RS}$ 13. $\angle X$ 14. point *P*   15. $\overline{OP}$ 16. $\angle QRS$

Write the letter of the correct answer.

a. line   **b.** angle   **c.** line segment   **d.** ray   **e.** plane   **f.** point

17. I am sometimes identified by my vertex.

18. I cannot continue infinitely. I am named by my endpoints.

19. I continue infinitely in one direction.

20. I continue infinitely in two directions.

21. I am flat and continue infinitely in all directions.

22. I am an exact location in space.

ANOTHER LOOK

Divide.

1. $3.1\overline{)27.59}$ 2. $4.4\overline{)37.4}$ 3. $0.5\overline{)9.5}$ 4. $0.16\overline{)64}$ 5. $0.2\overline{)16.7}$

6. $0.29\overline{)153.7}$ 7. $0.8\overline{)2.8}$ 8. $1.5\overline{)8.79}$ 9. $0.006\overline{)0.504}$ 10. $0.01\overline{)0.125}$

11. $0.016\overline{)3.98}$ 12. $0.004\overline{)36}$ 13. $3.6\overline{)14.85}$ 14. $24\overline{)0.48}$ 15. $35\overline{)0.875}$

Angles

A. More than 4,000 years ago, Egyptian architects designed the Great Pyramids. Their knowledge of angles helped them build these structures. The pyramids are still one of civilization's great achievements.

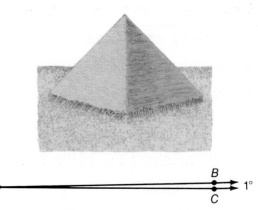

Angles are measured in **degrees** (°). ∠BAC measures 1°.

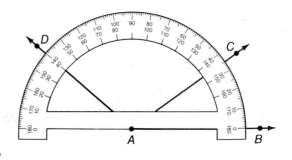

You can classify angles by their measures.

| **straight angle** | **right angle** | **obtuse angle** | **acute angle** |

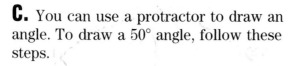

measures 180°   measures 90°   measures more than 90° but less than 180°   measures less than 90°

B. You can use a **protractor** to measure an angle.

1. Place the center of the protractor on the vertex of the angle.

2. Place the edge of the protractor so that one side of the angle crosses the zero mark on one of the scales.

3. Read the measure of the angle where the other side crosses the same scale.

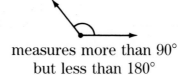

4. ∠CAB measures 35°. ∠DAB measures 140°.

C. You can use a protractor to draw an angle. To draw a 50° angle, follow these steps.

1. Draw $\overrightarrow{XY}$.

2. Place the center of the protractor on X. Make sure the zero mark of one scale is on $\overrightarrow{XY}$.

3. Find the 50° mark on the same scale, and draw point Z.

4. Draw $\overrightarrow{XZ}$.

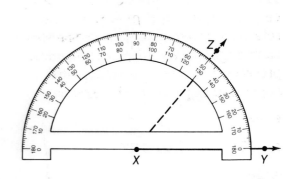

Refer to the figure to answer Exercises 1–4.

1. Name six acute angles.

2. Name two obtuse angles.

3. Name five right angles.

4. Name one straight angle.

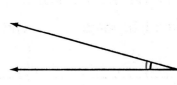

Use a protractor to measure each angle.

5.

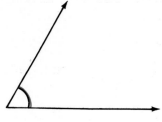

6.

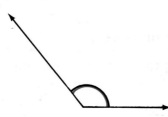

7.

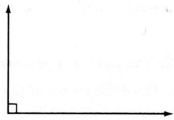

8.

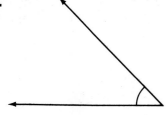

9.

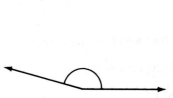

10.

Use a protractor to draw each angle.

11. 45°   12. 120°   13. 70°   14. 130°

15. 165°   16. 52°   17. 68°   18. 180°

FOCUS: ESTIMATION

This protractor shows the location of certain important angles. Use it as a reference to estimate the measure of each angle below. Do *not* use a real protractor. Write the name of the angle that matches each measure.

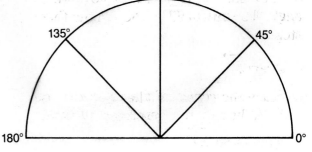

1. 48°   2. 85°

3. 125°   4. 140°

5. 20°

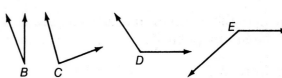

More Practice, page 453

Perpendicular and Parallel Lines

A. One of the Seven Wonders of the Ancient World was the marble Temple of Artemis. It had 106 columns around a base that was larger than a football field. To make sure that the columns were parallel was a great challenge to the builders.

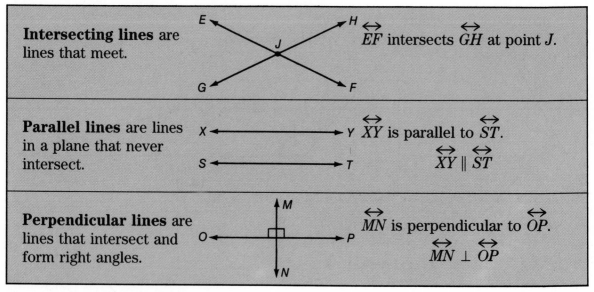

Intersecting lines are lines that meet.	$\overleftrightarrow{EF}$ intersects $\overleftrightarrow{GH}$ at point J.
Parallel lines are lines in a plane that never intersect.	$\overleftrightarrow{XY}$ is parallel to $\overleftrightarrow{ST}$. $\overleftrightarrow{XY} \parallel \overleftrightarrow{ST}$
Perpendicular lines are lines that intersect and form right angles.	$\overleftrightarrow{MN}$ is perpendicular to $\overleftrightarrow{OP}$. $\overleftrightarrow{MN} \perp \overleftrightarrow{OP}$

B. You can use a **compass** and a **straightedge** to construct perpendicular lines.

1. Draw a line, and label a point P. Place the point of the compass at P, and make marks on both sides of P. Label the points A and B.

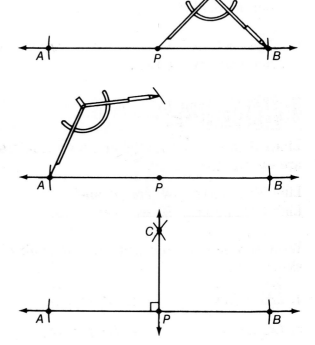

2. Open the compass wider. Place the compass point on A. Draw a mark above the line. Use the same compass opening, and repeat this for point B.

3. Label the point where the two marks intersect C. Draw $\overleftrightarrow{CP}$. $\overleftrightarrow{CP} \perp \overleftrightarrow{AB}$

Write *parallel* or *intersecting* to describe each pair
of lines.

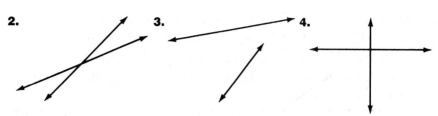

Write *perpendicular* or *not perpendicular* to describe
each pair of lines.

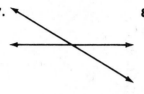

Refer to the figure at the right to answer Exercises 9–12.

9. Name two pairs of parallel lines.

10. Name two pairs of perpendicular lines.

11. Name eight right angles.

12. Name six pairs of intersecting lines that are not
perpendicular.

13. Draw a line. Construct a line perpendicular to the
line you have drawn.

CHALLENGE

Lines that are not parallel and do not intersect
are called **skew lines.**

Line *MN* and line *OP* are parallel.
Line *OQ* and line *NP* are skew lines.

Write *yes* or *no* to tell whether each pair of lines are
skew lines.

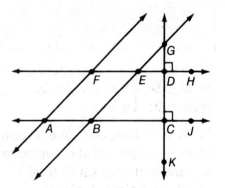

1. $\overleftrightarrow{MO}$ and $\overleftrightarrow{NP}$
2. $\overleftrightarrow{OP}$ and $\overleftrightarrow{TR}$
3. $\overleftrightarrow{RT}$ and $\overleftrightarrow{MO}$
4. $\overleftrightarrow{ST}$ and $\overleftrightarrow{OP}$
5. $\overleftrightarrow{OQ}$ and $\overleftrightarrow{ST}$
6. $\overleftrightarrow{NT}$ and $\overleftrightarrow{OQ}$
7. $\overleftrightarrow{QR}$ and $\overleftrightarrow{ST}$
8. $\overleftrightarrow{QS}$ and $\overleftrightarrow{PR}$

PROBLEM SOLVING
Drawing a Picture

Sometimes you may have trouble understanding a problem. Drawing a picture can often help you understand the problem and find a solution.

A group of archeologists mapped some ruins in an ancient forum. The forum is a square that measures 150 feet on a side. The archeologists entered the forum through a gate in the exact center of one side. They walked along a path straight toward the opposite side for 80 feet until they reached a temple. At the temple, they turned left and walked 60 feet to an amphitheater. They turned left again and walked 45 feet to a villa. At the villa, they turned left and walked back to their original path from the gate. Then they turned right and walked back to the gate. How many feet did they walk from the villa to the gate?

Draw a picture.

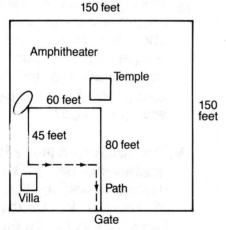

You can see from your picture that the archeologists walked 60 feet to go from the villa back to the path. Since they had already walked back 45 of the 80 feet of the path, they had to walk only 35 feet after they returned to the path in order to reach the gate.

To find the total, add. 60 + 35 = 95

They walked 95 feet from the villa to the gate.

Write the letter of the drawing you would use to solve
each problem.

1. Jan is exploring a temple. The
temple is a rectangle that measures
50 feet by 30 feet. The long sides of
the temple face north and south. Jan
enters the exact center of the south
side and walks 20 feet north to label
a column. She then walks 15 feet
east to label another column. How
far is she from the eastern side of
the temple?

2. Jan starts at the exact center of the
temple. She walks 5 feet to the
west, where she finds an artifact.
She then walks 8 feet to the south,
where she finds some ancient coins.
Then she walks 1 foot east and 11
feet north to the altar stone. How
far is the altar stone from the
northern side of the temple?

A.

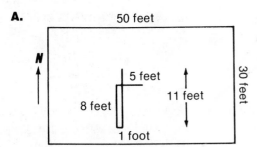

B.

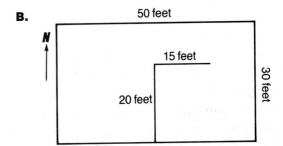

Draw a picture, and solve each problem.

3. A temple has 8 columns along one
side. Each column is 3 feet wide, and
they are spaced 7 feet apart. The
columns at each end of the row are
12 feet from the edges of the temple.
How wide is the temple?

4. The front steps of a villa extend 20
feet from the wall of the building.
There is a statue 15 feet from the
bottom step. The statue is 4 feet
wide. A path is 24 feet from the
statue. How far is the path from the
wall of the villa?

5. An archeologist is searching the
inside of a pyramid. Entering the
pyramid at ground level, he walks
4.5 m straight into the pyramid. The
passage then rises for 3 m and then
is straight for 5.5 m. Suddenly, the
passage drops 1 m and then opens
into a chamber. How far above
ground level is the chamber?

★6. The Senate Forum is a building that
has two extensions. The central
building is a square that measures
90 feet on a side. On the west side,
there is an extension that measures
40 feet by 30 feet. The extension on
the south side measures 50 feet by
50 feet. Add the lengths of all the
sides to find the distance around
the Senate Forum.

Triangles

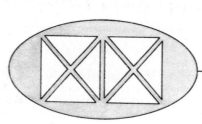

A. If you stand close to the Eiffel Tower, you can see how the tower's huge iron structure consists of hundreds of triangles. The unique design helps make the tower an unmistakable landmark in Paris.

A triangle can be named according to the lengths of its sides.

equilateral triangle

2 cm 2 cm
2 cm

All sides
are congruent.

isosceles triangle

3 cm 3 cm
2 cm

At least two sides
are congruent.

scalene triangle

5 cm
4 cm
2 cm

No sides
are congruent.

B. A triangle can be named according to the measures of its angles.

acute triangle

60°
80°
40°

three acute angles

right triangle

40°
90° 50°

one right angle

obtuse triangle

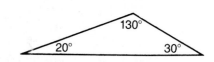

130°
20° 30°

one obtuse angle

C. If you were to make a drawing of a triangle, you could cut off the three angles and put them together to form a straight angle. **The sum of the measures of the angles of a triangle is 180°.**

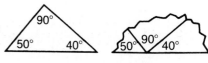

90°
50° 40°

50° 90° 40°

If you know the measures of two angles in a triangle, you can find the measure of the third angle.

Find the measure of $\angle A$.
The measure of $\angle A + 75° + 55° = 180°$.
The measure of $\angle A + 130° = 180°$.
The measure of $\angle A = 180° - 130°$.
The measure of $\angle A = 50°$.

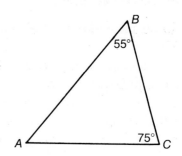

B
55°
A
75° C

Name each triangle according to the lengths of its sides.

1.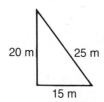

2.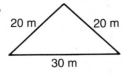

3.

Name each triangle according to the measures of its angles.

4.

5.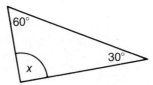

6.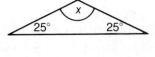

Find the measure of the missing angle.

7.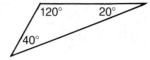

8.

9.

★**10.** Find each missing angle.

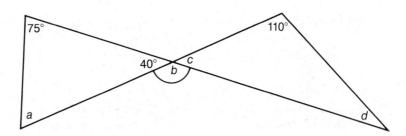

FOCUS: REASONING

Label these statements *true* or *false*.

1. Some isosceles triangles are equilateral triangles.
2. All right triangles are acute triangles.
3. No scalene triangles are right triangles.
4. No equilateral triangles are scalene triangles.

Use the words *some*, *none (no)*, and *all* to write five more true statements about triangles.

PROBLEM SOLVING
Practice

Professor Twilley is planning an archeological expedition. The circle graph shows her projected yearly budget.

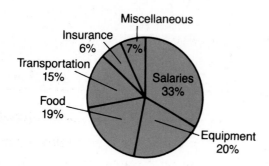

Using information from the graph, choose between estimating or finding the exact answer. Write *estimate* or *exact*.

1. About what fraction of the entire budget is used for salaries?

2. How much does insurance for the year cost?

Write the letter of the correct proportion.

3. Jane needs recipes for the expedition. Her cornbread recipe serves 6 people. It calls for 2 eggs and 1 cup milk. To serve 18 people, how many eggs will Jane need?

a. $\frac{6}{18} = \frac{n}{2}$ **b.** $\frac{2}{18} = \frac{n}{6}$ **c.** $\frac{2}{6} = \frac{n}{18}$

4. Jane's French-bread recipe calls for 6 cups of flour. Each bag of flour contains 12 cups of flour. How many servings of bread can be made from each bag of flour?

a. $\frac{6}{2} = \frac{12}{n}$ **b.** $\frac{2}{6} = \frac{12}{n}$ **c.** $\frac{2}{12} = \frac{n}{6}$

Solve. Write a simpler problem if necessary.

5. Professor Twilley found that a set of digging tools costs $45.25 at one store and $33.75 at another store. She must buy 12 sets of tools. How much money will she save by buying at the second store?

6. Professor Twilley found out that the price of insurance is 1.8% higher than the expected price. If the expected price was $50,000, how much will the insurance actually cost?

Use the map at the right to solve.

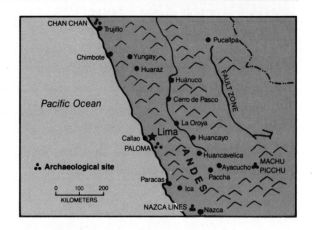

7. How far apart are the archeological sites at Paloma and Nazca?

8. How far apart are the sites at Chan Chan and Paloma?

9. How far apart are the cities of Lima and Paracas?

Solve. Use the circle graph if you need to.

10. The archeologists made a drawing of an ancient house that they excavated. The scale of the drawing was 1:8. On the drawing, the dimensions of the house are height, $1\frac{1}{2}$ feet; length, $3\frac{1}{2}$ feet; width, 2 feet. What were the dimensions of the actual house?

11. An archeologist made a drawing of a temple that he believes once stood on a certain site. The scale of the drawing is 2 feet to 4 meters. On the drawing, the dimensions of the temple are height, $3\frac{1}{2}$ feet; length, 2 feet; width, $1\frac{1}{2}$ feet. What were the dimensions of the actual temple?

12. It cost $1,200 to transport each of the 46 employees to the dig site. It cost $120,000 to ship supplies and equipment to the site. If the entire budget was $1,400,000, how much is left in the transportation budget?

13. If 83% of the transportation budget has already been spent and the entire budget was $1,400,000, is there enough money left in the transportation budget to buy 2 land rovers that cost $5,000 each?

★14. The original budget was planned for 46 people. Professor Twilley found that she needed to hire 14 more employees. If the entire budget is $1,400,000, by what percent should she increase the salary budget to pay the new employees the same salaries earned by the original employees?

★15. A large number of artifacts have been uncovered. The university will take 30% of the profits, the museum will take 25%, private investors will take 15%, and the professor will take the rest. If the total profit was $250,000, how much will each party receive? What percent of the profits will Professor Twilley receive?

Quadrilaterals

The Lighthouse of Alexandria is considered to be one of the Seven Wonders of the Ancient World. Its light was visible for hundreds of miles and guided ships into the harbor for more than 1,000 years. The sides of the lighthouse were covered with quadrilateral shapes.

A **quadrilateral** is a figure that has four sides. Some quadrilaterals have special names.

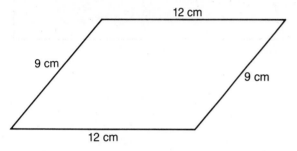

A **parallelogram** has two pairs of parallel sides and two pairs of congruent sides.

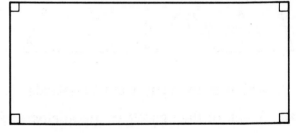

A **rhombus** is a parallelogram that has four congruent sides.

A **rectangle** is a parallelogram that has four right angles.

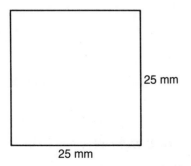

A **square** is a rectangle that has four congruent sides.

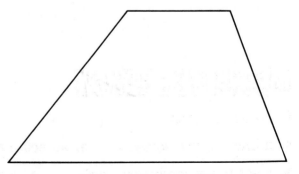

A **trapezoid** has exactly one pair of parallel sides.

Write the name that best describes each figure.

1. 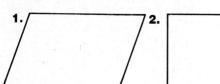 **2.** 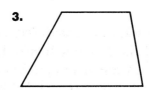 **3.** 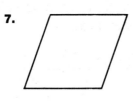 **4.**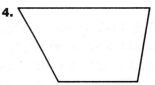

5. 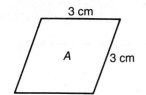 **6.** 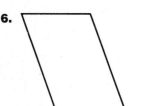 **7.** 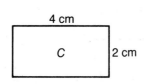 **8.**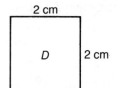

Use the figures to answer Exercises 9–12.

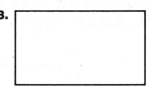

3 cm
A
3 cm

B

4 cm
C
2 cm

2 cm
D
2 cm

9. Which of the figures are trapezoids?

10. Which of the figures are parallelograms?

11. Which of the figures are rectangles?

12. Which of the figures are rhombuses?

MIDCHAPTER REVIEW

Draw each figure.

1. a line   **2.** a ray   **3.** an acute angle   **4.** a right angle

5. a set of perpendicular lines   **6.** a set of parallel lines

7. an isosceles triangle   **8.** a scalene triangle

Other Polygons

A. This Persian carpet was made in the nineteenth century. The artists used different kinds of polygons to lend order and simplicity to the pattern.

A **polygon** has sides that are line segments. It is a **closed figure** because you can trace its boundaries without reaching an endpoint. A polygon can be named according to the number of its sides.

Triangles and quadrilaterals are polygons. A regular polygon has congruent sides and congruent angles.

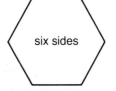
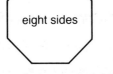

five sides   six sides   eight sides   ten sides

regular pentagon   **regular hexagon**   **regular octagon**   **regular decagon**

B. A **diagonal** is a line segment that is not a side and that joins two vertices of a polygon.

You can use diagonals to find the sum of the angles in a polygon.

Draw all of the diagonals from one vertex. The number of triangles formed is 2 less than the number of sides of the polygon.

Think: The sum of the angles of a triangle is 180°.

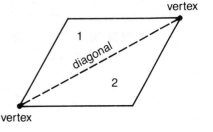

So, the sum of the angles of the polygon equals the number of sides minus 2, times 180°.

The sum of the angles of the polygon is 360°.

Number of sides − 2
↓
$(4 - 2) \times 180° = n$

Number of triangles
↓
$2 \times 180° = 360°$

Write the name of each polygon.

1.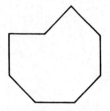

2.

3.

4.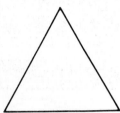

5.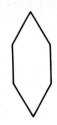

6.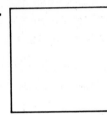

Find the sum of the angles of each figure.

7. a pentagon   **8.** an octagon   **9.** a decagon   **10.** a trapezoid

★11. Draw (or trace from page 320) each polygon listed in the chart. Draw all of the diagonals you can from only one vertex of each polygon. Copy and complete the chart. Can you discover a pattern?

Name of polygon	Number of sides	Number of diagonals from one vertex
Triangle	3	0
Quadrilateral	▧	▧
Pentagon	▧	▧
Hexagon	▧	▧
Octagon	▧	▧

ANOTHER LOOK

Divide. Write the answer in simplest form.

1. $\frac{7}{8} \div \frac{8}{7}$

2. $\frac{3}{8} \div \frac{4}{3}$

3. $\frac{3}{4} \div \frac{3}{5}$

4. $\frac{2}{5} \div \frac{3}{2}$

5. $\frac{5}{12} \div \frac{1}{6}$

6. $\frac{9}{10} \div 3$

7. $4 \div \frac{1}{8}$

8. $7 \div \frac{2}{3}$

9. $8 \div \frac{2}{5}$

10. $6\frac{1}{2} \div 4$

11. $2\frac{3}{8} \div 4$

12. $5\frac{1}{4} \div 2\frac{1}{3}$

13. $3\frac{1}{3} \div 1\frac{2}{3}$

14. $2\frac{2}{3} \div 1\frac{1}{4}$

15. $3\frac{2}{3} \div 2\frac{1}{6}$

Congruence and Symmetry

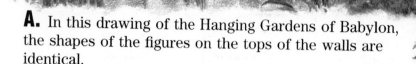

A. In this drawing of the Hanging Gardens of Babylon, the shapes of the figures on the tops of the walls are identical.

A tracing of one figure would match exactly the tracing of any other figure.

Figures that have exactly the same shape and size are **congruent.**

Figure A is congruent to Figure B.

$A \cong B$

The symbol $\cong$ means "is congruent to."

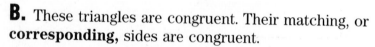

B. These triangles are congruent. Their matching, or **corresponding,** sides are congruent.

$\overline{AB} \cong \overline{DE}, \overline{CA} \cong \overline{FD}, \overline{BC} \cong \overline{EF}$

Their corresponding angles are congruent.

$\angle A \cong \angle D, \angle B \cong \angle E, \angle C \cong \angle F$

C. The figures on the tops of the walls are also **symmetrical.** If you fold the tracing along the dotted line, one half would fit exactly over the other. The dotted line is called a **line of symmetry.**

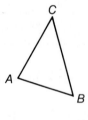

line of symmetry

Other examples:

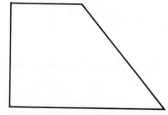

trapezoid
no lines of symmetry

isosceles triangle
one line of symmetry

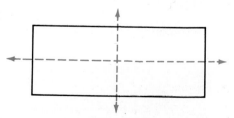

rectangle
two lines of symmetry

322

Write the letter of each polygon that is congruent to
the given polygon.

1.   **a.**   **b.**   **c.**

2.   **d.**   **e.**   **f.**

3.   **g.**   **h.**   **i.**

Trapezoid *ABCD* ≅ trapezoid *EFGH*. Copy and
complete the chart.

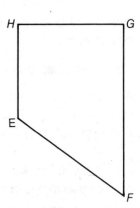

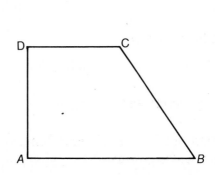

4.	$\overline{AB}$	≅	▨
5.	$\overline{BC}$	≅	▨
6.	▨	≅	$\overline{CD}$
7.	∠B	≅	▨
8.	∠C	≅	▨
9.	▨	≅	∠D

Trace each figure, and draw all the possible lines of symmetry.

10.   **11.**   **12.**   **13.**

CHALLENGE

Complete.

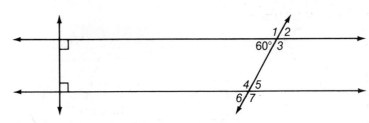

1. measure of ∠1 = ▨

2. measure of ∠2 = ▨

3. measure of ∠3 = ▨

4. measure of ∠4 = ▨

5. measure of ∠5 = ▨

6. measure of ∠6 = ▨

7. measure of ∠7 = ▨

323

Similar Figures

A. This colossal ivory-and-gold statue of Zeus was perhaps the most famous statue of the ancient world. How are these drawings of the statue the same? How are they different?

Figures that have the same shape, but not necessarily the same size, are **similar.**

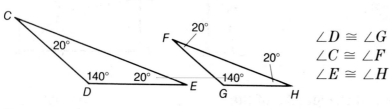

Figure *A* is similar to Figure *B*. *A* ~ *B*. The symbol ~ means "is similar to."

B. Similar figures have corresponding angles that are congruent.

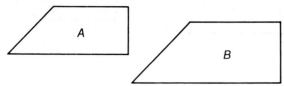

$\angle D \cong \angle G$
$\angle C \cong \angle F$
$\angle E \cong \angle H$

C. In similar figures, the ratios of the lengths of corresponding sides are equal.

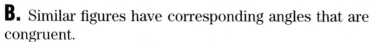

length of $\overline{JK} \to 4$ $\dfrac{}{}$ $5 \leftarrow$ length of $\overline{JL}$
length of $\overline{PQ} \to 8$ $=$ $\dfrac{}{10} \leftarrow$ length of $\overline{PR}$

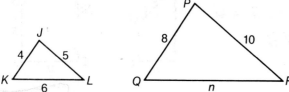

You can use equal ratios to find the length of $\overline{QR}$.

length of $\overline{JK} \to 4$ $=$ $6 \leftarrow$ length of $\overline{KL}$
length of $\overline{PQ} \to 8$ $n \leftarrow$ length of $\overline{QR}$

Solve for n.

$$4 \times n = 6 \times 8$$
$$4 \times n = 48$$
$$n = 48 \div 4$$
$$n = 12$$

The length of $\overline{QR}$ is 12.

Write the letter of the figure that is similar to each of
Figures 1–4.

1.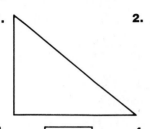

2.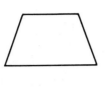

a.

b.

3.

4.

c.

d.

5. Figure *LMNOP* ~ Figure *QRSTU*
Name the corresponding sides.

6. Figure *ABCD* ~ Figure *EFGH*
Name the corresponding angles.

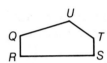

Figure *ABCD* ~ Figure *EFGH*
Find the measure of the angles and the lengths of the
sides.

7. measure of $\angle B$ = ▨

8. measure of $\angle D$ = ▨

9. measure of $\angle E$ = ▨

10. measure of $\angle G$ = ▨

11. length of $\overline{AD}$ = ▨

12. length of $\overline{GH}$ = ▨

13. length of $\overline{BC}$ = ▨

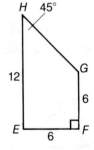

CHALLENGE

Complete. Draw models to help you find the answer.

1. Are all equilateral triangles similar?

2. Are all regular hexagons similar?

3. Are all regular polygons that have the same number
of sides similar? How do you know?

Circles

A. The circle is a figure that was often used in ancient art. This Egyptian cameo is one example. It is symbolic of the Nile River's wealth.

A **circle** consists of all the points in a plane that are the same distance from one point, called the **center.** Point R is the center of circle R.

B. Parts of circles have special names.

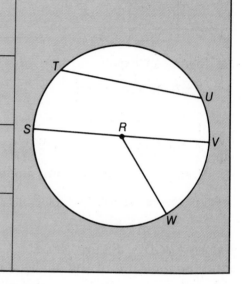

A **chord** is a line segment that has endpoints on the circle. $\overline{TU}$ is a chord.	
A **radius** of a circle is a line segment that joins the center of the circle with any point on the circle. $\overline{RW}$ is a radius.	
A **diameter** is a chord that passes through the center of a circle. It is twice the length of the circle's radius. $\overline{SV}$ is a diameter.	
A **central angle** is an angle that has its vertex at the center of the circle. $\angle SRW$ is a central angle.	

C. To construct a circle with a given radius, open a compass to the length of the desired radius. Place the compass point where you want the center of the circle. Turn the compass completely around.

Write *chord*, *diameter*, or *radius* for each line segment.

1.  segment

2.  se diame

3.  chord

4. 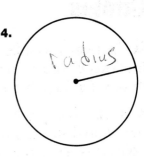 radius

Use the circle to complete Exercises 5–12.

5. Name the circle.

6. Name the center.

7. Name two chords.

8. Name the diameter.

9. Name three radii.

10. Name three central angles.

11. Name an obtuse central angle.

12. Name an acute central angle.

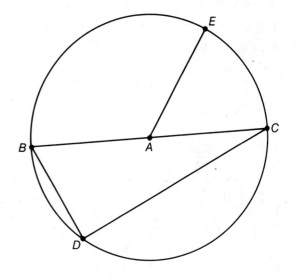

Use a compass to construct each circle.

13. radius = 22 mm

14. radius = $1\frac{1}{2}$ in.

★15. diameter = 7.5 cm

Solve.

16. If circle L is congruent to circle M and has a diameter of 14 cm, what is the radius of circle M?

17. How many diameters are needed to divide a circle into six equal parts?

18. Use your compass to construct a circle that has center A. Choose a point B on the circle, and construct another circle that has the same radius. Label a point C where the circles intersect. Draw the triangle that is formed by points A, B, and C. What type of triangle is $\triangle ABC$?

19. Use your compass to construct a circle that has center 0. Draw a diameter and label it RS. Choose a point T on the circle. Draw triangle RST. What type of triangle is it? Try this with other points on the circle. What do you discover about the triangles?

More Practice, page 454

Translations, Rotations, Reflections

A. Ancient Greece was well known for producing beautiful pottery. Many of the vases were covered by complex geometric patterns made up of one figure positioned in many different ways.

You can change the position of a figure in several ways.

You can **slide** the figure along a straight line. The new figure is called a **translation image**.

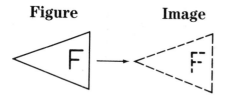

B. You can **turn** the figure on a curved path around a point. The new figure is called a **rotation image**.

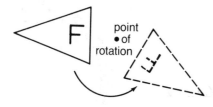

C. You can **flip** the figure along a line of symmetry. The new figure is called a **reflection image**.

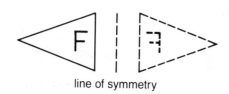

328

Write *translation, rotation,* or *reflection* to describe
the relationship of Figure B to Figure A.

1.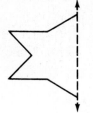

2.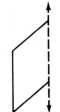

3.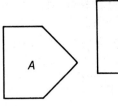

Trace each figure. Then draw its reflection on the line
of symmetry to make a symmetrical figure.

4.

5.

6.

Trace each figure. Then draw its image after it has been
rotated a half turn around point P.

7.

8.

9.

Solve. For problems 10–12, use the Infobank.
Look at the figure. Use the information on page 435
and write the letter of the figure that is

10. a translation.　　**11.** a rotation.　　**12.** a reflection.

Look at the figure. Use the information on page 435

CALCULATOR

You can see lines of symmetry in some digits on a
calculator display.

Use a calculator to find each answer. Then find how
many lines of symmetry each answer has.

1. $202{,}020.2 \times 5$

2. $46{,}662 \div 14$

3. $855 \div 5$

4. $16{,}665.5 \times 2$

5. $222{,}202 \times 4$

6. $33{,}564{,}333 \div 3$

PROBLEM SOLVING
Looking for a Pattern

If you are asked to find what should be next in a group of numbers, letters, or shapes, you should look for a pattern between the first and second items; and the second and third items; and so on.

> On a dig in Mexico, Dr. Mavis Sourte found an ancient mosaic. It was set in a pattern of tiled circles. The first circle is made up of 4 tiles. The next 7 circles have 9, 5, 10, 15, 11, 22, and 27 tiles. The rest of the tiles show the continuation of this pattern. How many tiles are there in the ninth circle?

To solve, you need to look for a pattern. Look at the series of numbers.

4, 9, 5, 10, 15, 11, 22, 27, ■

You need to find a series of operations that will produce this pattern. You can write the possible operations for each step of the pattern.

$$4 \quad 9 \quad 5 \quad 10 \quad 15 \quad 11 \quad 22 \quad 27$$

$$+5 \quad -4 \quad +5 \quad +5 \quad -4 \quad +11 \quad +5$$
$$\qquad\qquad \text{or} \qquad\qquad\qquad \text{or}$$
$$\qquad\qquad \times 2 \qquad\qquad\qquad \times 2$$

You can see a pattern. But the pattern only works when the third and sixth operations are $\times 2$. The series of operations used to produce the pattern is $+5, -4, \times 2$.

Once you know the pattern, you can figure out what the next number will be. The seventh operation was $+5$. So, the eighth is -4.

$$27 - 4 = 23$$

There are 23 tiles in the ninth circle.

Solve by finding the pattern.

1. Dr. Sourte discovered a row of carvings on the wall of a building. The first carving was 12 inches from the east end of the wall. The next carving was 6 inches from the first carving. The distances between the next 6 carvings were 18, 20, 10, 30, 32, and 16 inches. What series of operations produced this pattern?

2. If the pattern were continued, how many inches would separate the ninth and the tenth carvings?

3. How far would the ninth carving be from the east end of the wall?

4. If the wall was 350 inches long, how many carvings were there in the row?

★5. Dr. Sourte found symbols that stand for numbers carved on a stone. The chart shows the number each symbol represents.

◊ = 1   ⋁ = 1,000
☉ = 10   ● = 10,000
▭ = 100   △ = 100,000

On one wall of the building, she finds five groups of symbols representing numbers. These are the groups.

▭ ☉ ☉ ☉ ☉ ☉ ☉ ☉

▭ ▭ ☉ ☉ ☉ ☉ ☉ ☉ ☉ ◊

⋁ ⋁ ▭ ▭ ▭ ▭ ▭ ▭ ▭ ▭ ☉

⋁ ⋁ ▭ ▭ ▭ ▭ ▭ ▭ ▭ ▭ ▭ ☉ ◊

● ● ⋁ ⋁ ⋁ ⋁ ⋁ ⋁ ⋁ ⋁ ⋁ ▭ ☉

What number does each group represent? What is the pattern of the numbers?

★6. What are the next two numbers in the pattern? What two groups of symbols would represent these numbers?

READING MATH

Vocabulary

Read these two paragraphs.

The pianist played a <u>scale</u> in <u>G major</u> and an <u>arpeggio</u> in the <u>relative minor, e</u>.

The book editor checked the <u>folios</u> on the <u>F and G's</u> against the book's <u>TOC</u>.

Do you know the meaning of the underlined words and phrases? These are special words and phrases used by musicians and book editors, respectively. If you wanted to become a musician or a book editor, you would need to know what they mean.

When you read problems in geometry, you need to know what the special words and phrases mean. You've studied some of them already. Now see how many words you can match with their meanings.

1. isosceles
2. rhombus
3. intersecting
4. translation
5. perpendicular
6. segment
7. line
8. vertex
9. equilateral
10. symmetrical
11. ray
12. scalene

a. a triangle that has no sides equal in length

b. lines that cross

c. a triangle that has three sides equal in length

d. a figure that has two halves exactly alike

e. sliding a figure along a straight line to another position

f. part of a line that begins at an endpoint and continues in one direction

g. the endpoint for the rays of an angle

h. lines that intersect and form right angles

i. a triangle that has two sides of equal length

j. a parallelogram that has four equal sides

k. a straight path of points

l. part of a line that begins at one point and ends at another point

GROUP PROJECT

The Pyramid Problem

The problem: You and your classmates are studying Ancient Egypt. You decide to build a model of the Great Pyramid. Your model will include all the rooms, passageways, and secret entrances. Use the information below to help you make a plan of the model.

Key Facts

- The Great Pyramid originally stood 481 feet tall.
- The base of the pyramid covers 13 acres.
- The pyramid contains more than 2 million stone blocks.
- You have $23 in the class treasury to buy materials to build the pyramid.
- Scale models are usually built on a ratio of 8 ft to 1 in.

Key Questions

- What scale will you use? Will you use the 8:1 ratio?
- What materials will you use to build the model?
- Who will draw the plans?
- Who will build the model?
- Where will you build the model? display it?

CHAPTER TEST

Name each figure. (page 306)

Write the measure of each angle. Then classify it as
acute, obtuse, right, or *straight.* (page 308)

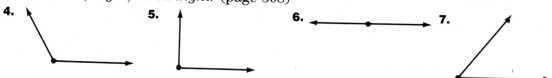

Write *parallel, perpendicular,* or *intersecting* for each
pair of lines. (page 310)

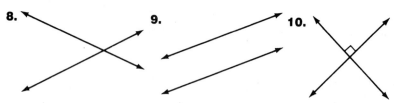

Write the name that best describes each
figure. (pages 314, 318, and 320)

Find the measure of the missing angle.
(page 314)

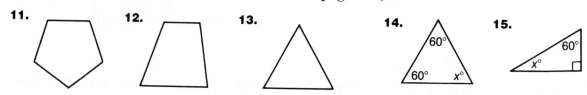

Write the letter of each polygon that is congruent to
the given polygon. (page 322)

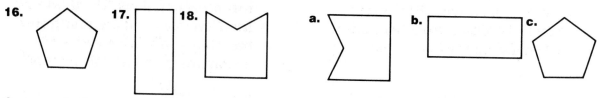

Copy each figure and draw all the lines of symmetry. (page 322)

$\triangle ABC \sim \triangle DEF$. Use the figures to complete Questions 21–24. (page 324)

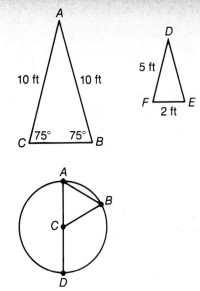

21. What is the measure of $\angle CAB$?

22. What is the measure of $\angle DEF$?

23. What is the measure of $\overline{DE}$?

24. What is the measure of $\overline{BC}$?

Use circle C to complete Questions 25–27. (page 326)

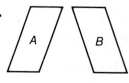

25. Name three radii.

26. Name the diameter.

27. Name one chord.

Write *translation, rotation,* or *reflection* to describe the relationship of Figure B to Figure A. (page 328)

28.

29.

30.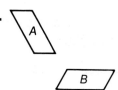

31.

Solve. (pages 312 and 330)

32. Allison's paper-delivery route first takes her 12 blocks west of her house, then 7 south, 4 east, 3 north, 3 east, 4 south, 3 east, and finally 5 blocks north again. How many blocks is Allison from her house when she finishes her route?

33. Edward is examining a photo of an Egyptian statue that has many rows of carvings. The first row has 8 symbols of animals. The second row has 14 symbols. The third row has 7 symbols, and the fourth row has 21 symbols. What series of operations produced this pattern?

BONUS

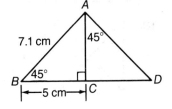

What is the measure of

1. $\angle BAC$?

2. $\angle ADC$?

3. $\angle BAD$?

4. $\overline{BD}$?

5. $\overline{AD}$?

RETEACHING

A. Figures that have exactly the same size and the same shape are called *congruent figures*. △ABC is congruent to △DEF. △ABC ≅ △DEF
The matching sides of congruent figures are called corresponding sides. These triangles are congruent. Their corresponding sides are $\overline{AB} \cong \overline{DE}$, $\overline{CA} \cong \overline{FD}$, $\overline{BC} \cong \overline{EF}$.

Corresponding angles are congruent.
$\angle A \cong \angle D$, $\angle B \cong \angle E$, $\angle C \cong \angle F$

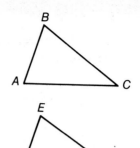

B. Figures that have the same shape, but not necessarily the same size, are *similar figures*. △GHI is similar to △JKL. △GHI ~ △JKL
Similar figures have corresponding angles that are congruent.
$\angle G \cong \angle J$, $\angle H \cong \angle K$, $\angle I \cong \angle L$

In similar figures, the ratios of the lengths of corresponding sides are equal.
You can use equal ratios to find the length of $\overline{JK}$.

$$\frac{\text{length of } \overline{HI} \to 4}{\text{length of } \overline{KL} \to 8} = \frac{7 \leftarrow \text{length of } \overline{GH}}{n \leftarrow \text{length of } \overline{JK}}$$

Solve for n. $4 \times n = 7 \times 8$
$n = 56 \div 4 = 14$

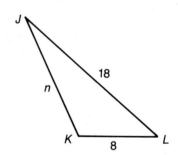

Pentagon *ABCDE* ≅ Pentagon *FGHIJ*. Name the corresponding parts from each figure.

1. $\overline{AB} \cong$ ▨   **2.** ▨ $\cong \overline{FJ}$

3. $\overline{CD} \cong$ ▨   **4.** ▨ $\cong \overline{IJ}$

5. $\angle B \cong$ ▨   **6.** ▨ $\cong \angle J$

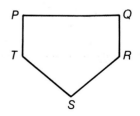

Pentagon *KLMNO* ~ Pentagon *PQRST*. Name the corresponding parts from each figure.

7. $\overline{KL} \sim$ ▨   **8.** ▨ $\sim \overline{RS}$

9. $\overline{KO} \sim$ ▨   **10.** ▨ $\sim \overline{QR}$

11. $\angle M \sim$ ▨   **12.** ▨ $\sim \angle T$

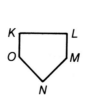

ENRICHMENT

Constructing Congruent Angles

To construct congruent angles, all you need is a
compass and a straightedge.

To construct an angle congruent to ∠CAB:

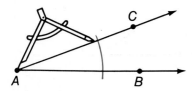

Make an arc through the angle with
your compass.

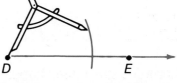

Draw a ray and make the same arc
through it.

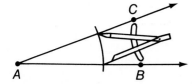

With a compass, measure the angle.

Place the sharp point of the compass
on the point where the arc intersects
the ray. Draw an arc.

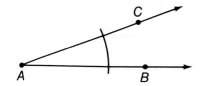

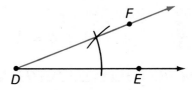

Draw a ray connecting the endpoint
and the intersection.

$$\angle CAB \cong \angle FDE$$

Construct congruent angles.

1.

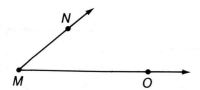

2.

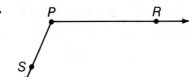

TECHNOLOGY

Look at this LOGO procedure. It will draw a square that has sides of any length.

```
TO SQUARE :SIDE
REPEAT 4 [FD :SIDE RT 90]
END
```

The variable :SIDE allows you to plug in any length for a side. The command SQUARE 50 to the turtle will cause it to draw a square whose sides are 50 steps long.

You can use more than one variable in a LOGO procedure. This procedure would change the size of the angles as well as the length of the sides.

```
TO SHAPE :SIDE :ANGLE
REPEAT 4 [FD :SIDE RT :ANGLE]
END
```

But you must be careful when choosing the size of the angle, or the figure the turtle draws will not be a regular polygon.

You can calculate the number of degrees in each angle of any regular polygon. For example, there are three angles in a triangle. Each angle is the same size as the others. Since the sum of the angles in a triangle is 180°, each angle is equal to 180° ÷ 3, or 60°.

You can also find the measure of each turn the turtle makes. The turtle turns 360° in one complete trip around any polygon. So, the size of each turn it makes in the triangle is 360° ÷ 3, or 120°.

Number of sides	3	4	5
Measure of each turn	120°	90°	72°

1. What is the measure of each turn in a hexagon?

2. Identify the type of figure drawn by this procedure.

```
TO SOMESHAPE
REPEAT 180 [FD 2   RT 2]
END
```

Write a procedure to draw each of the following.

3. A square whose sides are 17 steps long

4. A pentagon whose sides are 50 steps long

5. A hexagon whose sides are 90 steps long

6. An octagon that has any length sides

7. A nonagon that has any length sides

★**8.** Any number of parallel lines

CUMULATIVE REVIEW

Write the letter of the correct answer.

1. Another way to write the ratio $\frac{2}{5}$ is ■.

   a. 20%   **b.** 2:5

   c. 5:2   **d.** not given

2. Which is the equivalent ratio for $\frac{7}{8}$?

   a. 70%   **b.** $\frac{21}{24}$

   c. $\frac{14}{8}$ **d.** not given

3. Solve the proportion: $\frac{3}{n} = \frac{12}{16}$.

   a. 4   **b.** 16

   c. 36   **d.** not given

4. Which fraction in simplest form is the same as 60%?

   a. $\frac{1}{5}$ **b.** $\frac{4}{8}$

   c. $\frac{2}{3}$ **d.** not given

5. Which decimal represents 58%?

   a. 0.058   **b.** 0.508

   c. 0.58   **d.** not given

6. Find 40% of 75.

   a. 24   **b.** 30

   c. 185   **d.** not given

7. Which percent is equivalent to the shaded region?

   a. 33%   **b.** 67%

   c. 100%   **d.** not given

8. The factors of 23 are 1 and 23. Therefore, 23 is a ■ number.

   a. composite   **b.** prime

   c. even   **d.** not given

9. $8\overline{)0.328}$

   a. 0.041   **b.** 0.410

   c. 31   **d.** not given

10. 4.389×100

   a. 43.89   **b.** 438.9

   c. 4,389   **d.** not given

11. Round $33.72 to the nearest dollar.

   a. $33   **b.** $33.50

   c. $34   **d.** not given

12. $3\frac{3}{5} \times \frac{5}{7}$

   a. $\frac{18}{35}$ **b.** $2\frac{4}{7}$

   c. $12\frac{6}{7}$ **d.** not given

13. Which unit would you use to measure the amount of water in a swimming pool?

   a. pints   **b.** quarts

   c. gallons   **d.** not given

14. Sara made a scale model of the Gateway Arch in St. Louis. She used the scale 1 in. : 20 ft. Her model is $31\frac{1}{2}$ in. tall. How tall is the real Gateway Arch?

   a. 430 ft   **b.** 630 ft

   c. 1,260 ft   **d.** not given

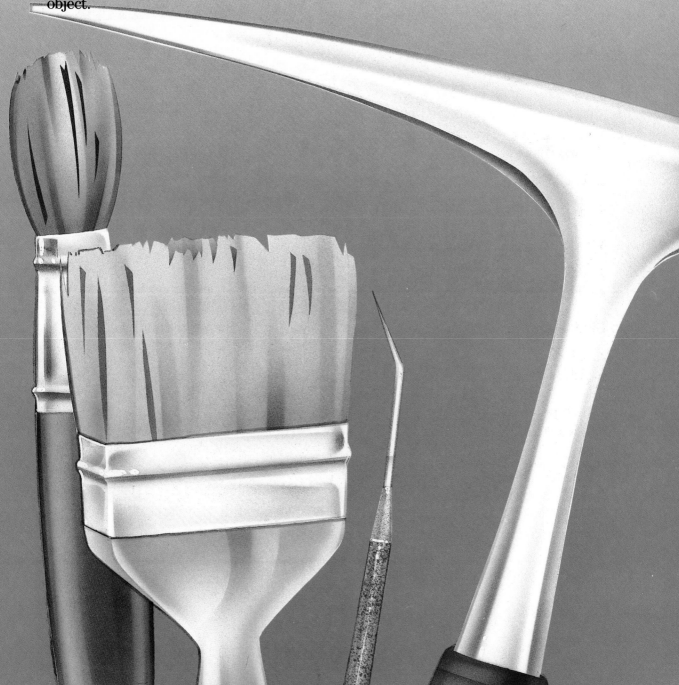

You are an archeologist who has been working on a major dig in a very remote, mountainous region of Europe. You discover what appears to be an ancient stone wheel. Write a detailed description of this object without mentioning the word *wheel*. Do not use a drawing or a diagram. Find out whether someone can produce a drawing or a model that will match your description of the object.

10 PERIMETER AREA, VOLUME

Perimeter of Polygons

A. Archeologists measured the ancient, irregular-shaped floor of an Incan stone house. The four sides measured 8 meters, 7 meters, 6 meters, and 6 meters. What was the distance around the floor?

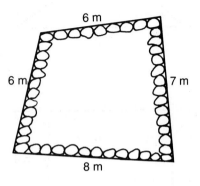

The distance around a polygon is called the **perimeter.** You can find the perimeter of a polygon by finding the sum of the lengths of its sides.

P = sum of lengths of sides
$P = 8 + 7 + 6 + 6$
$P = 27$

The distance around the floor was 27 m.

B. Since a rectangle has two pairs of congruent sides, use this formula to find its perimeter:

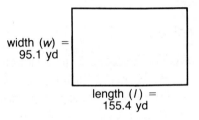

$P = (2 \times \text{length}) + (2 \times \text{width})$ or $P = 2l + 2w$
$P = (2 \times 155.4) + (2 \times 95.1)$
$P = 310.8 + 190.2$
$P = 501 \text{ yd}$

C. Since a square has four equal sides, multiply the length of one side by 4 to find the perimeter.

$P = 4 \times \text{length of side}$ or $P = 4s$
$P = 4 \times 6\frac{1}{2}$
$P = 26 \text{ ft}$

length of side $(s) = 6\frac{1}{2}$ ft

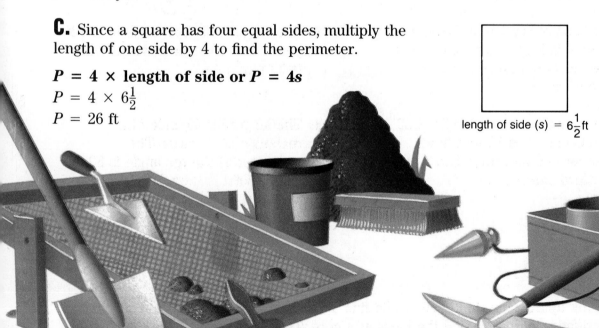

Find the perimeter of each polygon.

1.
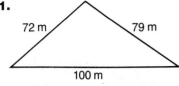
72 m 79 m
100 m

2.
16 cm
10 cm 10 cm
26 cm 26 cm

3.
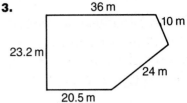
36 m
23.2 m 10 m
24 m
20.5 m

4.
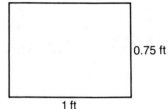
0.75 ft
1 ft

5.
11 ft
35.2 ft

★6.
10 ft 5 ft
15 ft
30 ft

Solve.

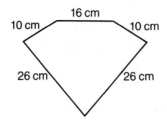

7. The Pentagon in Arlington, Virginia, is the world's largest office building. Its shape is a regular pentagon. Find its perimeter.

281 m

8. The base of the Great Pyramid of Cheops in Egypt is square. Each side measures 115 m. Find its perimeter.

9. The length of a football field is 120 yards. It is 53.3 yards wide. What is its perimeter?

★10. The perimeter of a triangle is 25 feet. One side is 10 feet long. Another is 6 feet long. How long is the third side?

★11. The length of one side of a rectangle is 30 yards. The perimeter of the rectangle is 80 yards. What is the width of one side of the rectangle?

CHALLENGE

If you took apart a baseball, you would find 1,080 feet of yarn tightly wound around the baseball's core. That is enough yarn to go around the perimeter of a baseball infield 3 times. What is the perimeter of this baseball infield?
What is the length of each side of the infield?

PROBLEM SOLVING
Using Broken-Line Graphs and Bar Graphs

A broken-line graph can show how something has changed over a period of time. The graph shows the distances traveled in the campaign of Alexander the Great.

- The title of the graph at the right tells you that the graph shows the number of miles traveled by Alexander the Great from 334 B.C. to 329 B.C.

- The labels at the left side of the graph show the number of miles traveled. The labels at the bottom show the years.

- To find the number of miles Alexander traveled in a particular year, locate that year. Then, find the dot above this year. The placement of the dot helps you read the number of miles traveled because it directs your attention to the scale at the left.

A bar graph can also help you find information.

- The title tells you that the bar graph at the right shows the number of miles Alexander the Great traveled between 328 B.C. and 323 B.C.

- The labels at the left show the number of miles traveled. The labels at the bottom show the years.

- To find the number of miles Alexander traveled in a particular year, locate that year. The height of the bar above the year shows the number of miles traveled that year. You can read the height by using the scale at the left.

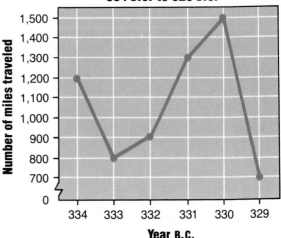

YEARLY MILEAGE OF FIRST HALF OF ALEXANDER THE GREAT'S CAMPAIGN 334 B.C. to 329 B.C.

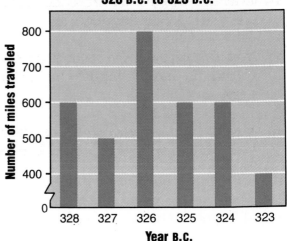

YEARLY MILEAGE OF SECOND HALF OF ALEXANDER THE GREAT'S CAMPAIGN 328 B.C. to 323 B.C.

Can you use the broken-line graph and the bar graph on page 344 to answer these questions? Write *yes* or *no*.

1. How many miles did Alexander travel in 323 B.C.

2. How many miles did Alexander travel in the summer of 327 B.C.?

Solve.

3. How far did Alexander travel in 328 B.C.?

4. In which year did Alexander travel the greatest distance?

5. In which year did Alexander travel the least distance?

6. Did Alexander travel more in the first or in the second year of the campaign?

7. If Alexander had traveled 200 miles farther in 333 B.C., would he have traveled farther than he did in 334 B.C.?

8. Did Alexander travel more in 330 B.C. than in 326 B.C.?

9. How many miles did Alexander travel in the first three years of his campaign?

10. How many miles did Alexander travel in the last four years of the campaign?

11. In which year did the number of miles traveled change the most from the number traveled in the previous year?

12. What was the average distance Alexander traveled between 334 B.C. and 329 B.C.? between 328 B.C. and 323 B.C.?

Circumference

A. The Aztec Empire in Mexico was famous for its sculpture. One of the most elaborate sculptures was the calendar stone. The **diameter** of this circular stone measures about 4 yards.

What is the **circumference** of, or distance around, the stone?

If you divide the circumference of any circle by its diameter, the quotient will always be the same. This quotient is given the name *pi* and is shown by the Greek letter π. Two approximate values of π are 3.14 and $\frac{22}{7}$.

Since the ratio of the circumference (C) of a circle to its diameter (d) equals π, you can multiply π by a circle's diameter to find its circumference.

$$\frac{C}{d} = \pi$$
$$C = \pi \times d$$

$C = \pi \times d$

$C \approx 3.14 \times 4$

$C \approx 12.56$

| ≈ means "is approximately equal to" |

$C = \pi \times d$

$C \approx \frac{22}{7} \times 4$

$C \approx 12\frac{4}{7}$

The circumference of the calendar stone is approximately 12.56 yd, or $12\frac{4}{7}$ yd.

B. Since the diameter of a circle is twice the radius, you can use this formula to find the circumference when the radius is given.

$C = \pi \times 2 \times \textbf{radius}; \; C = \pi \times 2 \times r \; \text{or} \; C = 2\pi r$

$C \approx \frac{22}{7} \times 2 \times 14$

$C \approx \frac{22}{7}^{1} \times \overset{4}{28} \approx 88$

14 m

The circumference is approximately 88 m.

Find the circumference. Use $\frac{22}{7}$ for π.
Write the answer in simplest form.

1.

2.
5 ft

3.
35 in.

4.
$6\frac{1}{2}$ in.

5. $d = 14$ ft

6. $r = 4$ ft

7. $d = 28$ ft

8. $r = 13\frac{1}{2}$ in.

Find the circumference. Use 3.14 for π.
Round to the nearest hundredth.

9.
42 m

10.
28 cm

11.
49.8 m

12.
28.34 m

13. $d = 7$ cm

14. $r = 25$ mm

15. $d = 8.5$ m

16. $r = 54.2$ m

Solve. Use 3.14 for π. Round to the nearest centimeter.

17. The Aztec made circular shields from gold, woven reeds, and feathers. The famous Coyote Shield has a radius of 35 cm. What is its circumference?

18. The pictures on many of the Aztec shields that have survived tell a story. One shield shows the jagged Mexican mountains. The shield is 62.9 cm in diameter. What is its circumference?

CHALLENGE

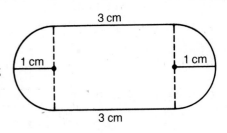
3 cm
1 cm   1 cm
3 cm

You can find the perimeter of this figure by dividing it into 2 half-circles and 2 line segments. Use 3.14 for π.

$P = (\pi \times 2 \text{ cm}) + 3 \text{ cm} + 3 \text{ cm}$, or 12.28 cm

Find the perimeter.

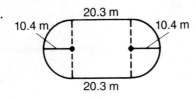
20.3 m
10.4 m   10.4 m
20.3 m

Area of Rectangles and Squares

A. Pompeii was an ancient Roman city that lay buried for centuries under ashes from the eruption of Mount Vesuvius. Some walls, covered with colored tiles, have been rediscovered. What is the area of this wall?

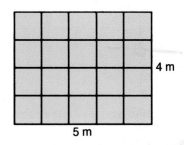

4 m

5 m

The **area** of a polygon is the number of square units needed to cover the polygon.

Think of how many square tiles that measure 1 meter on each side would fit on a wall 4 meters high and 5 meters wide. Along the height of the wall, 4 tiles would fit. The width of the wall would equal 5 of the tiles.

Since a rectangle has two pairs of equal sides, you can multiply the length by the width to find the area.

$A = \textbf{length} \times \textbf{width}$ or $A = lw$
$A = 5 \times 4$
$A = 20$

The area of this wall is 20 square meters (m^2).

B. Since a square has four congruent sides, you can multiply the length of one side by itself to find the area.

$A = \textbf{side} \times \textbf{side}$ or $A = s^2$
$A = 6.2 \times 6.2$
$A = 38.44$ square feet (ft^2)

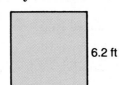

6.2 ft

Checkpoint Write the letter of the correct answer.

Find the area.

1.

3.4 cm

5.6 cm

a. $A = 18$ cm^2
b. $A = 18.04$ cm^2
c. $A = 19.04$ cm^2
d. $A = 1,904$ cm^2

2.

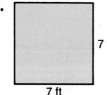

7 ft

7 ft

a. $A = 14$ ft
b. $A = 28$ ft^2
c. $A = 49$ ft^2
d. $A = 72$ ft^2

Find the area of each figure.

1.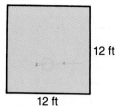
12 ft
12 ft

2.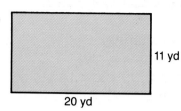
11 yd
20 yd

3.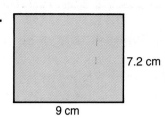
7.2 cm
9 cm

Find each area.

4. $l = 18$ ft; $w = 10$ ft

5. $l = 8.7$ m; $w = 6.3$ m

6. $l = 142$ cm; $w = 139$ cm

7. $l = 120$ yd; $w = 120$ yd

8. $l = 7.4$ in.; $w = 5.6$ in.

9. $l = 12$ cm; $w = 0.8$ cm

Solve.

This scale drawing shows the rooms of a Roman house that was uncovered at Pompeii. Copy the table. Use the scale drawing to help you complete the table.

	Room	Length (m)	Width (m)	Area (m²)
10.	Garden	10	4	▨
11.	Courtyard (with patio)	▨	▨	▨
12.	Patio (with fountain)	▨	▨	▨
★13.	Reception hall	▨	▨	▨
★14.	Entire house	▨	▨	▨

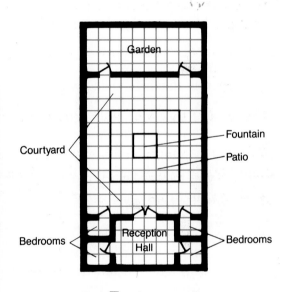

Each ☐ = 1 square meter.

ANOTHER LOOK

Find the product. Write the answer in simplest form.

1.
$$\begin{array}{r} 56 \\ \times\ 1.3 \\ \hline \end{array}$$

2.
$$\begin{array}{r} 3.8 \\ \times\ 26 \\ \hline \end{array}$$

3.
$$\begin{array}{r} 14.6 \\ \times\ 2.8 \\ \hline \end{array}$$

4.
$$\begin{array}{r} 0.215 \\ \times\ 1.18 \\ \hline \end{array}$$

5.
$$\begin{array}{r} 2.31 \\ \times\ 2.22 \\ \hline \end{array}$$

6. $\frac{3}{4} \times \frac{5}{6}$

7. $\frac{7}{8} \times 9$

8. $\frac{1}{3} \times 4\frac{3}{4}$

9. $5 \times 2\frac{9}{10}$

10. $6\frac{2}{3} \times 7\frac{5}{8}$

More Practice, page 455

PROBLEM SOLVING
Choosing/Writing a Sensible Question

Rosario and José are interested in archeology. Not far from their home in Farmington, New Mexico, are ruins of the ancient communities of the Anasazi. To learn more about these people, Rosario and José decide to visit one of the ruins with a group of other students. Two of the biggest ruins are Pueblo Bonito at Chaco Canyon and Cliff Palace at Mesa Verde.

The group has to decide which ruin to visit. Answering which of these questions will help them make a decision?

- How far from Farmington are Cliff Palace and Pueblo Bonito?

  Knowing how far away the ruins are is important. If one ruin is much farther away than the other, the group might want to visit the closer ruin.

- Can you enter the ruins?

  This is an important question, because a ruin in which you can walk around is more fun and more interesting to visit than one that you cannot enter.

- How many people have visited the ruins?

  This is not an important question. The number of people who have visited the ruins does not affect the group's decision to visit the ruins.

- Can you drive to the ruins?

  This is an important question. The group may not want to hike a long way to a ruin that is far from a road.

The group decided to go to Cliff Palace at Mesa Verde National Park. These ruins are closer to Farmington and are easier to reach by car.

Read each statement. For each statement, write two questions that should be answered before making a decision.

1. Before setting out on the trip to Cliff Palace, Rosario looked at the map. He found out that there were several possible ways to drive to the ruins.

2. When they arrived at Cliff Palace, everyone wanted to go in different directions. They decided to split up and then meet for lunch.

3. At the end of the day, José was very excited. He wanted to share with his family what he had seen with his friends. He wanted to make a model of Cliff Palace as it looked when it was built 1,000 years ago.

4. Daisy wanted to draw a map that would show all the important Anasazi communities. She wanted to show Cliff Palace and its ancient neighbors.

5. Tina studied the agriculture and the foods of ancient civilizations. She wanted to prepare for José, Daisy, and Rosario a meal that included one of the foods of the Anasazi.

6. Rosario noticed a help-wanted sign in the visitors center. The center needed 2 students to work on an archeological dig at a small ruin.

7. Daisy wanted to learn more about the history of the Anasazi. She wanted to do a report for her class.

8. Tina wanted to learn about the language of the Anasazi. She wanted to write a book report about the Anasazi language.

Area of Parallelograms and Triangles

A. You can use what you know about the area of a rectangle to help you find the area of a parallelogram.

A parallelogram can be reshaped to form a rectangle that has the same area.

The formula for finding the area of a rectangle is

A = length × width, or $A = lw$.

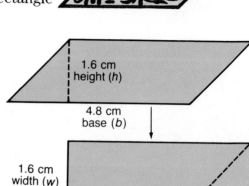

So, the formula for finding the area of a parallelogram is

A = base × height, or $A = bh$.
$A = 4.8 \times 1.6$
$A = 7.68$

The area of the parallelogram is 7.68 cm².

B. You can use what you know about the area of a parallelogram to find the area of a triangle.

Draw the diagonal of a parallelogram. It divides the parallelogram into two congruent triangles.

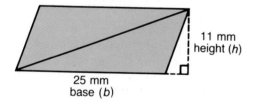

So, the area of the triangle is *half* the area of the parallelogram.

The formula for finding the area of a parallelogram is

$A = bh$.

So, the formula for finding the area of a triangle is

$A = \frac{1}{2} bh$.
$A = \frac{1}{2} \times 25 \times 11$
$A = \frac{1}{2} \times 275$
$A = 137.5$

The area of the triangle is 137.5 mm².

Find the area of each figure.

1.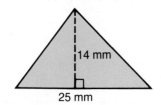
2 ft
4 ft

2.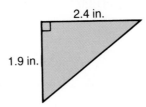
12 cm
5.5 cm

3.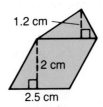
1.6 cm
14.3 cm

4.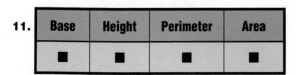
14 mm
25 mm

5.
2.4 in.
1.9 in.

★6.
1.2 cm
2 cm
2.5 cm

Find the area of the parallelogram.

7. $b = 24$ cm; $h = 14$ cm

★8. $h = 3$ ft; $b = 4\frac{1}{7}$ ft

Find the area of the triangle.

9. $b = 266$ mm; $h = 165$ mm

★10. $b = 5\frac{1}{2}$ in.; $h = 7$ in.

Copy each table. Use the figures to complete.

11.

Base	Height	Perimeter	Area
■	■	■	■

8 mm
5 mm   4 mm   5 mm
8 mm

12.

Base	Height	Perimeter	Area
■	■	■	■

1.7 cm   2.5 cm
1.5 cm
2.8 cm

13.

Base	Height	Perimeter	Area
■	■	■	■

5 m   12 m
13 m

FOCUS: MENTAL MATH

Find the area of each figure. Compute mentally.

1. rectangle
$l = 600$ ft
$w = 80$ ft

2. parallelogram
$b = 100$ cm
$h = 75$ cm

3. triangle
$b = 90$ in.
$h = 60$ in.

4. triangle
$b = 120$ mm
$h = 50$ mm

Area of a Circle

A. "Pieces of eight" were Spanish coins minted in Mexico during the 1700's. The coins could be chopped into smaller pieces, called *bits*. You can use the bits to find the area of one side of the coin.

The pieces of the coin can be put together to form a figure that looks like a parallelogram.

$\frac{1}{2} \times C$

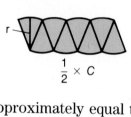

$\frac{1}{2} \times C$

So, the area of the circle is approximately equal to the area of the parallelogram.

Area of the circle ≈ Area of the parallelogram

$A \approx$ base × height

$A \approx \frac{1}{2} \times C \times r$ $\boxed{C = 2\pi r}$

$A \approx \frac{1}{2} \times (2\pi r) \times r$

$A \approx \pi r^2$

The radius of a piece of eight is 18 mm. Find the area.

Area of a circle $= \pi r^2$
Area of a circle $\approx 3.14 \times 18^2$
Area of a circle $\approx 3.14 \times 324$
Area of a circle $\approx 1{,}017.36$, or about 1,017

The area is about 1,017 mm².

B. You can use the diameter of a circle to find its area. Find the area of the circle.

$A = \pi r^2$

$A \approx \frac{22}{7} \times 7^2$ $\boxed{\begin{array}{l}\text{If } d = 14, \\ \text{then } r = 7.\end{array}}$

$A \approx 22 \times 7$

$A \approx 154$

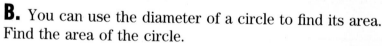

14 ft

The area is about 154 ft².

354

Find the area. Use 3.14 for π. Round to the nearest hundredth.

1.
8 mm

2.
62 cm

3.
4.2 m

4.
9.8 m

5.
13.05 mm

6.
36.2 cm

7.
6.22 mm

8.
13 m

9. $r = 15.3$ m

10. $d = 98$ mm

11. $d = 4.8$ cm

Find the area. Use $\frac{22}{7}$ for π. Write the answer in simplest form.

12. $r = 1\frac{3}{4}$ in.

13. $d = 10\frac{1}{2}$ yd

14. $d = 4\frac{1}{5}$ ft

Solve. For Problem 16, use the Infobank.

15. A group of pirates searched for buried treasure. Here is a copy of the map they used. What is the area of the section they searched?

16. Use the information on page 435 to solve. The pirates found a trunk that was full of coins. The coins came from all over the world. Find the area of a reale.

★17. The pirates chose a lookout to walk in a circle around the section they searched. The diameter of the lookout's circle was 6 m longer than the diameter of the section they searched. Find the circumference of the lookout's circle.

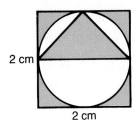
36 m

Search here.

CHALLENGE

1. Find the area of the square.

2. Find the area of the circle. (Use 3.14 for π.)

3. Find the area of the triangle.

★4. Find the area of the shaded region.

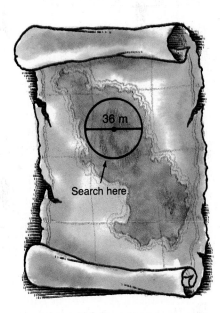
2 cm

2 cm

PROBLEM SOLVING
Choosing a Formula

Sometimes you must choose and use a formula to solve a problem.

Some students are making a bulletin-board display about the discovery of sunken ships. The bulletin board is 10 feet long and 5 feet tall. If the students want to cover the board with blue paper, how many square feet of paper will they need?

To solve the problem, you must choose the right formula. Think about these questions.

- Which geometric figure is described in the problem?
- Which measurements are given in the problem?
- Which measurement do you need to solve for?
- In which unit of measurement should the answer be expressed?

The problem describes a rectangular bulletin board. The board measures 10 feet by 5 feet. You need to find the area of the board. The area will be expressed in square feet.

To solve a problem by using a formula, follow these general rules.

1. Choose the correct formula and the correct form of the formula. Look at the formulas in the table. Since you are going to find the area of a rectangle, $A = lw$ is the formula you will use.

2. Substitute values in the formula. In this problem, $l = 10$ and $w = 5$.

3. Solve for the formula. Write the answer.
$A = lw$
$A = 10 \times 5 = 50$

The students will need 50 ft^2 of paper.

FORMULAS

Area		
$A = lw$		$A = \frac{1}{2} bh$
$A = s^2$		$A = \pi r^2$
$A = bh$		
Circumference		
$C = \pi d$		$C = 2\pi r$
Perimeter		
$P = $ sum of the lengths of the sides		
$P = 2l + 2w$		
$P = 4s$		

Write the letter of the correct formula to use in solving the problem.

1. Deep-sea divers dug a rectangular trench around a sunken ship. The trench was 435 feet long and 145 feet wide. What was the total distance around the trench?

   a. $A = lw$
   b. $p = 2l + 2w$
   c. $A = \pi d$

2. One of the divers drew a circle 4 inches in diameter to show on a map the location of the sunken ship. What was the area of the circle the diver drew?

   a. $A = \pi r^2$
   b. $C = \pi d$
   c. $A = S^2$

Use the correct formula to help you solve the problem.

3. Pluto is the smallest planet in our solar system. It has a diameter of about 1,880 miles. What is the approximate distance around Pluto?

4. One of the largest bicycles ever built has a front wheel that is 64 inches in diameter. What is the distance around the wheel of the bicycle?

5. One of the largest flags ever made is the Great American Flag. It is 411 feet long and 210 feet wide and was meant to fly from the Verrazano Bridge in New York City. How much fabric was used to make the flag?

6. A blanket was made from 20,160 different pieces of knitting. It measured 68 feet by 100 feet. If it were divided by a diagonal into 2 right triangles, how much knitted fabric would there be in 1 triangle?

7. Among the treasures found in a sunken ship were some gold coins. Each coin measured 2.40 cm in diameter. What was the area of each coin?

8. The divers also found an old rectangular treasure chest that contained coins and jewelry. The chest was 34 inches long and 25 inches wide. What was the distance around the chest?

★9. The front wheel of one of the largest bicycles ever built is 24 inches in diameter. The rear wheel of the bicycle is 20 inches in diameter. What is the difference between the areas of the two wheels?

10. On a trip to see Mount McKinley, the highest mountain in North America, the Smiths drove 328 miles the first day. They drove $2\frac{1}{4}$ times as far the next day. On the third day, they drive 279 miles. How far did they travel?

Solid Figures

A. In 1503, a Spanish ship sank in the Atlantic Ocean. The ship was carrying precious jewels of various geometric shapes. Many years later, the jewels were recovered. How many faces, edges, and vertices does this jewel have?

A **solid figure,** or a space figure, is a three-dimensional figure.

This jewel is a solid figure that has four faces, six edges, and four vertices.

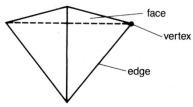

B. These solid figures are **polyhedrons** because their faces are polygons.

You can identify a **prism** by the shape of its base.

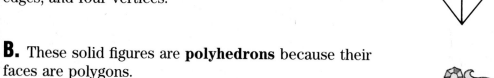

cube   triangular prism   rectangular prism

The bases of a prism are congruent.

You can also identify a **pyramid** by the shape of its base.

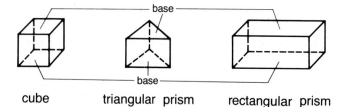

triangular
pyramid

square
pyramid

C. These solid figures are not polyhedrons. Their faces are not polygons.

cone   cylinder   sphere

Copy and complete the chart.

	Solid figure	Name of solid figure	Number of faces	Number of edges	Number of vertices
1.			■	6	■
2.			6	■	■
3.			■	■	■
4.			■	■	12

Name each figure.

5.

6.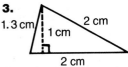

7.

MIDCHAPTER REVIEW

Find the perimeter and the area of each figure.

1.  6 mm, 7 mm, 5 mm

2. 10 cm

3. 1.3 cm, 1 cm, 2 cm, 2 cm

4. 15 cm, 30 cm

Find the circumference and the area of each circle.
Use 3.14 for π. Round to the nearest hundredth.

5.  1.2 cm

6. 7.5 m

7. 24 cm

8. 42 mm

Surface Area

A. A museum wants to display ancient stone boxes inside thin glass covers. Each glass cover measures 4 feet wide by 3 feet high by 6 feet long. How much glass is needed to cover an entire box?

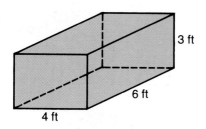

To find the **surface area** of a cover, find the area of each face. Then find the sum of these areas.

Face	Length	Width	Area
A	6 ft	4 ft	24 ft²
B	6 ft	3 ft	18 ft²
C	6 ft	4 ft	24 ft²
D	6 ft	3 ft	18 ft²
E	4 ft	3 ft	12 ft²
F	4 ft	3 ft	12 ft²
		Surface Area	108 ft²

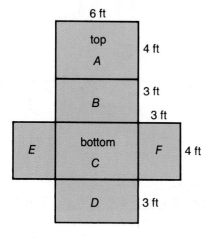

To cover a box, 108 ft² of glass will be needed.

B. To find the surface area of a cylinder, find the area of its bases (K and L) and its curved side (M). Then find the sum of these areas.

Area of $K = \pi r^2$

$\quad A \approx 3.14 \times 4^2$

$\quad A \approx 50.24$ cm²

> **Think:** circle $K \cong$ circle L. So, area of K = area of L.

Area of $M = lw$

$\quad A = (2 \times \pi \times r) \times w$

$\quad A \approx 2 \times 3.14 \times 4 \times 9$

$\quad A \approx 226.08$ cm²

> **Think:** The length of M is the circumference of the base.

The surface area of K and L is about $50.24 + 50.24$, or 100.48 cm².

The surface area of M is about 226.08 cm².

The surface area of the cylinder is about $100.48 + 226.08$, or about 326.56 cm².

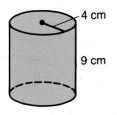

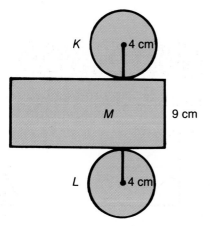

Find the surface area of each figure.
Use 3.14 for π.

1.

3 cm
8 cm
5 cm

2.

2 m
2 m
2 m

3.

2 cm
6 cm
6 cm

4.

5 cm
2 cm

5.

3 mm
9 mm

6.

6 m
6 m

7.

4 cm
10 cm
7 cm

8.

5 m
10 m

★9.

4 cm
5 cm
8 cm
6 cm

Solve.

10. A collection of old Egyptian texts was discovered in a rectangular box that measured 5 feet by 7 feet by 14 feet. What is the surface area of the box?

11. Some scrolls were stored in a cylindrical container. A museum wants to cover the cylinder with a thin layer of glass that measures 18 inches high and 8 inches in diameter. How much glass is needed to cover the entire cylinder?

★12. Imagine that you have built the box shown in the diagram. You want to cover the surface of the box with a brightly colored cloth. How many square feet of cloth will you need?

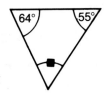

1 ft
$1\frac{1}{2}$ ft
2 ft
4 ft
7 ft

ANOTHER LOOK

Find the missing measure.

1.

45°
90°

2.

62° 62°

3.

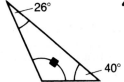

26°
40°

4.

64° 55°

Volume

A. Atahuallpa was a ruler of the Inca Empire. In 1533, a group of Spanish soldiers captured Atahuallpa. To free their leader, the Inca filled a room 22 feet long, 17 feet wide, and 8 feet high with gold. What volume of gold did the room contain?

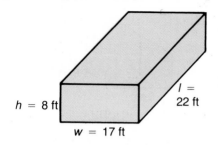

You can find how much gold the room contained by finding the volume of the room.

Think of how many gold cubes measuring 1 foot on each side would fill the room.

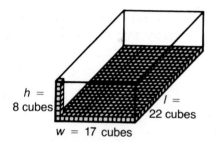

The cubes could be placed in layers that are 22 cubes long by 17 cubes wide. The layers could be stacked 8 cubes high.

Think of the room as a rectangular prism. To find the volume of a rectangular prism, multiply length by width by height.

$V = $ **length** × **width** × **height** or $V = lwh$
$V = 22 \times 17 \times 8$
$V = 2,992$
The volume of the gold was 2,992 ft^3.

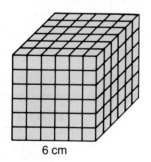

B. A cube has the same length, width, and height. You can multiply the dimensions, or cube the measure of an edge, to find the volume of a cube.

$V = $ **(length of edge)**^{3} or e^3
$V = 6^3$, or $6 \times 6 \times 6$
$V = 216$

The volume of this cube is 216 cm^3.

6 cm

Find the volume of each figure.

1.

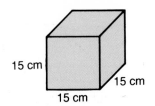

15 cm · 15 cm · 15 cm

2.

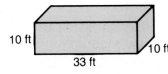

10 ft · 33 ft · 10 ft

3.

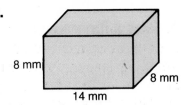

8 mm · 14 mm · 8 mm

Find each volume.

4. $l = 2$ in.; $w = 1$ in.; $h = 2$ in.

5. $l = 3$ m; $w = 1$ m; $h = 1$ m

6. $l = 4$ ft; $w = 4$ ft; $h = 7$ ft

7. $l = 16$ mm; $w = 12$ mm; $h = 13$ mm

8. $l = 8$ yd; $w = 7$ yd; $h = 11$ yd

9. $l = 3$ m; $w = 4.3$ m; $h = 5$ m

Solve.

10. The Inca used relay runners to carry messages. They could travel as far as 240 miles per day. If 160 runners traveled a total of 240 miles, what was the average distance traveled by each runner?

11. Imagine an Inca jewelry case in the shape of a cube. Each edge of the case measures 75 cm. What is the volume of the case?

12. The Inca used llamas to transport most of their goods. The llamas carried their loads in baskets. Find this basket's volume.

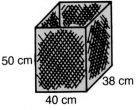

50 cm · 38 cm · 40 cm

★13. Corn grown by the Inca was stored in granaries. Find the total volume of this granary.

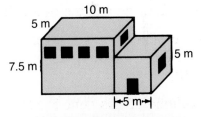

10 m · 5 m · 7.5 m · 5 m · 5 m

Edge	Volume
3 in.	27 in.³
6 in.	▦
▦	▦
▦	▦
▦	▦

CALCULATOR

Copy the table. Use a calculator to complete the table.

Find the volume of a cube 3 inches along its edge. Then double the length of the edge. Keep doubling. What happens to the cube's volume?

More Practice, page 456

PROBLEM SOLVING
Making a Diagram

Making a diagram can help you solve some kinds of problems. You can use a diagram to help you find the perimeter, the surface area, and the volume of irregular figures.

> Sellena is drawing up plans for an imaginary city. The watchtower in the city has the shape of a cylinder 20 ft tall and 7 ft in diameter. A room, in the shape of a cube 7 ft wide, is located at the top of the tower. The watchtower will be covered with gold leaf. To the nearest 0.1 ft^2, how much gold leaf will it take to cover the tower?

Make a diagram so that you can visualize the problem. Include the dimensions. Break the problem down into steps.

1. Find the surface area of the cube. Remember to subtract the circular area on the base that will not be covered with gold leaf.

Surface area of cube $= (5 \times \text{one face}) + \text{area of base}$
$= 5 \times (l \times w) + (l \times w) - \pi r^2$
$= 5 \times (7 \times 7) + (7 \times 7) - 3.14 \times (3.5)^2$
$= 245 + 49 - 38.5$
$= 255.5 \text{ ft}^2$

2. Find the surface area of the cylinder.

Surface of cylinder $= \text{circumference} \times \text{height}$
$= 2\pi r \times 20$
$= 2 \times 3.14 \times (3.5) \times 20$
$= 439.6 \text{ ft}^2$

3. Add the surface areas of the cube and the cylinder.

Surface of tower $= \text{surface of cube} + \text{surface of cylinder}$
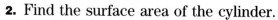
$= \quad\quad 255.5 \quad\quad + \quad\quad 439.6$
$= \quad 695.1 \text{ ft}^2$

It will take 695.1 ft^2 of gold leaf to cover the tower.

Write *always*, *sometimes*, or *never* for each statement.
Make a diagram to decide.

1. A quadrilateral with four equal sides is called a *square*.

2. A right triangle is also an equilateral triangle.

3. A hexagon is a regular polygon.

4. All circles are similar.

Make a diagram, and solve each problem.
Use 3.14 for π.

5. In Sellena's city, the royal family stores their jewels in a stone keep. The keep has a rectangular floor that is 20 ft by 45 feet. Its walls are 16 ft tall. On top of the keep is a roof in the shape of a triangular prism that is 5 ft tall and as long as the building. What is the total volume of the keep?

6. In the center of the city is the Festival Park. It has the shape of 4 regular octagons placed together to form a square. A fountain has been placed in the square to fill the space between the octagons. Each side of the octagons is 3 yards long. What is the perimeter of the park?

7. The mayor lives in the Mayor's Mansion. The mansion has a central building that is 42 ft by 42 ft and 3 stories tall. On either side of the central building are 2 wings, each of which measures 25 ft by 40 ft and 2 stories tall. What is the total floor area of the mansion?

★8. In the Royal Gardens is a glass menagerie. The central portion of the menagerie has the shape of a rectangular prism 25 ft wide, 30 ft tall, and 50 ft long. On either side of the central portion are 2 portions that have the same shape and the same width and length dimensions but are half as tall. How many square feet of glass is needed for the outer surface of the menagerie?

LOGICAL REASONING

Members of the Ryansport Rockhounds Club collect jasper, obsidian, and agate rocks to make jewelry. Of the members, 11 collect jasper, 15 collect obsidian, and 12 collect agate. No one in the club collects all 3 stones, but 6 of these members collect agate and obsidian, 3 of them collect jasper and obsidian, and 4 collect jasper and agate. How many members does the club have?

This Venn diagram can be used to solve the problem. To show the number of members who collect all three kinds of rocks, write the number (0) in the region that is *inside all three circles*.

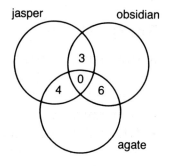

To show the numbers of members who collect two kinds of rocks, write the numbers in the regions that are *inside both circles*.

To find the numbers of members who collect only one kind of rock, you can subtract.

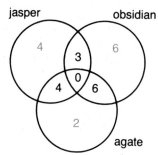

Number collecting jasper *only* = 11 − (4 + 0 + 3) = 4
Number collecting obsidian *only* = 15 − (3 + 0 + 6) = 6
Number collecting agate *only* = 12 − (4 + 0 + 6) = 2

0 + (3 + 4 + 6) + (4 + 6 + 2) = 25 members in the club.

Draw Venn diagrams and complete. Use two circles.

1. In the Rock and Shell Club
14 members collect rocks.
9 members collect shells.
6 of these members collect both rocks and shells.

The club has _____ members.

2. In the Chess and Checkers Club
15 members play chess.
8 members play *only* chess.
12 members play *only* checkers.

The club has _____ members.

Draw a Venn diagram and complete. Use three circles.

The class did a survey of the pets that each student had. 19 had dogs, 18 had cats, and 11 had fish. No one had both cats and fish, but 12 had dogs and cats, and 7 had dogs and fish.

3. How do you know that no one had dogs, cats, and fish?

4. How many students had a dog, a cat, or a fish as a pet?

GROUP PROJECT

Popcorn Power

The problem: You and your classmates are in charge of the annual popcorn-popping festival. You want to create the biggest box of popcorn the festival has ever seen. You have a plastic bin that is 10 ft × 8 ft × 6 ft. You need to plan for this big day. Use the following information to help you.

Key Questions

- How much unpopped popcorn will you need? When it is popped, what will its volume be?
- How much oil will you need?
- How much will everything cost?
- Who will make the popcorn?
- Who will fill the bin?
- How long will it take to fill the bin?
- How will you transport the bin to the festival?
- If you decided to sell some of the popcorn, how would you go about it?

CHAPTER TEST

Find the perimeter. (page 342)

1.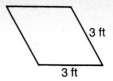
3 ft
3 ft

2.
14 cm

3.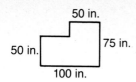
50 in.
50 in.
75 in.
100 in.

Find the circumference. Use 3.14 for π. Round to the nearest hundredth. (page 346)

4.
1.6 m

5.
92 mm

Find the area. (pages 348 and 352)

6.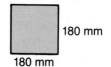
180 mm
180 mm

7.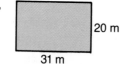
20 m
31 m

8.
0.9 in.

9.
2.2 cm
2.5 cm

10.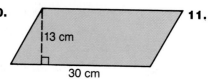
13 cm
30 cm

11.
0.75 in.
1.29 in.

Find the area. Use 3.14 for π. Round to the nearest hundredth. (page 354)

12.
34.2 cm

13.
19 ft

Copy and complete the chart. (page 358)

	Solid figure	Name of solid figure	Number of faces	Number of edges	Number of vertices
14.		___			
15.		___			

Find the surface area. Use 3.14 for π. (page 360)

16.

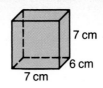
7 cm
6 cm
7 cm

17.

4 ft
4 ft
4 ft

18.

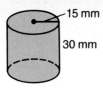
15 mm
30 mm

Find the volume. (page 362)

19.

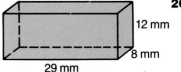
12 mm
8 mm
29 mm

20.

1.7 in.
1.7 in.
1.7 in.

21.

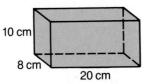
10 cm
8 cm
20 cm

22. Read the statement. Then formulate questions that should be answered before making a decision. (page 350)

Steven went shopping for a birthday present for his father. He looked at some ties, a tool set, and a record album.

23. Write the correct formula for solving the problem. (page 356)

Dawn wants to build a backyard pen for her dog Fang. She wants the pen to be 30 feet long and 10 feet wide. How long will the fence around the pen be?

24. Look at the bar graph and solve. (page 344)

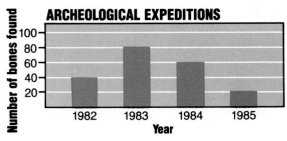

ARCHEOLOGICAL EXPEDITIONS
Number of bones found
100
80
60
40
20
1982 1983 1984 1985
Year

How many more bones were found on the 1984 expedition than in 1982?

25. Make a diagram and solve. (page 364)

An archeologist unearthed an ancient two-room house. The main room was 12 feet long by 9 feet high by 8 feet wide. The second room was 6 feet long by 7 feet high by 8 feet wide. What was the perimeter of the house?

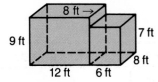
8 ft →
9 ft
7 ft
8 ft
12 ft   6 ft

BONUS

Find the total volume of the swimming pool.

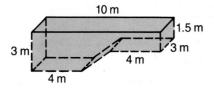
10 m
1.5 m
3 m
3 m
4 m
4 m

RETEACHING

A. A circle can be reformed into a parallelogram that has approximately the same area.
So, the formula for finding the area of a circle is based on the formula for the area of a parallelogram.

Area of circle $= \pi r^2$

Remember: $\pi \approx 3.14$ or $\frac{22}{7}$.

The radius of this circle is 7 cm. Find the area.

$A = \pi r^2$
$A \approx 3.14 \times 7^2$
$A \approx 3.14 \times 49$
$A \approx 153.86 \text{ cm}^2$

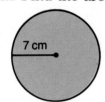
7 cm

B. If you know the diameter of a circle, you can find its area.

$A = \pi r^2$
$A \approx \frac{22}{7} \times 6^2$ **If $d = 12$, then $r = 6$.**
$A \approx \frac{22}{7} \times 36$
$A \approx 113\frac{1}{7} \text{ in.}^2$

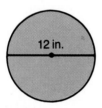
12 in.

Find the area. Use 3.14 for π. Round to the nearest hundredth.

1.
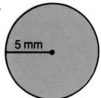
5 mm

2.
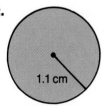
1.1 cm

3.
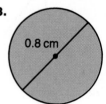
0.8 cm

★4.
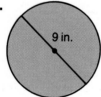
9 in.

Find the area. Use $\frac{22}{7}$ for π.

5.
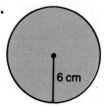
6 cm

6.

14 in.

7.
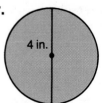
4 in.

8.
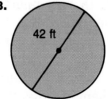
42 ft

ENRICHMENT

Indirect Measure

What is the height of this ancient column? If you cannot measure something's height directly, you can compare its shadow to the shadow of something you can measure. In this example, it is the young tree.

Triangles *XYZ* and *ABC* are similar. The ratio of the column's height to its shadow is equal to the ratio of the tree's height to its shadow.

column height $\rightarrow \dfrac{XY}{YZ} = \dfrac{AB}{BC} \leftarrow$ tree height
column's shadow $\rightarrow$ $\qquad\quad \leftarrow$ tree's shadow

Write a proportion.

$$\frac{n}{42} = \frac{4}{6}$$

Use cross multiplication to find the value of *n*.

$$n \times 6 = 42 \times 4$$
$$n \times 6 = 168$$
$$n = 168 \div 6$$
$$n = 28$$

The column is 28 feet tall.

Find the value of *h*.

1.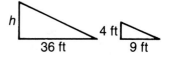

2.

3.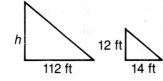

Find the height of each object.

4. Steve wants to know the height of a column whose shadow is 32 feet long. A pole nearby is 3 feet high. Its shadow is 8 feet long. What is the height of the column?

5. Darleen is measuring a stone statue. Its shadow is 28 feet long. A 13-foot tree nearby has a 26-foot shadow. How high is the statue?

6. Fred wants to know the height of an ancient temple. Its shadow is 96 feet long. An ancient wall next to the temple is 10 feet tall. Its shadow is 16 feet long. How tall is the temple?

7. Carla has to measure a tall pillar. Its shadow is 135 feet long. A nearby tree is 27 feet tall. Its shadow is 81 feet long. What is the height of the pillar?

371

TECHNOLOGY

Here's a BASIC program that contains a new statement. See whether you can guess what it does.

```
10   LET N1 = 6
20   PRINT "GUESS A NUMBER BETWEEN 1 AND 10"
30   INPUT N2
40   IF N2 = N1 THEN PRINT "YOU GOT IT!!"
```

You could have your friend RUN this program. Your screen might look like this.

```
GUESS A NUMBER BETWEEN 1 AND 10
?   4
```

Your screen might also look like this.

```
GUESS A NUMBER BETWEEN 1 AND 10
?   6
YOU GOT IT!!
```

The IF ... THEN statement in line 40 compares the values of N2 and N1. IF they are equal, THEN it does the rest of the line; it prints a message.

In the first run of the program, the computer puts the number 6 in variable N1. Then it asks you for a number. You type a 4 and press RETURN or ENTER. The computer stores the 4 in N2. Now line 40 checks to see whether the 6 in N1 is equal to the 4 in N2. Because they are not equal, the computer skips the second half of the IF ... THEN statement. It does not print anything.

In the second run of the program, because the values of N1 and N2 are equal, the computer prints YOU GOT IT!!

Let's add two more lines to this program.

```
10   LET N1 = 6
20   PRINT "GUESS A NUMBER BETWEEN 1 AND 10"
30   INPUT N2
40   IF N2 = N1 THEN PRINT "YOU GOT IT!!"
50   IF N2 < N1 THEN PRINT "YOUR NUMBER IS TOO LOW"
60   IF N2 > N1 THEN PRINT "YOUR NUMBER IS TOO HIGH"
```

Line 50 checks to see whether the number you typed is less than 6. If it is, then the TOO LOW message will print.

Line 60 checks to see whether the number you typed is greater than 6. If it is, then the TOO HIGH message will print.

When you RUN this program, your screen might look like this.

GUESS A NUMBER BETWEEN 1 AND 10
? 4
YOUR NUMBER IS TOO LOW

1. What would your screen look like if you ran this program and typed the number 8 after the question mark?

   10   LET A = 5
   20   LET B = 7
   30   LET C = A + B
   40   PRINT "WHAT IS" A "PLUS" B
   50   INPUT S
   60   IF S = C THEN PRINT "GOOD WORK!"

2. Add two more lines to this program. If you type in a wrong answer, the computer should tell you that your answer is TOO HIGH or TOO LOW.

3. Rewrite this program so the computer asks for two numbers, and then asks you for the sum. Your screen might look like this.

TYPE IN A NUMBER
? 4
TYPE IN ANOTHER NUMBER
? 6
WHAT IS 4 PLUS 6
? 9
YOUR NUMBER IS TOO LOW

CUMULATIVE REVIEW

Write the letter of the correct answer.
Use the figure below to answer
Exercises 1 and 2.

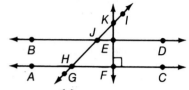

1. $\overleftrightarrow{KF}$ is ▦ to $\overleftrightarrow{AC}$.

  a. parallel   **b.** skew
  c. perpendicular   **d.** not given

2. Which angle is a right angle?

  a. $\angle AHI$ **b.** $\angle EFC$
  c. $\angle BJI$ **d.** not given

3. Find the measure of $\angle A$.

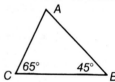

  a. 45°   **b.** 70°
  c. 80°   **d.** not given

Use the figures below to answer
Exercises 4 and 5.

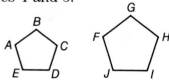

4. These figures are ▦.

  a. hexagons   **b.** quadrilaterals
  c. pentagons   **d.** not given

5. Both figure $ABCDE$ and figure
$FGHIJ$ are regular polygons;
therefore, they are ▦.

  a. congruent   **b.** similar
  c. symmetric   **d.** not given

6. What kind of angle is this?

  a. acute   **b.** obtuse
  c. right   **d.** not given

7.
$$8 \text{ h } 42 \text{ min} + 6 \text{ h } 30 \text{ min}$$

  a. 14 h 12 min   **b.** 15 h 12 min
  c. 14 h 2 min   **d.** not given

8. What is the least common multiple
of 8, 24, and 48?

  a. 2   **b.** 3
  c. 8   **d.** not given

9. $0.73\overline{)0.06716}$

  a. 0.0897   **b.** 0.092
  c. 0.093   **d.** not given

10. Solve for n. $n \times 5 = 60$.

  a. 6   **b.** 11
  c. 12   **d.** not given

11.
$$67.05 \times 17$$

  a. 113.985   **b.** 1,139.85
  c. 1,178.85   **d.** not given

12. Reggie owns 47 toy cars. He also
owns 5 storage cases. Each case
can hold 9 cars. How many of the
cars are *not* stored in a case?

  a. 2   **b.** 9
  c. 45   **d.** not given

You have just elected a new class government. Take a poll of all the class members to determine what they think the government should try to accomplish. You might list five possibilities, and have the class members choose the one they favor most. Compile your statistics into a report for the class government to use.

11 STATISTICS AND PROBABILITY

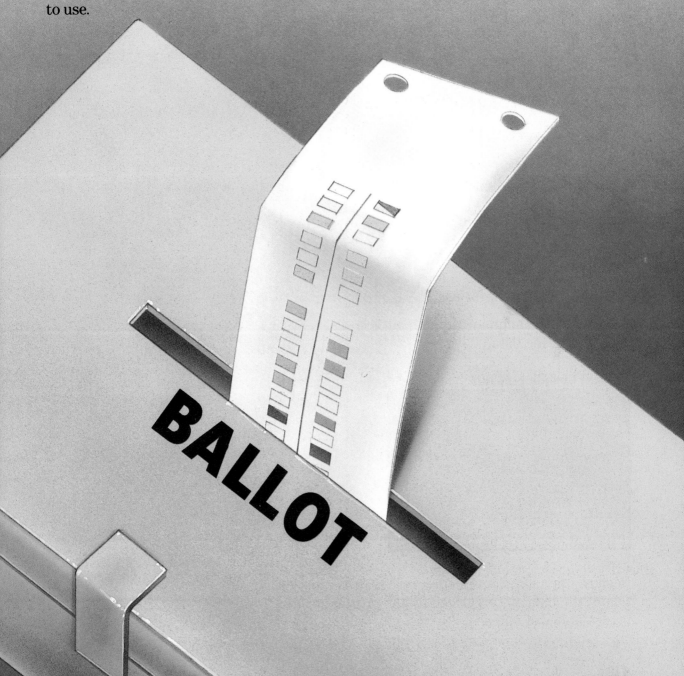

Recording Data on a Table

A. A sixth-grade class at the Herrick School held a student-council election. To count the votes for the candidates in an organized way, the students made a tally of the votes.

To make a tally:

1. Make a list of the candidates.

2. Make a mark on the list for each vote that each candidate received.

Bill	卌 ||
Al	卌	
Lori	卌	
Joan	卌 ||||

B. This election data will be easier for others to read if you organize it as a table.

To make a table:

1. Make one column for each type of data.

2. Fill in the columns with the data from the tally. Organize the data.

STUDENT COUNCIL ELECTION

Candidate	Votes
Joan	9
Bill	7
Lori	6
Al	6

Because the table lists election results, it is most easily read if the data are organized by the greatest to the least number of votes.

Solve.

1. The sixth-grade class is having a party. Their teacher tells them they will need 3 of each of the following: salads, gallons of juice, bowls of fruit or raw vegetables, hot dishes, and desserts. Use the information from the chalkboard at right to make a tally of what each class member has agreed to bring.

   Of what categories of party food will there be enough?

   What will still be needed?

2. Choose one of these projects. Collect the data, tally it, and then put it in a table.

   Project 1: Interview your classmates to find out which U.S. President is their favorite. How many chose Presidents other than Washington, Jefferson, Lincoln, or Kennedy?

   Project 2: Make a list of the top 5 popular songs of the week. Interview your classmates to find out which of the 5 songs is their favorite. Compare the results to the actual rankings. (HINT: Will two columns be enough?)

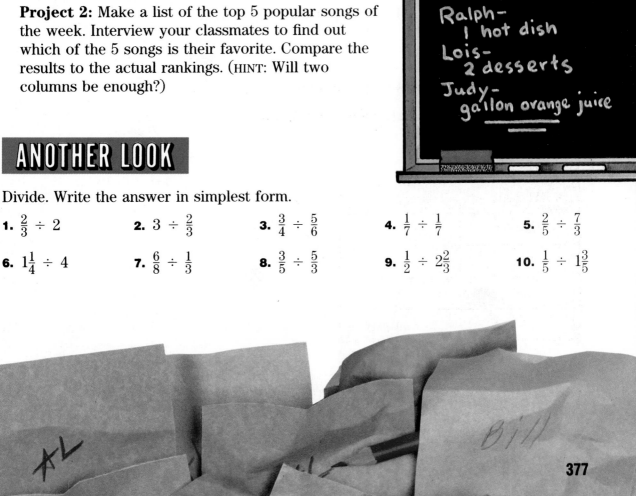

Sal–
  a bowl of carrots
Rhea–
  potato salad
Marilyn –
  gallon apple juice
Catherine –
  1 dessert
Eddie–
  a bowl of grapes
Dottie–
  macaroni salad
Patty–
  a bowl of broccoli
Joe–
  gallon grape juice
Cindy–
  gallon apple juice
Kevin–
  1 hot dish
Ralph–
  1 hot dish
Lois–
  2 desserts
Judy–
  gallon orange juice

ANOTHER LOOK

Divide. Write the answer in simplest form.

1. $\frac{2}{3} \div 2$

2. $3 \div \frac{2}{3}$

3. $\frac{3}{4} \div \frac{5}{6}$

4. $\frac{1}{7} \div \frac{1}{7}$

5. $\frac{2}{5} \div \frac{7}{3}$

6. $1\frac{1}{4} \div 4$

7. $\frac{6}{8} \div \frac{1}{3}$

8. $\frac{3}{5} \div \frac{5}{3}$

9. $\frac{1}{2} \div 2\frac{2}{3}$

10. $\frac{1}{5} \div 1\frac{3}{5}$

Interpreting Information

A. The students at the Herrick School held a mock mayoral election. Find to the nearest tenth the **mean,** or average, number of votes cast by each grade.

Grade	1	2	3	4	5	6
Votes	55	54	50	53	54	49

You can find the mean of a set of numbers by adding and then dividing the sum by the number of addends.

$55 + 54 + 50 + 53 + 54 + 49 = 315$

$315 \div 6 = 52.5$

The mean number of votes cast was 52.5.

B. If you order a set of numbers from the least to the greatest, the number in the middle is the **median.** If there is an even number of numbers in the set, then the mean of the two middle numbers is the median.

49, 50, 53, 54, 54, 55

$(53 + 54) \div 2 = 53.5$

The median of this set of numbers is 53.5.

C. The **mode** is the number that occurs most often. The mode of this set of numbers is 54.

D. The **range** is the difference between the greatest number and the least number.

$55 - 49 = 6$

The range of this set of numbers is 6.

Copy and complete the table.

Set	Mean	Median	Mode	Range
1. 6, 12, 11, 12, 14	▦	▦	▦	▦
2. 32, 51, 47, 10, 10	▦	▦	▦	▦
3. 75, 33, 51, 33, 98	▦	▦	▦	▦
4. 59, 44, 59, 12, 59, 3, 44	▦	▦	▦	▦
5. 11, 9, 3, 7, 3	▦	▦	▦	▦
6. 4.2, 57.6, 4.2	▦	▦	▦	▦

Solve. For Problem 8, use the Infobank.

7. Walter Rivera is running for mayor. For his fund-raising dinners, tickets are sold both in advance and at the door. For previous dinners, the range of ticket sales at the door has been 15, with the fewest tickets sold being 5. If the advance sale for the next dinner is 85, what is the greatest number of people Mr. Rivera's staff could reasonably expect?

★8. Use the information on page 436 to solve. Mr. Rivera has held 5 rallies so far in his campaign for mayor. His campaign manager needs to predict the number of people who will attend the final rally. Will the mean or the median give a more accurate idea of the number of people at past rallies? Why?

CHALLENGE

Mr. Rivera goes on TV's *Newsforum* show to be interviewed by 3 local journalists. The journalists' mean age is 42, their median age is 45, and the range of their ages is 23. What are their ages?

Making a Pictograph

Pictographs use symbols to represent large numbers. You can make a pictograph to show the information in this table about the 1984 Presidential election.

THE 1984 PRESIDENTIAL ELECTION

State	Total votes
Arizona	995,277
Massachusetts	2,512,880
New York	6,538,787

To make a pictograph:
1. Round the numbers in the table to a convenient place. For this graph, round each number to the nearest 500,000.

Total votes	Votes (rounded)
995,277	1,000,000
2,512,880	2,500,000
6,538,787	6,500,000

2. List the states vertically as in the table. Title the graph.

THE 1984 PRESIDENTIAL ELECTION

State	Total votes
Arizona	
Massachusetts	
New York	

3. Choose a symbol to represent an approximate number of votes.

Let ☐ = 1,000,000 votes.

Let ◿ = 500,000 votes.

Replace the numbers with symbols to complete the graph.

You can see from the pictograph how voters turned out in these states during the 1984 Presidential election.

THE 1984 PRESIDENTIAL ELECTION

State	Total votes
Arizona	☐
Massachusetts	☐ ☐ ◿
New York	☐ ☐ ☐ ☐ ☐ ☐ ◿

Each ☐ = 1,000,000 votes.

Solve.

1. Copy and complete the pictograph. Use the data in the table.

PROFESSIONS OF OUR PRESIDENTS

Profession	Number of Presidents
Actor	1
Businessman	4
Farmer	2
Lawyer	24
Soldier	6
Teacher	3

PROFESSIONS OF OUR PRESIDENTS

Profession	Number of Presidents
Actor	
Businessman	
Farmer	
Lawyer	
Soldier	
Teacher	

Each ⊕ = 4 Presidents.

2. According to your graph, what was the profession of most of the Presidents?

3. Use the following information to draw your own pictograph: Over the years, the number of representatives in Congress has increased as more states have been admitted to the Union. When the Constitution was first adopted, in 1787, there were 65 representatives. By 1820, that number had increased to 213. In 1850, the House had 237 members; in 1880, 332; and by 1910, it had reached its present membership of 435.

4. According to your graph, about how many times has the House increased in size since 1820?

MIDCHAPTER REVIEW

Test Date	Score
Sept. 20	92
Nov. 3	94
Dec. 14	73
Feb. 1	98
Mar. 17	89
Apr. 28	85
May 29	85

Use the information to prepare a table that lists Fran's test scores from the lowest to the highest. Then find the mean, median, and mode of her test scores.

Making a Bar Graph

A **bar graph** helps a reader compare different quantities. You can use a bar graph to show the information in this table about the 1860 Presidential election.

To make a bar graph:

1. Round the numbers in the table to a convenient place. For this graph, round each number to the nearest hundred thousand.

THE 1860 PRESIDENTIAL ELECTION

Candidate	Popular votes	Votes (rounded)
Abraham Lincoln	1,866,352	1,900,000
Stephen Douglas	1,375,157	1,400,000
John Breckinridge	845,763	800,000
John Bell	589,581	600,000

2. Draw and label the vertical and horizontal axes. Choose intervals between the numbers that best display the data. For this graph, intervals of 200,000 would be reasonable. Title the graph.

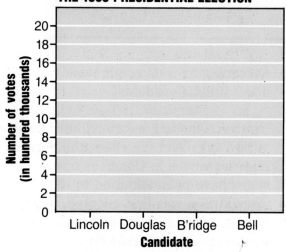

3. Draw vertical bars to represent each number.

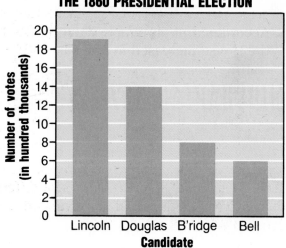

Solve.

1. Use the information in this table about the 1912 Presidential election to draw a bar graph.

THE 1912 PRESIDENTIAL ELECTION

Candidate	Popular votes
Woodrow Wilson	6,286,214
Theodore Roosevelt	4,216,020
William H. Taft	3,483,922

2. According to your graph, if $\frac{1}{3}$ of Taft's supporters had voted for Roosevelt, would Roosevelt have won the popular vote?

3. Use the following information to make a bar graph: Electoral votes determine who wins the Presidency. The candidates who received the greatest number of electoral votes are Ronald Reagan with 525 in 1984, Franklin Roosevelt with 523 in 1936, Richard Nixon with 520 in 1972, and Ronald Reagan again with 489 in 1980.

4. According to your graph, if a future candidate received 500 electoral votes, which place would he or she hold on the list?

5. Take a poll of students in your class to find out which of the last four Presidents they like most. Make a bar graph to show the results.

CHALLENGE

Make another bar graph that shows the results of the 1860 Presidential election, but use a different scale on the vertical axis. Make the intervals on the vertical axis equal to 0.3 million.

Does Lincoln's margin of victory shrink?

More Practice, page 457

PROBLEM SOLVING
Making a Table To Find a Pattern

You can often make a table to help you find a pattern that will help you solve a problem.

> One city is counting votes after an election. At one point, 15,500 votes were counted. 15 minutes later, a total of 16,250 votes were counted. After 30 minutes, 17,050 votes in all were counted. After 45 minutes, 17,900 votes were counted. If this pattern continues, how many votes would be counted in $1\frac{1}{2}$ hours?

VOTES COUNTED

Minutes	0	15	30	45	
Votes	15,500	16,250	17,050	17,900	

The count is reported at 15-minute intervals of time. The next number of minutes would be 60.

To find the pattern in the number of votes, look at how the numbers differ from one another. First, find the difference between the first two counts. The difference is 750. Now, add 750 to the second number to see whether you get the third number on the table, 17,050.

$$16,250 + 750 = 17,000 \neq 17,050$$

So, the pattern does not involve adding 750 to each number.

Try another way. Find the difference between *each* pair of numbers. The number of votes counted the first three times increases by 750, 800, and 850. So, the pattern involves adding 50 more votes to the number counted in the previous 15 minutes and adding this sum to the total.

So, if this pattern continues, in 90 minutes, or $1\frac{1}{2}$ hours, 20,750 votes would be counted.

Copy and complete the table.

1. There are 2 voting machines and 6 workers at one voting station. At the next station, there are 2 machines and 8 workers. The next station has 2 machines and 11 workers, and the next has 2 machines and 13 workers. The city has 14 machines. What is the total number of workers?

Machines	2	2	2	2			
Workers	6	8	11	13			

Solve. Make a table if needed.

2. One candidate greeted 10 people in 6 seconds. After 12 seconds, he greeted 18 people. After 18 seconds, he greeted 26 people. At the end of 24 seconds, he greeted 34 people. At this rate, how many people will he greet in 42 seconds?

3. What is the total number of people that the candidate greets in 1 minute?

4. The polls open at 6:00 A.M. By 6:15 A.M., 12 people have voted. By 6:30 A.M., 24 people have voted, and by 6:45 A.M., 36 people have voted. By what time will 60 people have voted?

5. Polly hands out political flyers. She has given out 20 flyers after one minute, 23 flyers after two minutes, 26 after three minutes, and 29 after four minutes. If she continues in this pattern to give out her entire supply of 65 flyers, in how many minutes will she have given out all of them?

6. An inspector must visit each voting station in order. It takes him about 1 hour 12 minutes to visit 3 stations. If he starts at 6:00 A.M., at what time will he visit his eighteenth station?

Making a Broken-Line Graph

A **broken-line graph** is used to show a continuing trend over a period of time. You can make a broken-line graph to show the information in this table about the money spent on a candidate's television ads.

To make a broken-line graph:

1. Round the numbers in the table to a convenient place. For this graph, round each number to the nearest $1,000.

MONEY SPENT ON TV CAMPAIGN ADS

Month	Actual amounts	Rounded amounts
May	$36,427	$36,000
June	$43,840	$44,000
July	$38,921	$39,000
Aug.	$32,085	$32,000
Sept.	$56,780	$57,000
Oct.	$62,010	$62,000

2. Draw and label the vertical and horizontal axes. Choose intervals between the numbers that best display the data. For this graph, intervals of $5,000 would be reasonable. Title the graph. Note that the ragged line shows where part of the scale is missing.

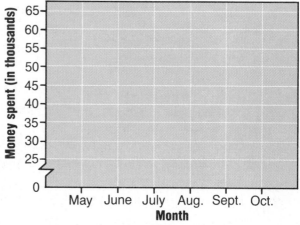

3. Place the points on the graph. Then connect all the points with line segments.

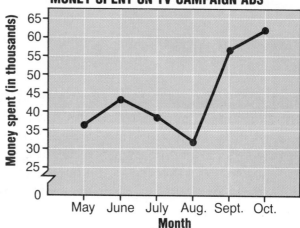

386

Solve.

1. Copy and complete the broken-line graph.

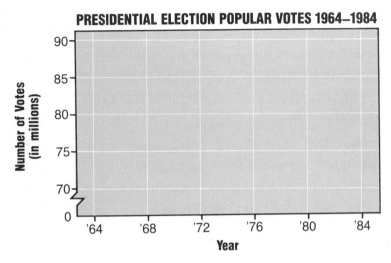

PRESIDENTIAL ELECTION POPULAR VOTES 1964–1984

Year	Number of votes
1964	70,303,305
1968	72,967,119
1972	76,336,008
1976	79,977,869
1980	85,100,120
1984	89,060,410

2. According to your graph, did the popular vote decline from one election to the next between 1964 and 1984?

3. Use the following information to make a broken-line graph: In the 1956 Presidential election, 59.3% of all those who were eligible voted. In 1960, that percentage rose to 62.8. The percentage was 61.9 in 1964, 60.9 in 1968, 55.2 in 1972, 53.5 in 1976, 54.0 in 1980, and 53.3 in 1984.

4. According to your graph, in which years did the percentage of eligible voters who voted rise from the previous election?

FOCUS: REASONING

Sara White, Hillary Brown, and Steven Green were sitting reading the election results. Sara said, "Our shirts are the colors of our names, but none of us is wearing the color shirt that matches our name. Isn't that funny?" The student in the brown shirt said, "I don't think that's funny." What color shirt was each student wearing?

PROBLEM SOLVING
Practice

Write the letter of the formula you would use to solve
each problem.

1. The conference room of Pilar
   Sierra's campaign headquarters
   measures $11\frac{1}{2}$ feet long by $12\frac{1}{4}$ feet
   wide. She wants to buy a rug that
   will end $\frac{1}{2}$ foot from the wall. What
   size rug should she buy for the
   room?
   a. $A = lw$
   b. $A = \frac{1}{2}bh$
   c. $A = 2\pi r$

2. During a campaign parade, the
   marching band paraded around a
   circular playing field once. If the
   diameter of the field is 150 meters,
   how far did the band march?
   a. $P = 2l + 2w$
   b. $P = 4x$
   c. $C = 2\pi r$

3. Sarah wants to cover her garden
   with a plastic tarpaulin to protect it
   from frost. The garden measures 24
   feet long by 15 feet wide. What size
   tarpaulin should Sarah buy?
   a. $A = 2\pi r$
   b. $A = lw$
   c. $A = \frac{1}{2}bh$

4. Jim and Barry need to buy paper for
   the kite they are making. The kite
   has a triangular shape. Its height is
   4 feet. Its base is 2 feet. What is the
   least amount of paper that Jim and
   Barry should buy?
   a. $A = \frac{1}{2}bh$
   b. $A = lw$
   c. $P = 4x$

Read each statement. Then write a sensible question
about the situation.

5. Carlos and Luis go to the library to
   look at books about the history of
   their state. They want to give a
   report to their class on their state
   and its history.

6. Rose went on a trip to Alaska and
   learned about several American
   Indian groups. After she returned
   home, she wanted to do a report in
   class about a group of American
   Indians.

7. Jeannette and Susan are planning a
   weekend camping trip. They are
   trying to decide which of 2 state
   parks they should visit.

8. James wants to write a report on
   famous mathematicians. He goes to
   the library to look for books on the
   subject.

Use the bar graph to answer each question.

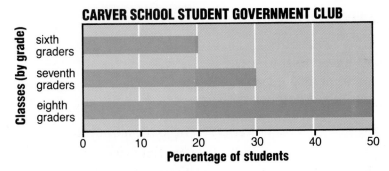

CARVER SCHOOL STUDENT GOVERNMENT CLUB

Classes (by grade): sixth graders, seventh graders, eighth graders

Percentage of students: 0, 10, 20, 30, 40, 50

9. There are 50 students in the Carver Student-Government Club. How many of the students are seventh graders?

10. If there are 50 students in the club, how many fewer sixth graders than eighth graders are there in the club?

Solve.

11. The block association raised $1,896.40 for a political candidate. What was the average amount, to the nearest cent, raised by each of the 29 people who worked with the block association?

12. A politician budgeted $598,675 for his election campaign. The actual cost of the campaign was $687,950. How much more than the budgeted amount was that?

13. Sean wants to make and hang campaign banners. He has $12\frac{1}{2}$ yards of material. He uses $1\frac{1}{4}$ yards to make 1 banner. He wants to make 8 banners. Does he have enough material?

14. While fund-raising, Deidre rode her bike 15 miles. Then she had a flat tire and had to walk 4 miles. If she cycled at 20 miles per hour and walked at 3 miles per hour, about how long did the trip take her?

15. A campaign debate is being held on a baseball field that is in the shape of a pentagon. If each of 2 sides is 72 m long and each of the remaining sides is 120 m long, what is the perimeter of the baseball field?

★16. In the mayoral race, Dave Herbert ran against Judy Longstreet. The results of the election were 23,251 votes for Herbert, 26,828 votes for Longstreet, and 9,539 votes for other candidates. What percent of the votes did each candidate receive? Who won? by what percent of the vote?

PROBLEM SOLVING
Checking That the Solution Answers the Question

You *always* need to pay special attention to the question asked in a word problem. Some problems require an answer that is more than just a number with a label.

> In 1944, Franklin Delano Roosevelt was reelected President of the United States. He received 432 votes from the electoral college. In 1948, Harry Truman, Roosevelt's successor, received 304 electoral votes. Did Roosevelt receive 130 more electoral votes than Truman?

Which is the correct answer?

a. Franklin Roosevelt received 128 more electoral votes.

b. No, Roosevelt did not receive 130 more electoral votes.

c. Yes, Roosevelt received many more electoral votes than Truman.

Think about what the question asks. You need to subtract to find the difference in votes. The difference is 128. Choice *a* states that the difference is 128, but this is not the answer to the question. Choice *c* also does not answer the question. The correct answer is *b*. If you are not sure why, carefully reread the question that was asked in the problem.

Write the letter of the correct answer.

1. At Merrill Academy, Bob Jones received 75% of the total votes for student council president. If 512 people voted, how many votes did Bob receive?

   a. Bob won the election.
   b. Bob received 384 votes.

2. Mayor Len of Ridgetown spent $1,500 on his reelection campaign. His opponent, Carol Ladd, spent 4 times as much money. How much money did Carol Ladd spend?

   a. Carol Ladd spent $4,500 more.
   b. Carol Ladd spent $6,000.

Solve.

3. The Presidential term of office in the United States is 4 years. Franklin Delano Roosevelt served as President for $3\frac{1}{4}$ terms. For how many years did Roosevelt serve as President?

4. Bob Richmond won his town's mayoral election. For every 3 votes that he received, his rival received 2 votes. If Bob's rival received 14,560 votes, how many votes did Bob receive?

5. The ages of the candidates in Newcombe's city elections are 35, 37, 44, 56, 37, and 49. What is the mean age of the candidates? What is the median age? What is the mode?

6. Maytown has 15,284 eligible voters. The Women's League of Voters did a study and found out that $\frac{3}{4}$ of those eligible voters actually vote in elections. How many people in Maytown do not vote?

7. Each of the 3 candidates for public office in Franklin City spent the maximum amount allowed for TV advertisements—$1,275.50. How much money was spent on TV advertisements by the 3 candidates?

8. Andrew Pymm was elected city clerk of Rislow. He received 55% of the total vote. If 62,540 people voted, how many votes did Andrew Pymm receive?

9. Franklin Delano Roosevelt was elected to his first term as president in 1932 with 22,821,857 popular votes. He was elected to a second term with 27,751,597 popular votes. For his third and fourth terms he received 27,244,160 and 25,602,504 votes respectively. In what year did Roosevelt receive the most popular votes?

10. Carl, Amy, Steven, and Martha ran for class president. Martha received one more vote than Carl. Amy received twice as many votes as Steven. Steven received three more votes than Martha. Who won the election?

Probability and Expectation

A. James, Sue, Dan, Jon, and Laurie are running for class president. Their names are printed on strips of paper and put into a hat. The first name picked will appear first on the ballot. What is the **probability** that Sue's name will be picked first?

It is **equally likely** that any one of the names will be picked. Since there are more boys' names than girls' names, it is more likely that a boy's name will be picked.

Probability can be shown as a fraction.

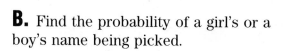

$$\frac{\text{number of favorable outcomes (Sue's name)}}{\text{number of possible outcomes (all the names)}} = \frac{1}{5}$$

There is 1 chance in 5 that Sue's name will be picked first. The probability is $\frac{1}{5}$.

B. Find the probability of a girl's or a boy's name being picked.

Favorable outcomes: 5
Possible outcomes: 5
Probability: $\frac{5}{5}$, or 1

It is **certain** that either a girl's or a boy's name will be picked.

Find the probability of Ted's name being picked.

Favorable outcomes: 0
Possible outcomes: 5
Probability: $\frac{0}{5}$, or 0

It is **impossible** for Ted's name to be picked.

C. James polls the students in the class and finds that 1 of every 2 students says that they will vote for him. There are 30 students in the class. Based on this poll, how many votes can James expect?

To find the expected number of votes, multiply the probability of a student's voting for James by the total number of votes that will be cast.

The probability equals 1 of 2, or $\frac{1}{2}$.

Multiply the probability by the total. $\frac{1}{2} \times 30 = 15$

James can expect 15 students to vote for him.

Use this information to solve Exercises 1 through 7.

José, Tanya, Richie, Flo, Michelle, and Betty all want to count the votes on election day. Ms. Miller wants only one person to count the votes. She writes all the names on a spinner and spins the dial once to pick a name.

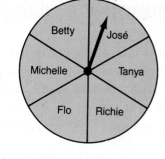

1. Is it more likely or less likely that a boy's name will be picked?

What is the probability that the name picked will be

2. a boy's?

3. a girl's?

4. Fred's?

5. Michelle's?

6. a girl's or a boy's?

★7. José's or Flo's?

Solve.

8. Each of the 5 candidates forms a party. If it is equally likely for any of the 30 students to join any party, how many students can Jon expect to join his party?

9. On election day, the 5 candidates give speeches. By mutual consent, James will speak first and Sue will speak second. Everybody else wants to speak last, and so they draw lots. What is the probability that Laurie will speak last?

★10. Poll some of the students in your class to determine whom they would vote for if there was an election for class president. Find each candidate's probability of winning and how many votes each could expect to receive.

FOCUS: ESTIMATION

To estimate the total attendance, think:

All the numbers are about 6,000. Multiply the estimated daily attendance by the number of days.

$5 \times 6,000$ Estimate: 30,000

Fair Attendance	
Mon.	5,736
Tues.	6,814
Wed.	6,523
Thurs.	5,963
Fri.	6,419

Estimate.

1. 8,250 + 7,838 + 7,985 + 8,058

2. 87,955 + 90,457 + 91,293

Independent Events

A. Claudia is running for the student council. She has to choose the colors to use on her campaign buttons and her pennants. The buttons come with either red or white backgrounds, and the pennants come with red, white, or blue backgrounds. From how many different arrangements of button and pennant colors does Claudia have to choose?

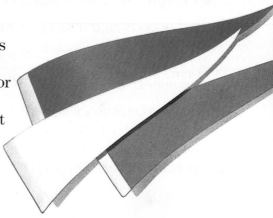

You can use a tree diagram to show the possible arrangements.

Button color	Pennant color	Possible arrangement
red	red	red button, red pennant
	white	red button, white pennant
	blue	red button, blue pennant
white	red	white button, red pennant
	white	white button, white pennant
	blue	white button, blue pennant

Claudia can choose from 6 different arrangements.

B. You can also find the total number of possible arrangements by multiplying the number of choices for each item.

button colors		pennant colors		
2	×	3	=	6

C. Claudia writes the button colors on slips of paper and then picks one at random. She does the same with pennant colors. What is the probability that Claudia will choose red for buttons and white for pennants?

The choice of button color does not affect the choice of pennant color, and so the two events are independent. To find the probability that two **independent events** will both occur, multiply the probability of each event occurring.

Red button

Favorable outcomes: 1
Possible outcomes: 2
Probability: $\frac{1}{2}$

White pennant

Favorable outcomes: 1
Possible outcomes: 3
Probability: $\frac{1}{3}$

Red button and white pennant

$\frac{1}{2} \times \frac{1}{3} = \frac{1}{6}$

The probability that Claudia will choose red for buttons and white for pennants is 1 in 6 or $\frac{1}{6}$.

Use the spinner to solve Exercises 1 through 3.

A spinner such as the one at right is spun twice.

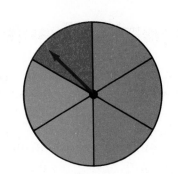

1. What is the probability that the first spin will be green? green or blue?

2. What is the probability that both spins will be red? that the first will be red and the second blue?

3. How many possible outcomes are there?

Solve.

4. Eric has to choose the color and shape of his campaign posters. They come in white, yellow, green, or blue and can be square, rectangular, or triangular. Use a tree diagram to show all the possible arrangements.

5. Before the election, Lina and Bob plan to debate. They flip a coin twice, once to decide who will speak first and once to decide who will be first on the ballot. What is the probability that Bob will win both times?

6. Jean's campaign manager is ordering pamphlets. She must decide on the arrangement of paper color, ink color, and typeface. From how many arrangements does she have to choose?

Paper	Ink	Typeface
white	black	bold
cream	blue	italic
blue	red	gothic

ANOTHER LOOK

Complete.

1. What is 50% of 36?

2. What percent of 50 is 15?

3. What percent of 90 is 9?

4. 80% of ■ is 160.

5. 25% of ■ is 120.

6. What is 30% of 60?

More Practice, page 458

READING MATH

Scanning

English is written and read from left to right. We are used to moving our eyes from left to right.

As we read mathematics our eyes move in all directions. When we read tables, graphs, charts, or diagrams our eyes move up, down, left or right.

Look at the graph below. Read the letters in alphabetical order. As you read, think about how your eyes moved around the page.

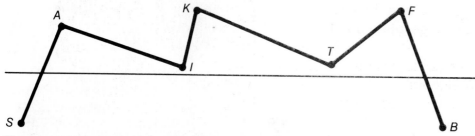

Your eyes probably moved all around the graph. You were **scanning** to find the next letter.

Learning to scan can help you read mathematics. You don't read all the information. Your eyes move around until you find the information you want.

1. Scan the graph above. Write all the vowels you find.

2. Scan the table below to find the product of 17 and 19.

3. Scan the table to find two numbers that have a product of 483.

4. Scan the graph below to find the color that was chosen most often.

5. Scan the graph to find a color chosen by 25 people.

×	17	19	21	23	27
17	289	323	357	391	459
19	323	361	399	437	513
21	357	399	441	483	567
23	391	437	483	529	621
27	459	513	567	621	729

Favorite Colors			
	X		⟩
⟩	X		X
X	X	⟩	X
X	X	X	X
X	X	X	X
Red	Blue	Green	Yellow

Each X stands for 10 people.

GROUP PROJECT

Surveying Voters

The problem: The editor of a local newspaper has asked your class to take a survey of voters in your community. The lists below include the main points to cover. Read the lists carefully. Then prepare your questionnaire. When you're ready, take the survey, and tally the results. Each student in your class should try to survey at least 5 people.

Key Questions

- How many people voted in the last election? How many people did not vote?
- How many people do/do not plan to vote in the next election?
- Why might a person choose not to vote?
- Which political party, if any, is each person associated with?

Other Questions to Consider

- Do young voters give answers different from those of older voters?
- Do males give answers different from those of females?

Results to Tally

- Based on your survey, what percent of the population voted in the last election?
- Based on your survey, what percent is likely to vote in the next election?
- What reasons did people give for not voting?
- Which political party seems to have more followers than any other party in your community?

CHAPTER TEST

1. Organize the following information in a table. Use the data in the table to make a pictograph. (pages 376 and 380)

Students at the Cranston School travel to school in different ways. 89 students walk. 22 are driven by their parents. 31 ride bicycles, and 193 ride the bus.

2. Use the data in the table to make a bar graph. (page 382)

THE NUMBER OF CALORIES IN SOME SNACK FOODS

Food	Calories per serving
Apple	80
Celery	5
Cheddar cheese	115
Grapes	35
Milk	150
Watermelon	110

3. Use the data in the table to make a broken-line graph (page 386) and answer Questions 4–7. (page 378)

CRANSTON SCHOOL STUDENTS SICK AT HOME, BY MONTH

Month	Sept.	Oct.	Nov.	Dec.	Jan.	Feb.	Mar.	Apr.	May	June
Number of students Who missed a day of school	11	14	16	19	24	31	20	14	8	3

4. What is the mean number of students to stay home each month? _____

5. What is the median number? _____

6. What is the mode? _____

7. What is the range? _____

This spinner is spun once. Write as a fraction the probability that the arrow will land on   (page 392)

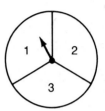

8. C.   **9.** B.   **10.** G.   **11.** A, B, C, or D.

12. If you spin the spinner 30 times, how many times can you expect the arrow to land on D?

Use the spinners with 1, 2, 3, green, red, and blue to solve exercises 13 through 16. (page 394)

13. Each spinner is spun once. Make a tree diagram to show all possible outcomes.

14. How many possible outcomes are there?

15. What is the probability that the first spinner will land on 1 and the second will land on red?

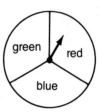

16. Use the tree diagram to find the probability that the first spinner will land on 1 or 2 and the second spinner will land on green?

Solve. Be sure you answer the question asked. (pages 384 and 390)

19. In the election of 1812, James Madison received 128 electoral votes. In 1816, Monroe received 183 electoral votes. Did Monroe receive 54 more electoral votes than Madison?

20. When Tina Estrom ran for school president, she handed out flyers. She handed out 17 flyers after 2 minutes, 28 flyers after 4 minutes, and 39 flyers after 6 minutes. If she continues in this pattern, how many flyers would she have handed out after 10 minutes?

BONUS

Each spinner is spun once. How many possible outcomes are there?

Each spinner is spun twice. How many possible outcomes are there?

Each spinner is spun once. What is the probability of black, A, 1 occurring?

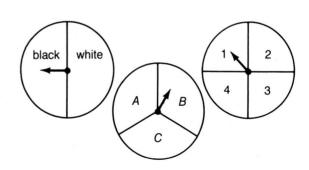

399

RETEACHING

You can use multiplication to find the probability that 2 independent events will both occur.

You need to choose an arrangement of colors for the band uniforms in your school. The colors of the hats can be blue or red. The colors of the shirts can be white, yellow, blue, or red. You write the hat colors and shirt colors on slips of paper and then pick one of each at random.

What is the probability that you will choose red for the hats and blue for the shirts?

You need to multiply the probability of each event occurring.

Red hat

Favorable outcomes: 1
Possible outcomes: 2
Probability: $\frac{1}{2}$

Blue shirt

Favorable outcomes: 1
Possible outcomes: 4
Probability: $\frac{1}{4}$

Red hat and blue shirt

$\frac{1}{2} \times \frac{1}{4} = \frac{1}{8}$

The probability that you will choose red for the hats and blue for the shirts is 1 in 8.

Use the spinner at the right to solve.
A spinner such as the one at right is spun twice.

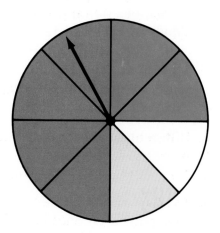

1. What is the probability that the first spin will be red?

2. What is the probability that the first spin will be either red or yellow?

3. What is the probability that both spins will be white? That the first will be red and the second green?

4. How many possible outcomes are there?

ENRICHMENT

Interpreting Statistics

Statistics can be used to make things seem true even if they are not. Here are three examples of how a statistic can be misinterpreted.

1. Sue's favorite baseball team won 97 games last year. Mike's favorite football team won only 14 games last year. Sue's favorite team is better than Mike's favorite team.

   How the statistic was misinterpreted: It is unfair to compare different groups of data. The total number of games in a professional baseball season is 162 games, while in a football season there are only 16 games.

2. Statistics show that 28 of every 30 students will miss at least 1 day of school because of colds. Mae's class had 30 students. 28 missed school because of colds. Therefore, Mae does not have to worry about catching a cold.

   The conclusion is wrong because the statistics show only a probability, not a certainty, that 28 of every 30 students will catch a cold.

3. Phil's mean test score this year was 91. Any score above 90 receives an A. Therefore, Phil received A's on all his tests.

   The conclusion is wrong because a mean was confused with the range. Phil's mean score was 91, but his range of scores may have included some that were less than 90.

For each story, write the letter that shows how the statistic was misused.

A. Different groups of data were compared.
B. A probability was treated as a certainty.
C. A mean was confused with the range of a set.

1. The Colts have won every game they have played on Saturdays. They play this Saturday. They will win.

2. Recipe A calls for $\frac{1}{4}$ cup sugar.
   Recipe B calls for $\frac{1}{2}$ cup sugar.
   Recipe B is sweeter than Recipe A.

3. Joan has seen 4 dogs this morning. Each has licked her hand. All the dogs Joan will see this morning will be friendly.

4. The mean height of the players on the team was 5 ft 6 in. Al is only 5 ft tall. Everyone on the team is taller than Al.

CUMULATIVE REVIEW

Write the letter of the correct answer.

1. What is the perimeter of the polygon?

   a. 16 m   **b.** 30 m
   c. 144 m   **d.** not given

2. What is the area of a rectangle 6 ft long and 3 ft wide?

   a. 9 ft^2 **b.** 18 ft
   c. 18 ft^2 **d.** not given

3. Find the area of the triangle.

   a. 150 mm^2 **b.** 300 mm^2
   c. 450 mm^2 **d.** not given

4. Find the area of the circle. Use 3.14 for π. Round to the nearest hundredth.

   a. 12.32 m^2 **b.** 24.62 m^2
   c. 28.28 m^2 **d.** not given

5. The solid figure pictured is a ▪.

   a. cone   **b.** cylinder
   c. sphere   **d.** not given

6. Find the volume of the cube.

   a. 16 m^3 **b.** 32 m^3
   c. 64 m^3 **d.** not given

7. The line segment drawn through the center of the circle is a ▪.

   a. radius   **b.** center
   c. circumference   **d.** not given

8. The percent represented by $\frac{4}{20}$ is ▪.

   a. 20%   **b.** 40%
   c. 80%   **d.** not given

9. 40 min 32 s = 39 min ▪ s

   a. 22   **b.** 32
   c. 62   **d.** not given

10. Write $\frac{42}{140}$ in simplest form.

    a. $\frac{3}{10}$ **b.** $\frac{6}{20}$
    c. $\frac{1}{3}$ **d.** not given

11. 709.43 ÷ 1,000

    a. 0.70943   **b.** 7,094.3
    c. 70,943   **d.** not given

12. 12)$34.56

    a. $2.88   **b.** $3.88
    c. $28.80   **d.** not given

13. The Browns own a swimming pool that is 10 feet wide and 15 feet long. They buy a tarp to cover it. To find the area of the tarp, which formula would you use?

    a. $A = 2l + 2w$ **b.** $A = s^2$
    c. $A = l \times w$ **d.** not given

14. **BUDGET OF THE PHOTOGRAPHY CLUB**

    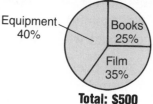

    How much money is used for film?

    a. $125   **b.** $175
    c. $200   **d.** not given

The world's record for the coldest temperature is -128.6°F, recorded in Antarctica on July 21, 1983. The record for the hottest temperature is 136°F, recorded in North Africa on September 13, 1922. Find out how the record temperatures in your area compare with these world records. Then set up your own system for keeping track of the temperature each day.

12 INTEGERS

Integers

A. During the launch of a spacecraft, time must be measured precisely. The clocks show the time before and after lift-off.

The time before lift-off is $^-5$ s.
Lift-off time is 0.
The time after lift-off is $^+5$ s.

Numbers such as $^-5$ and $^+5$ are called **integers.**

Integers can be used to show opposites.
Score 2 points: $^+2$.   Lose 2 points: $^-2$.
$10°$ above zero: $^+10$. $10°$ below zero: $^-10$.

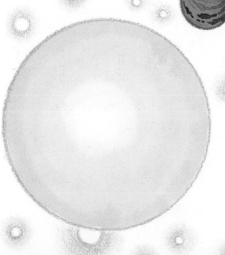

B. Integers can be shown on a number line.

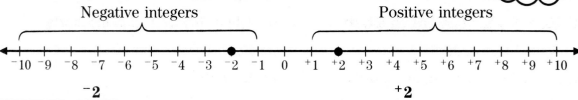

Negative integers   Positive integers

$^-10$ $^-9$ $^-8$ $^-7$ $^-6$ $^-5$ $^-4$ $^-3$ $^-2$ $^-1$ 0 $^+1$ $^+2$ $^+3$ $^+4$ $^+5$ $^+6$ $^+7$ $^+8$ $^+9$ $^+10$

$^-2$
● is 2 units to the left of 0.
● is read as "negative 2."

$^+2$
● is 2 units to the right of 0.
● is read as "positive 2."

$^-2$ and $^+2$ are opposite integers.
0 is neither positive nor negative.
However, 0 is an integer.

Checkpoint Write the letter of the correct answer.

Find the opposite of the integer.

1. $^-3$

a. 0
b. $^+1$
c. $^+3$
d. $^+6$

2. $^+6$

a. $^-12$
b. $^-6$
c. 0
d. $^+12$

3. $^-5$

a. $^-10$
b. 0
c. $^+2$
d. $^+5$

4. $^+8$

a. $^-16$
b. $^-8$
c. $^+4$
d. $^+16$

Identify the integers *A–F* on the number line.

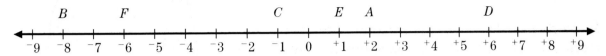

	B		F					C		E	A				D			
⁻9	⁻8	⁻7	⁻6	⁻5	⁻4	⁻3	⁻2	⁻1	0	⁺1	⁺2	⁺3	⁺4	⁺5	⁺6	⁺7	⁺8	⁺9

1. *A*   **2.** *B*   **3.** *C*   **4.** *D*   **5.** *E*   **6.** *F*

Write an integer to describe each situation.

7. 28° below zero

8. Win $12.

9. 845 feet above sea level

10. Increase the speed by 10 mi/h.

11. a withdrawal of $750

12. Dig a hole 4 feet deep.

13. Score 3 points.

14. Stock market drops 7 points.

Write the opposite situation and the opposite integer.

15. 10 steps downstairs

16. Up 8 floors in an elevator

17. Move 3 seats forward on a bus

18. 1 hour before ball game starts

19. Sank 3 feet under

20. Up 4 flights of stairs

21. 2 members join a club

22. Lose $5

23. Climb 9 yards up

24. Score 6 points

25. Increase the price by $7

26. To gain 5 yards in football

Solve.

27. An increase of 2° in the temperature of the spacecraft's cabin is shown by the integer ⁺2. Which integer would show a decrease of 2°?

28. The astronauts drilled 9 feet below the moon's surface to reach lunar samples. If the surface is considered 0, which integer would show the depth of the astronauts' drilling?

ANOTHER LOOK

Find the mean. Round to the nearest tenth when necessary.

1. 79, 116, 125, 104, 141

2. 11, 64, 21, 80, 47

3. 248, 421, 288, 366, 475

4. 15.6, 30.4, 27, 53.8, 34.4

5. 6, 17, 22, 12, 30, 9

6. 179, 214.7, 361.3, 311

Comparing Integers

A. Mt. Whitney and Mt. Shasta are two of California's highest mountains. One day at noon, the temperature at the peak of Mt. Whitney was ⁻8°F. The temperature on Mt. Shasta was ⁻4°F. On which mountaintop was the temperature colder?

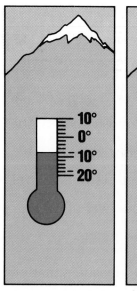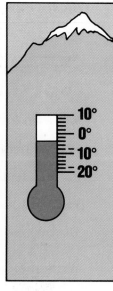

Compare the temperatures shown on the thermometers. On a thermometer, ⁻8°F is lower than ⁻4°F.

The temperature on Mt. Whitney, ⁻8°F, was colder.

B. You can use a number line to help you compare integers. Notice that the integers become greater as you move from left to right on the scale.

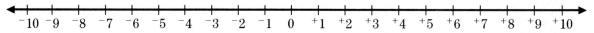

Compare ⁻3 and ⁻8.
Both integers are negative.
⁻3 is nearer to 0 than is ⁻8.
⁻3 is greater than ⁻8. ⁻3 > ⁻8

Compare ⁺7 and ⁺1.
Both integers are positive.
⁺7 is farther from 0 than is ⁺1.
⁺7 is greater than ⁺1. ⁺7 > ⁺1

> Given two negative integers, the one nearer to 0 is the greater.

> Given two positive integers, the one farther from 0 is the greater.

Compare ⁺1 and ⁻6.
⁺1 is to the right of 0.
⁻6 is to the left of 0.
⁺1 is greater than ⁻6. ⁺1 > ⁻6

> A positive integer or zero is always greater than a negative integer.

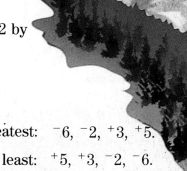

C. You can order the integers ⁻6, ⁺3, ⁺5, ⁻2 by comparing them.

Compare the negative integers. ⁻6 < ⁻2

Compare the positive integers. ⁺3 < ⁺5

Write them in order from the least to the greatest: ⁻6, ⁻2, ⁺3, ⁺5.

Write them in order from the greatest to the least: ⁺5, ⁺3, ⁻2, ⁻6.

Write >, <, or = for ●.

1. $^+5$ ● $^+7$
2. $^+3$ ● $^+8$
3. $^+6$ ● $^+4$
4. $^+5$ ● $^+3$

5. $^-5$ ● $^-2$
6. $^-10$ ● $^-10$
7. $^-3$ ● $^-7$
8. $^-8$ ● $^-6$

9. $^-2$ ● $^+3$
10. $^-7$ ● $^+4$
11. $^+5$ ● $^-10$
12. $^+9$ ● $^-6$

13. $^+19$ ● $^-13$
14. $^-7$ ● $^+11$
15. $^-6$ ● 0
16. $^+3$ ● $^+3$

17. 0 ● $^+12$
18. $^-17$ ● $^+9$
19. $^+10$ ● $^-11$
20. $^-1$ ● $^+1$

Write in order from the least to the greatest.

21. $^-10$, $^+5$, $^-5$
22. $^+8$, $^-7$, 0
23. $^+10$, $^-3$, $^-4$

24. $^+8$, $^-5$, $^+4$
25. $^-19$, $^+18$, $^+5$
26. 0, $^-6$, $^-8$

Write in order from the greatest to the least.

27. $^+25$, $^-5$, $^-9$, $^+8$
28. $^+85$, $^+52$, $^-53$, $^+71$

29. $^+13$, $^-74$, 0, $^+63$
30. $^-27$, $^+28$, $^+4$, $^+67$, $^-74$

Solve. Use the Infobank.

31. Use the information on page 436 to solve. The table lists the altitude of several places in the United States. Make a new table that lists the places in order from the highest altitude to the lowest altitude.

ANOTHER LOOK

Compare. Write <, >, or = for ●.

1. $\frac{1}{8}$ ● $\frac{4}{8}$
2. $\frac{10}{16}$ ● $\frac{12}{16}$
3. $\frac{3}{6}$ ● $\frac{4}{6}$
4. $\frac{7}{20}$ ● $\frac{4}{20}$

5. $\frac{1}{12}$ ● $\frac{1}{3}$
6. $\frac{3}{10}$ ● $\frac{3}{8}$
7. $\frac{2}{5}$ ● $\frac{2}{15}$
8. $\frac{7}{8}$ ● $\frac{7}{16}$

9. $\frac{3}{6}$ ● $\frac{5}{10}$
10. $\frac{2}{16}$ ● $\frac{1}{8}$
11. $\frac{2}{3}$ ● $\frac{3}{4}$
12. $\frac{4}{12}$ ● $\frac{5}{8}$

Adding Integers: Like Signs

A. Jeremy's science class took a trip to collect rock samples. Jeremy walked 3 yards from the starting point and found some slate. Then he walked another 6 yards to a spot where he found marble. How far did he walk from the starting point?

Add $^+3$ + $^+6$. Use the number line.

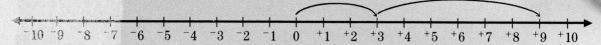

Start at 0. Move **right 3 spaces**. Move **right 6 more spaces**.

$^+3$ + $^+6$ = $^+9$

Jeremy walked 9 yards from the starting point.

B. You can add negative integers on the number line.

Add $^-2$ + $^-8$.

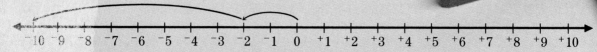

Start at 0. Move **left 2 spaces**. Move **left 8 more spaces**.

$^-2$ + $^-8$ = $^-10$

C. In each pair of equations, compare the signs of the addends to the sign of the sum. What do you notice?

$^+2$ + $^+3$ = $^+5$	$^+4$ + $^+3$ = $^+7$
$^-2$ + $^-3$ = $^-5$	$^-4$ + $^-3$ = $^-7$

> The sum of two positive integers is positive.
> The sum of two negative integers is negative.

Checkpoint   Write the letter of the correct answer.

Add.

1. $^+2$ + $^+9$

a. $^-11$
b. $^+7$
c. $^+11$
d. $^+18$

2. $^-2$ + $^-6$

a. $^-8$
b. $^-4$
c. $^+4$
d. $^+8$

Add.

1. $^+5 + {}^+15$ 2. $^+7 + {}^+6$ 3. $^+16 + {}^+7$ 4. $^+13 + {}^+8$

5. $^+5 + {}^+8$ 6. $^+16 + {}^+9$ 7. $^+20 + {}^+13$ 8. $^+7 + {}^+15$

9. $0 + {}^-8$ 10. $^-2 + {}^-8$ 11. $^-9 + {}^-8$ 12. $^-20 + {}^-15$

13. $^-9 + {}^-9$ 14. $^-8 + {}^-18$ 15. $^-12 + {}^-14$ 16. $^-11 + 0$

17. $^+9 + {}^+5$ 18. $^-18 + {}^-12$ 19. $^-13 + {}^-12$ 20. $^+6 + {}^+13$

21. $^-8 + {}^-6$ 22. $^-20 + {}^-12$ 23. $0 + {}^+20$ 24. $^-1 + {}^-16$

★25. $^+8 + {}^+5 + {}^+6$ ★26. $^-3 + {}^-6 + {}^-7$

Find n.

★27. $^-12 + {}^-10 = n$ ★28. $^-8 + n = {}^-14$ ★29. $n + {}^-19 = {}^-19$

Solve.

30. When the class started its science trip in the morning, the temperature was 58°F. By lunchtime, it had risen 7°. What was the temperature at lunchtime?

31. Terry descended 4 feet down a steep trail to reach a piece of mica. Then she descended 5 more feet and found a fossil. How far was she from her starting point?

32. Ed saw a trail marker as he hiked up Koy Hill. After walking 28 yards from the marker, he found a piece of slate. He saw another trail marker 32 yards after that. How far apart were the trail markers?

★33. Sue dug for fossils. She dug a hole 9 inches deep before lunch. After lunch, she continued to dig another 4 inches; then she stopped to sift some pebbles. She dug 7 more inches and found a fossil. How deep was the fossil buried?

MIDCHAPTER REVIEW

List the integers in order from the least to the greatest.

1. $^-6, 0, {}^+3, {}^-5$ 2. $^-9, {}^+9, {}^+3, {}^-2, {}^+4$ 3. $^+16, {}^-1, {}^+8, {}^-5, {}^+3$

Write $>$, $<$, or $=$ for ●.

4. $^+5 + {}^+3$ ● $^+4 + {}^+13$ 5. $^-3 + {}^-9$ ● $^-7 + {}^-5$

6. $^-2 + {}^-4$ ● $^-3 + {}^-1$ 7. $^+2 + {}^+6$ ● $^-8 + {}^-4$

SLATE

Adding Integers: Unlike Signs

A. When a jumbo jet took off, the temperature at the airport was $^+5°F$. As the jet climbed to 3,000 feet, the air temperature dropped 9°. What was the temperature at 3,000 feet?

Add $^+5 + {}^-9$. Use the number line.

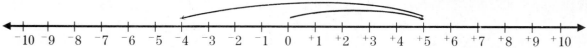

Start at 0. Move right 5 spaces. Move left 9 spaces.

$^+5 + {}^-9 = {}^-4$

The temperature at 3,000 feet was $^-4°F$.

B. Add $^-8 + {}^+6$. Will the sum be positive or negative? Use the number line to help you decide.

Start at 0. Move left 8 spaces. Move right 6 spaces.

$^-8 + {}^+6 = {}^-2$

> If you add integers with different signs, the sum has the same sign as the integer that is farther from zero.

Another example:

$^+10 + {}^-3 = {}^+7$

Checkpoint Write the letter of the correct answer.

Add.

1. $^+9 + {}^-4$
a. $^-13$
b. $^-5$
c. $^+5$
d. $^+13$

2. $^-4 + {}^+7$
a. $^-11$
b. $^-3$
c. $^+3$
d. $^+11$

3. $^+3 + {}^-9$
a. $^-12$
b. $^-6$
c. $^+6$
d. $^+12$

4. $^-8 + {}^+5$
a. $^-13$
b. $^-3$
c. $^+3$
d. $^+13$

Add.

1. $^-11 + {}^+19$ 2. $^-9 + {}^+14$ 3. $^-1 + {}^+13$ 4. $^-15 + {}^+20$ 5. $^-7 + {}^+13$

6. $^-18 + {}^+13$ 7. $^-5 + 0$ 8. $^-18 + {}^+9$ 9. $^-19 + {}^+13$ 10. $^-20 + {}^+8$

11. $^-12 + {}^+1$ 12. $^+14 + {}^-12$ 13. $0 + {}^+7$ 14. $^+18 + {}^-12$ 15. $^+16 + {}^-13$

16. $^+16 + {}^-17$ 17. $^+10 + {}^-13$ 18. $^+7 + {}^-12$ 19. $^+5 + {}^-13$ 20. $^+1 + {}^-15$

21. $^+9 + {}^+5$ 22. $^-5 + {}^+19$ 23. $^-12 + {}^+15$ 24. $0 + {}^-14$ 25. $^-16 + {}^+13$

★26. $^+6 + {}^-4 + {}^+7$ ★27. $^-9 + {}^-2 + {}^-8$ ★28. $^-4 + {}^-8 + {}^+11$

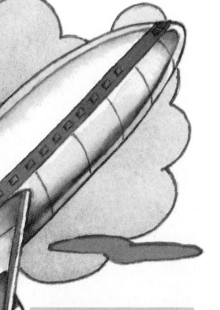

Solve.

29. A minisubmarine enters the Arctic Ocean, where the temperature is 7°C at sea level. It descends to 1,000 ft below sea level, where the temperature has fallen 6°C. What is the temperature?

30. On a Friday in December, the temperature is 21°F. Two days later, it is 32° warmer. What is the temperature?

31. In a laboratory test, the temperature of a solution is $^-4$°C. A chemist heats the solution, raising its temperature 7°. What is the temperature?

CALCULATOR

You can compute with integers using a calculator with a change sign key $\boxed{+/-}$. Study these examples.

Enter: $\boxed{3}$ $\boxed{4}$ $\boxed{+/-}$
Display: $34-$

Example	Keystrokes	Display	Answer
$78 + {}^-96$	$\boxed{7}$ $\boxed{8}$ $\boxed{+}$ $\boxed{9}$ $\boxed{6}$ $\boxed{+/-}$	$18-$	$^-18$
$^-52 - {}^-67$	$\boxed{5}$ $\boxed{2}$ $\boxed{+/-}$ $\boxed{-}$ $\boxed{6}$ $\boxed{7}$ $\boxed{+/-}$ $\boxed{=}$	15	$^+15$

Add or subtract.

1. $^+38 + {}^-72$ 2. $^+81 - {}^-66$ 3. $^-93 + {}^+19$ 4. $^-70 - {}^+26$

5. $^-98 - {}^-59$ 6. $^-46 + {}^-88$ 7. $^+473 + {}^+294$ 8. $^+283 - {}^+958$

Subtracting Integers

A. When a volcano erupts, its magma can rise to 3 miles above sea level. When it calms, the magma settles, dropping 5 miles from its highest point. At what level does the magma settle?

Subtract $^+3 - {}^+5$. Use the number line.

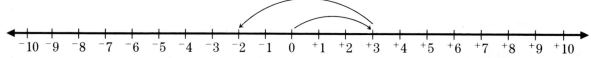

Start at 0. Move right 3 spaces. Move left 5 spaces.

$^+3 - {}^+5 = {}^-2$

> To subtract an integer, add its opposite.

$$^+3 - {}^+5 = n \qquad {}^-2 - {}^-8$$
$$^+3 + {}^-5 = {}^-2 \qquad {}^-2 + {}^+8 = {}^+6$$

The magma settles at 2 miles below sea level.

B. Apply the rule to subtract integers with unlike signs.

Subtract.
$$^-6 - {}^+9 \qquad\qquad {}^+4 - {}^-9$$
$$^-6 + {}^-9 = {}^-15 \qquad {}^+4 + {}^+9 = {}^+13$$

Checkpoint Write the letter of the correct answer.

Subtract.

1. $^-7 - {}^-3$

a. $^-10$
b. $^-4$
c. $^+4$
d. $^+10$

2. $^-2 - {}^+5$

a. $^-7$
b. $^-3$
c. $^+3$
d. $^+7$

3. $^+5 - {}^+8$

a. $^-13$
b. $^-3$
c. $^+3$
d. $^+13$

4. $^-10 - {}^+6$

a. $^-16$
b. $^-4$
c. $^+4$
d. $^+16$

Subtract.

1. $^+18 - {}^+10$
2. $^+7 - {}^+9$
3. $^+4 - {}^+14$
4. $^+19 - {}^+5$

5. $^-12 - {}^-5$
6. $^-5 - {}^-11$
7. $0 - {}^-4$
8. $^+2 - {}^-14$

9. $^-7 - {}^+14$
10. $^-17 - {}^+12$
11. $^-5 - {}^+18$
12. $^-16 - {}^+1$

13. $^-4 - {}^-13$
14. $^-6 - {}^-3$
15. $0 - {}^+11$
16. $^-15 - {}^+12$

17. $^-19 - {}^-20$
18. $^-16 - {}^+7$
19. $^+9 - {}^-18$
20. $^+17 - {}^+5$

21. $0 - {}^-12$
22. $^-10 - {}^+4$
23. $^+9 - {}^-9$
24. $^+15 - {}^+3$

25. $^+10 - {}^+15$
26. $^-7 - 0$
27. $^-15 - {}^-19$
28. $^-11 - {}^+14$

Find n.

★29. $^+7 - n = {}^-2$
★30. $n - {}^-6 = {}^+2$
★31. $^+5 - {}^-4 = n$

Solve.

32. On a cold morning in February, an Italian mountaineer climbs Vesuvius. At the foot of the volcano, the temperature is 4°F. When he reaches the top, the temperature is −6°F. By how many degrees did the temperature drop?

33. The highest air temperature recorded near the top of Mt. Fuji in Japan is $^+51°$. The lowest is $^-14°$. Find the difference between the highest and the lowest air temperatures.

CHALLENGE

Use the number line to find the mystery integers.

1. Integer A is 3 times as far from 0 as integer B. They are 12 units apart on the number line. Integer A is positive. Name integers A and B.

2. C, a positive integer, and D, a negative integer, are 6 units apart. C is half the distance that D is from 0. Name integers C and D.

3. Integer E is 3 times as far from 0 as integer F. They are 6 units apart on the number line. Integer E is positive. Name integers E and F.

4. Integer G and integer H are 4 units apart. G is 3 times as far from 0 as H. Both integers are negative. Name the integers G and H.

PROBLEM SOLVING
Using a Double-Line Graph

A double-line graph shows how two sets of information have changed over a period of time. This graph, for example, shows how the average monthly temperature changed in Chicago and in San Francisco.

Use the double-line graph to answer this question. Which city has a lower average temperature in the month of February?

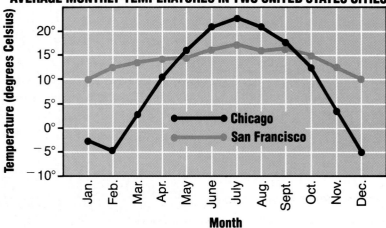

AVERAGE MONTHLY TEMPERATURES IN TWO UNITED STATES CITIES

- The labels at the left tell you the temperatures. Note that they are given in degrees Celsius. Also, note that the numbers given are both above and below zero.

- The labels at the bottom tell you the months of the comparison.

- The key tells you that temperatures for Chicago are given in black. Temperatures for San Francisco are given in green.

- Each point on this graph shows you the average temperature for that month. For example, notice the two points for February. The black line shows Chicago temperatures. The green line shows San Francisco temperatures. You can see that Chicago has a lower average temperature in February than San Francisco does.

Can you use the double-line graph to answer each question? Write *yes* or *no*.

1. What was the temperature in Chicago on July 4?

2. Was the temperature in San Francisco colder in January or in February?

Use the double-line graph to solve.

3. Which city has a greater range in temperature from January to December?

4. Which city is usually warmer during the year?

5. What is the warmest temperature shown on the graph?

6. In which month is Chicago's average temperature 16° Celsius?

7. Which city is likely to have higher heating costs?

8. On the average, is it cooler in January or in December in Chicago? What is the difference?

9. Between February and April, which city has cooler average temperatures?

10. Is the average temperature in July warmer in Chicago or in San Francisco?

11. If the average temperature in Chicago had been 1 degree cooler in February, what would it have been?

12. If the average temperature in San Francisco had been 2 degrees warmer in August, about what would it have been?

13. During which two months are the average temperatures in Chicago and San Francisco about the same?

14. In which city is the average temperature higher during the month of June?

Graphing Ordered Pairs

A dozen scientists will gather data on air pollution in Crystal City. They plan to set up 4 laboratories to collect samples in different sections of the city. They use a **coordinate grid** to divide the city into 4 sections.

CRYSTAL CITY

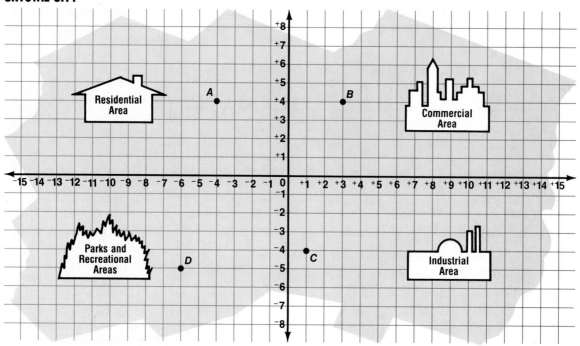

You can use an **ordered pair** of numbers to locate a point on a grid.

Locate the laboratory described by the ordered pair $(^-4,^+4)$.

- Start at 0.
- The first number shows how many units to move across. Move right if the number is positive, and left if the number is negative.
  $^-4$ means move left 4 units.
- The second number shows how many units to move up or down. Move up if the number is positive, and down if the number is negative.
  $^+4$ means move up 4 units.
- $(^-4,^+4)$ locates Lab A.

Write an ordered pair that locates Lab D.

- Start at 0.
- Write the integer that shows the number of units and the direction in which you move.
  D is 6 units to the left. Write $^-6$.
- Write the integer that shows the number of units you move up or down.
  D is 5 units down. Write $^-5$.
- $(^-6,^-5)$ locates lab D.

416

Scientists and architects are planning a new space center for the Saturn research program.

SATURN SPACE CENTER

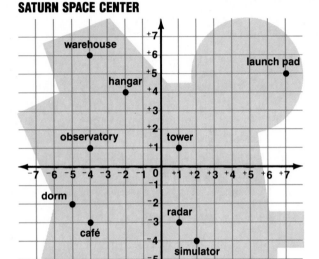

Write an ordered pair to describe the location of the

1. tower. **2.** hangar. **3.** café.

4. simulator. **5.** launch pad.

Write the name of the place identified by the ordered pair.

6. $(^-5, ^-2)$ **7.** $(^-4, ^+1)$ **8.** $(^+4, ^-7)$

9. $(^+1, ^-3)$ **10.** $(^-4, ^+6)$

CHALLENGE

Copy the grid at the right. Graph these points.

$(0,0)$ $(^+7, ^-4)$ $(^+7, ^+5)$ $(^+4, ^+2)$ $(0, ^+5)$

Connect them in order.
Change the first number in each ordered pair to its opposite.
Graph the new pairs in order. What do you notice?

Fold your drawing on the vertical axis. Have you discovered a line of symmetry?

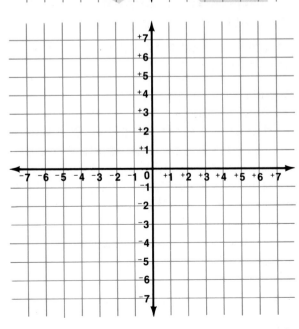

More Practice, page 460

PROBLEM SOLVING
Practice

Solve. Make a table if needed.

1. Alex is hydrolyzing water. He finds that for 0.8 L of water, he produces 0.8 L of hydrogen and 0.4 L of oxygen. For 0.6 L of water, he produces 0.6 L of hydrogen and 0.3 L of oxygen. How many liters of hydrogen does he produce when he produces 0.6 L of oxygen?

Solve. Make a guess, and check your answer.

2. Einsteinium is a human-made element named after Albert Einstein. Its atomic mass is a 3-digit number. It is evenly divisible by 2. The sum of the second two digits is 9. The first two digits are the product of a single digit multipled by itself. What is Einsteinium's atomic mass?

Solve. Draw a picture if needed.

3. A space shuttle leaves Jupiter and lands on Io. Io is the third satellite from Jupiter. Next, the shuttle lands on Europa, the fourth satellite. Then, it returns to Amalthea, the first satellite, and skips to Ganymede, the fifth satellite. If the shuttle skips 2 more satellites, it will land on Elara, the farthest satellite. How many satellites does Jupiter have?

Solve. Make a list if needed.

4. Dr. Roberts melts 1-g lumps of metals together to form 8-g slabs of new metal alloys. He has seven 1-g lumps of chromium and four 1-g lumps of magnesium. How many different mixtures of metals can he use to make one 8-g slab?

Solve.

5. Reggie fuses heavy elements at very high speeds to create new elements. He uses 4 different elements that have atomic weights of 255, 260, 279, and 284. If he fuses only two elements at a time, how many different weights could the new element have?

6. Eugene had a group of frog eggs. Of the group, 8 eggs did not hatch. Of those remaining, $\frac{1}{2}$ had hatched, but 2 tadpoles died. Eugene then had 4 tadpoles. How many frog eggs did he have originally?

7. Luis bought supplies for the lab. He spent $27 on test tubes. He spent $\frac{1}{2}$ the remaining money on glassware and $28 on test paper. He returned to the lab with $15. How much money did he begin with?

8. Calvin Doolittle is looking through a microscope at single-cell creatures. He finds that at higher magnifications, he sees fewer cells but greater detail. At 1 × magnification, he can see 160 cells, at 10 ×, he can see 80, and at 100 ×, he can see 40. How many cells can he expect to see at 1000 × magnification?

9. The periodic table is a chart that gives information about the elements, such as the number of electrons and the atomic weight of each known element. The number of elements listed in the table is a 3-digit prime number. The second digit is 0. The first digit is 6 fewer than the third digit, and their sum is eight. How many elements are listed in the table?

10. In a planetarium, Vinnie watched as an astronomer pointed to a group of stars that formed a row. The astronomer pointed to the first star in the pattern. Then, she skipped 2 stars and explained the fourth. She then went back 2 stars and explained the second star. Then, she skipped 6 stars to the last star. How many stars were there in the row?

11. To make salts, Silvia Jones mixes the positive ions lithium, sodium, and potassium with the negative ions fluorine, chlorine, and bromine. Each positive ion combines with only 1 negative ion. How many different salts can she make?

★12. From this lesson, choose one problem that you've already solved. Show how you could use another method to solve this problem.

CALCULATOR

Solve for n and x using numbers from the **Number Box**. Use your estimation skills and the calculator to help you.

Example $25 + {}^-19 + {}^-24 + n = 0$ $n = 18$

1. $41 + {}^-37 + {}^-28 + n = 0$

2. $57 + {}^-16 + {}^-23 + n = 0$

3. $24 + {}^-37 + {}^-12 + n = 0$

4. $39 - {}^-29 + {}^-48 + n = 0$

5. $51 - 38 - {}^-61 + n = 0$

6. $43 + {}^-27 - {}^-17 - n = 0$

7. $53 + {}^-28 + n + x = 0$

8. $17 + {}^-47 + n + x = 0$

9. $92 + {}^-28 + n - x = 0$

10. $43 + {}^-68 + n - x = 0$

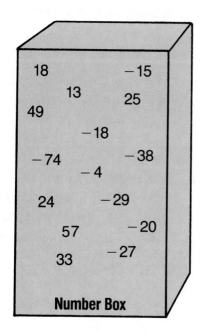

Number Box

18   -15
13   25
49
-18
-74 -38
-4
24   -29
57   -20
33   -27

Go through the maze from start to finish. Move only up and down or right to left. Add the numbers in colored boxes and subtract the numbers in the white boxes. Find the path that gives the least possible total. Use each number only once.

Start

36	37	38	39	40	41	42
35	34	33	32	31	30	29
22	23	24	25	26	27	28
21	20	19	18	17	16	15
8	9	10	11	12	13	14
7	6	5	4	3	2	1

End

GROUP PROJECT

Marvelous Möbius

The problem: A friend of yours says that there is no such thing as a one-sided object. If an object has a front, it has to have a back. You disagree, but how do you prove your point?

Easy. Follow these steps, and you'll find a one-sided object and an amazing mathematical oddity. It's called a Möbius strip.

Take a long strip of paper, and draw a dot at the top and a dot at the bottom of it. Holding both ends, twist one end of the strip, and then bring the two dots together. You will have something that looks like the drawing on this page. Use tape to secure the loop.

Do you see anything special about your loop? No? Then start anywhere on the loop, and draw a line down the middle. If this were a two-sided object, the line would go along one side only. What happens on your Möbius strip?

So, you've proved that a one-sided object can exist. But a Möbius strip can show more than that. Take scissors, and cut along the line you just drew. What usually happens when you cut something in half? What happened to the Möbius strip?

What do you think will happen if you cut your Möbius strip in half a second time? Try it.

Now make another Möbius strip. This time, add an extra twist. Cut the strip in half. What's the result?

CHAPTER TEST

Identify the integers *A–F* on the number line. (page 404)

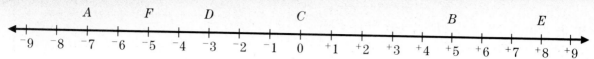

1. *A*
2. *B*
3. *C*
4. *D*
5. *E*
6. *F*

Write >, < or = for each ⬤. (page 406)

7. $^+4$ ⬤ $^-7$
8. $^-9$ ⬤ 0
9. $^-6$ ⬤ $^-6$
10. $^+3$ ⬤ $^-33$
11. $^-27$ ⬤ $^+29$
12. 0 ⬤ $^-68$
13. $^-52$ ⬤ $^-45$
14. $^+34$ ⬤ $^+34$

Write in order from the least to the greatest. (page 406)

15. $^+2, ^-2, ^-8, ^+8$
16. $^-15, ^+11, 0, ^-12$

Write in order from the greatest to the least. (page 406)

17. $^+8, ^-8, ^-10, ^+26$
18. $^-21, 0, ^+83, ^-74$

Add or subtract. (pages 408–410 and 412)

19. $^+4 + ^+16$
20. $^-7 + ^-9$
21. $^+32 + ^+2$
22. $^-18 + ^+11$
23. $^-13 + ^+13$
24. $^+14 + ^-7$
25. $^-14 - ^-14$
26. $^+20 - ^+3$
27. $^-38 - ^-8$
28. $^-51 - ^+32$
29. $^+30 - ^-5$
30. $^+34 - ^-14$

The graph at the right shows the relationship between the planets and the sun at one point in their orbits. Write an ordered pair to describe the location of each. (page 416)

31. the sun

32. Mars

33. Saturn

34. Earth

Write the name of the planet identified by the ordered pair. (page 416)

35. $(^-4, ^+4)$

36. $(^-1, ^+1)$

37. $(^+1, ^+2)$

38. $(^+2, ^-3)$

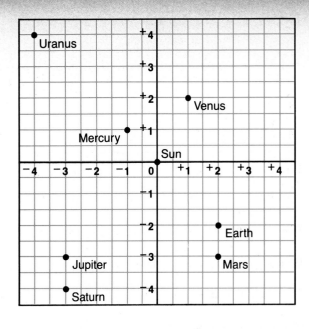

Use the graph at right to solve. (page 414)

39. Which agency, NASA or the Environmental Protection Agency (EPA), had a larger 1981 budget?

40. How much greater than the EPA budget was the NASA budget in 1982?

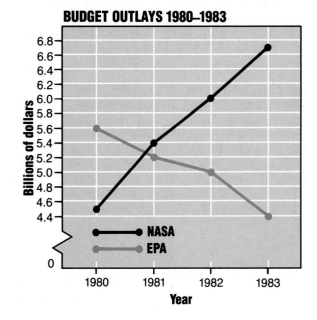

BONUS

Use the graph above to solve.
If the increase in NASA's budget from 1983 to 1984 is the same as the increase from 1981 to 1982, what would NASA's 1984 budget be?

RETEACHING

A. You can use a number line to help you add integers that have unlike signs. Move right on the number line to add a positive integer, and move left to add a negative integer.

Add $^+6 + {}^-5$.

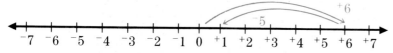

Start at 0. Move right 6 spaces. Then move left 5 spaces.

$^+6 + {}^-5 = {}^+1$

B. You can also show subtraction on a number line. You can use a shortcut to subtract an integer.

Subtract $^+5 - {}^-3$.

If you were adding $^-3$, you would move to the left. You are doing the opposite when subtracting. So, move right 3 spaces.

$^+5 - {}^-3 = {}^+8$

Add or subtract.

1. $^+5 + {}^-3$	**2.** $^+4 + {}^-10$	**3.** $^-8 + {}^+5$
4. $^-12 + {}^+13$	**5.** $^+7 + {}^-7$	**6.** $^+15 + {}^-5$
7. $^-20 + {}^+3$	**8.** $^-15 + 0$	**9.** $^+23 + {}^-17$
10. $^-18 + {}^+21$	**11.** $^+6 - {}^-2$	**12.** $^+3 - {}^-7$
13. $^-9 - {}^+8$	**14.** $^-10 - {}^+4$	**15.** $^+9 - {}^-1$
16. $^-17 - {}^+15$	**17.** $^-20 - 0$	**18.** $^+16 - {}^-13$
19. $^+11 - {}^-19$	**20.** $0 - {}^+6$	**21.** $^-10 + {}^-20$
22. $^-18 - {}^+12$	**23.** $^+17 - {}^-4$	**24.** $^-8 + {}^+22$
25. $^+10 - {}^-9$	**26.** $^+8 + {}^-6$	**27.** $^-7 - {}^+1$
28. $^-2 + {}^+4$	**29.** $^+8 + {}^-8$	**30.** $^-10 - {}^+10$

ENRICHMENT

Multiplying and Dividing With Integers

Here are the rules you need to multiply with integers.

Rule 1:	a positive integer	×	a positive integer	=	a positive integer
	$^+3$	×	$^+4$	=	$^+12$
Rule 2:	a negative integer	×	a negative integer	=	a positive integer
	$^-3$	×	$^-4$	=	$^+12$
Rule 3:	a negative integer	×	a positive integer	=	a negative integer
	$^-4$	×	$^+3$	=	$^-12$
Rule 4:	a positive integer	×	a negative integer	=	a negative integer
	$^+4$	×	$^-3$	=	$^-12$

Example:

```
←——+——+——+——+——+——+——+——+——+→
 ⁻12  ⁻9  ⁻6  ⁻3   0  ⁺3  ⁺6  ⁺9 ⁺12
```

Multiply.

1. $^+8 \times {}^-9$ **2.** $^-6 \times {}^-4$ **3.** $^+6 \times {}^-6$ **4.** $^-9 \times {}^-8$ **5.** $^+3 \times {}^+5$

6. $^-13 \times {}^+7$ **7.** $^+16 \times {}^-9$ **8.** $^-19 \times {}^-19$ **9.** $^+27 \times {}^-18$ **10.** $^+17 \times {}^-13$

Here are the rules you need to divide with integers.

Rule 1:	a positive integer	÷	a positive integer	=	a positive integer
	$^+24$	÷	$^+4$	=	$^+6$
Rule 2:	a negative integer	÷	a negative integer	=	a positive integer
	$^-24$	÷	$^-4$	=	$^+6$
Rule 3:	a negative integer	÷	a positive integer	=	a negative integer
	$^-24$	÷	$^+4$	=	$^-6$
Rule 4:	a positive integer	÷	a negative integer	=	a negative integer
	$^+24$	÷	$^-4$	=	$^-6$

Divide.

11. $^-35 \div {}^+5$ **12.** $^+20 \div {}^-4$ **13.** $^+72 \div {}^+8$ **14.** $^-16 \div {}^-4$ **15.** $^+45 \div {}^-5$

16. $^+36 \div {}^-12$ **17.** $^+300 \div {}^+15$ **18.** $^-221 \div {}^-13$ **19.** $^-780 \div {}^+4$ **20.** $^+676 \div {}^-52$

CUMULATIVE REVIEW

Write the letter of the correct answer.
Use this table for Exercises 1–3.

FAVORITE TYPE OF TV SHOW

Type of show	Votes
Sports specials	12
Movies	7
Comedies	12
News specials	8
Mysteries	4

1. What is the range of votes cast?

a. 8 b. $8\frac{3}{5}$

c. 12 d. not given

2. What is the mode of votes cast?

a. 7 b. 8

c. 12 d. not given

3. **FAVORITE TYPE OF TV SHOW**

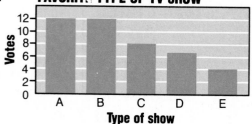

Which bar stands for News specials?

a. C b. D

c. E d. not given

4. $^{-}5 - {}^{+}15$

a. $^{-}20$ b. $^{+}10$

c. $^{+}20$ d. not given

5. Write the probability as a fraction:
Favorable outcomes: 3; Possible outcomes: 6.

a. $\frac{1}{3}$ b. $\frac{1}{2}$

c. 6 d. not given

6. The diameter of a circle is 4 in. Find its circumference. Use 3.14 for π.

a. 1.256 in. b. 12.56 in.

c. 125.6 in. d. not given

7. $27\frac{5}{8} - 12\frac{3}{4}$

a. $12\frac{7}{8}$ b. $15\frac{2}{8}$

c. $15\frac{7}{8}$ d. not given

8. Figure B is a ■ of Figure A.

a. reflection b. translation
c. rotation d. not given

9. The ages of the members of Zeke's family are 43, 39, 14, and 12. To find the median age, which equation would you use?

a. $108 \div 4 = n$ b. $43 - 12 = n$
c. $(39 + 14) \div 2 = n$ d. not given

10. Judy can hit a golf ball 5 times farther than she can throw a baseball. She can throw a baseball 50 yd. How far can she hit a golf ball?

a. 25 yd b. 250 yd
c. 2,500 yd d. not given

Help File

If you have trouble understanding the question, use one or more of these hints.

Formulating a sensible question
Think of a sensible question that could be answered with the numbers in the problem.

Finding needed/extra information
Some problems do not have all the facts you need. Find the facts you need from resource books or other sources. Some problems contain more facts than you need. Make a list. Cross out the facts you do not need.

Organizing information
It is sometimes easier to understand the question if you organize the information in the problem by writing it down or making a list or a table.

Working backward
Sometimes it helps to work backward from the results to solve the problem.

Rewriting the question
Think about the information in the problem. Sometimes it helps to rewrite the question in your own words. Make sure you know what you are being asked to do.

Drawing a picture or diagram
Drawing a picture or a diagram can help you to understand the information in a problem. Study the picture or diagram to decide how to solve the problem.

Choosing a formula
Think about the formulas you have studied. Look at the information in the problem. Can you use the information and a formula to answer the question?

Using proportions
Using the numbers in a problem to set up a proportion can help you see how to answer the question.

Finding information in the problem
Ask yourself what the question is asking you to find. Look at the information in the problem. Decide how to use them to answer the question.

Help File

You understand the question. To help you decide what you need to do, use one or more of these hints.

Writing an equation
Use the numbers in the problem to write an equation. This will help you see how to solve the problem.

Writing a simpler problem
Sometimes it helps to use simpler numbers. If you see how to use the simple numbers, you can use the actual numbers in the problem to find the actual answer.

Making a plan
Make a plan for multistep problems. Following your plan will help you use the information to find the answer.

Estimating
Sometimes you can use an estimate to answer a question. Sometimes you should find an exact answer.

Finding the pattern
Study the pattern you are given. It will help you find the missing items.

Making a table or a list
A table or a list can help you see the pattern that will enable you to solve a problem.

Guessing and checking
Try guessing at an answer. Check your guess. Adjust the guess up or down to find the exact answer.

Converting measurement
Be sure all the units of measure in the problem are the same before you begin to solve the problem.

Using graphs
Use the information in a graph to answer questions.

Using a scale drawing, recipe, map, or schedule
Use the information in the scale drawing, recipe, map, or schedule to answer the question.

Help File

If you have difficulty while you're solving the problem, use one or more of these hints. If you need more help, use the Table of Contents or the Index.

Dividing

When dividing, use an estimate for a 2-digit divisor. You may have to adjust your estimate up or down after you try the actual divisor. See pages 132–133.

$$35\overline{)910} \rightarrow 5\overline{)\,10}^{\,3}$$

Solving problems with decimals

When multiplying, count the digits to the right of the decimal point in both factors. There must be the same total number of digits to the right of the decimal point in the product. See pages 96–97.

$$\begin{array}{r} 0.85 \\ \times\, 0.02 \\ \hline 170 \\ 00 \\ \hline 0.0170 \end{array}$$

When dividing, you may have a remainder. Write zeros in the dividend, and continue to divide. See pages 156–157.

$$4\overline{)0.3} \rightarrow 4\overline{)0.300}^{\,0.075} \\ \begin{array}{r}28\\\hline 20\end{array}$$

Solving problems with fractions

When subtracting with mixed numbers, you sometimes have to rename a number. See pages 218–219.

$$\begin{array}{r} 3\frac{1}{4} \rightarrow \quad 2\frac{5}{4} \\ -\,1\frac{3}{4} \rightarrow -\,1\frac{3}{4} \\ \hline 1\frac{2}{4} = 1\frac{1}{2} \end{array}$$

When adding mixed numbers, make sure the sum is in simplest form. See pages 218–219.

$$\begin{array}{r} 2\frac{5}{8} \\ +\,1\frac{4}{8} \\ \hline 3\frac{9}{8} \rightarrow 3 + 1\frac{1}{8} \rightarrow 4\frac{1}{8} \end{array}$$

When multiplying or dividing mixed numbers, rewrite them as fractions, and multiply. Write your answer as a mixed number. See pages 238–241.

$$1\frac{1}{2} \times 1\frac{1}{4} \rightarrow \frac{3}{2} \times \frac{5}{4} \rightarrow \frac{15}{8}$$

Solving problems with percent

To find the percent of a number, write the percent as a decimal or a fraction, and multiply. See pages 286–287.

$$25\% \text{ of } 80 \rightarrow 0.25 \times 80$$
$$25\% \text{ of } 80 \rightarrow \frac{1}{4} \times 80$$

To find what percent one number is of another number, write an equation, and solve. See pages 288–289.

$$\begin{aligned} n\% \text{ of } 120 &= 60 \\ n\% &= 0.50 \\ n &= 50\% \end{aligned}$$

Adding and subtracting integers

Read the signs in front of the integers before you add or subtract. See pages 408–413.

$$^-3 + {}^+2 = {}^-1$$
$$^-3 + {}^-2 = {}^-5$$

Help File

When you want to know whether your answer is correct, use one or more of these hints.

Checking for a reasonable answer
Be sure your answer makes sense. Try estimation. If your estimated answer is very different from your solution, compute the problem again.

Checking that the solution answers the question
Some questions do not ask for number answers. Check to be sure that you have answered the question asked.

Checking the operations
For addition, subtract one addend from the sum. The difference should be the other addend.

$$\begin{array}{r} 4{,}057 \\ +\,2{,}183 \\ \hline 6{,}240 \end{array} \qquad \begin{array}{r} ^{13}\\ ^{1\,\cancel{3}\,10}\\ 6{,}2\,4\,\cancel{0} \\ -\,2{,}1\,8\,3 \\ \hline 4{,}0\,5\,7 \end{array}$$

For subtraction, add the difference to the number being subtracted. The sum should be the other number.

$$\begin{array}{r} 4{,}057 \\ -\,2{,}183 \\ \hline 1{,}874 \end{array} \qquad \begin{array}{r} ^{1\ 1}\\ 1{,}874 \\ +\,2{,}183 \\ \hline 4{,}057 \end{array}$$

For multiplication, divide the product by one of the factors. The quotient should be the other factor.

$$\begin{array}{r} 431 \\ \times\ 22 \\ \hline 9{,}482 \end{array} \qquad 22\overline{)9{,}482}\ \ ^{431}$$

For division, multiply the quotient by the divisor and add the remainder. The answer should be the dividend.

$$15\overline{)5{,}040}\ \ ^{336} \qquad \begin{array}{r} 336 \\ \times\ 15 \\ \hline 5{,}040 \end{array}$$

There are several ways to interpret remainders. Be sure you have answered the question asked.

$$15\overline{)5{,}042}\ \ ^{336\ R2} \qquad \begin{array}{r} 336 \\ \times\ 15 \\ \hline 5040 \\ +\ \ \ 2 \\ \hline 5{,}042 \end{array}$$

Checking decimals
Be sure your decimal point is placed correctly.

Checking fractions
To check addition and subtraction of fractions, be sure the fractions have like denominators. Remember to simplify your answer.

Checking integers
Check the signs on the integers to be sure you have completed the problem correctly.

Using outside sources
You can check some answers in outside sources such as reference books and periodicals.

Infobank

WHAT AMERICANS SPENT TO DINE OUT IN 1984

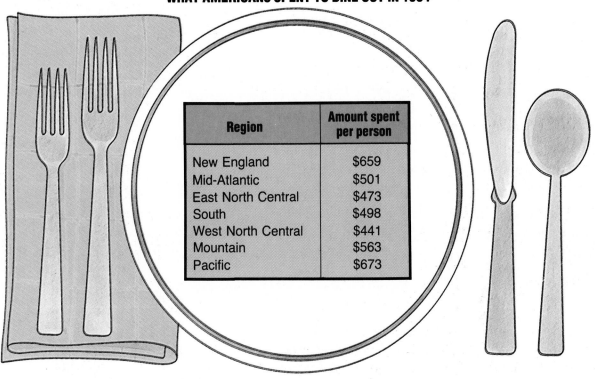

Region	Amount spent per person
New England	$659
Mid-Atlantic	$501
East North Central	$473
South	$498
West North Central	$441
Mountain	$563
Pacific	$673

MEN'S 100–METER BUTTERFLY RESULTS (IN SECONDS)

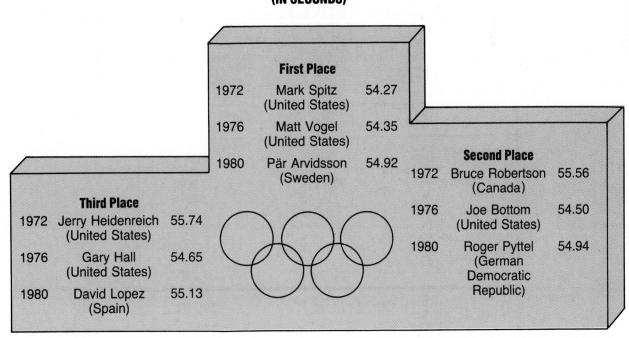

First Place

1972	Mark Spitz (United States)	54.27
1976	Matt Vogel (United States)	54.35
1980	Pär Arvidsson (Sweden)	54.92

Second Place

1972	Bruce Robertson (Canada)	55.56
1976	Joe Bottom (United States)	54.50
1980	Roger Pyttel (German Democratic Republic)	54.94

Third Place

1972	Jerry Heidenreich (United States)	55.74
1976	Gary Hall (United States)	54.65
1980	David Lopez (Spain)	55.13

YEARS OF SERVICE OF SOME UNITED STATES SENATORS

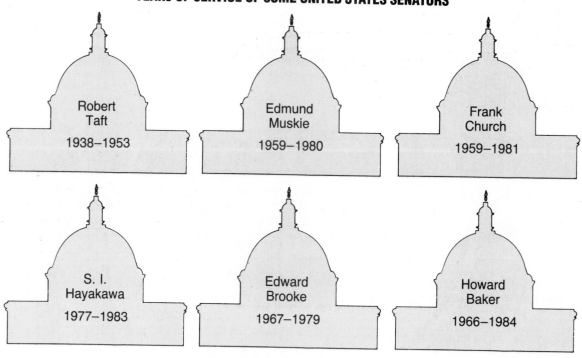

Robert Taft
1938–1953

Edmund Muskie
1959–1980

Frank Church
1959–1981

S. I. Hayakawa
1977–1983

Edward Brooke
1967–1979

Howard Baker
1966–1984

USE OF WATER IN THE UNITED STATES OVER A TYPICAL 20-HOUR PERIOD (IN MILLIONS OF GALLONS)

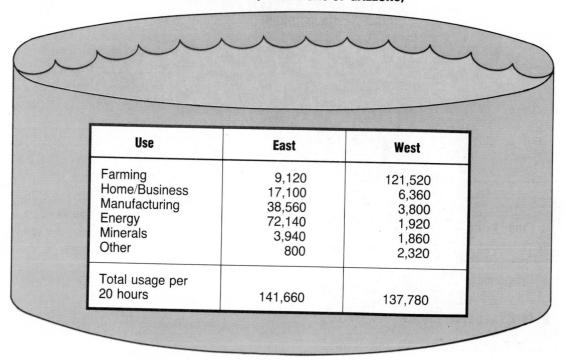

Use	East	West
Farming	9,120	121,520
Home/Business	17,100	6,360
Manufacturing	38,560	3,800
Energy	72,140	1,920
Minerals	3,940	1,860
Other	800	2,320
Total usage per 20 hours	141,660	137,780

DISTANCES BETWEEN SELECTED CITIES (IN MILES)

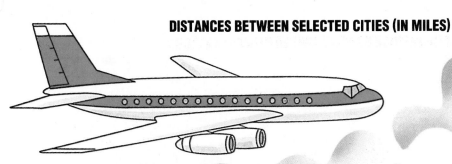

	Berlin, Germany	Bombay, India	Cape Town, South Africa	London, England	Los Angeles, United States	Mexico City, Mexico
Bombay, India	6,924	· · ·	8,626	7,182	14,004	15,645
Cape Town, South Africa	9,621	8,262	· · ·	9,663	16,044	13,698
London, England	924	7,182	9,663	· · ·	8,054	8,916
Los Angeles, United States	9,306	14,004	16,044	8,054	· · ·	2,481
Mexico City, Mexico	9,717	15,645	13,698	8,916	2,481	· · ·
Moscow, Union of Soviet Socialist Republics	4,602	5,040	10,128	2,493	9,765	10,764

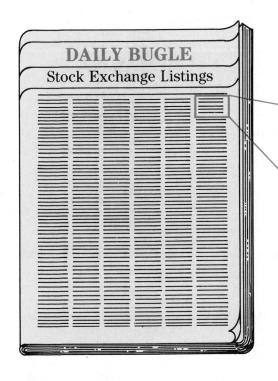

DAILY BUGLE

Stock Exchange Listings

Company	Price per share
Grow-Rite Company	$12\frac{1}{2}$
Happy Plants	$12\frac{3}{4}$
Sunshine Garden Co.	$12\frac{5}{8}$

HOURS WORKED					
Employee: Brenda Davis					
Date	Monday 4/9	Tuesday 4/10	Wednesday 4/11	Thursday 4/12	Friday 4/13
Hours worked	6 h 35 min	7 h 35 min	7 h 25 min	6 h 55 min	6 h 35 min

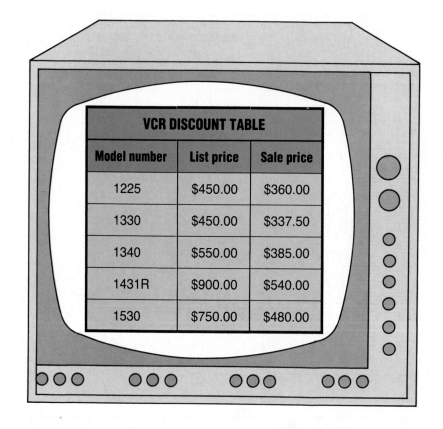

VCR DISCOUNT TABLE		
Model number	**List price**	**Sale price**
1225	$450.00	$360.00
1330	$450.00	$337.50
1340	$550.00	$385.00
1431R	$900.00	$540.00
1530	$750.00	$480.00

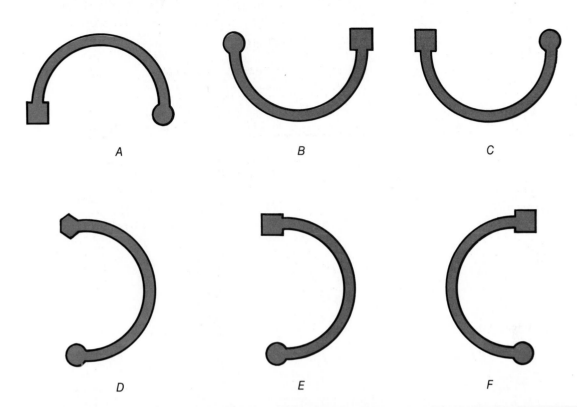

A

B

C

D

E

F

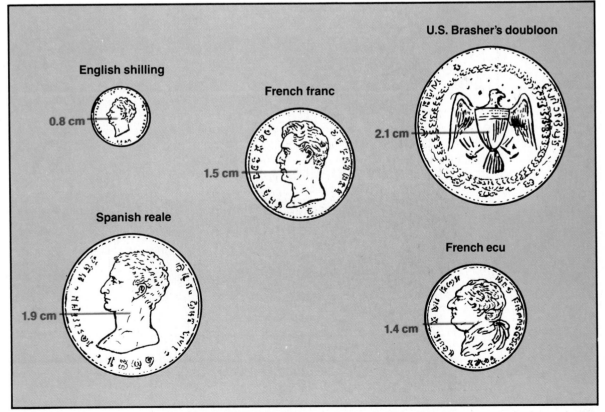

English shilling

0.8 cm

French franc

1.5 cm

U.S. Brasher's doubloon

2.1 cm

Spanish reale

1.9 cm

French ecu

1.4 cm

RIVERA CAMPAIGN RALLY ATTENDANCE

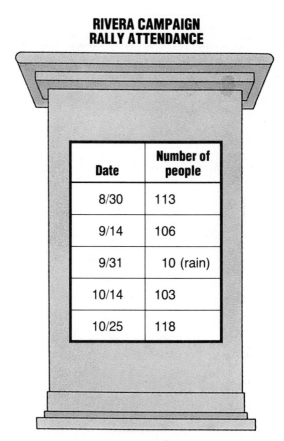

Date	Number of people
8/30	113
9/14	106
9/31	10 (rain)
10/14	103
10/25	118

ALTITUDES OF SELECTED PLACES IN THE UNITED STATES

Place	Distance above or below sea level
Mount Washington, New Hampshire	+6,288 ft
New Orleans, Louisiana	−5 ft
Eagle Mountain, Minnesota	+2,310 ft
Death Valley, California	−282 ft

More Practice

Chapter 1, page 3

Write the value of the blue digit.

1. 54,987   **2.** 605,302   **3.** 888,361   **4.** 76,256

Write the number in standard form.

5. three hundred ninety-five thousand, four hundred ten

6. 70,000 + 3,000 + 900 + 3

Write the number in expanded form.

7. 530,870   **8.** 210,376   **9.** 328,553   **10.** 328,631

Chapter 1, page 7

Compare. Write $>$, $<$ or $=$ for each ●.

1. 3,099 ● 3,900   **2.** 12,430 ● 12,413   **3.** 1,600 ● 1,499

4. 21,100 ● 2,999   **5.** 6,130 ● 5,630   **6.** 1,000,090 ● 999,999

7. 708 thousand, 312 ● 708 thousand, 312

Write in order from the least to the greatest.

8. 3,612; 45,000; 36,120   **9.** 67,301; 34,975; 1,000,443

Write in order from the greatest to the least.

10. 5,789,210; 909,386; 2,857,303   **11.** 67,202; 70,022; 42,134

Chapter 1, page 11

Identify the property used. Find the missing number.

1. $7 + 6 = \blacksquare + 7$ **2.** $\blacksquare + 4 = 4$ **3.** $2 + (9 + \blacksquare) = (2 + 9) + 7$

4. $\blacksquare + 0 = 8$ **5.** $9 + \blacksquare = 4 + 9$ **6.** $(6 + 5) + 3 = 6 + (\blacksquare + 3)$

7. $10 + 9 = 9 + \blacksquare$ **8.** $0 + 17 = 17 + \blacksquare$ **9.** $(7 + \blacksquare) + 8 = 7 + (9 + 8)$

Find the missing number.

10. $6 - \blacksquare = 2$ **11.** $\blacksquare - 4 = 5$ **12.** $9 + 8 = 8 + \blacksquare$

13. $9 - 0 = \blacksquare$ **14.** $10 - \blacksquare = 7$ **15.** $8 - 3 = \blacksquare$

16. $11 - 2 = \blacksquare$ **17.** $16 - \blacksquare = 0$ **18.** $\blacksquare + 5 = 5 + 7$

Chapter 1, page 15

Round to the nearest thousand.

1. 8,704   **2.** 52,489   **3.** 75,610   **4.** 983,299

Round to the nearest million.

5. 5,432,768   **6.** 37,502,914   **7.** 752,681,065   **8.** 9,518,387,163

Estimate. Write the letter of the best answer.

9. 5,849 + 3,976   **a.** less than 9,000   **b.** more than 9,000

10. $11.58 + $18.24   **a.** less than $30   **b.** more than $30

11. 68,791 − 49,508   **a.** less than 20,000   **b.** more than 20,000

12. $803.26 − $198.43   **a.** less than $600   **b.** more than $600

Chapter 1, page 21

Add.

1.
$$\begin{array}{r} 75 \\ 49 \\ + 54 \\ \hline \end{array}$$
2.
$$\begin{array}{r} 70 \\ 64 \\ + 94 \\ \hline \end{array}$$
3.
$$\begin{array}{r} 18 \\ 38 \\ + 84 \\ \hline \end{array}$$
4.
$$\begin{array}{r} \$38 \\ 81 \\ + 93 \\ \hline \end{array}$$
5.
$$\begin{array}{r} \$40 \\ 33 \\ + 37 \\ \hline \end{array}$$

6.
$$\begin{array}{r} 498 \\ 978 \\ + 8 \\ \hline \end{array}$$
7.
$$\begin{array}{r} 29 \\ 256 \\ + 54 \\ \hline \end{array}$$
8.
$$\begin{array}{r} 468 \\ 251 \\ + 148 \\ \hline \end{array}$$
9.
$$\begin{array}{r} \$ \ 52 \\ 4,710 \\ + 4 \\ \hline \end{array}$$
10.
$$\begin{array}{r} \$ \ 791 \\ 546 \\ + 17,651 \\ \hline \end{array}$$

11. 65 + 3,143 + 242 + 17,826   **12.** $395 + $11 + $448 + $3,758

13. 5,674 + 5 + 796 + 4,953   **14.** 99,524 + 5,256 + 48,908 + 4,164

Chapter 1, page 25

Subtract.

1.
$$\begin{array}{r} 20 \\ - 13 \\ \hline \end{array}$$
2.
$$\begin{array}{r} 104 \\ - 87 \\ \hline \end{array}$$
3.
$$\begin{array}{r} 906 \\ - 683 \\ \hline \end{array}$$
4.
$$\begin{array}{r} \$600 \\ - 287 \\ \hline \end{array}$$
5.
$$\begin{array}{r} \$900 \\ - 814 \\ \hline \end{array}$$

6.
$$\begin{array}{r} 800 \\ - 59 \\ \hline \end{array}$$
7.
$$\begin{array}{r} 700 \\ - 6 \\ \hline \end{array}$$
8.
$$\begin{array}{r} 806 \\ - 11 \\ \hline \end{array}$$
9.
$$\begin{array}{r} \$5,803 \\ - 431 \\ \hline \end{array}$$
10.
$$\begin{array}{r} \$2,068 \\ - 21 \\ \hline \end{array}$$

11. 9,079 − 2,665   **12.** 6,570 − 1,452   **13.** 98,078 − 3,464

14. 67,000 − 13,342   **15.** 30,996 − 21,624   **16.** 68,085 − 131

Chapter 2, page 41

Read each decimal. Give the value of the blue digit.

1. 5.329802   **2.** 0.67321   **3.** 4.87021   **4.** 11.43002   **5.** 22.9834

Write as a decimal.

6. nineteen and nineteen hundred-thousandths   **7.** forty-three thousandths

Write the short word name for each decimal.

8. 12.0607   **9.** 3.009   **10.** 21.78002   **11.** 9.43718

Chapter 2, page 45

Write >, <, or = for each ●.

1. 0.45355 ● 0.45535   **2.** 2.455 ● 2.4550   **3.** 6.0099 ● 6.0100

4. 5.34 ● 5.3400   **5.** 3.3099 ● 3.3010   **6.** 8.34 ● 8.3403

Write in order from the least to the greatest.

7. 25.1782; 25.172; 25.17; 25.2   **8.** 1.9; 1.89; 1.899; 2; 1.8988

Write in order from the greatest to the least.

9. 4.7666; 4.7706; 4.7607; 4.777   **10.** 2.1; 2.01; 2.001; 2.0011; 2.0101

Chapter 2, page 47

Round to the nearest whole number.

1. 8.85   **2.** 4.6   **3.** 7.33   **4.** 5.06   **5.** 7.2999   **6.** 3.502

Round to the nearest tenth.

7. 5.46   **8.** 4.055   **9.** 4.737   **10.** 5.77   **11.** 9.17   **12.** 8.91

Round to the nearest hundredth.

13. 2.074   **14.** 4.977   **15.** 2.468   **16.** 4.332   **17.** 6.103   **18.** 4.8719

Round to the nearest thousandth.

19. 7.8504   **20.** 5.8484   **21.** 1.6771   **22.** 6.1556

Round to the nearest ten-thousandth.

23. 7.60922   **24.** 28.71658   **25.** 5.24179   **26.** 1.96294

Estimate. Write > or < for each ●.

1. 5.71 + 3.04 ● 8   **2.** 4.56 + 7.31 ● 12   **3.** 9.18 + 15.87 ● 25

4. 8.972 + 10.853 ● 20   **5.** 17.638 + 12.129 ● 30   **6.** 47.803 + 2.516 ● 50

7. 6.27 − 3.89 ● 2   **8.** 14.72 − 6.59 ● 8   **9.** 22.05 − 12.08 ● 10

10. 8.615 − 4.234 ● 4   **11.** 7.394 − 6.409 ● 1   **12.** 17.898 − 5.167 ● 13

13. 2.89 + 1.97 ● 5   **14.** 10 − 3.83 ● 6   **15.** 12.46 + 9.15 ● 22

16. 9.015 − 7.346 ● 2   **17.** 18.215 + 8.539 ● 26   **18.** 56.214 − 15.847 ● 40

Find the sum.

1. 7.112 + 2.611   **2.** 4.73 + 3.05   **3.** 8 + 0.628

4. 9.6 + 3.2   **5.** 70.035 + 14.604   **6.** 1.711 + 3

7. 6.64 + 8.759   **8.** 6.043 + 7.418   **9.** 5 + 3.64

10. 8.351 + 0.371 + 64.133   **11.** 23.425 + 5.002 + 1.976

12. 1.3021 + 7.46 + 32.4   **13.** 5.0334 + 1.644 + 5.0355

Find the difference.

1. 81.17 − 4.06   **2.** 7.506 − 1.4518   **3.** $8.59 − $5.41

4. 88 − 42.840   **5.** 54.8 − 23.5   **6.** $6.57 − $1.52

7. 7.059 − 2.615   **8.** 9.4 − 2.3473   **9.** $3.98 − $2.10

10. 3.82 − 1.676   **11.** 8.9 − 1.94   **12.** $7.00 − $5.15

13. 95.108 − 3.3557   **14.** 38.6082 − 16   **15.** $51.53 − $5.70

Chapter 3, page 73

Find the product.

1.	30	**2.**	400	**3.**	60	**4.**	900	**5.**	7,000
	× 10		× 4		× 50		× 7		× 40

6. 8,000 × 500   **7.** 9,000 × 8,000   **8.** 400 × 500   **9.** 6,000 × 20

Chapter 3, page 75

Estimate. Then, if needed, write > or < to show how
you would adjust the estimate.

1. 42 × 21   **2.** 98 × 49   **3.** 614 × 72   **4.** 291 × 387

5. 209 × 328   **6.** 18 × 190   **7.** 590 × 780   **8.** 606 × 505

9. 995 × 387   **10.** 62 × 342   **11.** 101 × 821   **12.** 79 × 1,998

Chapter 3, page 83

Multiply.

1.	9,451	**2.**	6,718	**3.**	307	**4.**	$4,357	**5.**	$554
	× 885		× 446		× 301		× 47		× 153

6.	1,238	**7.**	7,527	**8.**	1,113	**9.**	$9,926	**10.**	$549
	× 102		× 712		× 714		× 67		× 131

11. 3,350 × 9   **12.** 1,674 × 632   **13.** 366 × 83   **14.** 4,182 × 209

15. 6,675 × 826   **16.** 8,170 × 33   **17.** 9,039 × 223   **18.** 651 × 57

Chapter 3, page 85

Write in exponent form.

1. seven to the third power   **2.** three to the sixth power

3. four squared   **4.** two to the sixth power

5. 6 × 6 × 6   **6.** 8 × 8 × 8 × 8 × 8 × 8 × 8 × 8

7. 3 × 3   **8.** 10 × 10 × 10 × 10

9. 4 × 4 × 4 × 4   **10.** 7 × 7 × 7 × 7 × 7

Write the product.

11. 9^3 **12.** 2^7 **13.** 7^3 **14.** 1^9 **15.** 12^2 **16.** 10^4

Multiply.

1. $\begin{array}{r} 0.0017 \\ \times\quad 100 \\ \hline \end{array}$	**2.** $\begin{array}{r} 8.947 \\ \times\quad 10 \\ \hline \end{array}$	**3.** $\begin{array}{r} 5.81929 \\ \times\quad 1{,}000 \\ \hline \end{array}$	**4.** $\begin{array}{r} 0.0094 \\ \times\quad 100 \\ \hline \end{array}$	**5.** $\begin{array}{r} \$6.71 \\ \times\quad 10 \\ \hline \end{array}$
6. $\begin{array}{r} 0.985 \\ \times\ 1{,}000 \\ \hline \end{array}$	**7.** $\begin{array}{r} 0.03426 \\ \times\quad 100 \\ \hline \end{array}$	**8.** $\begin{array}{r} 0.2191 \\ \times\quad 100 \\ \hline \end{array}$	**9.** $\begin{array}{r} 0.00002 \\ \times\quad 1{,}000 \\ \hline \end{array}$	**10.** $\begin{array}{r} \$43.22 \\ \times\quad 100 \\ \hline \end{array}$

11. 5.69033×10

12. $44.3169 \times 1{,}000$

13. $\$5.98 \times 10$

14. 2.96284×100

15. $0.0087 \times 1{,}000$

16. $\$47.67 \times 10$

Find the product.

1. $\begin{array}{r} 0.075 \\ \times\quad 6 \\ \hline \end{array}$	**2.** $\begin{array}{r} 0.103 \\ \times\quad 6 \\ \hline \end{array}$	**3.** $\begin{array}{r} 0.027 \\ \times\quad 2 \\ \hline \end{array}$	**4.** $\begin{array}{r} 1.496 \\ \times\quad 8 \\ \hline \end{array}$	**5.** $\begin{array}{r} 6.034 \\ \times\quad 9 \\ \hline \end{array}$
6. $\begin{array}{r} 9.404 \\ \times\quad 19 \\ \hline \end{array}$	**7.** $\begin{array}{r} 2.04 \\ \times\quad 46 \\ \hline \end{array}$	**8.** $\begin{array}{r} 9.59 \\ \times\quad 31 \\ \hline \end{array}$	**9.** $\begin{array}{r} 0.295 \\ \times\quad 12 \\ \hline \end{array}$	**10.** $\begin{array}{r} 0.037 \\ \times\quad 15 \\ \hline \end{array}$

11. 6.637×21

12. 0.366×12

13. 1.399×36

14. 11×0.028

15. 17×0.004

16. 25×0.31

Multiply.

1. $\begin{array}{r} 4.843 \\ \times\quad 0.3 \\ \hline \end{array}$	**2.** $\begin{array}{r} 9.025 \\ \times\ 5.496 \\ \hline \end{array}$	**3.** $\begin{array}{r} 0.007 \\ \times\quad 0.04 \\ \hline \end{array}$	**4.** $\begin{array}{r} 49.06 \\ \times\quad 4.63 \\ \hline \end{array}$	**5.** $\begin{array}{r} \$84.25 \\ \times\quad 0.4 \\ \hline \end{array}$
6. $\begin{array}{r} 21.2 \\ \times\quad 0.8 \\ \hline \end{array}$	**7.** $\begin{array}{r} 0.59 \\ \times\quad 4.2 \\ \hline \end{array}$	**8.** $\begin{array}{r} 0.006 \\ \times\ 0.001 \\ \hline \end{array}$	**9.** $\begin{array}{r} 0.358 \\ \times\quad 1.48 \\ \hline \end{array}$	**10.** $\begin{array}{r} \$67.40 \\ \times\quad 437 \\ \hline \end{array}$

11. 7.501×0.726

12. 0.04×0.02

13. $\$42.90 \times 5.7$

14. 5.066×0.44

15. 0.005×0.9

16. $\$32.50 \times 4.54$

Chapter 4, page 113

Compute.

1. $18 \div 2 + 15$
2. $5 \times 4 + 7$
3. $21 - 9 \div 3$
4. $16 - 4 \times 4$
5. $42 \div 6 + 1$
6. $24 - 6 \times 3$
7. $4 + 6 \times 10$
8. $76 - 4 \div 2$
9. $\dfrac{42 - 7 \times 5}{14 - 7}$
10. $(3 + 6) \div 3$
11. $3 + 6 \div 3$
12. $\dfrac{19 + 3}{22 \div 2}$
13. $2^3 + 3$
14. $43 - 4^2$
15. $(3 + 4)^2$
16. $64 \div 2^4$
17. $4 \times (3 \times 2)$
18. $(2^2 + 3) \times 5$
19. $7 - (12 \div 3)$
20. $(9 - 3^2) \times 6$

Chapter 4, page 125

Use short division to divide.

1. $5\overline{)271}$
2. $3\overline{)674}$
3. $2\overline{)407}$
4. $8\overline{)3,212}$
5. $5\overline{)\$1,520}$
6. $4\overline{)1,916}$
7. $7\overline{)5,026}$
8. $6\overline{)3,234}$
9. $7\overline{)3,866}$
10. $8\overline{)\$1,192}$
11. $2\overline{)811}$
12. $6\overline{)3,609}$
13. $3\overline{)2,426}$
14. $3\overline{)604}$
15. $2\overline{)\$1,214}$
16. $4\overline{)1,301}$
17. $4\overline{)2,279}$
18. $3\overline{)1,955}$
19. $7\overline{)1,901}$
20. $8\overline{)\$4,464}$
21. $7\overline{)5,348}$
22. $7\overline{)1,533}$
23. $5\overline{)4,940}$
24. $9\overline{)2,442}$
25. $4\overline{)\$648}$

Chapter 4, page 129

Divide.

1. $6\overline{)36}$
2. $6\overline{)360}$
3. $6\overline{)3,600}$
4. $60\overline{)3,600}$
5. $600\overline{)36,000}$
6. $10\overline{)200}$
7. $50\overline{)100}$
8. $70\overline{)490}$
9. $50\overline{)3,000}$
10. $40\overline{)1,600}$
11. $800\overline{)72,000}$
12. $900\overline{)2,700}$
13. $20\overline{)120}$
14. $80\overline{)240}$
15. $30\overline{)240}$
16. $70\overline{)2,800}$
17. $40\overline{)36,000}$
18. $30\overline{)1,800}$
19. $6\overline{)120}$
20. $300\overline{)1,500}$
21. $9\overline{)4,500}$
22. $70\overline{)420}$
23. $50\overline{)150}$
24. $20\overline{)60,000}$
25. $900\overline{)6,300}$

Chapter 4, page 133

Find the quotient.

1. $34\overline{)929}$ **2.** $24\overline{)672}$ **3.** $26\overline{)868}$ **4.** $33\overline{)627}$ **5.** $21\overline{)\$399}$

6. $23\overline{)919}$ **7.** $27\overline{)852}$ **8.** $31\overline{)680}$ **9.** $45\overline{)532}$ **10.** $37\overline{)\$814}$

11. $22\overline{)636}$ **12.** $32\overline{)892}$ **13.** $27\overline{)869}$ **14.** $35\overline{)765}$ **15.** $27\overline{)\$702}$

16. $927 \div 38$ **17.** $675 \div 25$ **18.** $501 \div 22$ **19.** $378 \div 27$ **20.** $\$928 \div 32$

21. $\frac{432}{24}$ **22.** $\frac{836}{22}$ **23.** $\frac{942}{43}$ **24.** $\frac{600}{32}$ **25.** $\frac{\$924}{28}$

Chapter 4, page 139

Divide.

1. $33\overline{)6,831}$ **2.** $95\overline{)57,264}$ **3.** $40\overline{)44,004}$ **4.** $53\overline{)\$31,906}$

5. $36\overline{)362,000}$ **6.** $99\overline{)29,931}$ **7.** $49\overline{)19,894}$ **8.** $79\overline{)\$32,074}$

9. $59\overline{)47,609}$ **10.** $88\overline{)53,049}$ **11.** $30\overline{)62,040}$ **12.** $26\overline{)10,556}$

13. $9,373 \div 91$ **14.** $1,546 \div 15$ **15.** $39,074 \div 96$ **16.** $\$40,000 \div 32$

17. $29,808 \div 49$ **18.** $10,341 \div 17$ **19.** $60,400 \div 67$ **20.** $\$18,584 \div 92$

21. $3,660 \div 12$ **22.** $12,707 \div 31$ **23.** $37,401 \div 62$ **24.** $\$10,246 \div 94$

Chapter 4, page 143

Find n.

1. $n \times 9 = 27$ **2.** $n \div 4 = 4$ **3.** $28 \div n = 7$ **4.** $5 \times n = 15$

5. $15 \div n = 3$ **6.** $n \times 8 = 16$ **7.** $7 \times n = 7$ **8.** $n \div 9 = 4$

9. $20 \div n = 5$ **10.** $8 \times n = 72$ **11.** $n \div 8 = 10$ **12.** $n \times 7 = 56$

13. $n \div 50 = 9$ **14.** $n \times 60 = 360$ **15.** $9 \times n = 900$ **16.** $140 \div n = 7$

17. $350 \div n = 50$ **18.** $n \div 60 = 8$ **19.** $n \times 80 = 640$ **20.** $70 \times n = 350$

Chapter 5, page 157

Divide.

1. $5\overline{)0.39}$ 2. $5\overline{)0.4}$ 3. $4\overline{)12.28}$ 4. $6\overline{)0.636}$ 5. $5\overline{)\$0.10}$

6. $6\overline{)0.3}$ 7. $2\overline{)1.7}$ 8. $4\overline{)24.2}$ 9. $3\overline{)96.726}$ 10. $5\overline{)\$0.40}$

11. $5\overline{)44.02}$ 12. $9\overline{)7.74}$ 13. $2\overline{)10.02}$ 14. $2\overline{)16.125}$ 15. $8\overline{)\$7.84}$

16. $0.737 \div 5$ 17. $0.357 \div 6$ 18. $0.1 \div 5$ 19. $\$31.20 \div 6$

20. $0.076 \div 8$ 21. $9.333 \div 9$ 22. $1.56 \div 2$ 23. $\$0.92 \div 4$

24. $0.139 \div 2$ 25. $10.23 \div 5$ 26. $2.6 \div 4$ 27. $\$20.48 \div 8$

Chapter 5, page 159

Divide.

1. $10\overline{)0.01}$ 2. $10\overline{)79.2}$ 3. $10\overline{)0.87}$ 4. $100\overline{)942.9}$ 5. $1,000\overline{)81.98}$

6. $1,000\overline{)0.06}$ 7. $10\overline{)47.86}$ 8. $100\overline{)36.29}$ 9. $10\overline{)0.7}$ 10. $1,000\overline{)22.85}$

11. $10\overline{)0.3}$ 12. $100\overline{)1.4}$ 13. $10\overline{)20.9}$ 14. $100\overline{)890.35}$ 15. $1,000\overline{)0.2}$

16. $88.06 \div 100$ 17. $143.22 \div 10$ 18. $7.57 \div 1,000$ 19. $1.39 \div 10$

20. $0.69 \div 1,000$ 21. $5.4 \div 100$ 22. $2.73 \div 10$ 23. $0.99 \div 1,000$

24. $725.6 \div 10$ 25. $1,032.71 \div 10$ 26. $4.7 \div 1,000$ 27. $0.09 \div 100$

Chapter 5, page 161

Divide.

1. $6.9\overline{)0.345}$ 2. $0.1\overline{)0.161}$ 3. $5.7\overline{)8.55}$ 4. $5.4\overline{)5.076}$ 5. $0.05\overline{)0.35}$

6. $8.3\overline{)5.146}$ 7. $6.8\overline{)0.0612}$ 8. $0.7\overline{)65.8}$ 9. $38.2\overline{)1.146}$ 10. $0.07\overline{)50.89}$

11. $0.2\overline{)15.96}$ 12. $35.6\overline{)110.36}$ 13. $65.9\overline{)527.2}$ 14. $9.3\overline{)0.0558}$ 15. $0.01\overline{)0.08}$

16. $172.44 \div 47.9$ 17. $0.0108 \div 0.2$ 18. $11.8296 \div 21.2$ 19. $171.60 \div 0.03$

20. $0.3636 \div 40.4$ 21. $6 \div 7.5$ 22. $61.9262 \div 9.8$ 23. $459.85 \div 0.05$

24. $172.84 \div 2.9$ 25. $3.156 \div 52.6$ 26. $0.8058 \div 5.1$ 27. $21,655.06 \div 0.07$

Round to the nearest tenth or to the nearest ten cents.

1. $6.389\overline{)4}$ 2. $0.058\overline{)0.547}$ 3. $0.71\overline{)1}$ 4. $0.044\overline{)6.921}$ 5. $0.76\overline{)\$0.46}$

Round to the nearest hundredth or to the nearest cent.

6. $0.162\overline{)2.5}$ 7. $6\overline{)4.357}$ 8. $0.015\overline{)6.5}$ 9. $4.3\overline{)0.08}$ 10. $3.247\overline{)\$1.05}$

Round to the nearest thousandth.

11. $8.04\overline{)0.038}$ 12. $0.17\overline{)0.1}$ 13. $0.96\overline{)0.707}$ 14. $0.003\overline{)0.01}$ 15. $4.2\overline{)6.7}$

Which unit would you use to measure? Write *cm*, *m*, or *km*.

1. a nail

2. a soccer field

3. the length of a shoelace

4. a stapler

5. the amount of thread in a spool

6. a bus route

7. a car race

8. the height of a tree

Write the letter of the correct measurement.

9. distance a baseball is hit   a. 15 cm   b. 15 m   c. 15 km

10. length of a straw   a. 19.5 cm   b. 19.5 dm   c. 19.5 m

Copy and complete each table.

	mL	L
1.	3,277	▨
2.	▨	8.723
3.	14,347	▨

	g	kg
4.	▨	7.514
5.	▨	5.903
6.	125	▨

	kg	g
7.	250.882	▨
8.	▨	94,772
9.	103.468	▨

Complete.

10. $84 \text{ L} = $ ▨ mL 11. $6.4 \text{ g} = $ ▨ mg 12. $1,654 \text{ mL} = $ ▨ L

Chapter 6, page 191

List the first six multiples of each number.

1. 3　　**2.** 7　　**3.** 11　　**4.** 13　　**5.** 16　　**6.** 18　　**7.** 24

Find the least common multiple.

8. 6 and 7　　　**9.** 7 and 8　　　**10.** 11 and 9　　　**11.** 25 and 15

12. 10 and 6　　**13.** 6 and 15　　**14.** 30 and 8　　**15.** 5 and 38

16. 38 and 8　　**17.** 6 and 29　　**18.** 10 and 16　　**19.** 9 and 29

20. 9 and 26　　**21.** 22 and 44　　**22.** 17 and 36　　**23.** 4 and 10

24. 6, 9, and 12　　　　**25.** 3, 8, and 10　　　　**26.** 5, 16, and 25

Chapter 6, page 199

Complete.

1. $\frac{9}{10} = \frac{63}{\blacksquare}$　　**2.** $\frac{7}{28} = \frac{1}{\blacksquare}$　　**3.** $\frac{1}{2} = \frac{\blacksquare}{64}$　　**4.** $\frac{15}{18} = \frac{\blacksquare}{6}$

5. $\frac{2}{8} = \frac{1}{\blacksquare}$　　**6.** $\frac{\blacksquare}{40} = \frac{9}{10}$　　**7.** $\frac{37}{74} = \frac{\blacksquare}{2}$　　**8.** $\frac{60}{96} = \frac{\blacksquare}{8}$

Compare. Write = or ≠ for each ●.

9. $\frac{3}{5}$ ● $\frac{5}{9}$　　**10.** $\frac{7}{10}$ ● $\frac{6}{7}$　　**11.** $\frac{5}{9}$ ● $\frac{45}{81}$　　**12.** $\frac{3}{4}$ ● $\frac{7}{9}$

13. $\frac{4}{7}$ ● $\frac{48}{84}$　　**14.** $\frac{3}{5}$ ● $\frac{2}{3}$　　**15.** $\frac{3}{8}$ ● $\frac{39}{104}$　　**16.** $\frac{9}{10}$ ● $\frac{6}{7}$

Chapter 6, page 205

Write each as a whole number or as a mixed number.

1. $\frac{66}{4}$　　**2.** $\frac{84}{4}$　　**3.** $\frac{96}{6}$　　**4.** $\frac{63}{4}$　　**5.** $\frac{61}{6}$

6. $\frac{120}{8}$　　**7.** $\frac{33}{6}$　　**8.** $\frac{13}{2}$　　**9.** $\frac{112}{8}$　　**10.** $\frac{57}{6}$

Write each as a fraction in simplest form.

11. 20　　**12.** $7\frac{1}{6}$　　**13.** $8\frac{1}{4}$　　**14.** $10\frac{1}{2}$　　**15.** $9\frac{1}{6}$

16. $5\frac{4}{5}$　　**17.** $16\frac{1}{4}$　　**18.** $5\frac{2}{3}$　　**19.** $11\frac{1}{2}$　　**20.** $3\frac{1}{3}$

Chapter 6, page 211

Add. Write the answer in simplest form.

1. $\frac{1}{5} + \frac{3}{5}$ 2. $\frac{5}{8} + \frac{1}{8}$ 3. $\frac{5}{9} + \frac{2}{9}$ 4. $\frac{1}{5} + \frac{4}{5}$ 5. $\frac{8}{9} + \frac{5}{9}$

6. $\frac{5}{6} + \frac{2}{6}$ 7. $\frac{1}{2} + \frac{3}{10}$ 8. $\frac{1}{4} + \frac{1}{8}$ 9. $\frac{1}{6} + \frac{1}{3}$ 10. $\frac{7}{10} + \frac{4}{5}$

11. $\frac{1}{9} + \frac{2}{9} + \frac{4}{9}$ 12. $\frac{3}{8} + \frac{7}{8} + \frac{1}{8}$ 13. $\frac{1}{2} + \frac{1}{5} + \frac{1}{10}$ 14. $\frac{1}{3} + \frac{5}{6} + \frac{7}{8}$

15. $\begin{array}{r}\frac{3}{10}\\ +\frac{4}{5}\\ \hline\end{array}$ 16. $\begin{array}{r}\frac{1}{6}\\ +\frac{1}{4}\\ \hline\end{array}$ 17. $\begin{array}{r}\frac{1}{3}\\ +\frac{1}{5}\\ \hline\end{array}$ 18. $\begin{array}{r}\frac{1}{9}\\ +\frac{1}{2}\\ \hline\end{array}$ 19. $\begin{array}{r}\frac{1}{4}\\ +\frac{1}{10}\\ \hline\end{array}$

Chapter 6, page 213

Subtract. Write the difference in simplest form.

1. $\frac{7}{8} - \frac{1}{2}$ 2. $\frac{7}{9} - \frac{6}{9}$ 3. $\frac{3}{5} - \frac{1}{5}$ 4. $\frac{9}{10} - \frac{4}{5}$ 5. $\frac{2}{3} - \frac{1}{6}$

6. $\frac{1}{3} - \frac{2}{9}$ 7. $\frac{1}{2} - \frac{1}{3}$ 8. $\frac{4}{5} - \frac{2}{3}$ 9. $\frac{3}{4} - \frac{1}{10}$ 10. $\frac{4}{5} - \frac{1}{2}$

11. $\begin{array}{r}\frac{2}{5}\\ -\frac{1}{5}\\ \hline\end{array}$ 12. $\begin{array}{r}\frac{4}{5}\\ -\frac{2}{5}\\ \hline\end{array}$ 13. $\begin{array}{r}\frac{1}{2}\\ -\frac{1}{10}\\ \hline\end{array}$ 14. $\begin{array}{r}\frac{2}{3}\\ -\frac{1}{2}\\ \hline\end{array}$ 15. $\begin{array}{r}\frac{6}{7}\\ -\frac{2}{3}\\ \hline\end{array}$

Chapter 6, page 219

Add or subtract. Write the answer in simplest form.

1. $6\frac{1}{4} + 4\frac{1}{4}$ 2. $9\frac{1}{3} + 4\frac{1}{2}$ 3. $20\frac{5}{6} - 15\frac{3}{6}$ 4. $9\frac{3}{6} - 4\frac{1}{6}$ 5. $1\frac{1}{2} + 3\frac{1}{7}$

6. $13 - 4\frac{1}{10}$ 7. $4\frac{3}{10} + 3\frac{1}{4}$ 8. $8\frac{1}{2} - 5\frac{2}{3}$ 9. $12 - 5\frac{6}{7}$ 10. $5\frac{1}{2} + 3\frac{1}{3}$

11. $\begin{array}{r}9\frac{1}{2}\\ -7\frac{2}{3}\\ \hline\end{array}$ 12. $\begin{array}{r}9\frac{2}{3}\\ +4\frac{3}{4}\\ \hline\end{array}$ 13. $\begin{array}{r}4\frac{3}{4}\\ +1\frac{1}{6}\\ \hline\end{array}$ 14. $\begin{array}{r}4\frac{1}{10}\\ -1\frac{1}{6}\\ \hline\end{array}$ 15. $\begin{array}{r}11\frac{1}{2}\\ -1\frac{5}{9}\\ \hline\end{array}$

Multiply. Write the answer in simplest form.

1. $72 \times \frac{7}{9}$ **2.** $10 \times \frac{3}{8}$ **3.** $\frac{5}{6} \times 4$ **4.** $\frac{4}{7} \times 21$ **5.** $25 \times \frac{13}{15}$

6. $\frac{5}{6} \times 14$ **7.** $\frac{8}{9} \times 9$ **8.** $\frac{1}{3} \times 3$ **9.** $8 \times \frac{7}{9}$ **10.** $7 \times \frac{8}{9}$

11. $\frac{4}{5} \times 20$ **12.** $\frac{3}{4} \times 5$ **13.** $64 \times \frac{3}{16}$ **14.** $\frac{5}{8} \times 4$ **15.** $\frac{7}{12} \times 8$

16. $\frac{3}{5} \times 25 \times \frac{7}{30}$ **17.** $\frac{1}{7} \times 18 \times \frac{28}{33}$ **18.** $42 \times \frac{5}{6} \times \frac{3}{35}$

Multiply. Write the answer in simplest form.

1. $\frac{1}{6} \times 1\frac{1}{2}$ **2.** $\frac{6}{7} \times 9\frac{1}{3}$ **3.** $\frac{3}{4} \times 4\frac{2}{3}$ **4.** $\frac{2}{7} \times 4\frac{1}{2}$ **5.** $\frac{4}{5} \times 6\frac{2}{3}$

6. $8 \times 10\frac{6}{7}$ **7.** $9\frac{3}{5} \times 5$ **8.** $7 \times 2\frac{5}{6}$ **9.** $9\frac{3}{4} \times 2$ **10.** $8 \times 3\frac{1}{3}$

11. $\frac{2}{3} \times 8\frac{4}{7}$ **12.** $\frac{9}{10} \times 8\frac{3}{4}$ **13.** $4 \times 6\frac{1}{8}$ **14.** $3 \times 7\frac{7}{10}$ **15.** $\frac{6}{7} \times 2\frac{4}{5}$

16. $6\frac{3}{8} \times 5$ **17.** $3\frac{5}{7} \times 4\frac{1}{2}$ **18.** $9\frac{2}{3} \times 2\frac{4}{7}$ **19.** $6\frac{1}{6} \times 9\frac{1}{3}$ **20.** $2\frac{4}{5} \times 1\frac{6}{7}$

Write the reciprocal of each number.

1. $10\frac{5}{7}$ **2.** 45 **3.** $3\frac{5}{7}$ **4.** $2\frac{5}{6}$ **5.** $\frac{1}{9}$

Divide. Write the answer in simplest form.

6. $50 \div \frac{8}{9}$ **7.** $\frac{2}{9} \div \frac{1}{3}$ **8.** $26 \div \frac{1}{4}$ **9.** $\frac{2}{5} \div \frac{1}{2}$ **10.** $\frac{5}{6} \div \frac{5}{9}$

11. $23 \div \frac{7}{8}$ **12.** $33 \div \frac{4}{9}$ **13.** $\frac{3}{4} \div \frac{4}{7}$ **14.** $\frac{1}{8} \div \frac{1}{5}$ **15.** $35 \div \frac{5}{6}$

16. $\frac{5}{9} \div 15$ **17.** $\frac{9}{10} \div 23$ **18.** $\frac{3}{5} \div 36$ **19.** $\frac{2}{9} \div 9$ **20.** $\frac{2}{5} \div 14$

Divide. Write the answer in simplest form.

1. $10\frac{1}{2} \div 5$ **2.** $\frac{1}{2} \div 4\frac{7}{10}$ **3.** $1\frac{1}{3} \div 6\frac{3}{4}$ **4.** $7\frac{1}{2} \div 10\frac{5}{6}$ **5.** $\frac{2}{3} \div 6\frac{1}{8}$

6. $9\frac{5}{6} \div 2$ **7.** $10\frac{1}{2} \div 4$ **8.** $4\frac{1}{2} \div 4$ **9.** $6\frac{2}{3} \div \frac{1}{2}$ **10.** $3\frac{2}{3} \div \frac{3}{5}$

11. $2\frac{1}{2} \div \frac{4}{7}$ **12.** $8\frac{1}{3} \div 1\frac{2}{3}$ **13.** $5\frac{2}{3} \div 8\frac{1}{2}$ **14.** $6\frac{3}{4} \div 1\frac{4}{5}$ **15.** $\frac{1}{6} \div 10\frac{8}{9}$

16. $8\frac{1}{2} \div \frac{1}{2}$ **17.** $7\frac{3}{7} \div \frac{1}{3}$ **18.** $\frac{1}{4} \div 6\frac{4}{9}$ **19.** $3\frac{1}{3} \div 3$ **20.** $7\frac{1}{4} \div 2$

Complete.

1. 16 ft = ■ in.   **2.** 648 in. = ■ ft   **3.** 69 ft = ■ yd   **4.** 89 yd = ■ ft

5. 10,560 yd = ■ mi   **6.** 3 mi = ■ yd   **7.** $3\frac{1}{2}$ yd = ■ in.   **8.** $2\frac{4}{5}$ mi = ■ ft

Compute.

9.
$$\begin{array}{r} 4 \text{ ft } 7 \text{ in.} \\ + 4 \text{ ft } 7 \text{ in.} \\ \hline \end{array}$$

10.
$$\begin{array}{r} 17 \text{ yd } 2 \text{ ft} \\ + 3 \text{ yd } 2 \text{ ft} \\ \hline \end{array}$$

11.
$$\begin{array}{r} 16 \text{ mi } 1{,}423 \text{ yd} \\ + 12 \text{ mi } 1{,}567 \text{ yd} \\ \hline \end{array}$$

12.
$$\begin{array}{r} 7 \text{ yd } 11 \text{ in.} \\ + \quad\quad 9 \text{ in.} \\ \hline \end{array}$$

13.
$$\begin{array}{r} 32 \text{ ft } 3 \text{ in.} \\ - 12 \text{ ft } 6 \text{ in.} \\ \hline \end{array}$$

14.
$$\begin{array}{r} 45 \text{ yd } 1 \text{ ft} \\ - 33 \text{ yd } 2 \text{ ft} \\ \hline \end{array}$$

15.
$$\begin{array}{r} 3 \text{ mi } 789 \text{ yd} \\ - 2 \text{ mi } 989 \text{ yd} \\ \hline \end{array}$$

16.
$$\begin{array}{r} 1 \text{ mi} \\ - 500 \text{ yd } 2 \text{ ft} \\ \hline \end{array}$$

Complete.

1. 34 c = ■ pt   **2.** 23 pt = ■ c   **3.** 14 pt = ■ qt   **4.** 40 qt = ■ pt

5. 128 qt = ■ gal   **6.** 41 gal = ■ qt   **7.** 208 oz = ■ lb   **8.** 39 lb = ■ oz

9. 108,000 lb = ■ T   **10.** 28 T = ■ lb   **11.** $4\frac{3}{4}$ gal = ■ qt   **12.** $10\frac{3}{8}$ lb = ■ oz

Choose the best measurement. Write the letter of the correct answer.

13. the gas tank of a car   **a.** 15 fl oz   **b.** 15 qt   **c.** 15 gal

14. a juice glass   **a.** 8 fl oz   **b.** 8 qt   **c.** 8 gal

15. a packet of powdered milk   **a.** 2 oz   **b.** 2 lb   **c.** 2 T

16. a jumbo jet   **a.** 50 oz   **b.** 50 lb   **c.** 50 T

Is the equation a proportion? Write *yes* or *no*.

1. $\frac{11}{8} = \frac{66}{48}$ **2.** $\frac{4}{16} = \frac{3}{16}$ **3.** $\frac{3}{5} = \frac{9}{15}$ **4.** $\frac{20}{7} = \frac{80}{28}$

5. $\frac{13}{3} = \frac{1}{2}$ **6.** $\frac{7}{14} = \frac{8}{15}$ **7.** $\frac{1}{13} = \frac{6}{78}$ **8.** $\frac{12}{16} = \frac{9}{8}$

9. $\frac{4}{3} = \frac{12}{9}$ **10.** $\frac{16}{15} = \frac{48}{45}$ **11.** $\frac{18}{5} = \frac{90}{25}$ **12.** $\frac{1}{4} = \frac{16}{8}$

Find the missing term.

13. $\frac{29}{4} = \frac{n}{8}$ **14.** $\frac{2}{n} = \frac{8}{92}$ **15.** $\frac{n}{36} = \frac{58}{72}$ **16.** $\frac{6}{n} = \frac{54}{63}$

17. $\frac{24}{2} = \frac{n}{6}$ **18.** $\frac{31}{15} = \frac{n}{45}$ **19.** $\frac{21}{n} = \frac{84}{4}$ **20.** $\frac{2}{6} = \frac{22}{n}$

Write the percent for each ratio.

1. $95 : 100$ **2.** $4 : 100$ **3.** $20 : 100$ **4.** $17 : 100$

5. 89 to 100 **6.** 22 to 100 **7.** 36 to 100 **8.** 16 to 100

Write as a percent.

9. $\frac{53}{100}$ **10.** $\frac{49}{100}$ **11.** $\frac{85}{100}$ **12.** $\frac{92}{100}$

13. $\frac{76}{100}$ **14.** $\frac{31}{100}$ **15.** $\frac{43}{100}$ **16.** $\frac{3}{100}$

17. 0.54 **18.** 0.09 **19.** 0.01 **20.** 0.43

21. 0.19 **22.** 0.63 **23.** 0.18 **24.** 0.74

Write a percent for each fraction.

1. $\frac{21}{50}$ **2.** $\frac{38}{50}$ **3.** $\frac{36}{75}$ **4.** $\frac{11}{25}$ **5.** $\frac{54}{75}$ **6.** $\frac{14}{25}$

7. $\frac{7}{42}$ **8.** $\frac{29}{30}$ **9.** $\frac{17}{37}$ **10.** $\frac{13}{15}$ **11.** $\frac{8}{17}$ **12.** $\frac{1}{11}$

13. $\frac{47}{49}$ **14.** $\frac{28}{29}$ **15.** $\frac{26}{36}$ **16.** $\frac{3}{49}$ **17.** $\frac{31}{36}$ **18.** $\frac{8}{44}$

19. $\frac{10}{32}$ **20.** $\frac{26}{32}$ **21.** $\frac{9}{24}$ **22.** $\frac{8}{24}$ **23.** $\frac{3}{48}$ **24.** $\frac{40}{49}$

Find the percent of each number.

1. 61% of 235   **2.** 20% of 543   **3.** 10% of 79   **4.** 59% of 8

5. 8% of 242   **6.** 18% of 185   **7.** 62% of 140   **8.** 58% of 33

Find the amount of each discount. Then find each sale price.

9. Price: $11.90
Discount: 10%

10. Price: $22.80
Discount: 15%

11. Price: $17.80
Discount: 35%

Find the amount of sales tax for each. Then find the total price.

12. Price: $42.00
Tax: 7%

13. Price: $14.60
Tax: 5%

14. Price: $25.00
Tax: 4%

Find the percent.

1. What percent of 25 is 16?   **2.** What percent of 60 is 27?

3. What percent of 20 is 16?   **4.** What percent of 50 is 46?

5. 17 is what percent of 20?   **6.** 24 is what percent of 75?

7. 45 is what percent of 125?   **8.** 36 is what percent of 225?

Find the rate of discount.

9. Sale price: $56.94
Original price: $78.00

10. Sale price: 57¢
Original price: 95¢

Complete.

1. 75% of what number is 45?   **2.** 4% of what number is 14?

3. 75% of what number is 72?   **4.** 23% of what number is 69?

5. 35% of what number is 21?   **6.** 25% of what number is 28?

7. 12% of what number is 57?   **8.** 40% of what number is 68?

9. 36% of what number is 90?   **10.** 8% of what number is 4?

Chapter 9, page 309

Measure and name each angle.

1.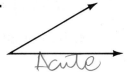
Acute

2.

3.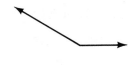

4.

Use a protractor to draw each angle.

5. $50°$

6. $130°$

7. $167°$

8. $90°$

Chapter 9, page 311

Use the figure at the right to answer
these exercises.

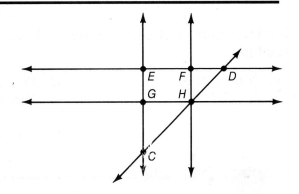

1. Name two pairs of perpendicular lines.

2. Name four right angles.

3. Name two pairs of intersecting lines
that are not perpendicular.

4. Name two pairs of parallel lines.

Chapter 9, page 315

Name each triangle according to the length of its sides.

1.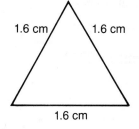
1.6 cm 1.6 cm
1.6 cm

2.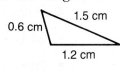
0.6 cm 1.5 cm
1.2 cm

3.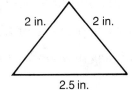
2 in. 2 in.
2.5 in.

Name each triangle according to the measure of its angles.

4.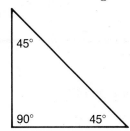
45°
90° 45°

5.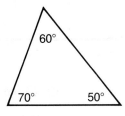
60°
70° 50°

6.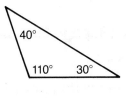
40°
110° 30°

Find the measure of the missing angle.

7. $\triangle ABC$: $\angle A = 65°$; $\angle B = 80°$;
$\angle C = $ ▇

8. $\triangle DEF$: $\angle D = $ ▇; $\angle E = 125°$;
$\angle F = 20°$

453

1. Figure *ABCDE* ~ *FGHIJ*. Name the corresponding sides and angles.

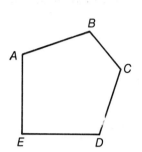

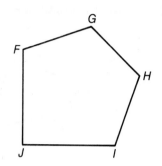

Figure *LMNO* ~ Figure *PQRS*.
Find the measure of the unmarked angles and the lengths of the unmarked sides.

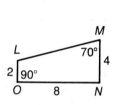

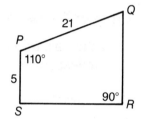

2. measure of ∠S

3. measure of ∠L

4. measure of ∠Q

5. measure of ∠N

6. length of $\overline{SR}$

7. length of $\overline{QR}$

8. length of $\overline{LM}$

Use the circle to complete Exercises 1–7.

1. Name the center.

2. Name three chords.

3. Name two radii.

4. Name a diameter.

5. Name the length of the diameter.

6. Name the circle.

7. Name two central angles.

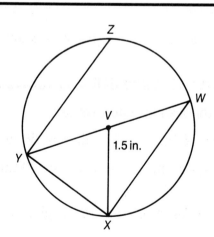

Solve.

8. Circle *A* has a radius of 10 cm. Circle *B* has a diameter twice that length. Are the two circles congruent?

9. How many diameters are needed to divide a circle into eight equal parts?

Chapter 10, page 343

Find the perimeter of each polygon.

1. a square with sides 32 cm long

2. a rectangle 16 ft by 51 ft

3. an isosceles triangle with sides of 73 mm and a base of 105 mm

4. a regular hexagon with sides of 53 in.

5.

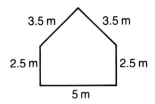

6.

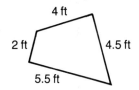

Chapter 10, page 347

Find the circumference. Use $\frac{22}{7}$ for π. Write the answer in simplest form.

1.

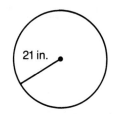

2.

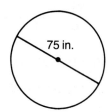

3.

4.

Find the circumference. Use 3.14 for π.

5. $d = 9$ cm

6. $d = 3$ m

7. $d = 14$ m

8. $d = 8$ mm

9. $r = 6$ cm

10. $r = 8$ mm

11. $r = 55$ mm

12. $r = 2$ m

Chapter 10, page 349

Find the area of each square.

1. $s = 26$ in.

2. $s = 50$ in.

3. $s = 3$ in.

4. $s = 27$ in.

5. $s = 4.2$ cm

6. $s = 70$ mm

7. $s = 14$ m

8. $s = 9$ cm

Find the area of each rectangle.

9. $l = 2$ ft, $w = 12$ ft

10. $l = 23$ ft, $w = 9$ ft

11. $l = 9$ in., $w = 24$ in.

12. $l = 5$ in., $w = 7.5$ in.

13. $l = 4$ mm, $w = 6.5$ mm

14. $l = 54$ mm, $w = 2$ mm

15. $l = 1.2$ cm, $w = 0.8$ cm

16. $l = 14$ m, $w = 0.7$ m

Chapter 10, page 353

Find the area of the parallelogram.

1. $b = 88$ in., $h = 2$ in.
2. $b = 74$ in., $h = 85$ in.
3. $b = 3$ ft, $h = 8$ ft
4. $b = 3$ ft, $h = 76$ ft

Find the area of the triangle.

5. $b = 59$ mm, $h = 42$ mm
6. $b = 6$ cm, $h = 36$ cm
7. $b = 84$ m, $h = 2$ m
8. $b = 1.4$ m, $h = 4$ m

Chapter 10, page 361

Find the surface area of each figure. Use 3.14 for π.

1.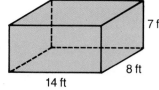
4 mm, 27 mm

2.
17 in., 17 in., 8 in.

3.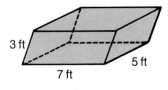
3 ft, 7 ft, 5 ft

4.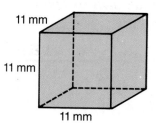
7 ft, 8 ft, 14 ft

5.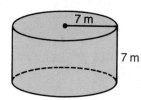
7 m, 7 m

6.
11 mm, 11 mm, 11 mm

Chapter 10, page 363

Find the volume of each cube.

1. $e = 16$ in.
2. $e = 5$ yd
3. $e = 12$ in.
4. $e = 8$ ft

Find the volume of each rectangular prism.

5. $l = 17$ cm, $w = 20$ cm, $h = 28$ cm
6. $l = 9$ mm, $w = 7$ mm, $h = 2$ mm
7. $l = 1.4$ m, $w = 5.2$ m, $h = 12$ m
8. $l = 7.3$ mm, $w = 4.8$ mm, $h = 9.5$ mm

456

Copy and complete the table.

	Set	Mean	Median	Mode	Range
1.	8, 17, 8, 9, 8	▦	▦	▦	▦
2.	65, 37, 42, 37, 19	▦	▦	▦	▦
3.	97, 101, 23, 97, 37	▦	▦	▦	▦
4.	51, 27, 51, 27, 105, 27	▦	▦	▦	▦
5.	19, 19, 13, 10, 24, 29	▦	▦	▦	▦
6.	11, 8, 7, 10, 11	▦	▦	▦	▦
7.	6, 13, 7, 15, 6, 19, 17, 9	▦	▦	▦	▦
8.	6.7, 5.2, 12.7, 5.2, 13.7	▦	▦	▦	▦
9.	27, 30.8, 31.4, 30.8, 3	▦	▦	▦	▦
10.	12.8, 10.3, 9.9, 10.3, 14.1, 22.4	▦	▦	▦	▦

Use the data on the table below to construct your own
bar graph.

LARSONVILLE MAYORAL ELECTIONS

Year	Total votes cast
1958	987
1962	1,416
1966	2,605
1970	2,890
1974	3,515
1978	4,918
1982	5,031
1986	5,602

The letters in the words *United States* are printed on cards. The cards are mixed up and placed into a hat. One card is selected at random. What is the probability that the card selected will show

1. the letter *T*?   **2.** the letter *N*?   **3.** the letter *S*?   **4.** the letter *I*?

5. a vowel?   **6.** a consonant?   **7.** the letter *O*?   **8.** a letter?

9. It is more or less likely that a vowel will be picked?

10. It is more or less likely that a consonant will be picked?

Make a tree diagram that shows all of the possible lunches. Each lunch should have one item from each part of this menu.

HILLSDALE SCHOOL LUNCH MENU

Soups	Main course	Vegetable	Dessert
Bean	Tuna	Corn	Apple
Pea	Ham	Potatoes	Prunes

Write > or < for each ●.

1. $^-8$ ● $^+26$
2. $^+13$ ● $^-57$
3. $^+22$ ● $^+69$
4. $^-45$ ● $^-11$
5. $^-41$ ● $^-73$
6. $^-7$ ● $^+60$
7. $^-69$ ● 0
8. $^+23$ ● $^+68$
9. $^-68$ ● $^-46$
10. $^+80$ ● $^-100$
11. $^+41$ ● $^+11$
12. $^+51$ ● 0

Write in order from the least to the greatest.

13. $^-86, ^-45, ^+91$
14. $^-12, ^-97, ^-50$
15. $^-62, ^-79, ^+88, ^-97$
16. $^+51, ^+48, ^-58$
17. $^-88, ^-19, ^+4$
18. $^+20, ^-56, ^+6, ^-16, ^+12$

Write in order from the greatest to the least.

19. $^-4, ^-52, ^+94$
20. $^-56, ^-46, ^-20$
21. $^+57, ^-18, ^+49, ^-16$
22. $^+44, ^+23, ^+55$
23. $^-1, ^+53, ^-56$
24. $^+1, ^-88, ^+11, ^-25, ^+15$

Add.

1. $^-12 + ^-12$
2. $^-16 + ^-7$
3. $^+3 + ^+3$
4. $^-1 + ^-9$
5. $^-5 + ^-5$
6. $^+6 + ^+5$
7. $^+16 + ^+15$
8. $^-14 + ^-1$
9. $^-16 + ^-19$
10. $^-18 + ^-2$
11. $^+7 + ^+2$
12. $^-11 + ^-16$
13. $^+8 + ^+2$
14. $^+10 + ^+6$
15. $^-14 + ^-20$
16. $^+16 + ^+13$

Find the sum.

1. $^+6 + ^-8$
2. $^+9 + ^-6$
3. $^+4 + ^-10$
4. $^+12 + ^-13$
5. $^-16 + ^+3$
6. $^-6 + ^+5$
7. $^-13 + ^+10$
8. $^-12 + ^+12$
9. $^+4 + ^-6$
10. $^+8 + ^-2$
11. $^-18 + ^+18$
12. $^+9 + ^-9$
13. $^-15 + ^+14$
14. $^+10 + ^-6$
15. $^+7 + ^-6$
16. $^+1 + ^-16$

Subtract.

1. $^+10 - ^-10$ 2. $^+16 - ^+5$ 3. $^-7 - ^+18$ 4. $^+20 - ^+11$

5. $^-13 - ^-2$ 6. $^-9 - ^-1$ 7. $^+9 - ^-3$ 8. $^+13 - ^+18$

9. $^-3 - ^-13$ 10. $^+11 - ^+12$ 11. $^-18 - ^-17$ 12. $^+8 - ^-11$

13. $^-7 - ^-7$ 14. $^-17 - ^-9$ 15. $^+5 - ^-14$ 16. $^-2 - ^-4$

17. $^-6 - ^+1$ 18. $^+3 - ^+6$ 19. $^+5 - ^+13$ 20. $^+8 - ^+7$

21. $^-4 - ^-4$ 22. $^+6 - ^+17$ 23. $^-8 - ^-18$ 24. $^+18 - ^-11$

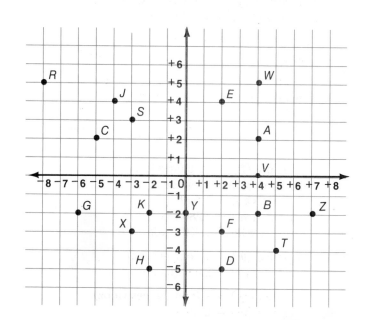

Write an ordered pair to describe the location of each point.

1. A 2. B 3. C 4. D 5. E

6. F 7. G 8. H 9. J 10. K

Write the letter of the point identified by each ordered pair.

11. $(^+5, ^-4)$ 12. $(^-3, ^-3)$ 13. $(^-8, ^+5)$ 14. $(0, ^-2)$

15. $(^+4, ^+5)$ 16. $(^-3, ^+3)$ 17. $(^+7, ^-2)$ 18. $(^+4, 0)$

TABLE OF MEASURES

TIME

1 minute (min) = 60 seconds (s)
1 hour (h) = 60 minutes
1 day (d) = 24 hours
1 week (wk) = 7 days
1 year (y) = 12 months (mo)
1 year = 52 weeks
1 year = 365 days

METRIC UNITS

Length

1 millimeter (mm) = 0.001 meter (m)
1 centimeter (cm) = 0.01 meter
1 decimeter (dm) = 0.1 meter
1 dekameter (dam) = 10 meters
1 hectometer (hm) = 100 meters
1 kilometer (km) = 1,000 meters

Mass

1 milligram (mg) = 0.001 gram (g)
1 kilogram (kg) = 1,000 grams

Capacity

1 milliliter (mL) = 0.001 liter (L)
1 kiloliter (kL) = 1,000 liters

Temperature

0° Celsius (C) . . . . . Water freezes
100° Celsius (C) . . . . . Water boils

CUSTOMARY UNITS

Length

1 foot (ft) = 12 inches (in.)
1 yard (yd) = 36 inches
1 yard = 3 feet
1 mile (mi) = 5,280 feet
1 mile = 1,760 yards

Weight

1 pound (lb) = 16 ounces (oz)
1 ton = 2,000 pounds

Capacity

1 cup (c) = 8 fluid ounces (fl oz)
1 pint (pt) = 2 cups
1 quart (qt) = 2 pints
1 quart = 4 cups
1 gallon (gal) = 4 quarts

Temperature

32° Fahrenheit (F). . . . . Water freezes
212° Fahrenheit (F). . . . . Water boils

FORMULAS

PERIMETER	Polygon	$P = $ sum of the sides
	Rectangle	$P = 2l + 2w$
	Square	$P = 4s$
CIRCUMFERENCE	Circle	$C = 2\pi r$, or $C = \pi d$
AREA	Circle	$A = \pi r^2$
	Parallelogram	$A = bh$
	Rectangle	$A = lw$
	Square	$A = s^2$
	Triangle	$A = \frac{1}{2}bh$
VOLUME	Cube	$V = e^3$
	Cylinder	$V = Bh$, or $V = \pi r^2 h$
	Rectangular Prism	$V = lwh$
	Triangular Prism	$V = \frac{1}{2}lwh$
OTHER	Diameter	$d = 2r$

SYMBOLS

$<$ is less than

$>$ is greater than

$\leq$ is less than or equal to

$\geq$ is greater than or equal to

$\neq$ is not equal to

$\approx$ is approximately equal to

$4 \div 2$ 4 divided by 2

5^4 5 to the fourth power

$0.\overline{36}$ 0.363636 …

$^{-}4$ negative 4

$\%$ percent

$3:5$ the ratio 3 to 5

$\$4/h$ the rate $4 per hour

$@$ at a certain amount each

$^{\circ}$ degree

A point A

$\overleftrightarrow{AB}$ line AB

$\overrightarrow{AB}$ ray AB

$\overline{AB}$ line segment AB

$\angle ABC$ angle ABC

$\triangle ABC$ triangle ABC

$\perp$ is perpendicular to

$\parallel$ is parallel to

$\cong$ is congruent to

$\sim$ is similar to

π pi (about 3.14)

$(5,3)$ the ordered pair 5,3

Glossary

Acute Angle An angle that measures less than 90°.

Acute triangle A triangle that has three acute angles.

Addends Numbers that are added.
Example: $8 + 6 = 14$

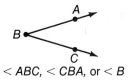

addends

Angle A figure formed by two different rays that have the same endpoint.

$< ABC$, $< CBA$, or $< B$

Area The number of square units needed to cover a surface.

Associative Property of Addition If the grouping of addends is changed, the sum remains the same.
Example: $(3 + 5) + 4 = 3 + (5 + 4)$

Associative Property of Multiplication If the grouping of factors is changed, the product remains the same.
Example: $(3 \times 3) \times 5 = 3 \times (3 \times 5)$

Average The average, or mean, of a set of numbers is the sum of the numbers divided by the number of addends.

BASIC *BASIC* stands for "Beginner's All-purpose Symbolic Instructional Code," a computer language.

Chord A line segment that has endpoints on a circle.

Circle A circle consists of all points in one plane that are the same distance from one point, called the *center*.

Circumference The distance around a circle.

Commutative Property of Addition If the order of two addends is changed, the sum remains the same.
Example: $7 + 2 = 2 + 7$

Commutative Property of Multiplication If the order of the factors is changed, the product remains the same.
Example: $7 \times 5 = 5 \times 7$

Composite number A composite number is a number that has more than two factors.
Example: 36 is a composite number because it has 8 factors: 1, 2, 3, 4, 6, 9, 12, and 18.

Cone A solid figure that has a circular base.

Congruent Figures that are exactly the same shape and size are congruent.

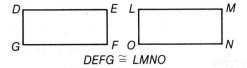

$DEFG \cong LMNO$

Cube A solid figure that has six square faces.

Cylinder A solid figure that has two congruent circular bases.

Debug To fix the problems in a computer program so that it will do what you want it to do.

Decimal A number that uses place value and a decimal point to show tenths, hundredths, thousandths, etc.
Examples: 0.04, 23.8517

Degree A unit of measure for circles, angles, and for temperature.

Denominator In $\frac{6}{7}$, 7 is the denominator. It tells the total number of parts or groups.

Diagonal A line segment that is not a side and that joins two vertices of a polygon.

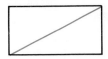

Diameter A chord that passes through the center of a circle.

Digit Any of the individual numerals 0, 1, 2, 3, 4, 5, 6, 7, 8, or 9, used to build the base-ten name for a number.

Distributive Property To find the product of a number times the sum of two addends, you can multiply each addend by the number, then add the products.
Example: $4 \times (9 + 3) = (4 \times 9) + (4 \times 3)$

Dividend The number divided to produce a quotient.

Divisible A number is divisible by another if it can be divided by that number with no remainder.
Example: 6 is divisible by 3, but not by 4.

Divisor The number by which the dividend is divided.

Edge Two faces of a solid intersect at an edge.

Equation A mathematical sentence that has an equal sign.

Equilateral triangle A triangle that has three sides of equal length.

Equivalent fractions Two or more fractions that name the same number.
Example: $\frac{2}{8} = \frac{1}{4}$

Expanded numeral A numeral expanded to show the value of each digit.
Example: $72{,}047 = 70{,}000 + 2{,}000 + 40 + 7$

Exponent An exponent tells how many times a number is multiplied by itself.
Example: $10^2 = 10 \times 10 = 100$
exponent

Face The flat surface of a prism.

Factors Numbers that are multiplied.
Example: $6 \times 3 = 18$
factors

Flip To move an object along a line of symmetry to form a reflection image.

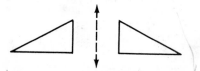

Flowchart A diagram that shows the steps to do something.

FOR/STEP/NEXT A three-part command that makes a computer repeat a step a given number of times.
Example: The program:
```
10   FOR N = 1 TO 10 STEP 3
20   PRINT N
30   NEXT N
```
makes a computer print the numbers 1, 4, 7, and 10.

Fraction A fraction is used to name parts of a whole, or parts of a group.

Gram A unit of mass in the metric system.

Greatest Common Factor The greatest common factor of two or more numbers is the greatest number that is a factor of each number.
Example: 8 is the greatest common factor of 16 and 24.

IF/THEN A command that tells a computer to make a decision.
Example: If N < 20 THEN 60 tells a computer to go to line 60 if the number in the storage place N is less than 20.

Inequality A number sentence that contains <, >, or =.

Integer A positive or negative whole number such as $^-5$ or $^+5$.

Intersecting lines Lines that meet or cross at one point.

Isosceles Triangle A triangle that has at least two congruent sides.

Latitude Used to locate a position on a globe or map, lines of latitude measure degrees north or south of the equator.

Least common denominator The least common multiple of the denominators of two or more fractions.
Example: For $\frac{1}{5}$ and $\frac{5}{6}$, 30 is the least common denominator.

Least common multiple The least common multiple of two or more numbers is the smallest number other than 0 that is a common multiple.
Example: For 3 and 4, 12 is the least common multiple.

Line A line is a straight path that goes on forever in two directions.

Line segment A line segment is a part of a line that begins at one point and ends at another point.

LIST A command that tells a computer to show the program lines that are stored in its memory.

Liter A unit of liquid capacity in the metric system.

Longitude Used to locate a position on a globe or map, lines of longitude measure degrees east or west of the prime meridian.

Mean The mean, or average, of a set of numbers is the sum of the numbers divided by the number of addends in the set.

Median The median is the middle number in an ordered set of numbers.

Meter A unit of length in the metric system.

Mixed Number A mixed number has a whole number part and a fraction part, such as $7\frac{3}{8}$.

Mode The mode is the number that occurs the most often in a set of numbers.

Multiple A multiple of a number is the product of that number and any other whole number. Example: 12, 18, and 24 are multiples of 6.

Number sentence An equation or inequality.
Examples: $12 - 5 = 7$ $n \times 7 = 42$
$4 \times 6 < 26$ $8 + 4 > 11$

Numerator In $\frac{3}{4}$, 3 is the numerator. It tells how many parts you are talking about.

Obtuse Angle An angle that measures more than 90° but less than 180°.

Obtuse triangle A triangle that has an obtuse angle.

Ordered pair A pair of numbers used to locate a point on a grid.

Parallel lines Lines in a plane that never intersect.

Parallelogram A quadrilateral that has two pairs of parallel sides and two pairs of congruent sides.

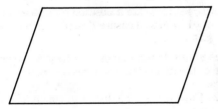

Perimeter The distance around a polygon, the sum of the lengths of its sides.

Periods A group of three digits in a numeral set off by commas.

Perpendicular lines Lines that intersect and form right angles.

Pi π The ratio of the circumference of a circle and its diameter equals pi. Pi is approximately 3.14 or $\frac{22}{7}$.

Plane A flat surface that continues infinitely in all directions.

Point A point is an exact location in space.

Polygon A closed figure formed by line segments.

Polyhedron A solid figure that has faces that are polygons.

Prime factorization A composite number can be shown to be the product of its prime factors. Example: The prime factorization of 24 is
$2 \times 2 \times 2 \times 3$.

Prime number A prime number has exactly two factors, itself and 1.

PRINT A command that tells a computer to output information on a screen or on paper.

Prism A solid that has congruent polygons as two parallel faces.

Probability A comparison of the number of favorable outcomes to the total number of possible outcomes.

Property of One for Multiplication If one factor is 1, then the product is always the other factor. Example: $8 \times 1 = 8$

Property of Zero for Addition If one of the addends is zero, then the sum is equal to the other addend.
Examples: $7 + 0 = 7; 0 + 9 = 9$

Property of Zero for Multiplication If one factor is 0, the product is always 0.
Examples: $9 \times 0 = 0; 8,561 \times 0 = 0$

Proportion A statement that two ratios are equal.
Examples: $\frac{3}{5} = \frac{9}{15}$

Protractor An instrument used to measure angles.

Pyramid A solid that has three or more faces that are triangles with a common vertex and one face that is a polygon.

Quadrilateral A polygon that has four sides.

Radius A line segment that has one endpoint on the circle and one endpoint on the center.

Range The difference between the greatest and the least number in a set of numbers.

Ratio A comparison between two numbers.

Ray A part of a line that begins at an endpoint and goes on forever in one direction.

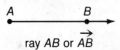

ray *AB* or $\overrightarrow{AB}$

Reciprocals Numbers whose products are 1.
Example: $4 \times \frac{1}{4} = 1$
4 and $\frac{1}{4}$ are reciprocals.

Rectangle A parallelogram that has four right angles.

Rectangular prism A three-dimensional figure that has six faces and eight corners. Its bases are rectangular.

Reflection image A flip of a figure forms a reflection image.

Rhombus A parallelogram that has four congruent sides.

Right angle An angle that measures 90°.

Right triangle A triangle that has one right angle.

RND(1) In a computer program, RND(1) makes a computer pick a random 9-place decimal between 0 and 1.

Rotation figure A turn of a figure around a point forms a rotation image.

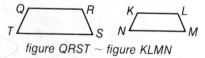

Scalene triangle A triangle that has no congruent sides.

Scientific notation A method for writing a number as the product of two factors. The first factor is a number between 1 and 10 and the second factor is a power of 10.
Example: $6{,}280{,}000 = 6.28 \times 10^{6}$

Similar figures Figures that have the same shape but not necessarily the same size.

figure QRST ~ figure KLMN

Simplest form A fraction is in simplest form if its numerator and denominator have no common factors other than 1.

Sphere A solid figure that has a surface with all points the same distance from its center.

Square A rectangle whose sides are all the same length.

Standard numeral The usual way to name a number.
Example: The standard numeral for seventy-three is 73.

Straight angle An angle that measures 180°.

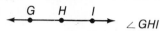
∠GHI

Symmetry A figure is symmetrical when there is a line about which the figure can be folded. The resulting figure matches the original.

Translation image A slide of a figure along a straight path forms a translation image.

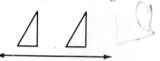

Trapezoid A quadrilateral that has exactly one pair of parallel sides.

Triangle A three-sided polygon.

Turn You can turn a figure on a curved path around a point to form a rotation image.

Vertex The common endpoint of the sides of an angle or two sides of a polygon.

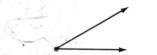

Volume The number of cubic units needed to fill a solid figure.

Whole number Any of these numbers:
0, 1, 2, 3, . . .

INDEX

Diawn
Palmer

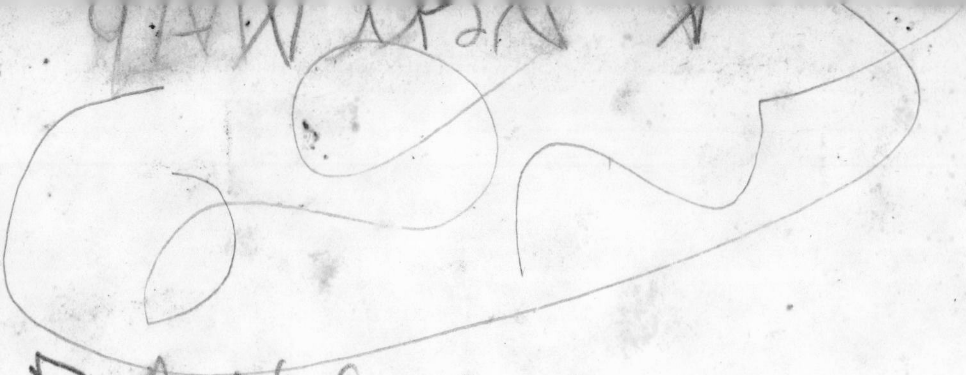

D A N G e r o u s
L I A S O N S

Dangerous
vrason
Dangerous
vrason

D A N G e R O U S

S U M P S O R